A Philosophical Companion
to First-Order Logic

A Philosophical Companion to First-Order Logic

Edited, with an Overview, by
R.I.G. Hughes

Hackett Publishing Company, Inc.
Indianapolis/Cambridge

Copyright © 1993 by Hackett Publishing Company, Inc.
All rights reserved
Printed in the United States of America

99   98   97   96   95   94   93   1   2   3   4   5   6   7

Cover and text design
   by Dan Kirklin

For further information, please address

Hackett Publishing Company, Inc.
P.O. Box 44937
Indianapolis, Indiana 46244-0937

Library of Congress Cataloging-in-Publication Data

A philosophical companion to first-order logic/[compiled and edited
   by] R.I.G. Hughes.
       p.   cm.
   Includes bibliographical references, index.
   ISBN 0-87220-182-1 (alk. paper)   ISBN 0-87220-181-3
   (pbk.: alk. paper)
     1. First-order logic.   I. Hughes, R.I.G.
   BC128.P55   1993
   160—dc20   93-14456
                                                                   CIP

The paper used in this publication meets the minimum requirements of
American National Standard for Information Sciences—Permanence of
Paper for Printed Library Materials, ANSI Z39.48-1984.
                              ∞

Contents

Preface

Although this collection of essays can be used in various ways, it was designed to accompany a one-term course in formal first-order logic. Two years ago, when I set out to compile it, I sent off a proposed table of contents, together with a letter explaining the project and a request for comments and suggestions, to about fifty philosophers in North America and elsewhere. The number who responded was very high, too high for me to list every one of them here. My thanks to them all; at my prompting they unearthed papers from bottom drawers, drew my attention to others that I had overlooked, and helped me to make up my mind about those I was already considering. (Nothing reinforces the feeling that a given direction is the way to go quite as effectively as the advice, "I wouldn't do that if I were you.") I apologize to individual correspondents whose favorite essays were left out; how much I owe to them collectively can be gauged by the fact that only five of the selections on my original list have survived.

The resulting anthology includes two introductory pieces, eleven papers dealing with specific topics (twelve, if the two by Dag Prawitz are considered separately), and two overviews. It provides, for each week n of a logic course ($1 \leq n \leq 12$), one or more essays dealing with the material covered in that week and accessible to students who have studied logic for precisely $n - 1$ weeks. In making the selection I have interpreted "dealing with" rather broadly. For example, none of the three essays listed in the table of contents under "Quantificational Logic: Semantics" deals primarily with semantics; two deal with ontology and one with the recursive syntax of quantified sentences. Each essay, however, adds a philosophical or a historical dimension to what is often presented in an exclusively formal way.

The essays differ in length, in degree of difficulty, and in emphasis. Thus the two introductory essays, each the opening chapter of a notable textbook, are representative of the two main tendencies within linguistic philosophy; one stresses the relation of logic to mathematics, the other its relation to natural languages. The essays which differ most in degree of difficulty are the two overviews. In including Ian Hacking's "What Is Logic?" I have gone beyond the brief I set myself. It is true that Hacking uses little in the way of technical apparatus that would be unfamiliar to a student after a one-term course in logic, and what he uses is explained within the paper; nevertheless, his paper is not one to be read and digested within a week. It is included, however, as one of the richest and most provocative studies of classical logic in recent years, for graduate students to work through at leisure when the course is over. In contrast, my essay "On First-Order Logic" has a decidedly modest aim: it reviews what the student has spent the term studying and gives it a history. This is the only essay written expressly for this volume. In the course of it I refer to others in the collection wherever appropriate, but do not go out of my way to do so. Nor do I assume familiarity with any of them. This means that certain topics, like the liar paradox, Gentzen's inversion principle, and the syntactic ambiguity of "flying kites" and "visiting relatives," get aired more than once in the volume, but it also makes the overview self-contained.

I am grateful to all the contributors, especially those whose essays are appearing for the first time and who acceded with good grace to editorial requests for revisions. Since I first mooted the idea to them, Jay Hullett and Paul Coppock of Hackett Publishing have been a great source of help and encouragement, and to them also I extend warm thanks.

R.I.G. Hughes
University of South Carolina

Introduction

W. V. Quine

Logic, like any science, has as its business the pursuit of truth. What are true are certain statements; and the pursuit of truth is the endeavor to sort out the true statements from the others, which are false.

Truths are as plentiful as falsehoods, since each falsehood admits of a negation which is true. But scientific activity is not the indiscriminate amassing of truths; science is selective and seeks the truths that count for most, either in point of intrinsic interest or as instruments for coping with the world.

Strictly speaking, what admit of truth and falsity are not statements as repeatable patterns of utterance, but individual events of statement utterance. For, utterances that sound alike can vary in meaning with the occasion of the utterance. This is due not only to careless ambiguities, but to systematic ambiguities which are essential to the nature of language. The pronoun 'I' changes its reference with every change of speaker; 'here' changes its reference with every significant movement through space; and 'now' changes its reference every time it is uttered.

The crucial point of contact between description and reality is to be sought in the utterance of a statement on the occasion of a stimulation to which that string of words has become associated. Not that the statement will refer to stimulation or sensation; it is apt to refer to physical objects. Language is a social institution, serving, within its limitations, the social end of communication; so it is not to be wondered that the objects of our first and commonest utterances are socially shared physical objects rather than private experiences. Physical objects, if they did not exist, would (to transplant Voltaire's epigram) have had to be invented. They are indispensable as the public common denominators of private sense experience.

The latest scientific pronouncement about positrons and the state-

This essay originally appeared in 1950 as the Introduction to W. V. Quine, *Methods of Logic.* It is reprinted here by permission of the author and of the publishers from *Methods of Logic,* by W. V. Quine (Cambridge, Mass.: Harvard University Press). Copyright 1950 © 1959, 1972, 1978, 1982 by W. V. Quine

ment that my pen is in my hand are equally statements about physical objects; and physical objects are known to us only as parts of a systematic conceptual structure which, taken as a whole, impinges at its edges upon observation. We have a network of statements that are variously linked with one another and some of which, out at the periphery of the network, are associated more or less strongly with sensory stimulation. Even the peripheral ones are mostly about physical objects: examples are 'My pen is in my hand', 'The mercury is at 80'.

A sensory stimulation elicits some closely associated statement and the associations then reverberate through the system of statements, activating at length another peripheral statement whose sensory associations make us expect some particular further stimulation. Such, schematically, is the mechanism of prediction. When prediction fails, we question the intervening network of statements. We retain a wide choice as to what statements of the system to preserve and what ones to revise; any one of many revisions will suffice to unmake the particular implication that brought the system to grief.

Normally the peripheral statements, closely associated to stimulations, are to be preserved from revision once the appropriate stimulations have occurred. If revision of the system should become necessary, other statements than these are to suffer. It is only by such an allocation of priority that we can hope to claim any empirical content or objective reference for the system as a whole.

There is also, however, another and somewhat opposite priority: the more fundamental a law is to our conceptual scheme, the less likely we are to choose it for revision. When some revision of our system of statements is called for, we prefer, other things being equal, a revision which disturbs the system least.

Where the two priorities come into conflict, either is capable of prevailing. Statements close to experience and seemingly verified by the appropriate experiences may occasionally be given up, even by pleading hallucination, in the extreme case where their retention would entail a cataclysmic revision of fundamental laws. But to overrule a multiplicity of such statements, if they reinforce one another and are sustained by different observers, would invite criticism.

The priority on law, considered now apart from any competition with the priority on statements verified by experience, admits of many gradations. Conjectures of history and economics will be revised more willingly than laws of physics, and these more willingly than laws of mathematics and logic. Our system of statements has such a thick cushion of indeterminacy, in relation to experience, that vast domains of law can easily be held immune to revision on principle. We can always turn to other quarters of the system when revisions are called for by unexpected experiences. Mathematics and logic, central as they are to the conceptual scheme, tend to be accorded such immunity, in view of our conservative preference for revisions which disturb the system least; and herein, perhaps, lies the "necessity" which the laws of mathematics and logic are felt to enjoy.

In the end it is perhaps the same to say, as one often does, that the laws of mathematics and logic are true simply by virtue of our conceptual scheme. For, it is certainly by virtue of that scheme that those laws are central to it; and it is by virtue of being thus central that the laws are preserved from revision at the expense of statements less strategically situated.

But it must now be remarked that our conservative preference for those revisions which disturb the system least is opposed by a significant contrary force, a force for simplification. Far-reaching revision of the fundamental laws of physics was elected in recent decades, by considerations of simplicity, in preference to the welter of *ad hoc* subsidiary laws which would otherwise have been needed to accommodate the wayward experiences of Michelson and Morley and other experimenters. Continued experiment "confirmed" the fundamental revisions, in the sense of increasing the simplicity differential.

Mathematical and logical laws themselves are not immune to revision if it is found that essential simplifications of our whole conceptual scheme will ensue. There have been suggestions, stimulated largely by quandaries of modern physics, that we revise the true-false dichotomy of current logic in favor of some sort of tri- or *n*-chotomy. Logical laws are the most central and crucial statements of our conceptual scheme, and for this reason the most protected from revision by the force of conservatism; but, because again of their crucial position, they are the laws an apt revision of which might offer the most sweeping simplification of our whole system of knowledge.

Thus the laws of mathematics and logic may, despite all "necessity," be abrogated. But this is not to deny that such laws are true by virtue of the conceptual scheme, or by virtue of meanings. Because these laws are so central, any revision of them is felt to be the adoption of a new conceptual scheme, the imposition of new meanings on old words. [No such revolution, by the way, is envisaged in this book; there will be novelties of approach and technique in these pages, but at bottom logic will remain unchanged.]*

*Editor's note: Passages where Quine describes what the reader will encounter in *Methods of Logic* have been enclosed in square brackets.

I have been stressing that in large part our statements are linked only remotely to observation. It is only by way of the relations of one statement to another that the statements in the interior of the system can figure at all in the prediction of experience, and can be found deserving of revision when prediction fails. Now of these relations of statements to statements, one of conspicuous importance is the relation of logical implication: the relation of any statement to any that follows logically from it. If one statement is to be held as true, each statement implied by it must also be held as true; and thus it is that statements internal to the system have their effects on statements at the periphery.

But for implication, our system of statements would for the most part be meaningless; nothing but the periphery would make sense. Yet implication is not really an added factor; for to say that one statement logically implies a second is the same as saying that a third statement of the system, an 'if-then' compound formed from the other two, is logically true or "valid." Logical truths are statements on a par with the rest, but very centrally situated; they are statements of such forms as 'p or not p', 'If p then p', 'If p and q then q', 'If everything is thus and so then something is thus and so', and others more complex and less quickly recognizable. Their characteristic is that they not only are true but stay true even when we make substitutions upon their component words and phrases as we please, provided merely that the so-called "logical" words '$=$', 'or', 'not', 'if-then', 'everything', 'something', etc., stay undisturbed. We may write any statements in the 'p' and 'q' positions and any terms in the 'thus and so' positions, in the forms cited above, without fear of falsity. All that counts, when a statement is logically true, is its structure in terms of logical words. Thus it is that logical truths are commonly said to be true by virtue merely of the meanings of the logical words.

[The chief importance of logic lies in implication, which, therefore, will be the main theme of this book. Techniques are wanted for showing, given two statements, that the one implies the other; herein lies logical deduction. Such techniques will be developed, for increasingly inclusive portions of logic, as the book proceeds. The objects of deduction, the things related by implication, are statements; so statements will constitute not merely the medium of this book (as of most), but the primary subject matter.]

Strictly speaking, as urged earlier, what admit of truth and falsity are not the statements but the individual events of their utterance. However, it is a great source of simplification in logical theory to talk of statements in abstraction from the individual occasions of their utterance; and this abstraction, if made in full awareness and subject to a certain precaution, offers no difficulty. The precaution is merely that we must not apply our logical techniques to examples in which one and the same statement recurs several times with changed meanings, owing to variations in immediate context. But such examples are easily enough adjusted to the purposes of logic by some preliminary paraphrasing, by way of bringing the implicit shifts of meaning into explicit form.

Logic and mathematics were coupled, in earlier remarks, as jointly enjoying a central position within the total system of discourse. Logic as commonly presented, and in particular as it will be presented in this book, seems to differ from mathematics in that in logic we talk about statements and their interrelationships, notably implication, whereas in mathematics we talk about abstract nonlinguistic things: numbers, functions, and the like. This contrast is in large part misleading. Logical truths, e.g., statements of the form 'If p and q then q', are not about statements; they may be about anything, depending on what statements we put in the blanks 'p' and 'q'. When we talk *about* such logical truths, and when we expound implications, we are indeed talking about statements; but so are we when we talk *about* mathematical truths.

But it is indeed the case that the truths of mathematics treat explicitly of abstract nonlinguistic things, e.g., numbers and functions, whereas the truths of logic, in a reasonably limited sense of the word 'logic', have no such entities as specific subject matter. This is an important difference. Despite this difference, however, logic in its higher reaches is found to bring us by natural stages into mathematics. For, it happens that certain unobtrusive extensions of logical theory carry us into a realm, sometimes also called 'logic' in a broad sense of the word, which does have abstract entities of a special kind as subject matter. These entities are classes; and the logical theory of classes, or set theory, proves to be the basic discipline of pure mathematics. From it, as first came to be known through the work of Frege, Dedekind, Weierstrass, and their successors in the late nineteenth century and after, the whole of classical mathematics can be generated. [Before the end of the book we shall have ascended through four grades of logic in the narrower sense, and emerged into set theory; and here we shall see, as examples of the derivation of classical mathematics, how the concept of number and various related notions can be defined.]

Logical Appraisal

P. F. Strawson

1. When a man says or writes something, there are many different ways in which his performance may be judged. Among other things, we may question his truthfulness or criticize his style, we may assess the morality of what he says, or we may appraise its logic; though not all these types of assessment are appropriate to all kinds of utterance. The words 'logical' and 'illogical' are themselves among the words of logical appraisal. If you call a discourse logical, you are in some degree commending it. If you call it illogical, you are, so far, condemning it. Words and phrases which go with 'logical' are 'consistent', 'cogent', 'valid', 'it follows'; words and phrases which go with 'illogical' are 'inconsistent', 'self-contradictory', 'invalid', 'a *non sequitur*'. Part of our problem is to see what sort of appraisal these words are used for, to what kind of standards we appeal in using them. It is easy to see that these are not moral or aesthetic standards; that logical criticism is not, say, a kind of literary criticism. A slightly more difficult distinction is that between the criticism we offer when we declare a man's remarks to be untrue and the criticism we offer when we declare them to be inconsistent. In the first case we criticize his remarks on the ground that they fail to square with the facts; in the second case we criticize them on the ground that they fail to square with one another. The charge of untruth refers beyond the words and sentences the man uses to that in the world about which he talks. We deny his assertion, and, in doing so, make a counter-assertion of our own about the subject of his discourse. We contradict him. But the charge of inconsistency does not in this way refer to anything outside the statements that the man makes. We simply consider the way his statements hang together. Just from considering the sentences themselves, as they are used, we can, perhaps, see that not all the statements he makes can be true together. It is not that we contradict him, and in doing so, make a counter-assertion about the subject of his remarks; we assert that he has contradicted himself, and, in doing this, we make no appeal to the

This essay originally appeared as ch. 1 of P. F. Strawson, *Introduction to Logical Theory* (London: Methuen, 1952). It is reprinted here by permission of the author, and of Routledge.

facts and express no opinion about them. It is this kind of internal criticism that is appraisal of the logic of a piece of discourse.

I. INCONSISTENCY

2. Words of logical appraisal have connected meanings. To be clear about the meaning of one such word is to be clear about the meanings of the others. For example, in a proof or argument, one statement (the conclusion) is said to follow logically from, or to be logically implied by, others (the premises), if the argument is valid; and an argument is valid only if it would be inconsistent (or self-contradictory) to assert the premises while denying the conclusion; or, in other words, only if the truth of the premises is inconsistent with the falsity of the conclusion. A deductive argument is a sort of threat, which takes the form: if you accept these premises as true, then you must accept this conclusion as true as well, on pain of self-contradiction. From among the various concepts of logical appraisal, I shall select this notion of inconsistency or self-contradiction for detailed discussion. Other choices could have been made, but there are reasons, which will emerge as we go on, for making this choice.

3. What is inconsistency? It is better to approach this question indirectly, by asking a series of others. One might ask first: Why bother to avoid inconsistency? What is wrong with contradicting yourself? There is nothing morally wrong about it. It may not even be entirely pointless. Suppose a man sets out to walk to a certain place; but, when he gets half-way there, turns round and comes back again. This may not be pointless. He may, after all, have wanted only exercise. But, from the point of view of a change of position, it is as if he had never set out. And so a man who contradicts himself may have succeeded in exercising his vocal chords. But from the point of view of imparting information, of communicating facts (or falsehoods) it is as if he had never opened his mouth. He utters words, but does not say anything. Or he might be compared with a man who makes as if to give something away and then takes it back again. He arouses expectations which he does not fulfil; and this may have been his purpose. Similarly, it may have been the purpose of a man who contradicts himself just to create puzzlement. The point is that the *standard* purpose of speech, the intention to communicate something, is frustrated by self-contradiction. Contradicting oneself is like writing something down and then erasing it, or putting a line through it. A contradiction cancels itself and leaves nothing. Consequently one cannot explain

what a contradiction is just by indicating, as one might be tempted to do, a certain form of words. One might be tempted to say that a contradiction was anything of the form 'X is the case and X is not the case'. But this will not do. If someone asks you whether you were pleased by something, you may reply: 'Well, I was and I wasn't', and you will communicate perfectly well. Or there might be a convention that when one said anything of this form, the second part of the sentence was to be neglected. Then the minimum requirement for such a contradiction would be to say, first, 'X is the case and X is not the case' and, after that, 'X is not the case and X is the case'. Nevertheless, the temptation to explain a contradiction as anything of this form is, we shall see, not without point.

4. The next two questions to ask are more difficult. They are: (*a*) when we use these words of logical appraisal, what is it exactly that we are appraising? and (*b*) how does logical appraisal become possible? That is, we shall ask: what is it exactly that we declare to be inconsistent? and: what makes inconsistency possible? I have spoken of *statements* as being inconsistent with each other; and there is a temptation to think that in this context we mean by a statement the same thing as a sentence of a certain kind; or, perhaps, the meaning of such a sentence. But suppose I write on the blackboard the following two pairs of sentences: (i) 'I am under six foot tall' and 'I am over six foot tall'; (ii) 'The conductor is a bachelor' and 'The conductor is married'. In writing the sentences on the blackboard, I have, of course, not contradicted myself; for I may have written them there with a purely illustrative intention, in giving an English lesson. Someone might say: Nevertheless, the sentences in each pair *are* inconsistent with each other. But what would this mean? Would it mean that if they were ever uttered with the intention of making a statement, an inconsistency would result? But suppose the first two sentences were uttered by different people, or by the same person at an interval of years; and that the second two sentences were uttered in different omnibuses, or in the same omnibus, but on different days. Then there would be no inconsistency. Earlier, I paraphrased 'seeing that two statements are inconsistent' as 'seeing that they cannot both be true together'. And it is clear that that of which we can say that it is true or false is also that of which we can say that it is consistent or inconsistent with another of its kind. What these examples show is that we cannot identify that which is true or false (the statement) with the sentence used in making it; for the same sentence may be used to make quite different statements, some of them true and some of them

false. And this does not arise from any ambiguity in the sentence. The sentence may have a single meaning which is precisely what, as in these cases, allows it to be used to make quite different statements. So it will not do to identify the statement either with the sentence or with the meaning of the sentence. A particular statement is identified, not only by reference to the words used, but also by reference to the circumstances in which they are used, and, sometimes, to the identity of the person using them. No one would be tempted to say that the sentence 'I am over six foot tall' was inconsistent with the sentence 'You are under six foot tall'. But plainly they can be used, in certain circumstances, to make statements which are inconsistent with each other; i.e., in the case where the second sentence is addressed to the man by whom the first sentence is uttered.

It is easy to see why one is tempted to think of the sentence 'I am over six foot tall' as being inconsistent with the sentence 'I am under six foot tall'. One thinks of both sentences as being uttered, in the same breath, by the same person. In this case we should ordinarily regard that person as having contradicted himself, i.e., we should regard him as having said something and then unsaid it; and so as having said nothing. The important assumption is that the two expressions 'over six foot tall' and 'under six foot tall' are applied to the same person at the same time. Let us give the name 'incompatible predicates' to any pair of expressions the application of which to the same person or thing at the same time results in an inconsistency. Thus we can say that one of the ways in which it is possible to say something inconsistent is by applying incompatible predicates to the same person or thing at the same time.

5. But must a language have incompatible predicates in it? And what makes predicates incompatible? I want to answer the first question by saying, not that a language must have incompatible predicates in it; only that it is very natural that it should. And I want to answer the second question by saying that it is we, the makers of language, who make predicates incompatible. One of the main purposes for which we use language is to report events and to describe things and persons. Such reports and descriptions are like answers to questions of the form: what was it like? what is it (he, she) like? We describe something, say what it is like, by applying to it words that we are also prepared to apply to other things. But not to all other things. A word that we are prepared to apply to everything without exception (such as certain words in current use in popular, and especially military, speech) would be useless for the purposes of description. For when we

say what a thing is like, we not only compare it with other things, we also distinguish it from other things. (These are not two activities, but two aspects of the same activity.) Somewhere, then, a boundary must be drawn, limiting the applicability of a word used in describing things; and it is we who decide where the boundaries are to be drawn.

This metaphor of drawing boundaries is in some ways misleading. I do not mean by it that we often make conscious decisions of this kind (though we sometimes do); nor that our boundary-drawing is a quite arbitrary matter; nor that the boundaries are fixed and definite; nor that the decisions we make when we make them, are purely verbal decisions. The boundaries are more like areas of indeterminate ownership than frontier-lines. We show ourselves to be near such a boundary, and we show also its indeterminacy, when, in reply to such a question as 'Was it red?', we give such an answer as 'Well, I suppose you could call it red'. We show ourselves on the point of making a boundary-decision when, with all the facts before us, we hesitate over the application of a certain word. Does such and such an act constitute an act of aggression or not? This case shows, too, how our decision is not a purely verbal matter; for important consequences may follow from our deciding that it is, or is not, an act of aggression. What makes our decisions, for a word already in use, non-arbitrary, is this: that our normal purpose will be defeated if the comparison implicit in the use of the word is too unnatural, if the similarity is too tenuous.

We may say: two predicates are incompatible when they lie on different sides of a boundary we have drawn: 'under six foot tall' and 'over six foot tall'; 'red' and 'orange'; 'aggressive' and 'pacific'. But this needs some explanation. Suppose you draw a closed figure on a piece of paper and then someone indicates a point on the ceiling and says: 'Does this point lie inside or outside the boundaries of the figure?' Of course, one might answer by imagining the boundaries of the figure extended in another dimension, up to the ceiling. But you might refuse to answer the question, by saying that you were drawing the boundary line only in the plane of the paper. Whatever lay outside the line in the plane of the paper was excluded from the figure. Things lying in a different plane were not excluded from it, but neither were they included in it. The figure has a certain plane of exclusiveness. And so with a word: it has a certain range of incompatibilities. 'Under six foot tall' is incompatible with 'over six foot tall'; but neither is incompatible with 'aggressive'. The last expression has a different incompatibility-range from the other two. There may sometimes be objections of a logical kind to applying expressions with different incompatibility-ranges to the same thing; but these will not be the objection that inconsistency will result from doing so.

When we apply a predicate to something, we implicitly exclude from application to that thing the predicates which lie outside the boundaries of the predicate we apply, but in the same incompatibility-range. By this I mean that if we go on to apply to the thing, in the same breath, one of the predicates which lie outside those boundaries, we shall be taken to have contradicted ourselves and said nothing. (This might be taken as a definition of 'incompatible predicates'.) But there is a qualification to be made here. Just as we might reply to the query 'Were you pleased?' with the words 'Well, I was and I wasn't' without inconsistency, so we might apply to the same thing, in the same breath, two predicates, which would ordinarily be regarded as incompatible, without contradicting ourselves. If we do this, we invite the question 'What do you mean?'; and if we can explain what we mean, or show the point of saying what we say, then we have not contradicted ourselves. But if there is no way of doing this, we are inconsistent. Thus we might say, in answer to a question, 'He is both over six foot tall and under six foot tall', and then explain that he has a disease which makes him stoop, but that if he were cured and were able to stand upright, he would top the six-foot mark. This shows again that one cannot fully explain what self-contradiction is, just by reference to groupings of words.

6. So long as we bear this qualification in mind, we can safely speak of incompatible predicates and can safely say that, when we apply a predicate to something by way of describing it, we implicitly exclude from application to it any predicates incompatible with that which we apply. (We should be said to have contradicted anyone who had just applied any of those predicates to the thing.) When we notice that this function of exclusion is implicit in all descriptive uses of language, we should not find it surprising that language contains devices for rendering the function explicit; devices of which, in English, the word 'not' is the most prominent. There are many very different kinds of occasion on which our primary concern is with the explicit exclusion of a predicate; e.g., when we wish to contradict a previous assertion; or to correct a possible false impression; or to express the contrast between what had been expected, feared, suggested, or hoped, and the reality; sometimes, when we are answering a direct question; sometimes, when we grope towards the right description by eliminating the wrong ones. What is common to such cases is that they create a need or a motive for emphasizing a difference rather than a resemblance. It is instructive to compare the use of 'not' with the use of those words which begin with negative prefixes; like 'intolerable', 'unpretentious', 'impolite', 'non-aggressive'. These words bear their incompatibilities

on their faces as surely as any phrase containing 'not'; but one would hardly say of them that they have the same function of explicitly rejecting a suggested description. They do not point more emphatically to differences than to likenesses; they rather serve to underline the fact that the two are complementary. One might ask why some words have such manifest incompatibles (viz., words which are the same except for a negative prefix), while others do not; why we do not speak of things as 'unblue', for example. One might be inclined to suggest that it is because 'not being blue' is relatively so indeterminate; i.e., that, where there is a wide range of incompatible predicates, like colour-words, it is unnatural to have a single word expressly excluding one of them. But I do not think this is a complete answer. There is a wide range of races and nationalities, but we have words (e.g., 'foreign', 'non-English', 'non-European') to indicate 'not being of a particular nationality (or range of races)'. I think the answer is, rather, that if we had a constant and persistent interest in things not being blue, as opposed to such a temporary interest as may arise from, e.g., wishing to correct a false impression, then we *should* have a word for this. Then we might say that in calling a thing 'unblue' we should be as much emphasizing its likeness to other unblue things as its difference from blue things. (It was characteristic of those formal logicians who framed unnatural-looking negative terms, like 'non-blue', not to concern themselves with questions and differences of this kind.)

This discussion of the function of 'not' helps us to see part of the point of the saying, incorrect though it is, that a contradiction is simply something of the form 'X is the case and X is not the case'. The standard and primary use of 'not' is specifically to contradict or correct; to cancel a suggestion of one's own or another's. And there is no restriction on the sphere in which it may exercise this function. Not all predicates have corresponding negatively prefixed terms, and not all statements are of the kind in which we simply apply a descriptive predicate to some person or thing. But any statement, whether or not it is of this simple kind, can be contradicted by the use of 'not'. So we are strongly inclined to regard a statement involving something of the form 'X is the case and X is not the case' as a self-contradiction; though always the indeterminacy of the verbal boundaries we draw, the different points of view which may tempt us both to apply and to withhold an expression, allow of the possibility of a consistent meaning being given to something of this form.

7. It is, then, our own activity of making language through using it, our own determination of the limits of the application of words, that

makes inconsistency possible; and it is no accident that, when we want to form for ourselves a general pattern or type of inconsistency, we employ the two words 'and' and 'not', together with a repetition of some one phrase or expression. Since all concepts of logical appraisal may be explained in terms of inconsistency, it is not surprising that these two words should play an important role in logic.

But we can create the possibility of inconsistency in statement, and hence of validity in argument, in a way more deliberate and self-conscious than those I have so far discussed. We can deliberately fix the boundaries of some words in relation to those of other words. This is what we do when we *define*[1] words or phrases. To introduce or to accept a definition[1] is to announce or to agree that conjoining the defined (or defining) expression with the defining (or defined) expression by the words 'and' and 'not' in their standard use (or in any equivalent way), and referring this conjunction to one and the same situation, is to count as an inconsistency. Accepting a definition is agreeing to be bound by a rule of language of this kind.

8. Let us now return to the questions we asked earlier: namely, what is it to which we apply words of logical appraisal? and: what makes logical appraisal possible? We saw that the answer to the first question was not 'sentences or groups of words', but 'statements or groups of statements'. It is statements and not sentences that are inconsistent with one another, follow from one another, etc. We see that the answer to the second question is: the boundaries of application that we draw between one expression and another, the rules we come to observe for using expressions of all kinds.[2] And the answer to the second question shows the full point of the temptation to answer the first by talking of sentences (groups of words) as being inconsistent. Behind inconsistencies between statements, stand rules for the use of expressions. If one understands this relationship, a lot of things which have puzzled people become clear. One sees how a linguistic

1. The words 'define' and 'definition' have many connected, though distinguishable, uses, of some of which what I say here is not true. I use the words here in a 'strict' sense.

2. But we must notice that, as far as ordinary speech is concerned, and apart from the introduction of words by *definition*, this talk of 'rules' may mislead us. We do not *generally* (in ordinary speech) draw up rules and make our practice conform to them; it is rather that we extract the rules from our practice, from noticing when we *correct* one another, when we are inclined to say that something is *inconsistent*, and so on.

rule for expressions in a particular language can lead to a general statement of logical appraisal which transcends individual languages altogether. Suppose someone says: 'A statement to the effect that a certain person is someone's son-in-law is inconsistent with the statement that he has never been married'. Let us call the statement he makes in saying this a general statement of logical appraisal or, for short, a logical statement. Now suppose someone says: 'In English the words "son-in-law of" mean the same as the words "married to the daughter of".' Let us call the statement he makes in saying this a linguistic statement. Now what is the relation between the logical statement and the linguistic statement? Well, suppose we translate into French the sentence used to make the logical statement. We shall obtain a sentence with no English words in it. If we also translate into French the sentence used to make the linguistic statement (i.e., the sentence beginning 'In English'), we shall obtain a French sentence, beginning 'En anglais', in which the expressions '"son-in-law of"' and '"married to the daughter of"' reappear unchanged. It seems that, whereas we are inclined to say that the French and English versions of the logical statement mean the same thing, or are used to make the same statement, we are not inclined to say that the English sentence used to make the linguistic statement means the same as the French sentence: 'En français les mots "gendre de" veulent dire la même chose que les mots "marié avec la fille de"'. For we are inclined to say that anyone uttering *this* sentence would be talking about a rule of French, whereas anyone uttering the English sentence used to make the linguistic statement would be talking about a rule of English. So these sentences are used to make quite different statements about quite different things, namely French words and English words. And if one says this, as one is strongly inclined to do, and also says that the French and English versions of the logical statement mean the same (are versions of the same statement), then, of course, it would seem to follow that the logical statement is not about what the linguistic statements are about, that the truth of the logical statement is independent of the truth of the linguistic statements; and from here it is an easy step to thinking of logical facts as independent of linguistic facts, and to adopting an attitude of reverence to logical facts. But to take this step is to forget that the fact that the English and French versions of the logical statement mean the same is itself in part the linguistic fact that 'son-in-law of' and 'married' in English mean the same as 'gendre de' and 'marié' in French. We might express this by saying that there is, after all, an alternative translation of the English sentence used for making the linguistic statement; namely the French sentence quoted above, beginning 'En français . . .' We might say that these were really different versions of the same rule; that in laying down inconsistency-rules in one language, we were implicitly laying down inconsistency-rules for the corresponding expressions in all languages; and that thus a linguistic statement *of the kind quoted* transcends the language of the words which it mentions. Only it is less natural to say this than to say that a logical statement transcends the language in which it is framed.

We see that there are difficulties in identifying logical statements with linguistic statements; in saying that sentences used to make logical statements mean the same as corresponding sentences used to make linguistic statements; and seeing this is apt to give us the illusion of an independent realm of logical facts, of which linguistic rules are merely the adventitious verbal clothing. We feel that, while it is a mere matter of linguistic history, which could easily have been different, that the expression 'son-in-law' means what it does mean, the statement we make when we say 'The statement that a man is a son-in-law is inconsistent with the statement that he has never been married' is one that could not be false, even though it is an historical accident that we make it in these words. But when we voice this feeling we are voicing the truism that a word could not both have the sense it in fact has (the sense in which we use it in making statements) and not have that sense.

The important thing is to see that when you draw the boundaries of the applicability of words in one language and then connect the words of that language with those of another by means of translation-rules, there is no need to draw the boundaries again for the second language. They are already drawn. (I am not suggesting that this is the order in which things are done; though it is the order in which things are learned.) This is why (or partly why) logical statements framed in one language are not just about that language.

It is important also to notice that this reason for not regarding statements of logical appraisal as about particular groups of words (e.g., sentences) is different from, though connected with, that which we have discussed earlier. Earlier we pointed out that it is not sentences which we say are inconsistent with one another, follow from one another, etc., but statements; the question of what statement is made, and of whether a statement is made at all, depends upon other things than simply what words are used. But rules about words lie behind all statements of logical appraisal; and it remains to be seen whether we can best do logic in terms of rules directly about representative expressions, or in terms of logical relations between statements.

II: REASONING

9. People often say that logic is the study of the principles of deductive reasoning. But this is too narrow, and includes irrelevant suggestions. Arguing, proving, inferring, concluding, solving a mathematical problem, might all be said to be kinds of reasoning. Their aims and purposes are different. The aim of argument is conviction; one tries to get someone to agree that some statement is true or false. You may get a man to agree that a statement is true by showing him that it follows from other statements which he already accepts. You may get him to agree that a statement is false because from it there follows another which he rejects. Proving is different: a man may argue successfully, and even validly, without proving; for an invalid argument may convince, and the premises of a valid argument may be false. Moreover, a man may prove something without arguing, without seeking to convince. When you prove a mathematical theorem in an examination, you are not trying to convince the examiner of its truth; your object is to exhibit your mathematical knowledge by writing down a set of statements of which the last is the theorem to be proved and of which each follows from the ones written down already, together with earlier theorems. Inferring, drawing conclusions, is different again. Here you know some facts or truths already, and are concerned to see what further information can be derived from them; to find out their logical consequences. Though inferring, proving, arguing have different purposes, they seem usually[3] to have also the common purpose of connecting truths with truths. The validity of the steps is, in general, prized for the sake of the truth of the conclusions to which they lead. But neither the common purpose, nor the different purposes, of arguing, proving, inferring, are a logical concern. The logical question, of the validity of the steps, is one that can be raised and answered independently of the question of whether these purposes are achieved. The validity of the steps does not alone guarantee the truth of the conclusion, nor their invalidity, its falsity. For to say that the steps are valid, that the conclusion follows from the premises, is simply to say

---

3. Not always. A child solves problems in applied arithmetic. What he aims at is not the *true* answer but the *right* answer. And what he is given marks for is not the answer, but the way he gets it.

that it would be inconsistent to assert the premises and deny the conclusion; that the truth of the premises is inconsistent with the falsity of the conclusion. The assessment of the reasoning as valid rules out a certain *combination* of truth and falsity; viz., truth in the premises and falsity in the conclusion. But it leaves open the possibility of other combinations: falsity with falsity and falsity with truth, as well as truth with truth. We are not told, when we are told that the reasoning is valid, that it would be inconsistent to deny both premises and conclusion or to assert the conclusion and deny the premises.

10. We often signalize a claim to be making a valid step in reasoning by the use of certain expressions to link one statement, or set of statements, and another. These are words and phrases like 'so', 'consequently', 'therefore', 'since', 'for', 'it follows that', &c. And other expressions are sometimes used to signalize steps, which we should rightly hesitate to call steps in reasoning, but which are of no less interest to the logician. I have in mind such expressions as 'that is to say', 'in other words', 'more briefly', 'I mean'. These are expressions which we sometimes (though not always or only) use on occasions on which we should describe ourselves, not as inferring or arguing, but rather as, say, putting into other words something that has already been said, or repeating it with something left out, or summarizing it, or making a *précis*. There is no sharply definite line separating those steps which we should call steps in reasoning, and those steps which we should describe in one of the alternative ways I have listed. Obviously, there are extremes, which we should classify without hesitation. Where the steps are numerous and intricate, we unhesitatingly apply such words as 'inference', or 'argument'; where something that has been said is simply repeated, in whole or in part, we unhesitatingly withhold these words. But there are borderline cases. A man who linked one part of his discourse with another by the phrase, 'in other words', thus disclaiming anything so portentous as an inference, might be met with the rejoinder 'But that doesn't follow', which imputes, and disallows, the claim to have validly inferred. The differences between the steps which are steps in reasoning and the steps we should not so describe are, from some points of view, important. From our present point of view, they are less important than the resemblances. What is common to all the cases I refer to is the claim, signalized by the linking expressions,[4] that it would be inconsistent to

4. Of course, the linking expressions I listed are not always used to make just this claim.

assert what precedes those expressions and to deny what follows them. The logician interests himself in cases in which this relationship holds between statements, irrespective of whether or not the transition from one statement to another so related to it is a transition which we should dignify by the name 'step in reasoning'; irrespective even of whether it is something we should acknowledge as a transition. . . . This explains why 'study of the principles of valid deductive reasoning' is too narrow a description of logic. A man who repeats himself does not reason. But it is inconsistent to assert and deny the same thing. So a logician will say that a statement has to itself the relationship he is interested in.

III. THE LOGICIAN'S SECOND-ORDER VOCABULARY

11. Most of the statements we make are not themselves about statements but about people or things. Statements which are not themselves about statements we shall call first-order statements; statements about first-order statements we shall call second-order statements; and so on. Since words of logical appraisal are used for talking about statements, the statements we make in using such words must at least be of the second order. We shall say that such words constitute a part of the logician's second-order vocabulary. Later, we shall speak analogously of first-order sentences (i.e., sentences used for making statements not about sentences or statements), and second-order sentences (i.e., sentences used for making statements about first-order sentences or first-order statements).

The phrases 'follows from' and 'logically implies' carry with them a suggestion of those mind-exercising situations in which we are prepared to talk of reasoning being carried on, of inferences being made, &c. The word 'valid', applied to a group of statements linked by some expression (e.g., 'therefore') signalizing the claim that one of the statements follows from the others, carries the same suggestion. We want a word, to signify that one statement is so related to another that it would be inconsistent to assert the first and deny the second, which does not carry this suggestion. It is customary to use the word 'entails' for this purpose. But, when it is convenient to do so, I shall license myself also to use ordinary words and phrases of logical appraisal in a manner which disregards the suggestion that reasoning-situations are involved. Such a departure from ordinary usage need not be misleading, if it is self-conscious.

12. I want now to discuss the relations to one another of some words of the logician's second-order vocabulary. First we must dis-

criminate between two kinds of inconsistency, between a wider and a narrower sense of 'contradiction'.

Suppose someone says of a certain man that he is over six foot tall, and someone else says of the same person that he is under six foot tall. Let us say that the first speaker makes the statement that o; and then let us abbreviate the phrase 'the statement that o' to 'S_o'. And let us say that the second speaker makes the statement that u; and then let us abbreviate the phrase 'the statement that u' to 'S_u'. Then, unless explanations are produced to show that the contradiction is only apparent, we shall properly say that the second speaker has contradicted the first, that S_u is inconsistent with S_o. A third speaker may say, of the man discussed, that he is just six foot tall; and in doing so he contradicts both previous speakers. Let us say that he makes S_j (the statement that the man under discussion is just six foot tall); and that S_j is inconsistent both with S_o and with S_u.

But now let us suppose that the second speaker, instead of making S_u, had made S_{not-o} (the statement that the man under discussion was not over six foot tall). Again, unless explanations were produced to show that the contradiction was only apparent, we should say that he had contradicted the first speaker, that S_{not-o} was inconsistent with S_o. But the relation between S_o and S_{not-o} is not quite the same as the relation between S_o and S_u. For whereas a statement, viz., S_j, could be made, that was inconsistent with both S_o and S_u, there is no way of making a statement that is inconsistent with both S_o and S_{not-o}. We express this by saying that S_o and S_{not-o} are contradictories, whereas S_o and S_u are only contraries. To say of two statements that they are contradictories is to say that they are inconsistent with each other and that no statement is inconsistent with both of them. To say of two statements that they are contraries is to say that they are inconsistent with each other, while leaving open the possibility that there is some statement inconsistent with both. (This may be taken as a definition of 'contradictory' and 'contrary' in terms of 'inconsistent'.) But we say of a man that he 'contradicts' another (or himself) when they (or he) make (or makes) statements which are inconsistent with each other, whether or not they are contradictories.[5]

We have already discussed the question of how inconsistency is possible; and the same discussion helps us to see how contradiction, in the narrower sense, is possible; and how this sense underlies the natural choice of 'X is the case and X is not the case' as the general

---

5. I shall continue to use 'contradiction', 'self-contradictory', 'contradict' sometimes in the wider sense; but shall restrict 'contradictory' to the narrower.

form of a contradiction. We compared the incompatibility-range of a predicate with the plane of a closed figure. Two predicates were incompatible when they lay on different sides of a boundary we had drawn in a certain range of incompatibilities. Suppose two predicates lying on different sides of such a boundary are applied to the same thing, so that two inconsistent statements are made. Then we can make a statement inconsistent with both these by applying to that thing a predicate lying outside the boundaries of both these predicates, but in the same incompatibility-range. But suppose, between them, the predicate exhaust this range. Then there is no way of making a statement inconsistent with both the previous statements. (If half of the surface of a sheet of paper is coloured red and the other half blue, there is no way of finding a point on the surface of the paper which is in neither the blue nor the red area.) We saw that we had, in language, besides predicates which were incompatible, devices (like 'not') for explicitly excluding (rejecting, withholding) a predicate from application to something. Where such devices exist, it is easy to see how the range of incompatibilities can be exhausted, how it is possible for contradictory statements to be made. Where two inconsistent statements are made by the application of merely incompatible predicates to something, there remains open the possibility of making a statement inconsistent with both, by the application of a third predicate belonging to the same incompatibility-range. But where one statement is inconsistent with another because it explicitly rejects (withholds, excludes) the predicate which the other applies, this possibility vanishes. To say that a thing neither has nor has not a certain property (i.e., to attempt to say something inconsistent both with the statement that it has, and with the statement that it has not, that property) is like saying that it both has, and has not, that property. One would not know what it meant, unless an explanation were given; though the indeterminacy of the boundaries of words, or the different points of view from which we may be tempted to apply and to withhold expressions, may allow of our giving a meaning to such a form of words. One might say: two statements are contradictories when a man who asserts both and a man who denies both, will both be taken to have contradicted themselves and said nothing.

But there is another way in which we can understand someone who says that a thing neither has nor has not a certain property. E.g., 'Does he care about it?' 'He neither cares nor doesn't care; he's dead.' The answer shows that the question is inappropriate to the circumstances, that some assumption which the questioner is making is untrue. It does not show that the statement that he cared and the statement that he did not care would both be false; it shows rather that the question of which is true does not arise, because the conditions of its arising are not fulfilled. Many statements are made in this way, against a background of assumption which is not called in question when their truth or falsity is discussed, and the calling in question of which prohibits discussion of their truth or falsity. Comment on the logical relations of statements occurs against the same background, at the same level of assumption, as discussion of their truth or falsity.

Contradictory statements, then, have the character of being both logically exclusive and logically exhaustive. It is perhaps easier to imagine a language in which contradictory statements could not be made than a language in which merely inconsistent statements could not be made. If there were only two kinds of four-footed animals, namely lions and tigers, one would have less need of the word 'not' in discussing the identity of an animal. If people felt less impulse to talk with inadequate information, to ask certain kinds of questions, to approach experience with doubts, fears, hopes, and expectations, one would have less need of the word. But the occasions on which the need is felt for the explicit exclusion of a predicate, or the explicit rejection of a statement or suggestion, are in fact, many. And so we have contradictory statements. We rightly associate with contradiction (in the narrow sense) the following pairs of antithetical expressions or notions: 'Yes' and 'No'; assertion and denial; truth and falsity; 'it is the case' and 'it is not the case'; affirmation and negation. This association is harmless so long as we remember that 'Yes and no' may not be a self-contradictory answer; that 'it is and it isn't' (the conjunction of affirmation and negation) may be used to make a genuine statement; that we may hesitate to call a statement either true or false. 'Assertion' and 'denial' are in a slightly different position. They have contradictory opposition as part of their meaning. Though a man may say 'It is and it isn't' without self-contradiction, we should hesitate to describe this as assertion and denial of the same thing. We would not say that a man could, in the same breath, assert and deny the same thing without self-contradiction. Of these pairs of antithetical expressions, 'assert' and 'deny', 'affirmative' and 'negative', 'true' and 'false' belong, like the word 'statement' itself, to the logician's second-order vocabulary, though they are not words of logical appraisal; whereas 'yes' and 'no', 'it is' and 'it is not' belong to the first-order vocabulary, though they may figure in second-order contexts.

13. We are now in a position to deploy more systematically the logician's interrelated vocabulary of logical appraisal. For this purpose

it is convenient to introduce certain abbreviatory devices. To begin
with we shall make a new extension of an abbreviatory device we have
used already. In discussing the relation between the statement, made
with regard to a certain person, that he was over six foot tall, and the
statement, with regard to the same person, that he was under six foot
tall, we referred to the first statement by means of the expression 'S_o'
and to the second statement by means of the expression 'S_u'. But
when we discuss, in a general way, the inter-relations of the vocabulary of logical appraisal, we shall want to refer to statements in general
rather than to particular statements. For example, we introduced the
word 'entails', explaining its meaning roughly as follows: to say that
one statement entails another is to say that it would be inconsistent to
make the first and deny the second. This explanation, which refers not
to particular statements, but to statements in general, we shall express
as follows: to say that S_1 entails S_2 is to say that it would be inconsistent to make S_1 and deny S_2. Here the subscripts play the role of the
words 'one', 'another', 'first', and 'second' in the original explanation.

This explanation can be paraphrased further. The notion of denial
is, as we have seen, closely linked with that of contradictoriness. To
deny a statement has the same logical force as to assert its contradictory; the differences are here irrelevant. So we may paraphrase our
explanation as follows: to say that S_1 entails S_2 is to say that it would
be inconsistent both to assert S_1 and to assert the contradictory of S_2.
Now the negative form of a statement (say, a form which includes the
word 'not') is not always its contradictory, as we have seen. But it is so
sufficiently often to justify us in abbreviating the phrase 'the contradictory of S_2' to '*not*-S_2'. So we can re-paraphrase: to say that S_1
entails S_2 is to say that it would be inconsistent both to assert S_1 and
to assert *not*-S_2. If it would be inconsistent to make a certain pair of
statements, it would be inconsistent to make the conjunctive statement (employing, say, the word 'and') of which they were the conjuncts. So, abbreviating 'the conjunctive statement of which S_1 and
not-S_2 are the conjuncts' to 'S_1 *and not*-S_2', we shall reparaphrase: to
say that S_1 entails S_2 is to say that S_1 *and not*-S_2 is inconsistent.

This explanation of entailment is like a definition of 'entails'. We
are giving a rule for the use of the word. We may emphasize this
character of the proceeding by using inverted commas and writing:

'S_1 entails S_2' may be defined as 'S_1 *and not*-S_2 is inconsistent'

and this can be abbreviated to:

'S_1 entails S_2' $=_{Df}$ 'S_1 *and not*-S_2 is inconsistent'.

When we use inverted commas, we emphasize the fact that we are giving a rule for the use of a certain expression in a certain language. When we refrain from using them, we emphasize the fact that implicit in such a rule are rules for all synonymous expressions in all languages. The definition is related to the explanation somewhat as linguistic statement to logical statement. There are other differences between the explanation of entailment and the definition.[6] These will emerge later.

14. Variants on 'is inconsistent' are 'is self-contradictory', 'is logically impossible', 'is logically false'. Now suppose we deny, or assert the contradictory of, an inconsistent statement. We saw that a man who *makes* an inconsistent statement says, in a manner, nothing at all. His statement cancels itself. So what is said by a man who *denies* an inconsistent statement? It seems that he says nothing either: he, too, leaves things where they were. (Of course, one can separately deny two statements which are inconsistent with each other, provided they are not contradictories, and succeed in saying something: to the speakers who respectively make S_o and S_u we can say 'You are both wrong' and in saying this, we implicitly make S_j. But to deny the single statement, S_o *and* S_u, is to say nothing about the height of the man discussed; for to make S_o *and* S_u is to say nothing about his height.) Nevertheless, there may be a point in asserting the contradictory of an inconsistent statement. It may serve, for example, to remind someone of the rule that is broken in making it. It may show him he has got into a tangle in making it. It may help him to show us how he was not really making an inconsistent statement at all, but trying to describe an unusual situation or a borderline case. Or it may serve to remind *ourselves* of the rules, to help us to work something out, or to correct tangles of our own. It may have other purposes as well. When we assert the contradictory of an inconsistent statement, we are said to make a logically necessary statement. Variants on 'logically necessary statement' are 'analytic statement', 'necessary truth', 'logically true statement'.

It is evident that the purposes which I have said might be served by making a logically necessary statement in the form of a contradictory of an inconsistent statement could be served equally well by making it in the form of a second-order statement of logical appraisal. These would, in fact, be different ways of saying the same thing, or of making the same appraisal. Instead of saying 'He is not both over and under six foot tall', we could say 'The statement that he is over six foot

---

6. The symbol 'S_1' changes its character.

tall is inconsistent with the statement that he is under six foot tall', or 'The statement that he is over six foot tall entails the statement that he is not under six foot tall'. Or we might adopt a form of words intermediate between the quoted first-order form and the quoted second-order forms. We might say: 'He *can't* be both over and under six foot tall' or 'It's *impossible* for him to be both over and under six foot tall'. Of these forms of words, those which employ the logical-appraisal words 'entails' and 'inconsistent' are the least apt to be philosophically misleading. The first form is too reminiscent of the form of words in which we give information about the height of a man, and is apt to make us think that anyone using this sentence would be giving very reliable information of this kind. The last two forms are too reminiscent of those sentences in which we discuss the physical and practical impossibilities of life, and are apt to make us think that we have here an instance of laws more adamant than even Nature gives, though of that kind.

To say that a statement is necessary, then, is to say that it is the contradictory of an inconsistent statement. We should notice that there is an oddity in using the word 'statement' at all in this connexion, and that we only do so by a kind of analogy. When a man makes an ordinary statement (ordinary statements, i.e., statements which are neither inconsistent nor logically necessary, are sometimes called 'contingent' or 'synthetic'), there is, or may be, a question as to whether what he says is true or false; and to determine the answer to it, we must turn our attention from the words he uses to the world, towards whatever it is that he is talking about. We may have to conduct experiments. But when a man makes a necessary or self-contradictory statement, there is no comparable question and no comparable procedure. We should not know where to look, or what experiments to conduct. How could we determine the truth or falsity of an inconsistent statement, when a man who makes such a statement says nothing? Of course, there are resemblances between the man who makes an inconsistent, and the man who makes an ordinary, statement. They both utter (or write) words; and they both use words which *can* be used to inform (or to misinform). The difference is that the man who makes an inconsistent statement arranges these words in such a way that we regard him as having said something which cancels itself. This is an unsatisfactory way of using words, and we compare this with the unsatisfactoriness of the way in which we use words when we make a false statement. For the general and standard purpose of making statements is to communicate information, to state facts. This purpose is frustrated when something false is said. It is also frustrated, though in a quite different way, when a man contradicts himself. So we compare the two ways of failing to state facts; and by analogy with the case of a man who makes a false statement, we say, of the man who contradicts himself, that he too, makes a false statement, only a *logically* false statement. And since we say that the man who asserts the contradictory of a false statement makes a true statement, we easily take the step of talking of a man who negates the form of words used in making the inconsistent statement as having uttered a true statement, only a *logically* (or *necessarily*) true statement. And then we are misled by the analogy: either into thinking of a special set of extra-linguistic facts or realities (logical necessities) described by logically true statements; or, when we see that what lie behind logical appraisals are rules of language, into thinking of necessary statements as, straightforwardly, statements *about* words. But they are neither; it is a corrective to both views to say, from time to time: the word 'statement' is misapplied in this connexion.

But there is no need to say it all the time. So I shall continue to talk of necessary statements. This conception enables us to give a further explanation of entailment, this time in terms of logical necessity. To say that S_1 entails S_2 is to say that the contradictory of S_1 *and not-*S_2 is logically necessary. Using the convention of abbreviating 'the contradictory of' to '*not-*', and using brackets to indicate that it is the contradictory of the single statement, S_1 *and not-*S_2, that we are talking of, we have: to say that S_1 entails S_2 is to say that *not-*$(S_1$ *and not-*$S_2)$ is logically necessary. By analogy with a practice of logicians which will be discussed later, the expression '*not-*$(S_1$ *and not-*$S_2)$' may be abbreviated by the use of the symbol '$\supset$' to '$S_1 \supset S_2$'. Writing the explanation as a definition, we have

$$\text{'}S_1 \text{ entails } S_2\text{'} =_{Df} \text{'}S_1 \supset S_2 \text{ is logically necessary'.}$$

If we eliminate all the abbreviations and write the latest form of the explanation in full, we have: to say that one statement entails another is to say that the contradictory of the conjunction of the first statement with the contradictory of the second is a necessary statement.

15. These two definitions of 'S_1 entails S_2' as 'S_1 *and not-*S_2 is inconsistent' and as '$S_1 \supset S_2$ is logically necessary' raise a problem. Suppose we have two statements, of which one is inconsistent and the other synthetic. We might, say, have the statement with regard to a certain person, that he both was and was not over six foot tall (we will refer to this as S_t) and the statement that Xmas Day, 1900, was a fine

day (we will refer to this as S_f). Are we, on the strength of the fact that S_t is inconsistent, to say that anyone who makes S_t *and not-*S_f makes an inconsistent statement? If we say this, and adhere to our definition of 'entails', we shall have to say that S_t entails S_f. But we wanted to give a meaning to 'entails' such that saying that one statement entailed another meant the same as saying that the second statement followed logically from the first; except that the suggestion of mind-exercising processes of inference which perhaps adheres to 'follows from' was to be omitted. But we should certainly not say that S_f followed from S_t. 'He is and is not over six foot tall; therefore (so, consequently, in other words, that is to say) Xmas Day, 1900, was a fine day' strikes us as nonsensical, and the use of any of the linking expressions as quite unjustified. Generally, if we *both* adhere to our definition of 'entails' *and* agree to call any conjunctive statement inconsistent simply on the ground that one or both of its conjuncts is inconsistent, we shall be committed to saying that an inconsistent statement entails any statement whatever (whether synthetic or not) and that a necessary statement is entailed by any statement whatever (whether synthetic or not). Equally, we can avoid these consequences either by making it a rule for the use of 'inconsistent' that no conjunctive statement is to be called inconsistent simply on the ground that one or both of its conjuncts is inconsistent; or by adding to our definition of 'S_1 entails S_2' as 'S_1 *and not-*S_2 is inconsistent' the proviso that the inconsistency of the conjunctive statement does not result simply from the inconsistency of one or both of its conjuncts. Between these alternatives we are free to choose.

16. And now to conclude the catalogue of words of logical appraisal. First, we may note that, allowing ourselves the terminological license claimed at the beginning of this part of the chapter, we shall have as variants on 'S_1 entails S_2' the following expressions: 'S_1 logically implies S_2'; 'S_2 follows from S_1'; 'the step from S_1 to S_2 is valid'; 'S_2 is deducible from S_1'. Second, we shall introduce and define the notion of logical equivalence as follows: 'S_1 is logically equivalent to S_2' $=_{Df}$ 'S_1 entails S_2 and S_2 entails S_1'. An alternative definition would be: 'S_1 and *not-*S_2 are contradictories'. It is evident that the introduction of any *definition* leads to a statement of logical equivalence. The definition of 'S_1 entails S_2' as 'S_1 is inconsistent with the contradictory of S_2' for example, leads to the following statement of equivalence: the statement that one statement entails another is logically equivalent to the statement that the first is inconsistent with the contradictory of the second. Third, we may define 'S_1 is the subcon-

trary of S$_2$' as follows: '*not*-S$_1$ is inconsistent with *not*-S$_2$'. This may be compared with the definition of 'S$_1$ is the contrary of S$_2$' as 'S$_1$ is inconsistent with S$_2$'. Two statements are contraries when it is logically impossible for them both to be true; subcontraries when it is logically impossible for them both to be false. These definitions of 'contrary' and 'subcontrary' leave it open whether statements which stand in either of these relations to each other are contradictories or not. Finally, two very useful additions to the logician's vocabulary are the phrases 'necessary condition' and 'sufficient condition'. When one statement entails another, the truth of the first is a sufficient condition of the truth of the second, and the truth of the second a necessary condition of the truth of the first.

Do Conditionals Have Truth-Conditions?

Dorothy Edgington

1. INTRODUCTION

In the first part of this paper (Sects. 2 and 4) I rule out the possibility of truth-conditions for the indicative conditional 'If A, B' which are a truth-function of A and B. In the second part (Sect. 6) I rule out the possibility that such a conditional has truth-conditions which are *not* a truth-function of A and B; I rule out accounts which appeal, for example, to a stronger-than-truth-functional 'connection' between antecedent and consequent, which may or may not be framed in terms of a relation between possible worlds, in stating what has to be the case for 'If A, B' to be true. I conclude, therefore, that the mistake philosophers have made, in trying to understand the conditional, is to assume that its function is to make a statement about how the world is (or how other possible worlds are related to it), true or false, as the case may be. Along the way (Sects. 3 and 5) I develop a positive account of what it is to believe, or to be more or less confident, that if A, B, in terms of which an adequate logic of conditionals can be developed. The argument against truth-conditions is independent of this positive account of the conditional, as I show that any truth-conditional account has counterintuitive consequences, as well as clashing with my positive thesis. But the positive account prevents the essay from merely having created a paradox, or a vacuum.

The essay is inspired by Ernest Adams's book, *The Logic of Conditionals*.[1] My positive thesis is a less technical variant of his. He proves

This essay first appeared in *Crítica: Revista Hispanoamericana de Filosofía*, XVIII, 52 (1986). It is reprinted here by permission of the author and the Editorial Board of *Crítica*.

1. Ernest Adams (1975). Some historical background: Robert Stalnaker (1970) was, I believe, the first to suggest that insight into the semantics of conditionals might be gained from the probability theorist's notion of a conditional probability, $P(B/A)$ (the probability of B given A). Judgements about how probable it is that if A, B, seem to coincide with judgements about the

the negative result too, but hardly perspicuously. My aim, in trying to extract an intuitively compelling argument from a somewhat baffling piece of algebra, is not only to make this way of thinking about conditionals more widely, and more deeply, appreciated. It is also, by weakening the assumptions, to provide a stronger proof of the negative result. I hope to render the positive thesis more plausible, too, by presenting it less technically.

It should not need emphasis that in the conditional we have an indispensable form of thought, which plays a large part in both theoretical reasoning about what is the case and practical reasoning about what to do. Its basic role may be described thus: we are not omniscient; we do not know as much as it would be useful for us to know. We are constantly faced with a range of epistemic possibilities—things that, as far as we know, may be true, when the question whether they are true is relevant to our concerns. As part of such practical or theoretical reasoning, it is often necessary to *suppose* (or assume) that some epistemic possibility is true, and to consider what else would be the case, or would be likely to be the case, given this supposition. The conditional expresses the outcome of such thought processes. It is worth remembering that any type of speech act can be performed within the scope of a supposition. There are conditional questions, commands, etc., as well as conditional assertions.

> If he phones, what shall I say?
> If I'm late, don't stay up.
> If you're determined to do it, you ought to do it today.

To assert or believe that if A, B is to assert (believe) B within the scope of the supposition, or assumption, that A.[2] This is bland

---

probability of B given A. Stalnaker suggested that we should define the conditional as that proposition whose probability is so measured. David Lewis (1976) was the first to prove that there is no such proposition. As a result, Stalnaker and Lewis rejected the equation of the probability of a conditional with a conditional probability, the former defending a non-truth-functional account, the latter the truth-functional account of indicative conditional propositions. Adams, instead, retains the equation, and denies that the conditional is, strictly speaking, a proposition. In this essay I support Adams. I am also indebted, in the proof of sect. 6, to I. F. Carlstrom and C. Hill's review of Adams (1975) in *Philosophy of Science* (1978).

2. I take this formulation from Mackie (1973), ch. 4. Mackie had the right idea, but did not have adequate arguments for his rejection of truth-conditions.

enough, it would seem, to be not worth denying. Now, from a truth-conditional perspective, this double illocutionary force—an assumption, and an assertion within its scope—is eliminable—is reducible to, or equivalent to, a plain assertion. If conditionals have truth-conditions, to assert 'If A, B' is to assert that its truth-conditions obtain. One way of presenting the conclusion of this essay, then, is that the double illocutionary force is *in*eliminable; there is no proposition such that asserting *it* to be the case is equivalent to asserting that B is the case given the *supposition* that A is the case. For any proposed truth-condition, I shall show that there are epistemic situations in which there is a divergence between assent to the proposition with that truth-condition and assent to the conditional.

The main argument of the essay concerns indicative conditionals. The thesis extends to subjunctive or counterfactual conditionals, but I shall not have space to argue that here.[3] The distinction, from the present perspective, is not between two types of conditional connection, but between two types of supposition, or better, two kinds of context in which a supposition is made. One can suppose that A, taking oneself to know that not-A; and one can suppose that A, not taking oneself to know that not-A. Typically, the subjunctive or counterfactual conditional is the result of the first kind of supposition, the open or indicative conditional the result of the second kind. An apparent difficulty which actually clarifies the point: I take myself to know that the carpet I am now looking at is not red. I may say 'If it had been red, it would have matched the curtains.' But I may also say 'If it *is* red—well, I have gone colour-blind or am suffering some sort of delusion'. In the subjunctive, I am taking it for granted that I am right in thinking it is not red. In the indicative, I am supposing that I am wrong. I am considering it to be an epistemic possibility that it is red, despite appearances. The importance of this for present purposes is that the positive account of indicative conditionals to follow assumes that the antecedent is always treated as epistemically possible by the speaker. When that condition is not satisfied, the conditional will be treated as a subjunctive, in the extension of the thesis. It will not matter if this distinction between two kinds of supposing does not match perfectly the grammatical distinction. It is enough if any conditional thought can be explained in one of the two envisaged ways.

One further remark about the methodology of this essay: while it is no part of my purpose to deny that some conditionals are certain, on a priori or other grounds, the argument hinges upon the undeniable

3. See Adams (1975), ch. 4. More support for a unified theory of indicative and counterfactual conditionals is found in Ellis (1978 and 1984).

fact that many conditionals, like other propositions, are assented to or dissented from with a degree of confidence less than certainty. We are frequently uncertain whether if A, B, and our efforts to reduce our uncertainty often terminate, at best, in the judgement that it is probable (or improbable) that if A, B. Of course, the truth-conditions theorist does not have to deny these undeniable facts. For him, to judge it more or less probable that if A, B is to judge it more or less probable that its truth-conditions obtain. But this pinpoints his mistake. I show that uncertainty about a conditional is not uncertainty about the obtaining of any truth-conditions. If a conditional had truth-conditions, it would be. Therefore, a conditional does not have truth-conditions. That is the structure of the argument to follow.

2. THE TRUTH FUNCTIONAL ACCOUNT

There are sixteen possible truth-functions of A and B. Only one is a candidate for giving the truth-conditions of 'If A, B'. Indeed, the following two assumptions are sufficient to prove that *if* 'If A, B' is truth-functional, it has the standard truth-function (that is, it is equivalent to '~(A & ~B)' and to '~A ∨ B'). (1) 'If P & Q then P' is true, whatever the truth-values of P and of Q; (2) Sentences of the form 'If A, B' are sometimes false, i.e. are not all tautologies. So we may safely speak of *the* truth-functional account.

It is important to recognize that there are powerful arguments in favour of the truth-functional account. Here are two. First, take any two propositions, B and C. Information that at least one of them is true seems sufficient for the conclusion that if C is not true, B is true. The converse inference is uncontroversial.[4] Let C be ~A, and we appear to have vindicated the equivalence between '~A ∨ B' and 'If A, B'. Second, information that A and C are not both true seems to license the inference that if A is true, C is not. Again, the converse implication is uncontroversial. Let C be ~B, and we appear to have vindicated the equivalence between '~(A & ~B)' and 'If A, B'. (I shall show later that my positive account will preserve the force of these arguments, while no account in terms of non-truth-functional truth-conditions can.)

But alas, there are well known difficulties for the truth-functional account: ~A entails ~(A & ~B), for any B. B entails ~(A & ~B), for any A. So, according to this account,

The Labour Party will not win the next election

---

4. Suppose that if C is not true, B is true. Then, either C is true or (it isn't, in which case) B is true.

entails

> If the Labour Party wins the next election, the National Health
> Service will be dismantled by the next government.

Anyone who accepts the former and rejects the latter is (on this
account) inconsistent.
   Similarly,

> The Conservative Party will win the next election

entails

> If a horrendous scandal emerges during the campaign involving the
> Prime Minister and most of the Cabinet, the Conservative Party will
> win the next election.

Again, anyone who accepts the former and rejects the latter has, on
this account, inconsistent beliefs.
   H. P. Grice (1975) argued that the truth-functional account can
withstand these objections, provided that we are careful to distinguish
the false from the misleading but true. There are many ways in which
one can speak the truth yet mislead. One way is to say something
weaker than some other relevant thing one is in a position to say.
Consider disjunctions. I am asked where John is. I firmly believe he is
in the bar, and I know that he never goes near libraries. Inclined to be
unhelpful but not wishing to lie, I say

> He is either in the bar or in the library.

I could go on: or at the opera or at the church or . . .)
   My hearer naturally concludes that this is the most precise information I am in a position to give, and also concludes from the truth (let
us assume) that I told him

> If he's not in the bar he is in the library.

The conditional, like the disjunction, according to Grice, is true
provided that he's in the bar, but misleadingly asserted on these
grounds.
   I shall now show that this defence of the truth-functional account
fails. Grice drew our attention to the existence of propositions which

a person *has grounds to believe true* but which it would be unreasonable, in normal contexts, to assert. A contrast is invoked between what one may reasonably *believe* and what one may reasonably *say,* given one's grounds. I do not dispute that it is important to recognize this phenomenon. It does, I think, correctly explain the behaviour of disjunctions. Being sure that John is in the bar, I cannot consistently *disbelieve* the proposition 'He is either in the bar or in the library'; indeed, if I have any epistemic attitude to that proposition, it should be one of belief, however inappropriate it is for me to assert it.

A good enough test of whether the Gricean story fits the facts about disjunctions is this: I am asked to respond, 'Yes', 'No', or 'No opinion', to the disjunction. Being sure of one disjunct, I should surely answer 'Yes'.

Here there is a striking contrast between disjunctions and conditionals. Imagine an opinion poll shortly before an election. Again, the subject is asked to respond 'Yes' if he thinks a proposition true, 'No' if he thinks it false, 'No opinion' otherwise. The subject is honest and prides himself on his consistency. Here are some of his responses:

1. The Labour Party will win (L) ....   No
2. The Labour Party won't win (~L) ....   Yes
3. Either the Labour Party won't win or _____ (~L ∨ _) (Fill in the   Yes
   blank as you will: If he accepts that (2) is true, he must, if rational,
   accept that at least one of two propositions, of which (2) is one, is
   true.)
4. If the Labour Party wins, the National Health Service will be
   dismantled by the next government (If L, N) ....   No

Now, on the truth-functional account, this person has blatantly inconsistent beliefs. His saying 'Yes' to (2) and 'No' to (4) is on a par with someone's saying 'Yes' to 'It's red and square' and 'No' to 'It's red'. The parallel is exact, for, on the truth-functional account, to deny (4) is equivalent to accepting L & ~N; he cannot consistently accept this yet deny L. But it is surely quite clear that our subject, in accepting (2) and rejecting (4), is not contradicting himself.

In the case of disjunctions, the predicted Gricean contrast between what it is reasonable to believe and what it is reasonable to say, given one's grounds, is discernible. In the case of conditionals, it is not. (I do not mean that the distinction does not apply to conditionals, but that it fails as a defence of the truth-functional account.) The purpose of the opinion poll is simply to elicit someone's opinions, irrespective of whether they would constitute appropriate remarks in an ordinary conversational interchange. We can stipulate that the subject is honest and serious. We must either accuse him of gross inconsistency, or accept that the conditional is not truth-functional.

This case against the truth-functional account cannot be made in terms of beliefs of which one is *certain*. Someone who is 100 per cent certain that the Labour Party won't win has (on my account of the matter) no obvious use for an *indicative* conditional beginning 'If they win'. But someone who is, say, 90 per cent certain that they won't win can have beliefs about what will be the case if they do. The truth-functional account has the immensely implausible consequence that such a person, if rational, is at least 90 per cent certain of any conditional with that antecedent.

The principle I am appealing to is this:

> If A entails B, it is irrational to be more confident of A than of B.

For instance, it is irrational to be more confident that a thing is red than that it is coloured. If the entailment is one-way, any way of rendering A true renders B true, but not conversely. B may be true when A is not. B has more chance of being true than A.[5]

Given that some entailments are exceedingly complex, the principle, in its full generality, no doubt has the consequence that no one is fully rational. But here we are dealing with a simple, decidable, truth-functional entailment of the most basic kind. If the truth-functional account were correct, it would be a straightforward matter to get the subject to recognize that he has inconsistent beliefs.

3. WHAT IT IS TO JUDGE THAT IF A, B

The critique of the truth-functional account has yet to be completed, but it is useful here to introduce, by way of contrast, my positive account of the consistent judgements our subject *is* making when he accepts (2) and rejects (4). Figure 1 is a diagrammatic representation of how likely he considers the various possibilities, L, ~L, N, ~N, L & N, L & ~N, etc., to be, vertical height representing probability. In considering whether if L, N, the subject assumes L; that is, he ignores the ~L-possibilities, the lower part of the diagram. Considering just those possibilities above the wide line, he asks how likely it is that N. Answer: very unlikely. On the other hand, he is committed to

---

5. The principle is provable in probability theory: writing '$\leftrightarrow$' for logical equivalence, $B \leftrightarrow (A \& B) \vee (\sim A \& B)$. So $P(B) = P(A \& B) + P(\sim A \& B)$. If A entails B, $A \leftrightarrow A \& B$. So $P(B) = P(A) + P(\sim A \& B) \geq P(A)$.

believing L ⊃ N, that is ~L ∨ N, to be slightly more probable than ~L, that is very likely.

FIG. 1

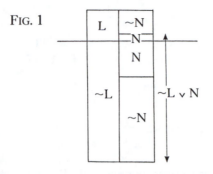

To judge it probable that A ⊃ B is to judge it improbable that A & ~B. To judge it probable that if A, B is not only to judge it improbable that A & ~B, but to judge this to be less probable than A & B. 'Is B likely given A?' is the question 'Is A & B nearly as likely as A?' (see Figure 2).

FIG. 2

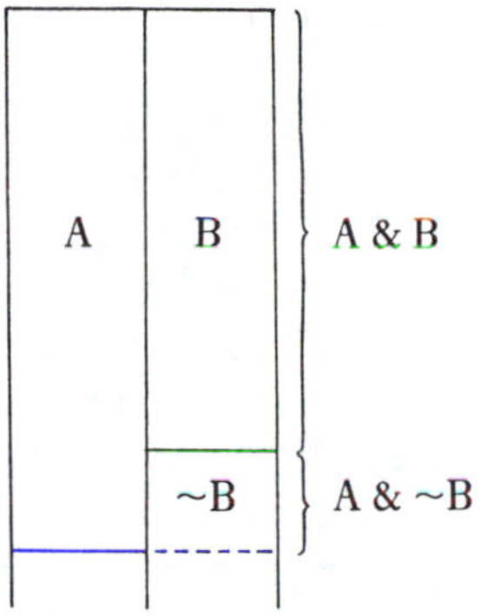

That A & ~B be small, which is necessary and sufficient for the conditional to be probable on the truth-functional account, is necessary but not sufficient on this account. If A & ~B is large, greater than ½, say, there isn't room for A & B to be larger still. However, A & ~B can be small and A & B smaller still, as in the original example. In such a case, the material implication is probable but the conditional is not.

A simple example of the contrast between the two accounts: How likely is it that if this (fair) die lands an even number, it will land six? On my approach, we assume that the die lands an even number; given that assumption, there are three equal possibilities, one of which is six. So the answer is ⅓. On the truth-functional approach, the answer is

⅔: if the die lands not-even or six, that is, if it lands, 1, 3, 5, or 6, the conditional is true. So the conditional has four chances out of six of being true.

4. THE CASE AGAINST TRUTH
FUNCTIONALITY CONTINUED

Let us continue our questionnaire to consider the second paradox of material implication:

5. The Conservative Party will win (C) .... Yes
6. Either _____ or the Conservative Party will win (__ ∨ C) (Fill in the blank as you like.) .... Yes
7. If a horrendous scandal emerges involving the Prime Minister and most of the Cabinet, the Conservative Party will win (If S, C) .... No

Such answers are not inconsistent. I grant that someone who is 100 per cent certain that the Conservatives will win will accept any conditional with an antecedent which he takes as an epistemic possibility and C as consequent. But that is not enough to prove the validity of the inference from C to 'If S, C'. Suppose our subject is 90 per cent certain that the Conservatives will win. He allows that they may not win, and that if certain, in his view unlikely, things happen, they will not win. So it is consistent to have a high degree of confidence that C and a low degree of confidence that if S, C. On the truth-functional account, this is, again, logically on a par with being very confident that it's red and square but very unconfident that it's square. On the other hand, his high degree of confidence in (5) does constrain him to at least that degree of confidence in (6) (see Figure 3).

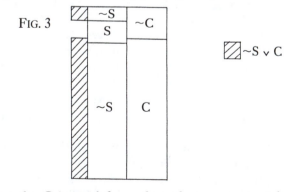

FIG. 3

I said that the Gricean defence depends on a contrast between when a conditional is fit to be believed and when it is fit to be asserted. I have shown that the conditions under which a conditional is believed do not fit the truth-functional account. So this defence fails. Frank Jackson (1979; 1980–1) defends the truth-functional account differently. His thesis is that for a conditional to be assertable, it must not only be believed that its truth-conditions are satisfied, but the belief must be *robust* or *resilient* with respect to the antecedent. This means that one would not abandon belief in the conditional if one were to discover the antecedent to be true. This ensures that an assertable conditional is fit for *modus ponens*. This condition is not satisfied if one believes A ⊃ B solely on the grounds that ~A. If one discovered that A, one would abandon one's belief that A ⊃ B, rather than conclude that B. I think this defence is open to the same objections as Grice's. There is simply no evidence that one *believes* a conditional whenever one believes the corresponding material implication, and then is prepared to *assert* it only if some further condition is satisfied.

I have been assuming that if a sentence is correctly assigned certain truth-conditions, a competent speaker believes that sentence if and only if he believes these conditions are fulfilled; and, provided that he is honest and has no wish to hide his opinion, will say so if asked 'Do you believe that A?' It may be objected that the distinction between its truth-conditions and other aspects of a sentence's use is more a theorist's, less a practitioner's distinction than I have allowed. If this is so, then we must ask, what theoretical purpose is served by the assignment of these truth-conditions? To explain the validity of inferences? But it does this very badly. I have shown this for the two simplest types of example, but these generate indefinitely many other counterintuitive 'valid' inferences. Here is a new 'proof' of the existence of God:[6] 'If God does not exist, then it is not the case that if I pray my prayers will be answered (by Him). I do not pray. (So it *is* the case that if I pray . . .) So God exists'. The extent to which the truth-functional account succeeds in capturing the validity of inferences is explained by the fact that the material implication is essentially weaker than the indicative conditional (see above) and so is the extent to which it fails.

Another suggestion is that the truth-functional account explains the behaviour of embedded conditions: it explains the contribution of the truth-conditions of 'If A, B' to those of '(If A, B) or (if C, D)', for example. But, unsurprisingly, the truth-functional account yields counterintuitive results for sentences containing conditionals as constituents. For example, it tells us that the following is a tautology:

6. I owe this example to W. D. Hart.

(If A, B) or (if not-A, B).

So anyone who rejects the first conditional must, on pain of contradiction, accept the second. So if I reject the conditional 'If the Conservatives lose, Thatcher will resign', I am committed to accepting 'If the Conservatives win, Thatcher will resign'![7]

We have not been able to find any theoretical purpose well served by these truth-conditions. There does not appear to be any indirect evidence in its favour to mitigate against the direct evidence against it—the fact that belief in a conditional and belief in a material implication do not coincide.

5. THE POSITIVE ACCOUNT CONTINUED

I outlined my positive account of belief in a conditional in Sect. 3. In considering how likely it is that if A, B, one assumes A, that is, ignores the possibility that $\sim$A. Relative to that assumption, one considers how likely it is that B (see Figure 2). This yields the following criterion:

> X believes that (judges it likely that) if A, B, to the extent that he judges that A & B is nearly as likely as A
> or, roughly equivalently, to the extent that he judges A & B to be more likely than A & $\sim$B.

If we were to make the idealizing assumption that a person's subjective probability judgements are precise enough to be assigned numbers between one and zero inclusive, we could be more precise and say that the measure of X's degree of confidence in the conditional 'If A, B' is the ratio

$$\frac{P_x(A \& B)}{P_x(A)}$$

This ratio is known in probability theory as *the conditional probability of B given A*. Our positive thesis could be stated, then

7. Lewis (1976) gives as his reason for rejecting the no-truth-conditions view that it cannot explain embedded conditionals. He goes on to defend the truth-functional account, attempting to explain away some of its paradoxical features. But he does not address the problem that the truth-functional account gives absurd results for embedded conditionals.

> A person's degree of confidence in a conditional, if A, B, is the conditional probability he assigns to B given A.

However, my argument does not depend upon the idealizing assumption of precise numerical values. Also, even if we grant numerical values, the ratio must not be taken as a reductive definition of the conditional probability, as though one first had to ascertain how probable it is that A and that A & B, and then divide the second by the first. Typically, one does not have to decide how likely it is that A in order to judge that B is likely given A. I may have given no thought to the matter of how likely it is that the Labour Party will win yet be confident that if they win public spending will increase; this latter confidence entails confidence that, however, likely it is that they win, it is nearly as likely that (they win and public spending increases). The non-reducibility is particularly obvious when, as part of some practical reasoning, one considers conditionals of the form 'If I do *x*, such-and-such will happen.' It would be absurd to hold that I have to know how likely it is that I will do *x* before I can assess such a conditional.

Let us consider some special cases. If I am certain of a conditional, for example that if he is a bachelor, he is unmarried, then, however likely it is that he is a bachelor, it is equally likely that he is a bachelor and unmarried. The ratio is 1. Given a conditional in which I have the lowest possible degree of confidence, for example, that if he's a bachelor, he's married, I assign probability 0 to the conjunction of antecedent and consequent, and hence to the ratio. If I think it is 50:50 that if you toss this coin, it will land heads, then, whatever the probability that you toss it, the probability that (you toss it and it lands heads) is half as much: the ratio is 1:2.

This measure has the advantage of allowing the probability of the conditional to be independent of the probability of the antecedent. On the truth-functional account, the probability that if you toss the coin it lands heads depends crucially on how probable it is that you toss it. Suppose it is much less likely now that you toss the coin than it was a minute ago. The probability of the material implication, which is equivalent to:

> Either you won't toss it, or (you will and it will land heads)

has greatly increased. But the probability of the consequent on the assumption that the antecedent is true has remained the same.

Non-truth-functional accounts of the truth-conditions of conditionals demand some sort of 'strong connection' between antecedent and consequent for the conditional to be true. Such a connection is clearly lacking in

> If you toss this (fair) coin, it will land heads.

On such accounts, the conditional is then certainly false. It should have probability 0. But surely, if someone is told 'the probability is 0 that if you toss it it will land heads', he will think it is a double-tailed or otherwise peculiar coin. Keeping the structure but changing the content of the example—a dog either bites or cowers when strangers approach, apparently at random, and with about equal frequency of each. Could one in good faith tell a stranger that the probability is zero (i.e. it is certainly false) that if he approaches, the dog will bite?

I think I have said enough to render plausible the claim that the measure of acceptability of a conditional 'If A, B' is the conditional probability of B given A. Without idealizing, the basic thesis that to assess how probable it is that if A, B, one assumes A, and considers how probable it is that B, under that assumption; and that that thought process is equivalent to considering whether A & B is nearly as likely as A. More evidence for the thesis comes from considering which inference-patterns involving conditionals are valid. There is not space to present this evidence fully,[8] but I shall end this section by saying something about the inference from 'A ∨ B' to 'If not-A, B'. As I said at the beginning of Sect. 2, if this inference were valid, the truth-functional account would be correct. And the inference appears very plausible. We shall see how to explain these facts.

FIG. 4

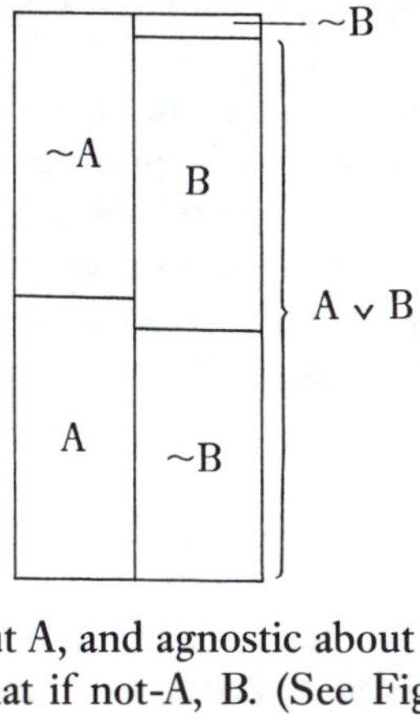

If I am agnostic about A, and agnostic about B, but confident that A or B, I must believe that if not-A, B. (See Figure 4. If in almost all

---

8. See Adams (1975), ch. 1.

possibilities, either A or B is true; and A and B are each true in approximately half the possibility-space; then in almost all not-A possibilities, B is true.) This is the normal situation in which a belief that A or B will play an active role in my mind, as a premiss or as anything else, for example, someone has told me that A or B, or I have eliminated all but these two possibilities.

On the other hand, if my belief that A or B derives solely from my belief that A, the inference is not justified. For example, I wake up and look at the clock. It says eight o'clock. It is fairly reliable but by no means infallible. I am 90 per cent confident that it is eight o'clock (within whatever degree of precision with which we make such statements). So, were I to consider the matter, I must be at least 90 per cent confident that it is either eight o'clock or eleven o'clock. But this gives me no grounds for confidence that if it is not eight, it is eleven (see Figure 5).

FIG. 5

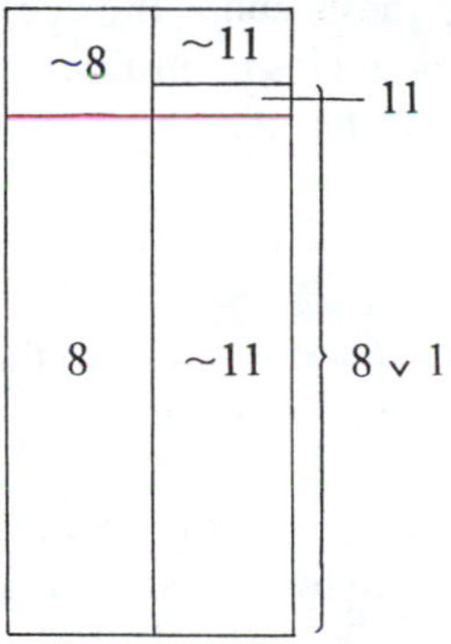

As it is rare and rather pointless to consider disjunctions in circumstances such as these, it is not surprising that we mistake 'A or B; therefore, if not-A, B' for a valid argument.

6. THE CASE AGAINST NON-TRUTH-FUNCTIONAL TRUTH CONDITIONS

If a conditional has truth-conditions, the probability of a conditional is the probability that those conditions obtain. Suppose that a conditional has truth-conditions which are not a truth-function of its antecedent and consequent. This means that the number of logically possible combinations of truth-values of A, B, 'If A, B' is between five and eight. That is, at least one and at most all four possible combinations of truth-values for A and B split(s) into two possibilities: 'If A, B'

true; 'If A, B' false. At most three of the following eight combinations
of truth-value can be ruled out a priori:

	A	B	If A, B
1a	T	T	T
1b	T	T	F
2a	T	F	T
2b	T	F	F
3a	F	T	T
3b	F	T	F
4a	F	F	T
4b	F	F	F

What follows is a 'tetralemma'. I shall now show that wherever
truth-functionality is assumed to fail, there are consequences incompatible with the positive thesis about the acceptance of a conditional;
and that where there is a clash, intuition continues to favour the
positive thesis rather than the non-truth-functional truth-conditions
thesis.

First, suppose

> Assumption 1: A conditional has truth-conditions which are not
> truth functional when A and B are both true.

Thus 1a and 1b are two distinct possibilities. On this assumption,
'If A, B' would be like 'A before B' and 'A because B'. For example,
the truth of 'John went to Paris' and of 'Mary went to Paris' leaves
open the question whether 'John went to Paris *before* Mary went to
Paris' is true; its truth depends on more than the truth-values of its
constituents.

Consequence of Assumption 1:

C_1: Someone may be sure that A is true and sure that B is true, yet not
have enough information to decide whether 'If A, B' is true; one may
consistently be agnostic about the conditional while being sure that
its components are true (as for 'A before B').

This consequence is central to my argument. I pause to clarify and
defend it. It does not *quite* follow *merely* from the assumption of non-
truth-functionality. There are exceptions to claims of the same form.
But the exceptions are special cases, which do not cast doubt on the
case of conditionals.

First exception: take the operator 'It is self-evident that . . .'. 'It is self-evident that A' is not a truth-function of A when A is true. But it does not follow that one may be sure that A yet agnostic about whether it is self-evident that A. For there is no room for uncertainty about propositions of this last form. However, such an operator clearly contrasts with the operators, 'if', 'before', 'because', which, in general, make contingent a posteriori claims, about which there is plenty of room for uncertainty. Of course there are self-evident conditionals, such as 'If he's a bachelor, he's unmarried'; but they owe their self-evidence to the particular contents of the constituent propositions. They are not self-evident just because of the meaning of 'if'.

It could be objected that my argument, resting on C_1, will not have shown that those conditionals which *are* self-evident don't have truth-conditions. But this would be to claim that 'if' is ambiguous: that it has a different meaning in 'If he's a bachelor he's unmarried' and 'If John is in Paris, so is Mary.' I see no grounds for an ambiguity. My positive thesis has the consequence that self-evident conditionals are certain—the consequent is certain on the supposition that the antecedent is true; and that conditionals about which one may be uncertain cannot be understood in terms of truth-conditions. It offers a unified account of indicative conditionals which is incompatible with a unified account in terms of truth conditions. Unified accounts are prima facie preferable to accounts which postulate ambiguities. In the absence of a strong case for ambiguity, then, my argument still applies to all conditionals.

A second counter-example to the general claim about non-truth-functionality I owe to Raúl Orayen: Interpret 'A*B' as 'I am sure that A and sure that B'. This is not a truth-function of A and B when A and B are both true. But it does not follow that I can be sure that A and sure that B yet agnostic about A*B. It could be replied that, as we do not have incorrigible access to our own beliefs, it *is* possible to be sure that A, sure that B, yet unsure about whether one is sure, i.e. unsure about A*B.[9] But in any case, any putative truth conditions of 'If A, B' will surely be unlike those of 'A*B' in being independent of the state of mind of any one individual. The hypothesis under consideration, Assumption 1, is that the truth of A and of B is insufficient to determine the truth of 'If A, B'. One doesn't have to be an extreme realist about truth to insist that whatever else is necessary is *in general* nothing to do with one individual's epistemic state. I say 'in general' because, as before, there will be special cases—conditionals which are

9. I owe this point to Raymundo Morado.

about the state of mind of some one individual; and *perhaps* to some of these, the individual concerned has incorrigible access. But, to repeat, we are in the business of interpreting 'If' for all conditionals. The contribution it makes to the (alleged) truth conditions of sentences in which it occurs makes no reference to my state of mind—though in special cases, the A or the B in 'If A, B' may do so.

C_1 still stands, then. Now C_1 is incompatible with our positive account. Being certain that A and that B, a person must think A & B is just as likely as A. He is certain that B on the assumption that A is true.

C_1 also conflicts with common sense. Admittedly, the conditional 'If A, B' is not of much interest to someone who is sure that both A and B are true. But he can hardly doubt or deny that if A, B, in this epistemic state. Establishing that the antecedent and consequent are true is surely one incontrovertible way of verifying a conditional. If you deny that if A, B, and I know that A and B are both true, I am surely in a position to correct you.

Assumption 1 must, then, be rejected. Truth-functionality cannot fail when A and B are both true. 'A & B' is sufficient for 'If, A, B'. Putative possibility 1b does not exist. We proceed to the second stage of the argument.

> Assumption 2: A conditional has truth-conditions which are not truth-functional when A is true and B is false.

Consequence of Assumption 2:

C_2:   Someone may be sure that A is true and sure that B is false yet not have enough information to settle whether 'If A, B' is true, and hence be agnostic about the latter.

As with C_1, this is incompatible with our positive account, and also with common sense. Such a person knows enough to reject the claim that B is true on the assumption that A. 'A & $\sim$B' is sufficient to refute 'If A, B'. Assumption 2 is false. Putative possibility 2a does not exist.

We have shown, then, that if a conditional has truth conditions, they are truth-functional for the two cases in which A is true. We shall now consider the cases in which A is false.

> Assumption 3: A conditional has truth-conditions which are not truth-functional when A is false and B is true.

Now suppose someone is sure that B but is uncertain whether A. On our positive account, he knows enough to be sure that if A, B: If B is certain, A & B is just as probable as A. This also accords with common sense. But according to Assumption 3, there are three possibilities—three ways the world may be—compatible with his knowledge:

A	B	If A, B
T	T	T
F	T	T
F	T	F

(I rely on the fact that we have established truth-functionality for the top line.)

A may be false, and if it is, some further condition has to be satisfied for 'If A, B' to be true, and he may not know whether it is satisfied. According to Stalnaker (1968), for instance, the further condition is that B be true in the closest possible world to the actual world in which A is true. And he might not know enough about the actual world to know whether this is so.

An example might help. I complain to John that he has not replied to my letter. He says he did—he posted the reply some weeks ago. I am not sure whether to believe him. Let A be 'He posted the reply' and B be 'I didn't receive it.' Our positive account has it that B is certain on the assumption that A, and so does common sense. But by Assumption 3, I should reason like this: 'I didn't receive the letter. Suppose he posted it: then the conditional is true. But suppose he didn't post it: this, together with the fact that I didn't receive it, is not sufficient for the conditional. It depends (say) on whether in the closest possible words in which he *did* post it, I still didn't receive it. And I can't be sure of that.'

Assumption 3, then, is incompatible with our positive account, and once more, intuition vindicates our account. Assumption 3 must be rejected. Putative possibility 3b does not exist.

> Finally, Assumption 4: Truth-functionality fails when 'A' and 'B' are both false.

Now consider someone who is sure that A and B have the same truth-value, but is uncertain which. For example he knows that John

and Mary spent yesterday evening together, but doesn't know whether
they went to the party. According to our positive account and according to common sense, he knows enough to be sure that if John went to
the party (J), Mary did (M). (J & M is as likely as J; M is certain on
the assumption that J.) But according to Assumption 4, he has to
consider three possibilities compatible with his knowledge:

J	M	If J, M
T	T	T
F	F	T
F	F	F

J and M may both be false, and if they are, some further condition has
to be satisfied for 'If J, M' to be true. Perhaps the further question, if
John and Mary didn't go, is whether Mary would have gone if John
had, and he can't be certain of that. Our positive account and Assumption 4 diverge, and intuition, once more, favours our account.
Assumption 4 must be rejected. Putative possibility 4b does not exist.

We have reached the end of our proof. That the conditional has
non-truth-functional truth-conditions entails that at least one of Assumptions 1 to 4 is true. But whichever we take, we can find conditionals whose acceptability (or unacceptability), both intuitively and in
terms of our positive account, conflicts with that assumption.

Given truth-conditions, we have a paradox. It is no accident that,
given truth-conditions, there is philosophical disagreement about
whether or not they are truth-functional. For there are acceptable
conditionals whose acceptability cannot be accommodated by any
non-truth-functional account. I have used some of these in the above
proof. And there are unacceptable conditionals whose unacceptability
cannot be accommodated by the truth-functional account. I used
these earlier in the case against truth-functionality. But our positive
account resolves this paradox. The mistake is to think of conditionals
as part of fact-stating discourse.

Perhaps we can get closer to the heart of the paradox with the
following case. I am wondering whether A and whether B. Someone
comes along who knows their truth-values, but feels unable to tell me all
he knows. He says 'The most I am able to tell you is this: $\sim$(A & $\sim$B).'
This is enough for me to conclude that if A, B. Now, $\sim$(A & $\sim$B) *does
not entail* 'If A, B'. That is the truth-functional account, with all its
difficulties. But *belief that* $\sim$(A & $\sim$B) *in the absence of belief that* $\sim$A

is sufficient for belief that if A, B (see Figure 6). No non-truth-functional truth-conditions can accommodate that fact.[10]

FIG. 6

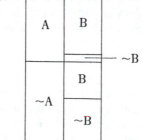

. . .

7. SOME CONCLUDING OBSERVATIONS

The argument makes no assumptions about what truth consists in—beyond the fact that one may take various epistemic attitudes to the question whether a given proposition has that property. Whatever 'true' means, to judge it likely that it applies to B on the assumption that it applies A is not equivalent to judging it likely that it applies to something else. The linguistic or mental act of *supposing* is ineliminable from conditionals, and they cannot be reduced to straight assertions or beliefs.

Another way of putting the conclusion is this. One can be certain or uncertain about a proposition, A. Uncertainty about A (~A, A ∨ B, etc.) has a structure which is not only compatible with the proposition's having one or other truth-value, but requires that it does. One can be certain or uncertain about whether if A, B. Uncertainty about a conditional has a structure which does not require that the conditional has one or other truth-value; moreover, it is incompatible with this.

There are several reasons why this argument is important. This is

---

10. This sentence conflicts with the thesis of Robert Stalnaker's "Indicative Conditionals" (1975). That paper and this one are both included in Jackson (1991), and the point at issue is discussed on pp. 198–99 of that version of my essay.

the most general one: a hard argument against (or for) the applicability of the concept of truth to a given area of discourse is a rare
thing. It is just possible that this one may shed light on controversies
about the applicability of the concept in other areas. Given certain key
features of the epistemology of discourse of the kind of question, we
can ask, does this epistemology fit with even a minimal metaphysics of
truth?

Another reason why the consequences of the argument are far-
reaching is that it has become increasingly fashionable to 'analyse'
other important philosophical concepts in terms of conditionals, for
example, causation, natural laws, dispositional properties, and more
recently, knowledge. The standard account of statements of the form
'All A's are B' is also a striking example. There is much that needs to
be re-examined in the light of this thesis.

Perhaps most importantly, the criterion for the validity of deductive
arguments needs to be restated in the light of this thesis. The standard criterion is that valid arguments preserve truth. But such arguments contain conditionals, and according to the thesis I have
defended, conditionals are not suitable candidates for truth. Now, our
interest in the validity of arguments is epistemological. A valid argument is one such that it is irrational to accept the premises and reject
the conclusion. Construing acceptance as high subjective probability,
and acceptance of a conditional in terms of high conditional probability, Adams has shown how to give a precise criterion of validity
along these lines, which coincides with the standard one for arguments without conditionals.[11] It explains why certain patterns of inference involving conditionals are valid; and it isolates the unusual
conditions under which others, which appear valid, fail. I discussed
one such example at the end of Sect. 5.

Finally, this argument should not be construed as part of a general
attack on truth-conditional semantics. It depends on a contrast between the roles of the constituent sentences of a conditional and the
conditional itself. It does not require, but fits well with a truth-
conditional account of our understanding of the former.

Indeed, this anti-realist argument about conditionals is more puzzling for a general anti-realist than for a philosopher with strong
realist tendencies. For the latter, let us say, a declarative sentence
identifies a possible state of affairs. It is true if and only if the state of

11. See Adams (1975), ch. 2. It is worth remarking that the existence of
logical consequences of moral judgements, rules, laws, etc. also suggests that
the classical account of validity is limited in scope.

affairs identified obtains. For him, the argument shows that there are no conditional states of affairs. For an anti-realist who construes truth along the lines of what is ideally rationally acceptable, it is much more puzzling that the notion cannot be applied to conditionals. But, as I said before, the argument itself makes no assumptions about the nature of truth.[12]

12. Earlier versions of this essay were read to the Oxford Philosophical Society in 1984 and the Conference on the Philosophy of Logic and Language in Leicester, 1985. It formed part of the material of a lecture course on Conditionals given at the Instituto de Investigacions Filosóficas, Universidad Nacional Autónoma de México in the summer of 1985. I am grateful to these audiences and many other people for useful comments, and especially to Raúl Orayen for his enthusiasm and constructive criticism.

4

What Do 'Q' and 'R'
Stand for Anyway?

Richard E. Grandy

1. THE QUESTIONS

The function of logical connectives, one may argue, is to permit the formation of complex sentences or statements or propositions from simple sentences or statements or propositions. But which of these three ways of thinking of the 'Q's and 'R's of formal logic should we prefer? In this paper I will concentrate on sentential or propositional letters which form such complexes as 'Q → R'. '→' is used here as a notation for a generic conditional whose properties need not be specified in full detail; I assume only that modus ponens is valid for it.

The standard range of answers to our question is the same as that for several other questions. It will put our inquiry into a better perspective to distinguish three:

 I. What are the objects of logic, i.e., what do 'Q', 'R' and the like stand for?
 II. What are the bearers of truth and falsehood? What kinds of things are true or false?
III. What are the objects of such verbs as 'believe', 'know' and their ilk?

"Propositions," "statements" and "sentences" are possible answers to all three of these questions, and it is not uncommon for philosophers to buttress direct arguments for an answer to one of these questions by appealing to the preferred answer to another. In this essay I will be concerned with the first question, though the conclusion may have indirect bearing on the other two.

2. SOME DISTINCTIONS

To pursue these questions intelligibly, it is prerequisite to make some terminological stipulations and to rehearse the general motivations for introducing statements and propositions.

Sentences: We begin with sentences and must first distinguish between types and tokens. The word 'radar' can be correctly said to have three letters or five in it. If one counts separately the two distinct occurrences of 'r' and 'a' then there are five; we are counting letter tokens. If the correct count is three, we are counting letter types. Similar distinctions must be observed with words and sentences. The sentence token you are now reading is an instance of the same type that occurs in each other copy of this essay, but those other copies have different tokens of this sentence. That much is standard philo- sophical lore. But we must go somewhat further in specifying termi- nology in order to carry out the detailed arguments later in this essay.

The following terminology is not standard—indeed none is in this area. I will reserve the term *utterance* for an audible sound pattern, and *inscription* for a visible pattern. Note that some philosophers and linguists use 'utterance' to cover both, and others reserve 'utterance' for an audible sound pattern. Another terminological distinction that must be considered is whether to count as a token of a sentence type of a language only patterns *produced by a speaker of that language as a token of that sentence type in that language*. In my usage no condition is placed on the method by which an utterance or inscription is pro- duced, so that tokens of English sentences might be produced by wind in the desert or by a random word generating program. Most fre- quently the tokens of interest are produced intentionally by humans, but they are occasionally produced by random natural events and are more frequently produced by machines. According to my terminology the sentence tokens will be a subset of the utterances and inscriptions.

Tokens are physical objects that are located (with some vagueness) in space-time. It is difficult to specify where the boundaries of an utterance are, or when an inscription is too faded to count any more. In contrast to tokens, types are abstract objects and do not exist in space-time. But it is important not to underestimate the abstract and theoretical properties that the tokens of sentence types have. In par- ticular considerable care must be taken in analyzing the relations between sentence types and utterances and inscriptions. Utterances and inscriptions are, by definition, readily observable entities. How- ever, the judgement that an utterance or inscription is a sentence token, as well as judgements about which sentence(s) they are tokens of, are highly theoretical, even if often instantaneous. This is often overlooked since it is assumed (or asserted) that tokens of the same sentence are similar or resemble each other. The sense of similarity is an important but abstract one, because 'rat', 'RAT', and many other variants are tokens of the same type. In addition to the variations among inscriptions which are respectively in upper case, lower case, cursive and dot matrix form, consider the resemblance between a spoken and a written token of a sentence! Since there is a great deal of variability in terminology, let us make explicit that in our use an ambiguous sentence inscription is an inscription of at least two sentence tokens of differing types. For example, "Visiting relatives can be boring" is a single token of two different types—the types differ with regard to whether the relatives or the speaker is visiting. Thus although tokens are readily observable physical objects, they have complicated theoretical properties. We will have more to say of ambiguity anon.

Statements: Philosophers (e.g., Lemmon 1966) have noted that one (or more) person(s) may make the same statement using different sentence types, or they may make different statements using two instances of the same type. Thus the concept of a statement is intended to capture what is in common to the various instances of speaking or writing. If Sam utters 'I am hungry' and Ralph utters 'Sam is hungry' then they have made the same statement with different sentences. If each utters 'I am hungry' then they have made different statements with different tokens of the same sentence type.

Propositions: Propositions in the modern sense entered the analytic vocabulary through the influence of Russell and Moore.[1] Both saw a need for objects of false belief—true beliefs could consist of relations between believers and facts, but in the case of false belief there is no such fact. Thus propositions were introduced and facts were analyzed as corresponding to true propositions. More recently, Church (1950) and others have argued the need for propositions on grounds more reminiscent of those for statements. Two persons who are monolingual speakers of different languages may have the same belief; Sam's belief that Seattle is north of Portland might be the same belief as Karl's belief that Seattle liegt nordlich von Portland even though Karl speaks no English and Sam no German. And within a single language, Sam's belief that Seattle is north of Portland may be the same as George's belief that Portland is south of Seattle. Thus sentences will not serve as the objects of belief, since sentences divide beliefs too finely.

3. CONDITIONS ON ANSWERS

These terminological preliminaries finished, we can consider in more detail the further questions that Question I involves. Our concern is the application of logic to ordinary languages such as English, and

1. That Moore and Russell introduced the modern sense of 'proposition' is clear, but what the modern sense is is not.

thus answers to our question must help us to answer questions about the relation between logic and language. From the point of view of the formal properties of sentential logic, calling one truth value 'true' and the other 'false' is window dressing. One could pick any two objects, say Paris and London, and let the atomic letters stand for one of these rather than the true and the false. One could then define a disjunction 'Q ∨ R' to stand for Paris if and only if at least one of the disjuncts does so. But this tells us nothing about the relation of logic and language.

More concretely, we are seeking an answer that will enable us to apply elementary observations about logical syntax and semantics to English.[2] The statement that modus ponens is a valid inference form (together with suitable auxiliary hypotheses) should tell us something about patterns of inference couched in English sentences. Similarly, the validity of excluded middle, non-contradiction and of the principle of addition,

$$\frac{Q}{Q \vee R}$$

should give us some insight into or information about English. In short, an answer to Question I should help us to understand discussions of the logical form of English inference patterns.

Both propositions and statements, as characterized above, are too crudely individuated to serve the function in question. Both are deliberately introduced in such a way as to blur many differences of formulation of word order, and even of language. This blurring is required in order to solve the problems about identity of belief or statement, but causes problems when applied to our Question I. For example, if we formulate the law of addition in terms of propositions as:

> Given a token of a true proposition Q, one may infer a sentence token that expresses the proposition which is a disjunction of Q and R.

we get as an alleged instance:

$$\frac{\text{Schnee ist weiß}}{\text{Snow is white or grass is green}}$$

2. The importance of this condition and the difficulty in meeting it seem to have first been noted in Nolan (1969).

Similarly, since the belief that 3 is odd and 7 is prime is the same belief as the belief that 7 is prime and 3 is odd, '3 is odd and 7 is prime' and '7 is prime and 3 is odd' express the same proposition and so the following is an instance of propositional modus ponens:

$$\frac{\text{If 3 is odd and 7 is prime, then 31 is perfect}}{\text{7 is prime and 3 is odd}}$$
$$\text{31 is perfect}$$

While this is a valid inference, it is not modus ponens. The inference figure modus ponens is justified by reference, not to the synonymy of sentences, but to the logical behaviour of the connective 'If . . . , then . . .'. Depending on exactly how one divides propositions, one may even get invalid inferences from the formulation of addition. For example, if being a mammal is part of the concept of being canine then 'Denbeigh is a mammalian canine' is the same proposition as 'Denbeigh is a canine', and so an instance of addition as formulated is:

$$\frac{\text{Denbeigh is a canine}}{\text{Denbeigh is a mammalian canine or 5 is even}}$$

A more thoughtful formulation of addition which would bring in tokens of sentences as well as propositions might fare better, and we will consider such an approach later. But for the moment I hope that I have at least raised some doubt about the simple and straightforward appeal to propositions or statements to answer our questions. Thus we turn next to the difficulties encountered in formulating an answer in terms of sentences.

4. QUINE'S ETERNAL SENTENCES

Quine (1950)[3] opts for utterances as the primary bearers of truth and falsity. In general, sentence tokens have one advantage over sentence types in this regard—they do not vary so much in truth value. The sentence type 'It is raining' has many true instances and many false ones. Inscriptions of sentences have less truth variance than types, but are hardly invariant. An inscription of 'You are trespassing' may persist for years and be read by many persons on many occasions. Utterances are not totally immune to such problems when orators address

3. Essay 1 in this volume.

crowds. And with the advent of radio, television and tape recorders, the notion of an utterance requires further clarification.

We need not enter into that quagmire here however, for neither utterances nor inscriptions alone help us much with our problem. Consider modus ponens in an utterance formulation:

> Given a true utterance Q and a true conditional utterance consisting of the first utterance Q as antecedent and an utterance R as consequent, the utterance R is also true.

This is totally inapplicable, for the *same* utterance cannot occur in isolation and as part of a conditional.[4] The most that the principle would tell us is that in a conditional 'if Q then R' if Q is true and the conditional is true then so is the consequent utterance R. But since we do not have a conclusion occurring separately from the major premise, we have no detachment to a conclusion, and thus no argument.

An alternative formulation that springs to mind is:

> Given a true token Q and a conditional formed from a token of the same type as Q as antecedent and another token R as consequent, then if the conditional is true so is any other token of the same type as R.

This has many applications but is incorrect. Since not all tokens of the same type need have the same truth value the token of type R which is the consequent can differ in truth value from the token of type R which is the conclusion.

Having brought types into the picture, let us try a formulation entirely in terms of them:

> For any true sentence type Q, and any conditional sentence type with Q as antecedent and R as consequent, sentence type R is also true.

This is correct but has relatively few applications since it requires that Q be true, i.e., that *all* instances of Q be uniformly true.

Considering the last two attempts together, we can see that for a

---

4. Since inscriptions are often fairly enduring particulars, it might occasionally be the case that the same inscription would occur in isolation and also at a different time as part of a larger inscription, but this is certainly not the usual case in the arguments we wish to evaluate.

subclass of sentences, those sentence types all of whose tokens have the same truth value, the two formulations both work, and indeed are equivalent. Now it may be that some sentence has only true tokens because it is only uttered once, truly, and is never uttered again. But our applications should not be contingent on such accidental facts. Rather we should be concerned with cases where we can know from the sentences themselves that all instances have the same truth value. Such sentences must have no essential deictic elements and no ambiguities—Quine calls them *eternal* sentences. So long as we restrict ourselves to the eternal sentences we have considerable latitude in the formulation of modus ponens:

> If every (any) token of Q is (would be) true, and every (any) token of the conditional formed from Q and R respectively is (would be) true, then so are (would be)(all) tokens of R.

The formulation of a satisfactory form of modus ponens leaves the question open as to whether we should consider the objects of logic to be eternal sentence types or tokens. The rule of Addition suggests that it must be types. In general, the existence of a token of sentence type R is not sufficient to guarantee that a token of sentence type R ∨ Q exists. (Choose your favorite two-hundred-word sentence as Q.) Thus unless we wish to qualify the principle of addition as conditional on the existence of R ∨ Q, we must opt for the eternal sentence *types*.

It may strike the reader that this secures the correctness of the logical principles at great cost to the scope of application—few sentences outside of mathematics will qualify as logically invariable. Quine would reply that this worry is excessive. To see this, I believe that a comparison with geometry may be helpful. As Plato noted some time ago, there are no true (Euclidean) geometric triangles in the world. Yet mathematics in general, and geometry in particular in still quite helpful. If, for the purposes at hand, a figure is sufficiently close to being a triangle, than we can treat it as one. That it is distinguishable from a true triangle in other contexts or by more refined measurement is irrelevant.

5. LOGIC AND ORDINARY SENTENCES

A more realistic approach still seems possible without departing from Quinean scruples about propositions and meanings. If we are concerned with evaluating or justifying a particular argument, it will suffice if the tokens of a given type all behave properly *in that context.*

Eternally impeccable behavior of all tokens at all times is not required. Thus our next formulation of modus ponens will be:

> If Q_1 and Q_2 are tokens of the same type of sentence and corresponding expressions occurring in them have the same extensions[5] and if R_1 and R_2 are tokens of the same type of sentence and corresponding component expressions occurring in them have the same extensions, and if S is the conditional containing Q_1 as antecedent and R_1 as consequent, then if Q_2 and S are true, so is R_2.

Notice that it is not sufficient that Q_1 and Q_2 be tokens of the same type, for they may contain indexical elements, such as 'I', 'now', 'tomorrow', or 'there', whose referents vary from token to token. And the co-extensiveness of the words is not alone sufficient, since Q_1 and Q_2 might still be tokens of different sentence types even if they contain different but co-extensive words in the same order. For example, since there are neither dragons nor unicorns, the words in the following two sentences have exactly corresponding extensions:

> All dragons have wings and scales.
> All unicorns have wings and scales.

If we are to use this proposal, or something like it, we must return to the issue of the relation between types and tokens and say rather more about types. On the usual understanding, a sentence type may be structurally ambiguous, and if this is the case our formulation is unsatisfactory. Coextensiveness of corresponding terms and being tokens of the same ambiguous type do not guarantee sameness of truth value of those tokens. What we are after are disambiguated sentence types, and as usual we need some distinctions, some technical terminology and some stipulations.

First, we need a set of basic elements, strings of which can represent the elementary properties of inscriptions and utterances. For English the alphabet is the obvious—though not unproblematic—choice.[6] To map an inscription onto an alphabetic string may seem trivial, but

5. Note that we need not know at all what the extensions of the expressions are, just that they are the same in the two occurrences. This seems to me to be a solution to Strawson's (1957) worry about how Quine can deal with ambiguity without invoking intensions.

6. Consider for example how to represent the *true* utterance approximated by "There are three tews in English."

is not in many cases, especially if the inscription is handwritten. And the first company that can develop a machine to produce alphabetic strings from utterances in English will become wealthy.

Secondly, we need a specification of a syntactic structure. Typically this fixes one of the possible syntactic structures of the string. Third we need a semantic interpretation, selecting as necessary among the semantic ambiguities. And finally, we need a specification of pragmatic structure. This last does not fix the reference of deictic elements, such as 'you', 'then', or 'here', but specifies the functions which, given a context, fix the references.

An ordered quadruple consisting of a string plus specifications of syntax, semantics, and pragmatics will be called a 'fully specified string' (abbreviated 'fss', pronounced 'fuss'). An utterance or inscription is a potential instance of a fss if it can reasonably be mapped onto the string of the fss. Thus my notion of a sentence type is ultimately replaced by the more exact notion of a fss. The issue of when something is actually an instance of a specific fss is a very complex matter that probably has to be relativized to persons. For example, an ambiguous utterance may be interpreted as an instance of one fss by the speaker and a different one by a hearer.

Fortunately, for purposes of logic we do not need to worry about exactly which fss is instanced. What we care about is constancy throughout the argument. Thus our penultimate formulation of modus ponens is:

> If, within the same context, Q_1 and Q_2 are respectively instances of the fss Q, R_1 and R_2 are instances of the fss R, and S is a conditional with Q_1 as antecedent and R_1 as consequent, then, in that context, if Q_2 and S are true, then so is R_2.

6. LOGIC AND GRAMMAR

Still our definition will not quite do because in some cases conditionals do not contain tokens of the minor premise or conclusion. The problem is more general, of course, and arises in all cases of excluded middle. The formal version, $Q \lor \sim Q$, contains two occurrences of the same sentence letter but the English version

> 'It is raining or it is not raining'

does not contain two tokens of the same sentence, unless we are inclined to take the quixotic path of seeing a second (discontinuous) token of 'it is raining' after the 'or'. Even if we do that, we have further difficulties with some conditionals. The conditional formed from 'Sam will go to Cambridge' and 'Sam will learn to punt' is 'If Sam goes to Cambridge, she will learn to punt' and it takes imagination, not simply blindness to a 'not', to see the relevant tokens in the conditional.

I think it preferable to face the fact that we need a theory about English that will tell us whether a token S_1 of S is of the type $Q \rightarrow R$, when Q_1 and R_1 are relevant tokens of Q and R. And similarly a theory will be required for the other connectives and quantifiers. How is such a theory to be tested? Presumably by comparison of semantic values of the conditional and the alleged components. Of course this is no simple matter—all of the problems of ambiguity and deixis are present here as well, although assumptions of linguistic generality and regularity will provide some leverage. All of these issues are at least implicitly familiar to anyone who has attempted to formalize any complex philosophical argument, but they are often overlooked when we theorize about logic.

Thus our final formulation of modus ponens is:

> If Q_1 is a token of a fss Q, R_1 a token of a fss R, and S_1 a token of $Q \rightarrow R$ and if corresponding elements of Q_1, R_1 and S_1 are coextensive, and if Q_1 and S_1 are true, then so is R_1.

Before celebrating too much, we should note that although we have a satisfactory formulation of modus ponens we have introduced a new technical notion, that of a fss which is a token of $Q \rightarrow R$, where Q and R are each a fss. In our formal language a complex type is formed by simply concatenating parentheses, tokens of the constituent types and a token of the logical operator. But English (and other natural languages) are not so straightforward: if the constituent types are those of 'Sam will go to Cambridge' and 'Sam will learn to punt' we have already noted one grammatical change that is required. Furthermore, it is arguable that

> If Sam goes to Cambridge, she will learn to punt.

conveys the intended conditional less ambiguously than

> If Sam goes to Cambridge, Sam will learn to punt.

And there is no reason to think that all tokens of $Q \rightarrow R$ will be tokens of the same English sentence. In addition to the above,

> If she goes to Cambridge, Sam will learn to punt.
> and
> Sam will learn to punt, if she goes to Cambridge.

are also candidates for being tokens of $Q \rightarrow R$.

To be a little more specific, an English expression is a token of $Q \rightarrow R$ just in case it stands in the appropriate semantic relations to appropriately related tokens of Q and R. Whether any English expressions, including those formed using 'if-then', are tokens of such a type is a difficult and much debated question that we shall not consider here.

7. CONCLUSIONS

I have argued for interpreting logic as being about sentences, though the application of logic to the evaluation of arguments is no more straightforward than is the application of geometry to carpentry. More precisely and technically, the fss is what logic is all about. It may be that the complexities that were involved in the notion of the type-token relation and in the concept of a token of a conditional type show that we would be better off with a simpler notion such as that of a proposition. This appeal to simplicity is, to my mind, very superficial. It is true that we could avoid all of the above complexities by simply requiring that the putative major premise in modus ponens express the conditional proposition with the appropriate propositions as antecedent and consequent. But if we wish to actually evaluate a specific argument, then we need to deal with the issue that propositions are expressed by a given inscription or utterance. And all of the structural analysis, contextual dependence and ambiguity resolution must be done. Propositional theories look simpler because they do not do the hard work, and if you do the hard work you do not need the propositions.

A very different kind of objection that might be raised to my approach is that it misplaces the locus of logic. I have written of logic as a matter of language, but there is a venerable tradition that holds that logic primarily governs thought and that language is but the outer sign of thought. Issues about the relation between thought and language are too complex to enter adequately in this essay, but my own view is a complex moderate position. Some thought seems to antedate language, but many of our thoughts, perhaps the majority, would be impossible without language. Thus logic would have an important role if only in analyzing linguistic matters. However, if the reader will consider the discussion of types, tokens and the like, it can be seen that if one were to add a third kind of token, internal representations, with the right kinds of structural properties and suitable complications, then there is no reason the analysis could not be extended to that realm. In such a case, the discussion may also be more directly relevant to our initial Question III.[7]

7. I am indebted to members of my Spring 1993 logic class and to the editor for helpful criticisms of earlier drafts.

5

Theories of Truth

Paul Horwich

The notion of truth occurs with remarkable frequency in our reflections on language, thought and action. We are inclined to suppose, for example, that *truth* is the proper aim of scientific inquiry, that *true* beliefs help us to achieve our goals, that to understand a sentence is to know which circumstances would make it *true*, that reliable preservation of *truth* as one argues from premises to a conclusion is the mark of valid reasoning, that moral pronouncements should not be regarded as objectively *true*, and so on. In order to assess the plausibility of such theses, and in order to refine them and to explain why they hold (if they do), we require some view of what truth is—a theory that would account for its properties and its relations to other matters. Thus there can be little prospect of understanding our most important cognitive faculties in the absence of a good theory of truth.

Such a thing, however, has been notoriously elusive. The ancient idea that truth is some sort of 'correspondence with reality' has still never been articulated satisfactorily: the nature of the alleged 'correspondence' and the alleged 'reality' remain objectionably obscure. Yet the familiar alternative suggestions—that true beliefs are those that are 'mutually coherent', or 'pragmatically useful', or 'verifiable in suitable conditions'—have each been confronted with persuasive counterexamples. A twentieth century departure from these traditional analyses is the view that truth is not a *property* at all—that the syntactic form of the predicate, "is true," distorts its real semantic character, which is not to *describe* propositions but rather to *endorse* them. This so-called 'deflationary' approach is also not without difficulties. However, there is some reason to think that they can be overcome and that deflationism is on the right track. If it is, then dramatic philosophical consequences are to be expected, since truth could not play the vital theoretical role in logic, semantics, epistemology and elsewhere that we are naturally inclined to give it.

1. TRADITIONAL THEORIES

The belief that snow is white owes its truth to a certain feature of the external world: namely, to the fact that snow is white. Similarly, the belief that dogs bark is true because of the fact that dogs bark. This sort of trivial observation leads to what is perhaps the most natural and popular account of truth, *the correspondence theory*, according to which a belief (statement, sentence, proposition, etc.) is true just in case there exists a fact corresponding to it (Wittgenstein 1961; Austin 1950). This thesis is unexceptionable in itself. However if it is to provide a rigorous, substantial, and complete theory of truth—if it is to be more than merely a picturesque way of asserting all equivalences of the form,

The belief *that p* is true ↔ *p*

—then it must be supplemented with accounts of what *facts* are, and what it is for a belief to *correspond* to a fact; and these are the problems on which the correspondence theory of truth has foundered. For one thing, it is far from clear that any significant gain in understanding is achieved by reducing "the belief that snow is white is true" to "the fact that snow is white exists"; for these expressions seem equally resistant to analysis and too close in meaning for one to provide an illuminating account of the other. In addition, the general relationship that holds in particular between the belief that snow is white and the fact that snow is white, between the belief that dogs bark and the fact that dogs bark, and so on, is very hard to identify. The best attempt to date is Wittgenstein's (1961) so-called "picture theory," whereby an elementary proposition is a configuration of primitive constituents, an atomic fact is a configuration of simple objects, an atomic fact *corresponds* to an elementary proposition (and makes it true) when their configurations are identical and when the primitive constituents in the proposition refer to the similarly-placed objects in the fact, and the truth value of each complex proposition is entailed by the truth values of the elementary ones. However, even if this account is correct as far as it goes, it would need to be completed with plausible theories of 'logical configuration', 'elementary proposition', 'reference', and 'entailment', none of which is easy to come by.

A central characteristic of truth—one that any adequate theory must explain—is that when a proposition satisfies its 'conditions of proof (or verification)' then it is regarded as *true*. To the extent that the property of *corresponding with reality* is mysterious, we are going to find it impossible to see why what we take to verify a proposition should indicate the possession of that property. Therefore a tempting alternative to the correspondence theory—an alternative which eschews obscure, metaphysical concepts and which explains quite straightforwardly why verifiability implies truth—is to simply *identify* truth with verifiability (Peirce 1932). This idea can take on various forms. One version involves the further assumption that verification is *holistic*—i.e. that a belief is justified (i.e. verified) when it is part of an entire system of beliefs that is consistent and 'harmonious' (Bradley 1914; Hempel 1935). This is known as the coherence theory of truth. Another version involves the assumption that there is, associated with each proposition, some specific procedure for finding out whether one should believe it or not. On this account, to say that a proposition is true is to say that it would be verified by the appropriate procedure (Dummett 1978; Putnam 1981). In the context of mathematics this amounts to the identification of truth with provability.

The attractions of the verificationist account of truth are that it is refreshingly clear compared with the correspondence theory, and that it succeeds in connecting truth with verification. The trouble is that the bond it postulates between these notions is implausibly strong. On the face of it, there could well exist several conflicting, yet internally coherent, systems of belief—suggesting that although coherence may confer plausibility, it is no guarantee of truth. We do indeed regard coherence, proof, and other forms of verification, as indicative of truth. But also we recognize the possibility that a proposition may be false in spite of there being excellent reasons to believe it, and that a proposition may be true even though we aren't able to discover that it is. Verifiability and truth are no doubt highly correlated; but surely not the same thing.

A third well known account of truth is known as *pragmatism* (James 1909; Papineau 1987). As we have just seen, the verificationist selects a prominent property of truth and considers it to be the *essence* of truth. Similarly the pragmatist focusses on another important characteristic—namely, that true beliefs are a good basis for action—and takes this to be the very nature of truth. True assumptions are said to be, by definition, those that provoke actions with desirable results. Again we have an account with a single attractive explanatory feature. But again the central objection is that the relationship it postulates between truth and its alleged analysans—in this case, utility—is implausibly close. Granted, true beliefs tend to foster success. But it happens regularly that actions based on true beliefs lead to disaster, while false assumptions, by pure chance, produce wonderful results.

2. DEFLATIONARY THEORIES

One of the few uncontroversial facts about truth is that the proposition that snow is white is true if and only if snow is white, the proposition that lying is wrong is true if and only if lying is wrong, and so on.

Traditional theories acknowledge this fact but regard it as insufficient and, as we have seen, inflate it with some further principle of the form, 'X is true if and only if X has property P' (such as, corresponding to reality, verifiability, or being suitable as a basis for action), which is supposed to specify *what truth is*. A variety of radical alternatives to the traditional theories result from denying the need for any such further specification (Ramsey 1927; Strawson 1950; Quine 1990). For example, one might suppose that the basic theory of truth contains nothing more than equivalences of the form, 'The proposition *that p* is true if and only if *p*' (Horwich 1990).

This sort of deflationary proposal is best presented in conjunction with an account of the *raison d'être* of our notion of truth: namely, that it enables us to compose generalizations of a special sort, that would otherwise call for 'infinite conjunction' or some other radically new logical device. Suppose, for example, you are told that Einstein's last words expressed a claim about physics, an area in which you think he was very reliable. Suppose that, unknown to you, his claim was the proposition that quantum mechanics is wrong. What conclusion can you draw? Exactly which proposition becomes the appropriate object of your belief? Surely not that quantum mechanics is wrong; because you are not aware that that is what he said. What is needed is something equivalent to the infinite conjunction:

> If what Einstein said was that $E = mc$, then $E = mc$, and if what he said was that quantum mechanics is wrong, then quantum mechanics is wrong, . . . and so on

—that is, a proposition, K, with the following properties: that from K and any further premise of the form, "Einstein's claim was the proposition that *p*" you can infer "*p*," whatever it is. Now suppose, as the deflationist says, that our understanding of the truth predicate consists in the stipulative decision to accept any instance of the schema, "The proposition *that p* is true if and only if *p*." Then your problem is solved. For if K is the proposition, "Einstein's claim is true," it will have precisely the inferential power that is needed. From it and "Einstein's claim is the proposition that quantum mechanics is wrong," you can use Leibniz' law to infer "The proposition that quantum mechanics is wrong is true," which, given the relevant axiom of the deflationary theory, allows you to derive "Quantum mechanics is wrong." Thus one point in favour of the deflationary theory is that it squares with a plausible story about the function of our notion of truth: its axioms explain that function without the need for any further analysis of 'what truth is'.

Further support for deflationism depends upon the possibility of showing that its axioms—instances of the equivalence schema—unsupplemented by any further analysis, will suffice to explain all the central facts about truth: for example, that the verification of a proposition indicates its truth, and that true beliefs have a practical value. The first of these facts follows trivially from the deflationary axioms. For given our *a priori* knowledge of the equivalence of "p" and "The proposition *that p* is true," any reason to believe that p becomes an equally good reason to believe that the proposition *that p* is true. The second fact can also be explained in terms of the deflationary axioms, but not quite so easily. Consider, to begin with, one's beliefs of the form,

(B)   If I perform act A, then my desires will be fulfilled.

Notice that the psychological role of such a belief is to bring about the performance of A. In other words, given that I do have belief (B), then typically

I will perform act A.

And notice also that when the belief is true then, given the deflationary axioms, the performance of A will in fact lead to the fulfillment of one's desires. I.e.

If (B) is true, then if I perform A, my desires will be fulfilled.

Therefore

If (B) is true, my desires will be fulfilled.

So it is quite reasonable to value the truth of beliefs of that form. But such beliefs are derived by inference from other beliefs and can be expected to be true if those other beliefs are true. So it is reasonable to value the truth of any belief that might be used in such an inference.

To the extent that such deflationary accounts can be given of *all* the facts involving truth, then the explanatory demands on a theory of truth will be met by the collection of all statements like, "The proposition that snow is white is true if and only if snow is white," and the sense that some deep analysis of truth is needed will be undermined.

However, there are several strongly felt objections to deflationism and these must be addressed. One reason for dissatisfaction is that the theory has an infinite number of axioms, and therefore cannot be completely written down. It can be *described* (as the theory whose axioms are the propositions of the form '*p* if and only if it is true that *p*'), but not explicitly formulated. This alleged defect has led some philosophers to develop theories which show, first, how the truth of any proposition derives from the referential properties of its constituents; and, second, how the referential properties of primitive constituents are determined (Tarski, 1943; Davidson, 1969). However, it remains controversial to assume that *all* propositions—including belief attributions, laws of nature, and counterfactual conditionals—depend for their true values on what their constituents refer to. Moreover there is no immediate prospect of a decent, finite theory of reference. So it is far from clear that the infinite, list-like character of deflationism can be avoided.

Another source of dissatisfaction with this theory is that certain instances of the equivalence schema are clearly false. Consider

(a)   THE PROPOSITION EXPRESSED BY THE SENTENCE IN CAPITAL LETTERS IS NOT TRUE.

Substituting this into the schema one gets a version of the 'liar' paradox: specifically,

(b)   The proposition *that the proposition expressed by the sentence in capital letters is not true* is true if and only if the proposition expressed by the sentence in capital letters is not true,

from which a contradiction is easily derivable. (Given (b), the supposition that (a) is true implies that (a) is not true, and the supposition that it is not true implies that it is.) Consequently, not every instance of the equivalence schema can be included in the our theory of truth; but it is no simple matter to specify the ones to be excluded (see Kripke, 1975). Of course, deflationism is far from alone in having to confront this problem.

A third objection to the version of the deflationary theory presented here concerns its reliance on *propositions* as the basic vehicles of truth. It is widely felt that the notion of proposition is defective and that it should not be employed in semantics. If this point of view is accepted then the natural deflationary reaction is to attempt a reformulation that would appeal only to *sentences*: for example,

"*p*" is true iff *p*.

But this so-called "disquotational theory of truth" (Quine 1990) comes to grief over foreign sentences and over indexicals, demonstratives and other terms whose referents vary with the context of use. It is not the case, for example, that *every* instance of "I am hungry" is true if and only if *I* am hungry. And there is no simple way of modifying the disquotational schema to accommodate these problems. A possible way out is to adopt a two-tier approach: first instantiate the disquotational schema, with sentences that don't exhibit context-sensitivity, and then extend the concept of truth via the principle that an utterance is true if its translation into (or interpretation within) that portion of the language is true. For example, my present utterance of "I am hungry" would be true in virtue of the fact that

> "P. H. is hungry at noon on 6th June 1991" is true iff P. H. is hungry at noon on 6th June 1991

> My present utterance may be translated as "P. H. is hungry at noon on 6th June 1991"

and

> P. H. is hungry at noon on 6th June 1991.

The trouble with this strategy is that if the notion of translation is going to be embraced, it is hard to see why propositions should have been avoided in the first place, since they could be defined as (or correlated with) equivalence classes of utterances under the translation relation. Such entities may well exhibit an unwelcome degree of indeterminacy, and may well defy reduction to familiar items. However they do offer a plausible account of belief (as relations to propositions) and, in ordinary language at least, they are indeed taken to be the primary bearers of truth.

3. FALSITY

The simplest plausible account of falsity is that a proposition is false just in case it is not true. An alternative formulation of this idea—one that parallels the equivalence schema for truth—is given by

> The proposition *that p* is false iff $\sim p$.

These two formulations are equivalent. For the logical expression "$\sim p$" is shorthand for "It is not the case that *p*." But there is no reason to distinguish *being true* and *being the case.* So "~*p*" means nothing more or less than "It is not true that *p*," which is presumably synonymous with "The proposition *that p* is not true."

From this natural account of falsity it follows that every proposition has a truth value; for to say of some proposition that it is neither true nor false would be to imply that it is both not true and *not* not true, which is a contradiction. This result has important ramifications in semantics, where it has often been found tempting to mark out certain 'odd' propositions as having no truth value.

One of the areas in which it has been popular to invoke truth-value-gaps is in the treatment of *vagueness.* It is often said, for example, that if John is a borderline case of baldness, then the proposition that John is bald is neither true nor false. But this approach leads to the contradiction just mentioned. An alternative strategy is to draw a distinction between truth and *determinate* truth (in terms of the idea that the latter, but not the former, implies the possibility of conclusive verification). One can then characterize what is special about vague propositions, without running afoul of the above theory of falsity, by saying that, although true or false, they lack *determinate* truth values.

A second type of proposition to which the 'no-truth-value' strategy has been applied are those, such as "Santa drives a sleigh," which contain nonreferring constituents. Again, there is an alternative policy: namely, regard such (logically simple) propositions as false. This can be sustained by converting names into predicates *à la* Quine, giving, in our example,

> The unique possessor of the property of being-Santa drives a sleigh,

and then employing Russell's theory of definite descriptions, to obtain

> There is exactly one thing possessing the property of being-Santa, and it drives a sleigh,

which is uncontroversially false.

Finally, there is a famous 'emotivist' account of ethics according to which, appearances to the contrary, moral pronouncements do not purport to assert facts but, rather, to express the feelings of the speaker, and therefore should not be regarded as true or false. However, there is no need to link the two components of this view. One might well agree that the peculiarity of ethical claims is that they are justified when the speaker has certain feelings. But this does not require us to say that they are neither true nor false—which, as we have seen, is a position best avoided. Once again we find no theoretical reason to depart from the simple account of falsity as absence of truth.

4. THE ROLE OF TRUTH IN LOGIC

Let us continue our examination of the implications of the deflationary theory for various areas of philosophical enquiry. Logic and truth might appear to be tightly associated with each other. For, in the first place, the principles of logic and metalogic invariably refer to truth:— viz. "No proposition is both true and false," "The laws of deductive inference preserve truth," etc. And, in the second place, the logical particles, "and," "not," etc. are typically defined in terms of truth and falsity, using truth-tables. Thus Frege (1956) came to the view that the laws of logic are about truth, in just the same sense that the laws of chemistry are about molecules. And in contemporary philosophy it is often supposed (e.g. by Dummett 1977 and Putnam 1978) that the choice between different logics boils down to a choice between different conceptions of truth.

In fact, however, logic and truth bear no such relations to one another. The reason that the notion of truth is used so much in logic is that logic is concerned with just the special sort of generalization which the notion of truth—as defined by the equivalence schema—is 'designed' to help us formulate. Suppose we wish to state the law of non-contradiction:

> Nothing is both green and not green, or both tall and not tall, or both fragile and not fragile, . . . and so on.

We need a single proposition that will be equivalent to this infinite conjunction. And we can obtain it as follows. The equivalence schema tells us that

> Nothing is both green and not green

is equivalent to

> The proposition that *nothing is both green and not green* is true

And similarly for the other conjuncts. Therefore our initial infinite list may be converted into another such list in which the same property, *truth*, is attributed to every member of an infinite class of structurally similar objects (propositions). And this second list can be captured as an ordinary generalization over objects:

Every proposition of the form 'Nothing is both F and not F' is true.

It is in just this role that the concept of truth figures so pervasively in logic. And notice that the notion of truth employed in formulating classical logic is exactly the same as the notion employed in other logics, such as intuitionistic logic and quantum logic: namely, the notion articulated by the equivalence schema.

A second source of the misimpression that truth and logic are peculiarly intertwined is the idea that our logical particles are best explained in terms of truth and falsity. A standard account of disjunction, for example, is the truth-table:

p	q	$p \vee q$
T	T	T
T	F	T
F	T	T
F	F	F

But in light of the equivalence schema this table is tantamount to the rules of inference:

$$\frac{p, q}{p \vee q} \qquad \frac{p, \sim q}{p \vee q} \qquad \frac{\sim p, q}{p \vee q} \qquad \frac{\sim p, \sim q}{\sim(p \vee q)}$$

$$\frac{}{(p \vee q) \vee (p \vee \sim q) \vee (\sim p \vee q) \vee (\sim p \vee \sim q)}$$

which, when combined with further rules derived similarly from the other truth tables, are equivalent to the propositional calculus. Thus the collection of rules of deductive inference helps to implicitly define the logical particles. The concepts of truth and falsity contribute nothing beyond ease of formulation.

5. THE ROLE OF TRUTH IN SEMANTICS

Following Davidson (1967), it is widely held that a sentence is given meaning by associating it with a condition for being true. For example, our understanding of the sentence "Snow is white" would consist in our commitment to the proposition *that "Snow is white" is true if and only if snow is white.* One frequently cited virtue of this so-called 'truth conditional theory' is that it dispenses with allegedly problematic notions such as "means that" in favor of the relatively clear ideas, "refers to" and "is true." Another supposed virtue is that it enables us to see how the meanings of composite expressions depend on the meanings of their parts, and to see therefore how it is possible for us, with our finite minds, to understand a potential infinity of compound expressions. For example, if our knowledge of the meanings of sentences "A" and "B" consists in knowing that

> "A" is true if and only if snow is white

and that

> "B" is true if and only if dogs bark,

then we can deduce that

> "A" is true and "B" is true
> if and only if snow is white and dogs bark.

But our understanding of "and" tells us that

> "A and B" is true
> if and only if "A" is true and "B" is true.

So we can conclude that

> "A and B" is true
> if and only if snow is white and dogs bark,

thereby deriving the truth condition (and, on this view, the meaning) of the compound expression from our knowledge of the meanings of its parts.

Criticism of the truth conditional theory of meaning comes from several directions. In the first place, it can be argued that understanding an expression consists merely in *associating* it with a meaning and need not involve any *knowledge* of that association. Such knowledge— e.g. that "A" means that snow is white, or that "A" is true if and only if snow is white—would require possession of the concepts, 'means that' or 'true'; yet it would seem that one might understand words like "snow" without yet having acquired those sophisticated semantic concepts. Moreover, any such explicit knowledge would have to be formulated in some language which the speaker already understands. Consequently, there must be some basic language whose understanding is not to be explained in terms of a knowledge of truth conditions. And so, then why should we have thought that such knowledge would ever be the basis of linguistic competence?

Secondly, the fact that a sentence, "A," is true if and only if snow is white does not entail that "A" expresses the proposition that snow is white. It entails merely that "A" and "snow is white" are either both true or both false. This difficulty may be mitigated by taking the words "if and only if" in the statement of truth conditions to convey a sufficiently *strong* relation of equivalence between ""A" is true" and "Snow is white." However, it is unclear that anything much weaker than *synonymy* will do, in which case the initial promise to have dispensed with the allegedly obscure notion of meaning will not be fulfilled.

A third criticism of the truth conditional theory accuses it of being not so much false as unhelpful—of explaining facts that are easy to explain without it, yet having nothing to say about the features of meaning that are most in need of illumination. According to this critique, the compositionality of meaning follows trivially from the fact that the meaning of an expression is a compound entity whose constituents are the meanings of the constituents of the expression and whose structure is determined by the expression's syntactic form. This shows, without the need for a truth conditional analysis, how we are able to figure out the meanings of complex expressions from the meanings of their parts.

Fourthly, the criticism continues, the most puzzling properties of meaning are not addressed at all by the truth conditional approach. For example, in virtue of which facts about the mind or linguistic behavior does a sentence come to have the particular meaning it has? It is all very well to cite our committing ourselves to some proposition of the form 'A is true iff p'; but this is empty in the absence of some indication of what state of mind such a commitment consists in. Similarly, another important fact about meaning is that if someone knows the meaning of a sentence then he knows something about what counts as evidence for and against its being true. Again, an interesting account of what it is to know the meaning of a sentence would shed light on this fact, but the truth conditional analysis leaves it in the dark. Perhaps the analysis can be supplemented with further theory and thereby explain these matters (see Davidson, 1990). How-

ever, questions will remain as to whether the truth conditional analysis
is itself doing any explanatory work. Insofar as the supplementary
theory does not deal separately with the elements of the analysans—
notably, "true" and the above mentioned, strong notion of "if and only
if"—but rather gives content to the analysans taken as a whole, then it
would be more straightforward to take the theory directly as an account of meaning, bypassing the truth conditional analysis.

6. THE ROLE OF TRUTH IN
METAPHYSICS AND EPISTEMOLOGY

It is commonly supposed that problems about the nature of truth are
intimately bound up with questions as to the accessibility and auton-
omy of facts in various domains: questions about whether the facts
can be known, and whether they can exist independently of our capacity to discover them (Dummett 1978; Putnam 1981). One might
reason, for example, that if 'T is true' means nothing more than 'T
will be verified' then certain forms of scepticism (specifically, those
that doubt the correctness of our methods of verification) will be
precluded, and that the facts will have been revealed as dependent on
human practices. Alternatively, it might be said that if truth were an
inexplicable, primitive, nonepistemic property, then the fact that T is
true would be completely independent of us. Moreover, we could, in
that case, have no reason to assume that the propositions we believe
actually have this property; so scepticism would be unavoidable. In a
similar vein, it might be thought that a special (and perhaps undesirable) feature of the deflationary approach is that truth is deprived of
any such metaphysical or epistemological implications.

On closer scrutiny, however, it is far from clear that there exists *any*
account of truth with consequences regarding the accessibility or au-
tonomy of non-semantic matters. For although an account of truth
may be expected to have such implications for facts of the form 'T is
true', it cannot be assumed without further argument that the same
conclusions will apply to the fact, T. For it cannot be assumed that T
and 'T is true' are equivalent to one another given the account of
"true" that is being employed. Of course, if truth is defined in the way
that the deflationist proposes, then the equivalence holds by definition.
But if truth is defined by reference to some metaphysical or epistemological characteristic, then the equivalence schema is thrown into
doubt pending some demonstration that the truth predicate, in the
sense assumed, will satisfy it. Insofar as there are thought to be
epistemological problems hanging over T that do not threaten 'T is

true', it will be difficult to give the needed demonstration. Similarly, if "truth" is so defined that the fact, T, is felt to be more (or less) independent of human practices than the fact 'T is true', then again it is unclear that the equivalence schema will hold. It would seem, therefore, that the attempt to base epistemological or metaphysical conclusions on a theory of truth must fail because, in any such attempt, the equivalence schema will be simultaneously relied on yet undermined.

The Justification
of Deduction

Susan Haack

1. It is often taken for granted by writers who propose—and, for that matter, by writers who oppose—'justifications' of *induction,* that *deduction* either does not need, or can readily be provided with, justification. The purpose of this paper is to argue that, contrary to this common opinion, problems analogous to those which, notoriously, arise in the attempt to justify induction, also arise in the attempt to justify deduction.

Hume presented us with a dilemma: we cannot justify induction deductively, because to do so would be to show that *whenever* the premises of an inductive argument are true, the conclusion must be true too—which would be *too strong*; and we cannot justify induction inductively, either, because such a 'justification' would be *circular.* I propose another dilemma: we cannot justify deduction inductively, because to do so would be, at best, to show that *usually,* when the premises of a deductive argument are true, the conclusion is true too—which would be *too weak*; and we cannot justify deduction deductively, either, because such a justification would be *circular.*

The parallel between the old and the new dilemmas can be illustrated thus:

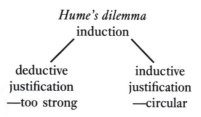

Hume's dilemma
induction

deductive justification —too strong

inductive justification —circular

This essay first appeared in *Mind,* 85 (1976). It is reprinted by permission of the author and of Oxford University Press

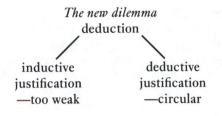

The new dilemma
deduction

inductive justification —too weak

deductive justification —circular

2. A necessary preliminary to serious discussion of the problems of justifying induction/deduction is a clear statement of them.

This means, first, giving some kind of characterisation of 'inductive argument' and 'deductive argument'. This is a more difficult task than seems to be generally appreciated. It will hardly do, for example, to characterise deductive arguments as 'non-ampliative' (Salmon 1966) or 'explicative' (Barker 1965), and inductive arguments as 'ampliative' or 'non-explicative'; for these characterisations are apt to turn out either false, if the key notion of 'containing nothing in the conclusion not already contained in the premisses' is taken literally, or trivial, if it is not.

Because of the difficulties of demarcating 'inductive' and 'deductive' inference, it seems more profitable to define an *argument:*

> An argument is a sequence $A_1 \ldots A_n$ of sentences $n \geq 1$), of which $A_1 \ldots A_{n-1}$ are the *premisses* and A_n is the *conclusion*

—and then to try to distinguish inductive from deductive standards of a 'good argument'.

It is well known that deductive standards of validity may be put in either of two ways: syntactically or semantically. So:

D_1 An argument $A_1 \ldots A_{n-1} \vdash A_n$ is deductively valid (in L_D) just in case the conclusion, A_n, is deducible from the premisses, $A_1 \ldots A_{n-1}$ and the axioms of L_D, if any, in virtue of the rules of inference of L_D (the syntactic definition).

D_2 An argument $A_1 \ldots A_{n-1} \vdash A_n$ is deductively valid just in case it is impossible that the premisses, $A_1 \ldots A_{n-1}$, should be true, and the conclusion, A_n, false (the semantic definition).

Similarly, we can express standards of inductive strength either syntactically or semantically; the syntactic definition would follow D_1 but with 'L_I' for 'L_D'; the semantic definition would follow D_2 but with 'it is improbable, given that the premisses are true, that the conclusion is false'.

The question now arises, which of these kinds of characterisation should we adopt in our statement of the problems of justifying deduction/induction? This presents a difficulty. If we adopt semantic accounts of deductive validity/inductive strength, the problem of justification will seem to have been trivialised. The justification problem will reappear, however, in a disguised form, as the question '*Are there any deductively valid/inductively strong arguments?*' If, on the other hand, we adopt syntactic accounts of deductive validity/inductive strength, the nature of the justification problem is clear: to show that arguments which are deductively valid/inductively strong are also truth-preserving/truth-preserving most of the time (i.e. deductively valid/inductively strong on the semantic accounts). On the other hand, there is the difficulty that we must somehow specify which systems are possible values of 'L_D' and 'L_I', and this will presumably require appeal to inevitably vague considerations concerning the intentions of the authors of a formal system.

A convenient compromise is this. There are certain forms of inference, such as the rule:

RI   From: m/n of all observed A's have been B's
         to infer: m/n of all A's are B's

which are commonly taken to be inductively strong, and similarly, certain forms of inference, such as

MPP   From: A $\supset$ B, A
         to infer: B

which are generally taken to be deductively valid. Analogues of the general justification problems can now be set up as follows:

> the problem of the justification of induction: show that RI is truth-preserving most of the time.
> the problem of the justification of deduction: show that MPP is truth-preserving.

My procedure will be, then, to show that difficulties arise in the attempt to justify MPP which are analogous to notorious difficulties arising in the attempt to justify RI.

3. I consider first the suggestion that deduction *needs* no justification, that the call for a proof that MPP is truth-preserving is somehow misguided.

An argument for this position might go as follows:

> It is analytic that a deductively valid argument is truth-preserving, for by 'valid' we mean 'argument whose premisses could not be true without its conclusion being true too'. So there can be no serious question whether a deductively valid argument is truth-preserving.

It seems clear enough that anyone who argued like this would be the victim of a confusion. Agreed, if we adopt a semantic definition of 'deductively valid' it follows immediately that deductively valid arguments are truth-preserving. But the problem was, to show that a particular form of argument, a form deductively valid in the syntactic sense, is truth-preserving; and *this* is a genuine problem, which has simply been evaded. Similar arguments show the claim, made e.g. by Strawson (1952, p. 257), that induction needs no justification, to be confused.

4. I argued in Section (1) that 'justifications' of deduction are liable *either* to be inductive and too weak, *or* to be deductive and circular. The former, inductive kind of justification has enjoyed little popularity (except with the Intuitionists? cf. Brouwer 1952). But arguments of the second kind are not hard to find.

(*a*) Consider the following attempt to justify MPP:

A1 Suppose that 'A' is true, and that 'A ⊃ B' is true. By the truth-table for '⊃', if 'A' is true and 'A ⊃ B' is true, then 'B' is true too. So 'B' must be true too.

This argument has a serious drawback: it is of the very form which it is supposed to justify. For it goes:

A1′ Suppose C (that 'A' is true and that 'A ⊃ B' is true). If C then D (if 'A' is true and 'A ⊃ B' is true, 'B' is true). So, D ('B' is true too).

The analogy with Black's 'self-supporting' argument for induction (1954) is striking. Black proposes to support induction by means of the argument:

A2 RI has usually been successful in observed instances.
∴ RI is usually successful.

He defends himself against the charge of circularity by pointing out that this argument is not a simple case of question-begging: it does not contain its conclusion as a premiss. It might, similarly, be pointed out that A1′ is not a simple case of question-begging: for *it* does not contain its conclusion as a premiss, either.

One is inclined to feel that A2 *is* objectionably circular, in spite of Black's defence; and this intuition can be supported by an argument, like Salmon's (1966), to show that if A2 supports RI, an exactly analogous argument would support a counter-inductive rule, say:

RCI   From: most observed A's have not been B's
       to infer: most A's are B's.

Thus:

A3   RCI has usually been unsuccessful in the past.
       ∴ RCI is usually successful.

In a similar way, one can support the intuition that there is something wrong with A1′, in spite of its not being straightforwardly question-begging, by showing that if A1′ supports MPP, an exactly analogous argument would support a deductively invalid rule, say:

       MM (modus morons);
       From: A ⊃ B and B
       to infer: A.

Thus:

A4   RI1Supposing that 'A ⊃ B' is true and 'B' is true, 'A ⊃ B' is true ⊃
       'B' is true.
       Now, by the truth-table for '⊃', if 'A' is true, then, if 'A ⊃ B' is true,
       'B' is true. Therefore, 'A' is true.

This argument, like A1, has the very form which it is supposed to justify. For it goes:

A4′   Suppose D (if 'A ⊃ B' is true, 'B' is true).
       If C, then D (if 'A' is true, then, if 'A ⊃ B' is true, 'B' is true).
       So, C ('A' is true).

It is no good to protest that A4′ does not justify *modus morons* because it uses an *invalid* rule of inference, whereas A1′ does justify *modus ponens*, because it uses a *valid* rule of inference—for to justify our conviction that MPP is valid and MM is not is precisely what is at issue.

Neither is it any use to protest that A1′ is not circular because *it* is an argument in the meta-language, whereas the rule which it is supposed to justify is a rule in the object language. For the attempt to save the argument for RI by taking it as a proof, on level 2, of a rule of level 1, also falls prey to the difficulty that we could with equal justice give a counter-inductive argument, on level 2, for the counter-inductive rule at level 1. And similarly, if we may give an argument using MPP, at level 2, to support the rule MPP at level 1, we could, equally, give an argument, using MM, at level 2, to support the rule MM at level 1.

(*b*) Another way to try to justify MPP, which promises not to be vulnerable to the difficulty that, if it is acceptable, so is an analogous justification of MM, is suggested by Thomson's discussion (1960) of the Tortoise's argument. Carroll's tortoise, in (1895), refuses to draw the conclusion, 'B', from 'A ⊃ B' and 'A', insisting that a new premiss, 'A ⊃ ((A ⊃ B) ⊃ B)' be added; and when that premiss is granted him, will still not draw the conclusion, but insists on a further premiss, and so *ad indefinitum*. Thomson argues that Achilles should never have conceded that an extra premiss was needed; for, he argues, if the original inference was valid (semantically) the added premiss is true but not needed, and if the original inference was invalid (semantically) the added premiss is needed but false. There is an analogy, here, again, with attempts to justify induction by appending a premiss—something, usually, to the effect that 'Nature is uniform'—which turns inferences in accordance with RI into deductively valid inferences. The required premiss would, presumably, be true but not needed if RI were deductively valid, false but needed if it is not.

Thomson's idea suggests that we should contrast this picture in the case of MPP:

A5 (1) $A \supset ((A \supset B) \supset B)$ (true but superfluous premiss)
    (2) A assumption
    (3) $(A \supset B) \supset B$ 1, 2, *MPP*
    (4) $A \supset B$ assumption
    (5) B 3, 4, *MPP*

with this picture in the case of MM:

A6 (1) $B \supset ((A \supset B) \supset A)$ (false but needed premiss)
    (2) B assumption
    (3) $(A \supset B) \supset A$ 1, 2, MPP
    (4) $A \supset B$ assumption
    (5) A 3, 4, MPP

Thomson's point is that in A5 premiss (1) is a tautology, so true; but it is not needed, since lines (2), (4) and (5) alone constitute a valid argument. In A6, by contrast, premiss (1) is *not* a tautology; but it is needed, because lines (2), (4) and (5) alone do not constitute a valid argument. But this is to assume that MPP, which is the rule of inference in virtue of which in A5 (2) and (4) yield (5), is valid; whereas MM, which is the rule of inference in virtue of which, in A6, (2) and (4) would yield (5), is *not* valid. But this is just what was to have been shown.

If A5 justifies MPP, which, after all, it uses, then the following argument equally justifies MM:

A7 (1) $(A \supset B) \supset (A \supset B)$ (true but superfluous premiss)
    (2) $A \supset B$ assumption
    (3) $A \supset B$ 1, 2, *MM*
    (4) B assumption
    (5) A 3, 4, *MM*

In A7 as in A5 the first premiss is a tautology, so true, but it is superfluous, since (if MM is accepted) lines (2), (4) and (5) alone constitute a valid argument.

(*c*) Nor will it do to argue that MPP is, whereas MM is not, justified 'in virtue of the meaning of "$\supset$".' For how is the meaning of '$\supset$' given? There are three kinds of answer commonly given: that the meaning of the connectives is given by the rules of inference/axioms of the system in which they occur; that the meaning is given by the interpretation, or, specifically, the truth-table, provided; that the meaning is given by the English readings of the connectives. Well, if '$\supset$' is supposed to be at least partially defined by the rules of inference governing sentences containing it (cf. Prior 1960, 1964) then MPP and MM would be exactly on a par. In a system containing MPP the meaning of '$\supset$' is partially defined by the rule, from 'A $\supset$ B' and 'A', to infer 'B'. In a system containing MM the meaning of '$\supset$' is partially defined by the rule, from 'A $\supset$ B' and 'B', to infer 'A'. In either case the rule in question would be justified in virtue of the meaning of '$\supset$', finally, since the meaning of '$\supset$' would be given by the rule. If, on the other hand, we thought of '$\supset$' as partially defined by its truth-table (cf. Stevenson 1961), we are in the difficulty discussed earlier ((*a*) above) that arguments from the truth-table to the justification of a rule of inference are liable to employ the rule in question. Nor would it do to appeal to the usual reading of '$\supset$' as 'if . . . then . . .', not just because the propriety of that reading has been doubted, but also because the question, why 'B' follows from 'if A then B' and 'A' but not 'A' from 'if A then B' and 'B', is precisely analogous to the question at issue.

(*d*) Our arguments against attempted justification of MPP have appealed to the fact that analogous procedures would justify MM. So at this point it might be suggested that we can produce independent arguments against MM. (Compare attempts to diagnose incoherence in RCI.) In particular, it might be supposed that it is a relatively simple matter to show that MM cannot be truth-preserving, since with MM at our disposal we could argue as follows:

A8 (1) $(P \& \sim P) \supset (P \vee \sim P)$
 (2) $P \vee \sim P$
 (3) $P \& \sim P$ $1, 2, MM$

So that a system including MM would be inconsistent. (This idea is suggested by Belnap's paper on 'tonk'.)

However, this argument is inconclusive because it depends upon certain assumptions about what else we have in the system to which MM is appended—in particular, that (1) and (2) are theorems. Now certainly *if* a system contained (1) and (2) as theorems, then (3) could be derived by MM, and the system would be inconsistent; but a system allowing MM can hardly be assumed to be otherwise conventional. (After all, many systems lack '$P \vee \sim P$' as a theorem, and minimal logic also lacks '$P \supset (\sim P \supset Q)$'.)

5. It might be suggested at this point that to direct our search for justification to a *form* of argument, or *argument schema*, such as MPP, is misguided, that the justification of the schema lies in the validity of its *instances*. So the answer to the question, 'What justifies the conclusion?' is simply 'The premises'; and the answer to the further question, what justifies the argument schema, is simply that its instances are valid.

This suggestion is unsatisfactory for several reasons. First, it shifts the justification problem from the argument schema to its instances, without providing any solution to the problem of the justification of the instances, beyond the bald assertion that they *are* justified. The claim that one can just *see* that the premises justify the conclusion is implausible in the extreme in view of the fact that people can and do disagree about which arguments are valid. Second, there is an *implicit generality* in the claim that a *particular* argument is valid. For to say that an argument is valid is not just to say that its premises and its conclusion are true—for that is neither necessary nor sufficient for (semantic) validity. Rather, it is to say that its premises *could not* be true without its conclusion being true also, i.e. that *there is no argu-*

ment of that form with true premisses and false conclusion. But if the claim that a particular argument is valid is to be spelled out by appeal to other arguments of that form, it is hopeless to try to justify that form of argument by appeal to the validity of its instances. (Indeed, it is not a simple matter to specify of what schema a particular argument is an instance. Our decision about what the logical form of an argument is may depend upon our view about whether the argument is valid.) Third, since a valid schema has infinitely many instances, if the validity of the schema were to be proven on the basis of the validity of its instances, the justification of the schema would have to be inductive, and would in consequence inevitably fail to establish a result of the desired strength. (Cf. Section 1.)

In rejecting this suggestion I do not, of course, deny the genetic point, that the *codification* of valid forms of inference, the *construction* of a formal system, may proceed in part via generalisation over cases—though in part, I think, the procedure may also go in the opposite direction. (This genetic point is, I think, related to the one Carnap (1968) is making when he observes that we could not convince a man who is 'deductively blind' of the validity of MPP.) But I do claim that the *justification* of a form of inference cannot derive from intuition of the validity of its instances.

6. What I have said in this paper should, perhaps, be already familiar—it is foreshadowed in Carroll (1895), and more or less explicit in Quine (1936) and Carnap (1968) ('. . . the epistemological situation in inductive logic . . . is not worse than that in deductive logic, but quite analogous to it', p. 266). But the point does not seem to have been taken.

The moral of the paper might be put, pessimistically, as that deduction is no less in need of justification than induction; or, optimistically, as that induction is in no more need of justification than deduction. But however we put it, the presumption, that induction is shaky but deduction is firm, is impugned. And this presumption is quite crucial, e.g. to Popper's proposal (1959) to replace inductivism by deductivism. Those of us who are sceptical about the analytic/synthetic distinction will, no doubt, find these consequences less unpalatable than will those who accept it. And those of us who take a tolerant attitude to nonstandard logics—who regard logic as a theory, revisable, like other theories, in the light of experience—may even find these consequences welcome.[1]

1. I have profited from comments made when an earlier version of this paper was read to the Research Students' Seminar in Cambridge, May 1972.

Meanings of
Implication

John Corcoran

In philosophical and mathematical discourse as well as in ordinary scholarly contexts the term 'implies' is used in several clear senses, many of which have already been noticed and explicated. The first five sections of this article codify and interrelate the most widely recognized meanings. Section 6 discusses a further significant and common use. Section 7 discusses and interrelates Tarski's notion of logical consequence, the "model-theoretic" notion of logical consequence, and Bolzano's two grounding relations. The eighth section employs the use-mention distinction to separate the three common grammatical categories of 'implies'. Section 8 also shows that criteria based on use-mention are not reliable indications of intended usage of 'implies'. The ninth and last section relates the above to the counterfactual and gives reasons for not expecting to find 'implies' used to express counterfactuals. A summary is provided.

1. It is already a widely recognized (and widely lamented) fact that mathematicians, needing a short single word to replace 'if . . . then' in its truth-functional sense, have adopted the term 'implies' for this purpose. In this sense "A implies B" means simply that A is false or B is true.[1] Let us use 'implies$_1$' to distinguish this sense from others to be noted below. Incidentally, as will become even more obvious below, it is only rarely, if at all, that 'implies' is used in this sense in current English. Some authors express 'implies$_1$' by the phrase 'materially implies'.

This essay was first published in *Diálogos* 25 (1973), 59–76. It is reprinted here by permission of the author and publisher.
©1973 Universidad de Puerto Rico. Reprinted by permission.

1. In order to avoid unnecessary intricacy, notation for the use-mention distinction is not strictly observed in the first seven sections. To some extent section 8 offers further justification for somewhat neglecting this otherwise important distinction.

2. "A implies B" is also used to mean that B is already logically implicit in A, i.e., that one would be redundant if he were to assert A and then also assert B in that asserting B would be making another statement without adding any new information (not already conveyed by A). For example, using 'implies' in this sense we would say that "The area of a triangle is one-half the base times the height" *implies* "The area of an isosceles triangle is one-half the base times the height." It is perhaps more usual to say "B is a logical consequence of A" or "A logically implies B" to mean that A implies B in this sense. We use 'implies$_2$' to distinguish this usage.

Clearly if A implies$_2$ B then A implies$_1$ B, but not necessarily conversely. For example, "Cats bark" *implies$_1$* "Dogs bark," but "Dogs bark" is certainly not a logical consequence of "Cats bark." Moreover, in the case of sentences which can have different truth-values at different times, a sentence which is true at a certain time has different implications$_1$ (at that time) than it has at a time when it is false. A false sentence implies$_1$ all sentences whereas a true sentence implies$_1$ only true sentences (Lewis and Langford 1959, p. 261). On the other hand, implication$_2$ is completely independent of the actual truth-value of A. A implies$_2$ the same sentences when true as when false. Implication$_2$ is a *logical* relation between sentences not a so-called material relation.

Another way that 'implies$_1$' and 'implies$_2$' may be contrasted is this: "A implies$_1$ B" amounts to "it is *not true* that A is true and B is false" whereas "A implies$_2$ B" amounts to "It is *logically impossible* that A is true and B is false" (Cf. Lewis and Langford 1959, pp. 243–44)

It is worth explicitly noting that logical implication is intimately related to the traditional notion of validity of a premise-conclusion argument. To say that A logically implies B is to say neither more nor less than that the argument (A,B) [premise A, conclusion B] is valid. And, as has often been noted, to say that (A,B) is valid is to say neither more nor less than that B simply "restates" part (or all) of what is said in A.

3. It also happens, both in mathematical contexts and in common parlance, but perhaps not as frequently, that "A implies B" is used to mean that B can be deduced (or derived or inferred) by logical reasoning from A. The reader should note that one logically deduces B from A for the sole purpose of establishing that B is already logically implicit in A, i.e., that A implies$_2$ B. It is usually taken for granted that A implies$_2$ B when B is correctly inferable from A (otherwise one could

not rely on logical reasoning). "A implies$_3$ B" is used to indicate "A implies B" in the sense of "B is logically derivable from A."

Suppose for the moment that B actually is logically deducible from A. Now suppose that a student, Mr. S., goes through the process of step-by-step deducing B from A. Does this mean that Mr. S. did the deduction correctly? Of course not. As we all know by experience in elementary geometry, often B is logically deducible from A even though the students do it incorrectly. Thus, to say that B is logically deducible from A is not to say that anyone who deduces B from A is doing it correctly. To say that B is logically deducible from A is to say that it is theoretically possible to carry out step-by-step, in a logically correct way, a process of deduction leading from A to B. There is no sufficient reason to think that B is logically deducible from A whenever A logically implies B. It is obvious that there could be cases where, although the deduction is theoretically possible, it is practically impossible for reasons of time. The deduction may require thousands of years to complete, for example. But, in a certain sense, the situation is worse than this. As a result of Gödel's work in the thirties, many mathematicians and philosophers believe that in some cases where A implies$_2$ B, A does not imply$_3$ B. These would be cases wherein a certain sentence B actually is a logical consequence of A (say the axioms of some branch of mathematics stated as a single sentence) but where it is impossible to deduce B from A.

Although Tarski has stated (1946, p. 410) that some logicians believed logical consequence (implies$_2$) to be sufficient as well as necessary for logical deducibility (implies$_3$), apart from some obvious confusions (e.g. Lewis and Langford 1959, p. 337; Wolf 1938, p. 40), none seem to have done so. In any case I have not been able to find any reference to corroborate Tarski's statements (cf. Corcoran 1972).

4. To compare the above three senses of 'implies' let us consider a particular example. Let A be one sentence which states Peano's postulates for arithmetic (Montague 1965, p. 135) *and* the definitions of addition, multiplication and prime number. Let B be Goldbach's conjecture "Every even number greater than two is the sum of two primes" (whose truth or falsity is yet unknown, see Forder 1958, p. 6). Now consider the following sentence.

(I) A implies B or A implies not-B

In the first sense of 'implies', statement I is a completely trivial remark whose truth is deducible by the law of excluded middle: If B is true then A implies$_1$ B and if not-B is true then A implies$_1$ not-B. But one or the other *is* true, hence statement I.

In the second sense of 'implies', statement I says, in effect, that Goldbach's conjecture is not logically independent of A.[2] Literally, statement I says: *either* Goldbach's conjecture is already logically implicit in A (so it would be redundant to add it as a new axiom) *or* the negation of Goldbach's conjecture is already logically implicit in A (so it would be redundant to add *it* as a new axiom). Under this reading I is not trivial. It is actually a rather deep statement involving the logical properties of the usual axiomatization of arithmetic. It so happens that statement I (in this sense) is known to be true.[3]

In the third sense of 'implies', statement I says, in effect, that *either* it is possible to deduce Goldbach's conjecture from the axioms and definitions of arithmetic *or* it is possible to deduce the negation of Goldbach's conjecture from the axioms and definitions of arithmetic. I think that it is safe to say that no one has any reason either to think that statement I, in this sense, is true *or* to think that it is false.

In summary, in the first sense statement I is trivially true, one need know essentially nothing to determine its truth; in the second sense it is true, but it is a fairly deep truth, knowledge of which involves a fairly extensive background in mathematics (say that of a college senior); in the third sense, it is a very deep statement whose truth (or falsity) is as yet not known. In fact, one mathematician (see Forder 1958, p. 6) writing in the 1920's seems to suggest that previous to his remarks on the subject *questions* of that sort had not even been discussed. As far as I know he is perfectly correct (cf. Corcoran 1972).

It is already obvious that no two of the above three notions of implication are intensionally the same, i.e. each has a distinct meaning. It can happen that distinct notions are nevertheless extensionally equivalent, i.e. that they apply truly to exactly the same things (or pairs of things in the case of relations). However, as we have just seen, no two of these are extensionally equivalent. The extension of implies$_3$ is

2. Since current usage of the term "independent" (and its variants) is not uniform, the following conventions of this essay should be noted. "B is logically independent of A" means that neither B nor its negation is a logical consequence of A. To say that a set of sentences is *independent* is to say that no one of them is a logical consequence of the rest. Saying that two sentences are independent is to say that the pair is independent.

3. See Forder (1958, *loc. cit.*). The basic fact needed to discover its truth can be gotten by combining the discussion of Peano's postulates in Birkhoff and Mac Lane (1953, pp. 54–56) with the general discussion of axiom systems in Forder (1958, pp. 1–12). Also cf. Montague (1965, p. 136).

properly included in that of implies$_2$ which itself is properly included in the extension of implies$_1$.

Russell was just one in a long line of otherwise sensitive philosophers who confused implies$_1$ (material implication) with implies$_2$ (logical implication). This is clear from many passages in Russell's writing where he uses "follows from" as indicating the converse of "implies." Remarkably, he is quite clear in his statement of the following three principles (Russell 1937, p. 15).

(1) A false proposition implies$_1$ every proposition.
(2) A true proposition is implied$_1$ by every proposition.
(3) Of any two propositions, one implies$_1$ the other.

Moreover, Russell would accept principle 4 below without hesitation; it is simply I (above) in the first sense discussed.

(4) For any two propositions, one implies$_1$ the other or else it implies$_1$ the negation of the other.

No one versed in elementary logic could accept Russell's identification of these two notions because, using the usual interconnection between logical consequence and validity of premise-conclusion arguments, principles 1 and 2 would imply that any argument with a false premise or a true conclusion is valid. No one versed in the history of mathematics could accept it because it would reduce the historically difficult, logical question of the independence of the parallel postulate to a triviality: principle 4 would say that no postulate is independent. Russell could save himself from this mistake by urging, with good reason, that the question of the independence of the fifth postulate is really about "implies$_3$," i.e., whether the fifth postulate and/or its negation is logically derivable from the conjunction of the other four. But what could he answer to the question of why anyone should care whether the fifth is independent (with respect to derivability) of the other four? If he were to answer that the real point is whether the fifth postulate and/or its negation is materially implied by the others, then he is caught in his triviality again.

My view is that no sense can be made of the importance of the problem of the independence of the parallel postulate without presupposing the notion of implies$_2$ (logical implication). My conclusion here is that Russell, for all his greatness, was insensitive to history and this insensitivity not only made possible his conflation of material and logical implication but it also effectively blocked his discovery of his error.

Needless to say, the four principles all become blatant falsehoods if 'implies$_2$' or 'implies$_3$' replaces 'implies$_1$'.

At the cost of seeming to flog a dead horse, I would like to discuss what I think are causes for confusing material implication and logical implication with (logical) derivability or deducibility.

There is a subtle fallacy involved in confusing material implication with derivability. Suppose we want to "show" that A materially implies B if and only if B is derivable from A. In the first place it is obvious enough and true besides that if B is derivable from A then A materially implies B. The fallacy comes in doing the converse. Suppose that A materially implies B. Then, if we also assume A we can derive B by modus ponens. This would seem to show that then B is derivable from A—but it doesn't! What it shows is that B is derivable from 'A materially implies B' *and* A (taken together), something that we did not need to be shown. (Cf. Russell 1937, p. 33 and Bolzano 1972, p. 209.)

Remember 'A materially implies B' means simply that A is false or B is true while 'B is derivable from A' means that it is theoretically possible to write out a deduction, possibly a very long one, which would show that B must be true were A true.

One confusion between logical implication and derivability seems to turn on a systematic ambiguity in English use of the suffix 'able' related to the ambiguity of the 'incorrect' use of 'can'. In the first place, deriving (inferring, deducing) B from A is not simply accomplished by pronouncing a performative, e.g. "I hereby infer B from A." Something must be done and it is usually something very complicated.

In a certain sense, logical implication is a warrant for derivation (inference, deduction). But even the presence of the warrant is no guarantee that the action can be carried out—either theoretically or actually. Of course, it is a tautology that if the warrant is present then the warrant is present. Interestingly enough, it is possible to use a word of the form *X-able* to indicate not the theoretical or actual possibility of doing X but merely that a warrant for doing X exists. For example, in a state park the mountain faces which have been approved for climbing could be called 'climbable' even though some of the so-called 'climbable faces' are not even theoretically possible to climb. Thus, if 'logically implies' is used as Russell (1937, p. 33) and others did use it, as indicating the existence of a warrant for logical deducibility, and if 'logically deducible' is also used to indicate the existence of the warrant—then the confusion results from an equivocation on the tautology: "A logically implies B if and only if B is logically deducible from A."

It is also relevant to note here that some writers seem to think that to deduce B from A is simply to form a belief that A logically implies B (where A actually does logically imply B). This use of "to deduce" would support the view that logical implication of B by A is a warrant for deducing B from A (cf. Lewis and Langford 1959, p. 337). This in turn would be consonant with using "deducible from" as a synonym for "logically implied by." However, it should be noted that analysis of philosophic, scientific and mathematical practice does not support the above use of "to deduce." Indeed, to deduce B from A *is* to form a belief that A logically implies B—but not simply that. In order to deduce B from A one must form the belief in a logically correct way which, in non-trivial cases, involves substantial logical discovery, discovery of a proof, a chain of logical reasoning from A to B. For example, Fermat *claimed* to have deduced his last "theorem," but to this day no one knows whether he did and no one has been able to do it (again?).* In any case, those of us who happen to believe that Fermat's last "theorem" does follow logically from the axioms and definitions of arithmetic do not say of others of similar belief that they have deduced the "theorem." Moreover, there are many people who believe true logical implications without having deduced them.

5. It has also already been noticed by others that "A implies B" is also sometimes used to mean that "A-and-C implies$_3$ B" where C is some "obvious" statement tacitly taken by the speaker to be presumed by anyone following the conversation. For example, one could say that "Marion is a football player" implies "Marion is a male" under the presumption that all football players are male. As another example, it is often noted in set-theory courses that the axiom of choice implies the well-ordering principle. Here the sentence C being presumed must express at least the definition of well-ordering and usually some of the more elementary axioms of set theory as well. To indicate this sense of 'implies' we could write "C-implies$_3$" where C indicates that a presumption is involved. Naturally, one would expect that "A implies B" is also used in the sense of "A-and-C implies$_2$ B" and in the sense of "A-and-C implies$_1$ B" where C indicates a presumption as above. We use "C-implies$_2$" and "C-implies$_1$" to indicate the last two senses.

It may well be the case that the three last-mentioned meanings of 'implies' account for the majority of actual usages. We call the last three usages *elliptical* or *enthymematic.* Enthymematic usage of 'implies' is particularly handy when it suits one's purpose to be vague while still conveying the idea of some sort of connection between two sentences.

---

* [Editor's note] A proof of the Fermat "theorem" by the British mathematician Andrew Wiles of Princeton University was announced in June, 1993 (*Nature*, vol. 364, 1 July 1993, pp. 13–14).

6. An additional class of uses I wish to discuss will at first seem very strange and perverse to those who carefully use 'implies' in one or more of the above senses. In one of the new senses, "A implies B" is used to mean that B can be logically concluded *as a fact* on the strength of A. In other words, "A implies B" means that A *is* sufficient evidence for B. As Frege insisted, nothing can be concluded as a fact on the strength of a false statement (cf. Jourdain 1912, p. 240) and, for that matter, a false statement cannot *be* evidence for anything although, of course, false statements are often (erroneously) accepted as evidence. In any case, if one knows that A is false (or at least does not know that A is true) then even if one knows that B follows logically from A one cannot conclude B as a fact on the strength of A. The point is that "A implies B" in this sense amounts to "A is true and A implies$_2$ B."

Another more general way of putting this involves the linguistic observation that when we say "The fact that A . . ." we intend to convey that A is true (plus whatever else is said). For example, "The fact that Samuel Clemens is alive implies that certain newspaper accounts are incorrect" means both that Samuel Clemens actually is alive and that a certain implication holds. Given this observation we can explain that "A implies B," in the senses of this section, means "The-fact-that-A implies B" which in turn is paraphrased "A is true and A implies B," where 'implies' is here taken to indicate ambiguously any one of the other senses (usually 'implies$_2$' or "C-implies$_2$"). This yields six new senses of 'implies'—one for each of the previous senses.

Each of these six present senses presupposes the truth of the antecedent sentence and it is only in these senses that "A implies B" presupposes the truth of A. In all other senses here considered, only a relation between A and B is asserted and no indication of the truth of A is suggested. Indeed, in the other senses the proposition "A implies A" is trivially true regardless of the truth-value of A whereas in the present senses "A implies A" logically implies A and so is false whenever A is false.

When I first became convinced that some students were actually using the term in one (or more) of the present senses I was at a loss to figure out exactly what, in their linguistic activity, had "induced" me to notice it. Then I made the following observations: (1) they were uncomfortable when I would say "A implies B" when A was obviously false, (2) one student actually said that a false sentence does not imply anything and (3) when A was obviously false they were reluctant to say "A implies B" but they often said "A *would* imply B" meaning, I suppose, that A would imply B if A were true.

The above is not conclusive evidence for my claim that 'implies' is actually used in the senses of this section. To make the claim more plausible—or at least more understandable—I will list a few other common ways of saying "A is true and A implies B" (usually "implies$_2$" or "C-implies$_2$").

(1) A; therefore, B.
(2) A; hence, B.
(3) A; consequently, B.
(4) A; thus B.
(5) A; so B.
(6) Since A, it follows that B.
(7) Since A; B.
(8) That A implies that B.

What this list is designed to show is that "A is true and A implies B" expresses a rather widely used idea.[4] This in turn makes it more plausible to think that 'implies' is sometimes used in some of these senses which, I repeat, are the only ones which presuppose the truth of the antecedent sentence.[5] Reflection on English usage will settle the matter.

"A implies B" in the sense of "A is true and A implies$_2$ B" is especially important in interpretation of Frege's views on logic. It may very well be the case that Frege developed only a logistic system (for proving logical truths) and did not go on to develop a system for deducing conclusions from (non-logical) premises because he was taking 'implies' in the latter sense. Going beyond a logistic system would have involved him in determination of truth-values of logically con-

4. There is nothing novel about this list. For example, Russell (1937, p. 14) discussed the first item and the rest are obvious once the relevant facts about the first are noticed.

5. It is already clear that I am using the term "presuppose" in one of its ordinary senses and *not* in the technical sense of Keenan (1973), Strawson (1952), and the modern linguistic semanticists according to which a sentence S presupposes P if and only if P must be true in order for S to have *either* truth-value. According to this usage, a sentence and its negation have the same presuppositions. For example, 'Fred was surprised that Mary won' and 'Fred was not surprised that Mary won' both presuppose 'Mary won.' I am by no means asserting that there is no use of "implies" in which "A implies B" presupposes A in Keenan's sense. On the contrary, such usage does exist. It is worth noting, however, that such use is not synonymous with the "genuine" conditional, "if A then B," which, even though it has a truth-value only when A is true, still does not presuppose the truth of A. In fact, the whole point of the genuine conditional is to avoid implying and/or presupposing the antecedent. Cf. Quine (1959, p. 12).

tingent sentences—thus exceeding the bounds of pure logic (cf. Jourdain 1912, esp. p. 240 and Russell 1937, p. 16). [No special notation will be used for the senses of this section.]

7. There is another class of meanings which might be attached to the term "implies." It is certain that some of them have been so attached and, if Bolzano's work ever gains the attention it deserves, several of the others will be also.

The easiest way of getting into this class of meanings is through some of Russell's remarks in *Principles of Mathematics* (1937). Russell considers the following sentence:

(1) Socrates is a man implies Socrates is mortal.

This appears to be a case of enthymematic implication where the presumption is that all men are mortal. But Russell says (1937, p. 14).

> . . . it appears at once that we may substitute not only another man, but any other entity whatever, in the place of Socrates. Thus although what is explicitly stated, in such a case, is a material implication ["implies$_1$" above], what is meant is a formal implication; and some effort is needed to confine our imagination to material implication.

By a formal implication Russell means a proposition of the following kind.

(2) For all values of x, $A(x)$ implies$_1$ $B(x)$.

In other words Russell is claiming that sentence 1 above would normally be understood, not as an enthymematic implication, but rather as equivalent in meaning to sentences 3 and 4 below.

(3) Everything which is a man is mortal.

(4) For every x, if x is a man then x is mortal.

At this point Russell is clear about formal implication, although he loses his clarity later on. Formal implication is a relation between propositional functions (or, in the terminology of this essay, between sentential expressions involving free variables) which holds when the universal closure of the appropriate conditional is true. In the above-quoted passage Russell says that it is natural to understand 'implies' between two sentences as indicating that formal implication holds between two sentential expressions gotten from the sentences by putting variables for terms (also cf. Bolzano 1972, p. 252). But Russell never bothered to say exactly which terms should be replaced by variables. There seem to be three obvious possibilities in explicating Russell. First, that there is no rule for determining which terms should be varied even in a given sentence. If the hearer is uncertain about what is being said in a given case the speaker must say which terms he wants to 'vary'. For example, sentence 5 below could be used to say that whoever eats fish likes fish, or that whatever Socrates eats he likes, or even that whatever anyone eats he likes.

(5) Socrates eats fish implies Socrates likes fish.

Given the character of *Principles of Mathematics* I think that this is the answer, i.e., that Russell was commenting on an ambiguous usage of 'implies'. The ambiguous usage tends to move the possibilities for 'implies' closer to the sense of logical implication by allowing some implications which would be false as logical implications to be counted as false. For example, sentence 6 is false when 'implies' means logical implication and it is false when taken in the sense of formal implication with 'meow' replaced by a variable; but, of course, it is a true material implication.

(6) Dogs meow implies cats meow.

A second way of understanding Russell is to let all shared terms vary. Here sentence 5 would mean that whatever anyone eats he likes. This has the advantage of being unambiguous. It also moves closer to logical implication but it still holds between sentences which are not related by logical implication. In this sense of 'implies', all generalizable material implications would hold as implications.

A third way of understanding Russell is to let all non-logical terms vary. Under this interpretation of 'implies' many of the generalizable material implications would fail and this would bring us very close to logical implication. Let us use 'implies$_4$' to indicate this sense of implies.

In fact, the last move brings us to a sense of implication which is consonant with Aristotelian logic to the extent that an Aristotelian argument is valid if and only if the conclusion is implied$_4$ by the conjunction of the premises. Moreover, Lewis and Langford (1959, pp. 342–46) offer something like implication$_4$ as an explication of the normal mathematical usage, and Tarski's explication (1956, pp. 410ff) differs from implication$_4$ only incidentally for the purposes of this article.[6]

Russell, Lewis-Langford and Tarski were all working in a framework of an interpreted language having a fixed universe of discourse. In addition, they all distinguished logical and non-logical terms. Finally, they all considered relations between A and B which hold when

6. From a broader perspective there are two highly significant further refinements in Tarski's work. In the first place Tarski recognized the possibility of a metalinguistic notion of implication (i.e. one not necessarily expressible in the object language in question) whereas Lewis and Langford followed Russell in trying to consider implication as an object language concept. Secondly, Tarski recognized the fact that in many scientific contexts implication relates sets (possibly infinite) of sentences to individual sentences.

universal closure of "A* implies$_1$ B*'" is true (where A* and B* are obtained by appropriately substituting variables for non-logical terms of A and B).

From the present point of view, the most significant refinement found in Tarski's explication is that all non-logical terms are to be varied. That Lewis and Langford did not explicitly lay down this requirement may be more of an oversight in exposition than an oversight in research— but this is unlikely given their comments (*op. cit.* on p. 340).

The explication of logical consequence which is most widely accepted today diverges from the above-mentioned Tarskian notion only by allowing universes of discourse "to vary." Using 'implies$_5$' for this notion restricted to sentences we would have that A implies$_5$ B if and only if the universal closure of A* implies$_1$ B* is true in every universe of discourse.[7] The reason for preferring "implies$_5$" to "implies$_4$" as an explication of logical consequence turns on an insight which was developed in the course of criticism of the axiom of infinity in type theory—viz. that the number of objects in the universe should not be a logical presupposition. A related reason for preferring "implies$_5$" is thought by some to be a reason for rejecting it—viz. that use of implication$_5$ makes clear that logic presupposes "logically possible worlds." This brings us to fringes of philosophy of logic which are beyond the compass of an essay designed to clarify the interrelations among the multitude of meanings of implication.

In connection with formal implication and Tarskian implication it would be unfair not to at least mention Bolzano's *Theory of Science* (1972), first published in 1837. Bolzano defined a notion which we may call relative implication. Let A and B be sentences and let S be a set of symbols, logical and/or non-logical. Bolzano's idea is to say that *A implies B relative to S* if and only if every uniform substitution for occurrences of members of S in A and B making A true makes B true (cf. Bolzano 1972, p. 209).

If S is taken to be empty then implication relative to S is material implication. If S is an appropriate set of non-logical terms shared by A and B then implication relative to S can be made to coincide with one reading of the ambiguous use of 'implies' which Russell thought he had noticed. If S is the set of all non-logical terms then implication relative to S is implication$_4$ or Tarskian implication. Bolzano let S be arbitrary and, consequently, he seems to have defined a notion which

---

7. This wording is adequate only for quantificationally closed languages which, like the language of type theory, contain universal generalizations of each sentence containing one or more nonlogical constants. For other languages the wording must be changed. (See, e.g. Quine 1959, p. 147).

was never studied before or since and which is much broader than any of the senses of implication mentioned above.

Bolzano did not believe that his notion of relative implication coincided with logical implication. He has devoted a section of his book to discussing the relation between relative implication and logical implication (1972, section 223). There he considers two examples of relative implication. He observes that they amount to generalized conditionals and he observes that knowledge of those implications is outside of the province of logic. One example is sentence 7 below as an implication relative to 'Caius'.

(7) Caius is a man implies Caius has an immortal soul.

This, of course, amounts to the sentence 9 below.

(8) For every x, if x is a man then x has an immortal soul.

He went on to indicate that for logical implication all except the logical concepts would have to be varied. Bolzano was explicit in these passages and all of his examples of logical implications clearly fall under Tarskian implication. In my opinion Bolzano thought that logical implication is implication$_4$ above. If this is so then Bolzano truly deserves credit for explication of logical consequence, if Tarski does, because in my opinion Bolzano offered precisely the same idea.[8]

Interestingly enough, Bolzano mentions two other places where 'implies' might be used. One is where Bolzano's "ground-consequence" relation holds. He explains that A is the ground of B (and B the consequence of A) when A and B are both true and A is the "reason why" B is true. The ground-consequence relation is not the same as logical implication because, as Bolzano himself points out, logical implication can hold between false sentences. He also points out that ground-consequence is not simply logical implication between true sentences, although he conjectures that whenever ground-consequence holds logical implication also holds (1972, pp. 274–75). The other place Bolzano mentions is where the "ground-judgment" relation holds, though he does not use these terms. Here we could say that *A yields B* if knowledge of A would be evidence for concluding B. Bolzano speaks of A being "the cause of knowing" B. He claims, with good argument, that this relation often goes in the opposite direction from the ground-consequence relation, i.e., that A is sometimes the ground of B (the "reason why" of B) when in fact B is "the cause of our knowledge" of A. For example, we know that it is hot outside because we know that a certain thermometer reads high but the rea-

8. The reason that I did not quote Bolzano is that the section in question (223) is not self-contained and Bolzano is not concise. Other passages which support my interpretation are found in *op. cit.*, pp. 38, 198, and 199.

son why the thermometer reads high is because it is hot outside. This is close to Bolzano's example. He uses the terms "real ground" and "ground of knowledge."

8. To some readers my failure to strictly observe the use-mention notation will seem unfortunate. It seems to me, however, that rigid observance of the distinction would add nothing to the paper and would actually detract from its clarity by making it unnecessarily intricate. Of course, the use-mention distinction and its accompanying notation are essential for avoiding certain kinds of confusion. But, as we will argue presently, the notation is not normally or necessarily observed and thus cannot be used as a sign indicative of intended meaning.

'Implies' can be used in all of the above senses in any and all of the grammatical categories of 'implies' usually distinguished by means of use-mention. There are three candidates for "the" grammatical category of "implies'. First, it can be used as a (binary) sentential connective—roughly a word which, when placed between two *sentences* of a language, forms a third sentence of the same language. Second, it can be used as a factive (or propositional) verb in the object language. This means that when placed between two factive (or propositional) noun phrases (usually "that . . .") of the object language it forms an object language sentence. Third, it can be used as a meta-linguistic verb, i.e., when placed between names of two object language sentences it forms a sentence of the metalanguage. 'Implies' actually occurs as a word in each category and in each category it can have a meaning corresponding to many of the distinctions made above.

To exemplify the use of 'implies' in each of the three categories let P and Q be (object language) sentences and let p and q be (object language) names of P and Q, respectively. Let 'q-implies-p' be a name of $\ulcorner q$ implies $p \urcorner$, also in the object language.

Connective

> $\ulcorner$P implies Q$\urcorner$
> $\ulcorner$P implies (Q implies P)$\urcorner$

Object language factive verb

> $\ulcorner$That P implies that Q$\urcorner$
> $\ulcorner$That P implies that that Q implies that P$\urcorner$

Metalinguistic verb

> $\ulcorner p$ implies $q \urcorner$
> $\ulcorner p$ implies q-implies-$p \urcorner$

I do not disagree with the logicians who believe that "implies$_1$" is best expressed with a connective and that "implies$_2$" and "implies$_3$" are best expressed by metalinguistic verbs. My point is that the preferred usage is conventional and that the convention has not been universally accepted. There is nothing to prevent "implies$_1$" from being expressed either as a factive verb or metalinguistically. More importantly, there is nothing to prevent "implies$_2$" from being expressed by a connective (necessarily non-truth-functional). Bolzano (1972, p. 44) seems to have thought that implication$_2$ was normally expressed by a connective. In *Prior Analytics*, especially in I.44, Aristotle seems to express a non-truth-functional implication by a connective. Even in current English we often express a non-truth-functional implication by "if A then necessarily B" and it may be possible to argue that 'if . . . then necessarily . . .' is a complex, discontinuous connective.

9. The so-called counterfactual conditionals have been left out of the discussion because the word 'implies' is not normally involved in them. In the first place, the counterfactuals presuppose the *negation* of "the antecedent" whereas none of the uses of 'implies' just considered does this.[9] Indeed, use of "A implies B" in a sense that presupposes the negation of A seems so perverse as to be outside of the range of acceptable English. In the second place, a counterfactual cannot be constructed grammatically in any of the three ways for constructing implicational sentences. The only construction deserving of mention is the one which involves use of a connective between two sentences and this cannot be the counterfactual construction because the antecedent and consequent are commonly *not sentences*. This can be seen from the following example.

If I were Hughes then I would be rich.

The counterfactual is probably derived grammatically by applying a (nonparaphrastic) transformation to an ordinary conditional.[10] For the example above, the transformation would be applied to the following.

If I am Hughes then I am rich.

9. It is truly remarkable that treatments of the counterfactual which leave this out of account could be called "preferred analyses." Indeed, it has been suggested that the counterfactual of A and B be explicated as "A C-implies$_2$ B" (cf. Craig and Mates 1970, p. 303).

10. Although existence of nonparaphrastic (meaning-changing) transformations had been denied by most linguists, Harris has recognized them in his latest books (1968, pp. 60–63).

If this is so then the problem of counterfactuals does not involve merely analysis of "if . . . then" but rather also analysis of the semantic effect of the transformation.

SUMMARY AND CONCLUSION: In the first five sections we have distinguished twelve uses of the term 'implies'. At the outset we distinguished: implies$_1$ (truth-functional), implies$_2$ (logical consequence) and implies$_3$ (logical deducibility). Next we distinguished three elliptical or enthymematic varieties of implication: C-implies$_1$, C-implies$_2$ and C-implies$_3$. In none of these six senses did "A implies B" presuppose the truth of A. Then we discussed the cases wherein "A implies B" is used to mean "The-fact-that-A implies B," which *does* presuppose the truth of A. We paraphrased the latter as "A is true and A implies B" where 'implies' indicates any of the previous six senses of the term. Thus, at that point, twelve senses of implies were distinguished, six which do not presuppose the truth of the implying sentence and six which do. Of the six which do, three are enthymematic.

In addition, the three original senses were carefully distinguished and interrelated, and possible causes of confusion were identified.

Then, building on some off-hand observations of Russell, we related the truth-functional use of 'implies' to two further notions which have been used as explications of traditional logical consequence. We also brought in Bolzano's relative implication and his two grounding relations.

We argued briefly that counterfactuals are not normally expressed using 'implies' and that the distinction between use and mention cannot be used as a test for distinguishing different meanings of 'implies'.

Use of 'implies' as a transitive verb taking a human subject has been ignored.[11]

11. I am grateful to the following persons for criticisms and suggestions: William Frank (Oregon State University), John Herring and Charles Lambros (SUNY/Buffalo), Jack Meiland (University of Michigan), Marshall Spector (SUNY/Stony Brook), Frank Jackson (Latrobe University, Australia), William Wisdom (Temple University). The final version of this paper was read at the University of Puerto Rico in March 1973. Previous versions were read at the University of Pennsylvania and at SUNY/Buffalo. [This paper appears in Spanish translation by José M. Sagüillo as "Significados de la implicación," *Agora* 5 (1985) 279–94.]

Truth and Proof

Alfred Tarski

The subject of this article is an old one. It has been frequently discussed in modern logical and philosophical literature, and it would not be easy to contribute anything original to the discussion. To many readers, I am afraid, none of the ideas put forward in the article will appear essentially novel; nonetheless, I hope they may find some interest in the way the material has been arranged and knitted together.

As the title indicates, I wish to discuss here two different though related notions: the notion of truth and the notion of proof. Actually the article is divided into three sections. The first section is concerned exclusively with the notion of truth, the second deals primarily with the notion of proof, and the third is a discussion of the relationship between these two notions.

1. THE NOTION OF TRUTH

The task of explaining the meaning of the term "true" will be interpreted here in a restricted way. The notion of truth occurs in many different contexts, and there are several distinct categories of objects to which the term "true" is applied. In a psychological discussion one might speak of true emotions as well as true beliefs; in a discourse from the domain of esthetics the inner truth of an object of art might be analyzed. In this article, however, we are interested only in what might be called the logical notion of truth. More specifically, we concern ourselves exclusively with the meaning of the term "true" when this term is used to refer to sentences. Presumably this was the original use of the term "true" in human language. Sentences are treated here as linguistic objects, as certain strings of sounds or written signs. (Of course, not every such string is a sentence.) Moreover, when speaking of sentences, we shall always have in mind what are called in grammar declarative sentences, and not interrogative or imperative sentences.

Whenever one explains the meaning of any term drawn from every-day language, he should bear in mind that the goal and the logical status of such an explanation may vary from one case to another. For instance, the explanation may be intended as an account of the actual use of the term involved, and is thus subject to questioning whether the account is indeed correct. At some other time an explanation may be of a normative nature, that is, it may be offered as a suggestion that the term be used in some definite way, without claiming that the suggestion conforms to the way in which the term is actually used; such an explanation can be evaluated, for instance, from the point of view of its usefulness but not of its correctness. Some further alterna-tives could also be listed.

The explanation we wish to give in the present case is, to an extent, of mixed character. What will be offered can be treated in principle as a suggestion for a definite way of using the term "true," but the offering will be accompanied by the belief that it is in agreement with the prevailing usage of this term in everyday language.

Our understanding of the notion of truth seems to agree essentially with various explanations of this notion that have been given in philo-sophical literature. What may be the earliest explanation can be found in Aristotle's *Metaphysics:*

> To say of what is that it is not, or of what is not that it is, is false, while to say of what is that it is, or of what is not that it is not, is true.

Here and in the subsequent discussion the word "false" means the same as the expression "not true" and can be replaced by the latter.

The intuitive content of Aristotle's formulation appears to be rather clear. Nevertheless, the formulation leaves much to be desired from the point of view of precision and formal correctness. For one thing, it is not general enough; it refers only to sentences that "say" about something "that it is" or "that it is not"; in most cases it would hardly be possible to cast a sentence in this mold without slanting the sense of the sentence and forcing the spirit of the language. This is perhaps one of the reasons why in modern philosophy various substitutes for the Aristotelian formulation have been offered. As examples we quote the following:

> A sentence is true if it denotes the existing state of affairs.

> The truth of a sentence consists in its conformity with (or correspondence to) the reality.

Due to the use of technical philosophical terms these formulations have undoubtedly a very "scholarly" sound. Nonetheless, it is my feeling that the new formulations, when analyzed more closely, prove to be less clear and unequivocal than the one put forward by Aristotle.

The conception of truth that found its expression in the Aristotelian formulation (and in related formulations of more recent origin) is usually referred to as the *classical,* or *semantic, conception of truth.* By semantics we mean the part of logic that, loosely speaking, discusses the relations between linguistic objects (such as sentences) and what is expressed by these objects. The semantic character of the term "true" is clearly revealed by the explanation offered by Aristotle and by some formulations that will be given later in this article. One speaks sometimes of the correspondence theory of truth as the theory based on the classical conception.

(In modern philosophical literature some other conceptions and theories of truth are also discussed, such as the pragmatic conception and the coherence theory. These conceptions seem to be of an exclusively normative character and have little connection with the actual usage of the term "true"; none of them has been formulated so far with any degree of clarity and precision. They will not be discussed in the present article.)

We shall attempt to obtain here a more precise explanation of the classical conception of truth, one that could supersede the Aristotelian formulation while preserving its basic intentions. To this end we shall have to resort to some techniques of contemporary logic. We shall also have to specify the language whose sentences we are concerned with; this is necessary if only for the reason that a string of sounds or signs, which is a true or a false sentence but at any rate a meaningful sentence in one language, may be a meaningless expression in another. For the time being let us assume that the language with which we are concerned is the common English language.

We begin with a simple problem. Consider a sentence in English whose meaning does not raise any doubts, say the sentence "snow is white." For brevity we denote this sentence by "S," so that "S" becomes the name of the sentence. We ask ourselves the question: What do we mean by saying that S is true or that it is false? The answer to this question is simple: in the spirit of Aristotelian explanation, by saying that S is true we mean simply that snow is white, and by saying that S is false we mean that snow is not white. By eliminating the symbol "S" we arrive at the following formulations:

(1)   "snow is white" is true if and only if snow is white.
(1') "snow is white" is false if and only if snow is not white.

Thus (1) and (1′) provide satisfactory explanations of the meaning of the terms "true" and "false" when these terms are referred to the sentence "snow is white." We can regard (1) and (1′) as partial definitions of the terms "true" and "false," in fact, as definitions of these terms with respect to a particular sentence. Notice that (1), as well as (1′), has the form prescribed for definitions by the rules of logic, namely the form of logical equivalence. It consists of two parts, the left and the right side of the equivalence, combined by the connective "if and only if." The left side is the definiendum, the phrase whose meaning is explained by the definition; the right side is the definiens, the phrase that provides the explanation. In the present case the definiendum is the following expression:

"snow is white" is true;

the definiens has the form:

snow is white.

It might seem at first sight that (1), when regarded as a definition, exhibits an essential flaw widely discussed in traditional logic as a vicious circle. The reason is that certain words, for example "snow," occur in both the definiens and the definiendum. Actually, however, these occurrences have an entirely different character. The word "snow" is a syntactical, or organic, part of the definiens; in fact the definiens is a sentence, and the word "snow" is its subject. The definiendum is also a sentence; it expresses the fact that the definiens is a true sentence. Its subject is a name of the definiens formed by putting the definiens in quotes. (When saying something of an object, one always uses a name of this object and not the object itself, even when dealing with linguistic objects.) For several reasons an expression enclosed in quotes must be treated grammatically as a single word having no syntactical parts. Hence the word "snow," which undoubtedly occurs in the definiendum as a part, does not occur there as a syntactical part. A medieval logician would say that "snow" occurs in the definiens *in suppositione formalis* and in the definiendum *in suppositione materialis.* However, words which are not syntactical parts of the definiendum cannot create a vicious circle, and the danger of a vicious circle vanishes.

The preceding remarks touch on some questions which are rather subtle and not quite simple from the logical point of view. Instead of elaborating on them, I shall indicate another manner in which any fears of a vicious circle can be dispelled. In formulating (1) we have applied a common method of forming a name of a sentence, or of any other expression, which consists in putting the expression in quotes. The method has many virtues, but it is also the source of the difficulties discussed above. To remove these difficulties let us try another method of forming names of expressions, in fact a method that can be characterized as a letter-by-letter description of an expression. Using this method we obtain instead of (1) the following lengthy formulation:

(2) The string of three words, the first of which is the string of the letters Es, En, O and Double-U, the second is the string of letters I and Es, and the third is the string of the letters Double-U, Aitch, I, Te, and E, is a true sentence if and only if snow is white.

Formulation (2) does not differ from (1) in its meaning; (1) can simply be regarded as an abbreviated form of (2). The new formulation is certainly much less perspicuous than the old one, but it has the advantage that it creates no appearance of a vicious circle.

Partial definitions of truth analogous to (1) (or (2)) can be constructed for other sentences as well. Each of these definitions has the form:

(3) "p" is true if and only if p,

where "p" is to be replaced on both sides of (3) by the sentence for which the definition is constructed. Special attention should be paid, however, to those situations in which the sentence put in place of "p" happens to contain the word "true" as a syntactical part. The corresponding equivalence (3) cannot then be viewed as a partial definition of truth since, when treated as such, it would obviously exhibit a vicious circle. Even in this case, however, (3) is a meaningful sentence, and it is actually a true sentence from the point of view of the classical conception of truth. For illustration, imagine that in a review of a book one finds the following sentence:

(4) Not every sentence in this book is true.

By applying to (4) the Aristotelian criterion, we see that the sentence (4) is true if, in fact, not every sentence in the book concerned is true, and that (4) is false otherwise; in other words, we can assert the equivalence obtained from (3) by taking (4) for "p". Of course, this equivalence states merely the conditions under which the sentence (4) is true or is not true, but by itself the equivalence does not enable us to decide which is actually the case. To verify the judgment expressed in (4) one would have to read attentively the book reviewed and analyze the truth of the sentences contained in it.

In the light of the preceding discussion we can now reformulate our main problem. We stipulate that the use of the term "true" in its reference to sentences in English then and only then conforms with the classical conception of truth if it enables us to ascertain every equivalence of the form (3) in which "*p*" is replaced on both sides by an arbitrary English sentence. If this condition is satisfied, we shall say simply that the use of the term "true" is adequate. Thus our main problem is: can we establish an adequate use of the term "true" for sentences in English and, if so, then by what methods? We can, of course, raise an analogous question for sentences in any other language.

The problem will be solved completely if we manage to construct a general definition of truth that will be adequate in the sense that it will carry with it as logical consequences all the equivalences of form (3). If such a definition is accepted by English-speaking people, it will obviously establish an adequate use of the term "true."

Under certain special assumptions the construction of a general definition of truth is easy. Assume, in fact, that we are interested, not in the whole common English language, but only in a fragment of it, and that we wish to define the term "true" exclusively in reference to sentences of the fragmentary language; we shall refer to this fragmentary language as the language *L*. Assume further that *L* is provided with precise syntactical rules which enable us, in each particular case, to distinguish a sentence from an expression which is not a sentence, and that the number of all sentences in the language *L* is finite (though possibly very large). Assume, finally, that the word "true" does not occur in *L* and that the meaning of all words in *L* is sufficiently clear, so that we have no objection to using them in defining truth. Under these assumptions proceed as follows. First, prepare a complete list of all sentences in *L;* suppose, for example, that there are exactly 1,000 sentences in *L*, and agree to use the symbols "s_1", "s_2", . . . , "$s_{1,000}$" as abbreviations for consecutive sentences on the list. Next, for each of the sentences "s_1", "s_2", . . . , "$s_{1,000}$" construct a partial definition of truth by substituting successively these sentences for "*p*" on both sides of the schema (3). Finally, form the logical conjunction of all these partial definitions; in other words, combine them in one statement by putting the connective "and" between any two consecutive partial definitions. The only thing that remains to be done is to give the resulting conjunction a different, but logically equivalent, form, so as to satisfy formal requirements imposed on definitions by rules of logic:

(5) For every sentence x (in the language L), x is true if and only if either
s_1, and x is identical to "s_1",
or
s_2, and x is identical to "s_2,"
....
....
or finally,
$s_{1,000}$, and x is identical to "$s_{1,000}$."

We have thus arrived at a statement which can indeed be accepted as the desired general definition of truth: it is formally correct and is adequate in the sense that it implies all the equivalences of the form (3) in which "p" has been replaced by any sentence of the language L. We notice in passing that (5) is a sentence in English but obviously not in the language L; since (5) contains all sentences in L as proper parts, it cannot coincide with any of them. Further discussion will throw more light on this point.

For obvious reasons the procedure just outlined cannot be followed if we are interested in the whole of the English language and not merely in a fragment of it. When trying to prepare a complete list of English sentences, we meet from the start the difficulty that the rules of English grammar do not determine precisely the form of expressions (strings of words) which should be regarded as sentences: a particular expression, say an exclamation, may function as a sentence in some given context, whereas an expression of the same form will not function so in some other context. Furthermore, the set of all sentences in English is, potentially at least, infinite. Although it is certainly true that only a finite number of sentences have been formulated in speech and writing by human beings up to the present moment, probably nobody would agree that the list of all these sentences comprehends all sentences in English. On the contrary, it seems likely that on seeing such a list each of us could easily produce an English sentence which is not on the list. Finally, the fact that the word "true" does occur in English prevents by itself an application of the procedure previously described.

From these remarks it does not follow that the desired definition of truth for arbitrary sentences in English cannot be obtained in some other way, possibly by using a different idea. There is, however, a more serious and fundamental reason that seems to preclude this possibility.

More than that, the mere supposition that an adequate use of the term "true" (in its reference to arbitrary sentences in English) has been secured by any method whatsoever appears to lead to a contradiction. The simplest argument that provides such a contradiction is known as the *antinomy of the liar;* it will be carried through in the next few lines.

Consider the following sentence:

(6) The sentence printed in red on page 65 of the June 1969 issue of *Scientific American* is false.

Let us agree to use "*s*" as an abbreviation for this sentence. Looking at that issue of the magazine, and the number of the page, we easily check that "*s*" is just the only sentence printed in red on page 65 of the June 1969 issue of *Scientific American.* Hence it follows, in particular, that

(7) "*s*" is false if and only if the sentence printed in red on page 65 of the June 1969 issue of *Scientific American* is false.

On the other hand, "*s*" is undoubtedly a sentence in English. Therefore, assuming that our use of the term "true" is adequate, we can assert the equivalence (3) in which "*p*" is replaced by "*s*". Thus we can state:

(8) "*s*" is true if and only if *s.*

We now recall that "*s*" stands for the whole sentence (6). Hence we can replace "*s*" by (6) on the right side of (8); we then obtain

(9) "*s*" is true if and only if the sentence printed in red on page 65 of the June 1969 issue of *Scientific American* is false.

By now comparing (8) and (9), we conclude:

(10) "*s*" is false if and only if "*s*" is true.

This leads to an obvious contradiction: "*s*" proves to be both true and false. Thus we are confronted with an antinomy. The above formulation of the antinomy of the liar is due to the Polish logician Jan Łukasiewicz.

Some more involved formulations of this antinomy are also known. Imagine, for instance, a book of 100 pages, with just one sentence printed on each page.

On page 1 we read:

> The sentence printed on page 2 of this book is true.

On page 2 we read:

> The sentence printed on page 3 of this book is true.

And so it goes on up to page 99. However, on page 100, the last page of the book, we find:

> The sentence printed on page 1 of this book is false.

Assume that the sentence printed on page 1 is indeed false. By means of an argument which is not difficult but is very long and requires leafing through the entire book, we conclude that our assumption is wrong. Consequently we assume now that the sentence printed on page 1 is true—and, by an argument which is as easy and as long as the original one, we convince ourselves that the new assumption is wrong as well. Thus we are again confronted with an antinomy.

It turns out to be an easy matter to compose many other "antinomial books" that are variants of the one just described. Each of them has 100 pages. Every page contains just one sentence, and in fact a sentence of the form:

> The sentence printed on page *00* of this book is *XX*.

In each particular case "*XX*" is replaced by one of the words "*true*" or "*false*", while "*00*" is replaced by one of the numerals "1," "2," . . . . , "100"; the same numeral may occur on many pages. Not every variant of the original book composed according to these rules actually yields an antinomy. The reader who is fond of logical puzzles will hardly find it difficult to describe all those variants that do the job. The following warning may prove useful in this connection. Imagine that somewhere in the book, say on page 1, it is said that the sentence on page 3 is true, while somewhere else, say on page 2, it is claimed that the same sentence is false. From this information it does not follow at all that our book is "antinomial"; we can only draw the conclusion that either the sentence on page 1 or the sentence on page 2 must be false. An antinomy does arise, however, whenever we are able to show that one of the sentences in the book is both true and false, independent of any assumptions concerning the truth or falsity of the remaining sentences.

The antinomy of the liar is of very old origin. It is usually ascribed to the Greek logician Eubulides; it tormented many ancient logicians and caused the premature death of at least one of them, Philetas of Cos. A number of other antinomies and paradoxes were found in antiquity, in the Middle Ages, and in modern times. Although many of them are now entirely forgotten, the antinomy of the liar is still analyzed and discussed in contemporary writings. Together with some recent antinomies discovered around the turn of the century (in particular, the antinomy of Russell), it has had a great impact on the development of modern logic.

Two diametrically opposed approaches to antinomies can be found in the literature of the subject. One approach is to disregard them, to treat them as sophistries, as jokes that are not serious but malicious, and that aim mainly at showing the cleverness of the man who formulates them. The opposite approach is characteristic of certain thinkers of the 19th century and is still represented, or was so a short while ago, in certain parts of our globe. According to this approach antinomies constitute a very essential element of human thought; they must appear again and again in intellectual activities, and their presence is the basic source of real progress. As often happens, the truth is probably somewhere in between. Personally, as a logician, I could not reconcile myself with antinomies as a permanent element of our system of knowledge. However, I am not the least inclined to treat antinomies lightly. The appearance of an antimony is for me a symptom of disease. Starting with premises that seem intuitively obvious, using forms of reasoning that seem intuitively certain, an antimony leads us to nonsense, a contradiction. Whenever this happens, we have to submit our ways of thinking to a thorough revision, to reject some premises in which we believed or to improve some forms of argument which we used. We do this with the hope not only that the old antinomy will be disposed of but also that no new one will appear. To this end we test our reformed system of thinking by all available means, and, first of all, we try to reconstruct the old antinomy in the new setting; this testing is a very important activity in the realm of speculative thought, akin to carrying out crucial experiments in empirical science.

From this point of view consider now specifically the antinomy of the liar. The antinomy involves the notion of truth in reference to arbitrary sentences of common English; it could easily be reformulated so as to apply to other natural languages. We are confronted with a serious problem: how can we avoid the contradictions induced by this antinomy? A radical solution of the problem which may readily occur to us would be simply to remove the word "true" from the

English vocabulary or at least to abstain from using it in any serious discussion.

Those people to whom such an amputation of English seems highly unsatisfactory and illegitimate may be inclined to accept a somewhat more compromising solution, which consists in adopting what could be called (following the contemporary Polish philosopher Tadeusz Kotarbiński) "the nihilistic approach to the theory of truth." According to this approach, the word "true" has no independent meaning but can be used as a component of the two meaningful expressions "it is true that" and "it is not true that." These expressions are thus treated as if they were single words with no organic parts. The meaning ascribed to them is such that they can be immediately eliminated from any sentence in which they occur. For instance, instead of saying

> it is true that all cats are black

we can simply say

> all cats are black,

and instead of

> it is not true that all cats are black

we can say

> not all cats are black.

In other contexts the word "true" is meaningless. In particular, it cannot be used as a real predicate qualifying names of sentences. Employing the terminology of medieval logic, we can say that the word "true" can be used syncategorematically in some special situations, but it cannot ever be used categorematically.

To realize the implications of this approach, consider the sentence which was the starting point for the antinomy of the liar; that is, the sentence printed in red on page 65 in that magazine. From the "nihilistic" point of view it is not a meaningful sentence, and the antinomy simply vanishes. Unfortunately, many uses of the word "true," which otherwise seem quite legitimate and reasonable, are similarly affected by this approach. Imagine, for instance, that a certain term occurring repeatedly in the works of an ancient mathematician admits of several interpretations. A historian of science who studies the works arrives at the conclusion that under one of these interpretations all the theorems stated by the mathematician prove to be true; this leads him naturally to the conjecture that the same will apply to any work of this mathematician that is not known at present but may be discovered in the future. If, however, the historian of science shares the "nihilistic" approach to the notion of truth, he lacks the possibility of expressing his conjecture in words. One could say that truth-theoretical "nihilism" pays lip service to some popular forms of human speech, while actually removing the notion of truth from the conceptual stock of the human mind.

We shall look, therefore, for another way out of our predicament. We shall try to find a solution that will keep the classical concept of truth essentially intact. The applicability of the notion of truth will have to undergo some restrictions, but the notion will remain available at least for the purpose of scholarly discourse.

To this end we have to analyze those features of the common language that are the real source of the antinomy of the liar. When carrying through this analysis, we notice at once an outstanding feature of this language—its all-comprehensive, universal character. The common language is universal and is intended to be so. It is supposed to provide adequate facilities for expressing everything that can be expressed at all, in any language whatsoever; it is continually expanding to satisfy this requirement. In particular, it is semantically universal in the following sense. Together with the linguistic objects, such as sentences and terms, which are components of this language, names of these objects are also included in the language (as we know, names of expressions can be obtained by putting the expressions in quotes); in addition, the language contains semantic terms such as "truth," "name," "designation," which directly or indirectly refer to the relationship between linguistic objects and what is expressed by them. Consequently, for every sentence formulated in the common language, we can form in the same language another sentence to the effect that the first sentence is true or that it is false. Using an additional "trick" we can even construct in the language what is sometimes called a self-referential sentence, that is, a sentence S which asserts the fact that S itself is true or that it is false. In case S asserts its own falsity we can show by means of a simple argument that S is both true and false—and we are confronted again with the antinomy of the liar.

There is, however, no need to use universal languages in all possible situations. In particular, such languages are in general not needed for the purposes of science (and by science I mean here the whole realm of intellectual inquiry). In a particular branch of science, say in chemistry, one discusses certain special objects, such as elements, molecules, and so on, but not for instance linguistic objects such as sentences or terms. The language that is well adapted to this discussion is a restricted language with a limited vocabulary; it must contain names of chemical objects, terms such as "element" and "molecule," but not names of linguistic objects; hence it does not have to be semantically universal. The same applies to most of the other branches of science. The situation becomes somewhat confused when we turn to linguistics. This is a science in which we study languages; thus the language of linguistics must certainly be provided with names of linguistic objects. However, we do not have to identify the language of linguistics with the universal language or any of the languages that are objects of linguistic discussion, and we are not bound to assume that we use in linguistics one and the same language for all discussions. The language of linguistics has to contain the names of linguistic components of the languages discussed but not the names of its own components; thus, again, it does not have to be semantically universal. The same applies to the language of logic, or rather of that part of logic known as metalogic and metamathematics; here we again concern ourselves with certain languages, primarily with languages of logical and mathematical theories (although we discuss these languages from a different point of view than in the case of linguistics).

The question now arises whether the notion of truth can be precisely defined, and thus a consistent and adequate usage of this notion can be established at least for the semantically restricted languages of scientific discourse. Under certain conditions the answer to this question proves to be affirmative. The main conditions imposed on the language are that its full vocabulary should be available and its syntactical rules concerning the formation of sentences and other meaningful expressions from words listed in the vocabulary should be precisely formulated. Furthermore, the syntactical rules should be purely formal, that is, they should refer exclusively to the form (the shape) of expressions; the function and the meaning of an expression should depend exclusively on its form. In particular, looking at an expression, one should be able in each case to decide whether or not the expression is a sentence. It should never happen that an expression functions as a sentence at one place while an expression of the same form does not function so at some other place, or that a sentence can be asserted in one context while a sentence of the same form can be denied in another. (Hence it follows, in particular, that demonstrative pronouns and adverbs such as "this" and "here" should not occur in the vocabulary of the language.) Languages that satisfy these conditions are referred to as formalized languages. When discussing a formalized language there is no need to distinguish between expressions of the same form which have been written or uttered in different places; one often speaks of them as if they were one and the same expression. The reader may have noticed we sometimes use this way of speaking even when discussing a natural language, that is, one which is not formalized; we do so for the sake of simplicity, and only in those cases in which there seems to be no danger of confusion.

Formalized languages are fully adequate for the presentation of logical and mathematical theories; I see no essential reasons why they cannot be adapted for use in other scientific disciplines and in particular to the development of theoretical parts of empirical sciences. I should like to emphasize that, when using the term "formalized languages," I do not refer exclusively to linguistic systems that are formulated entirely in symbols, and I do not have in mind anything essentially opposed to natural languages. On the contrary, the only formalized languages that seem to be of real interest are those which are fragments of natural languages (fragments provided with complete vocabularies and precise syntactical rules) or those which can at least be adequately translated into natural languages.

There are some further conditions on which the realization of our program depends. We should make a strict distinction between the language which is the object of our discussion and for which in particular we intend to construct the definition of truth, and the language in which the definition is to be formulated and its implications are to be studied. The latter is referred to as the metalanguage and the former as the object-language. The metalanguage must be sufficiently rich; in particular, it must include the object-language as a part. In fact, according to our stipulations, an adequate definition of truth will imply as consequences all partial definitions of this notion, that is, all equivalences of form (3):

"p" is true if and only if p,

where "p" is to be replaced (on both sides of the equivalence) by an arbitrary sentence of the object-language. Since all these consequences are formulated in the metalanguage, we conclude that every sentence of the object-language must also be a sentence of the meta-language. Furthermore, the metalanguage must contain names for sentences (and other expressions) of the object-language, since these names occur on the left sides of the above equivalences. It must also contain some further terms that are needed for the discussion of the object-language, in fact terms denoting certain special sets of expressions, relations between expressions, and operations on expressions; for instance, we must be able to speak of the set of all sentences or of the operation of juxtaposition, by means of which, putting one of two given expressions immediately after the other, we form a new expression. Finally, by defining truth, we show that semantic terms (expressing relations between sentences of the object-language and objects referred to by these sentences) can be introduced in the metalanguage by means of definitions. Hence we conclude that the metalanguage which provides sufficient means for defining truth must be essentially richer than the object-language; it cannot coincide with or be translatable into the latter, since otherwise both languages would turn out to be semantically universal, and the antinomy of the liar could be reconstructed in both of them. We shall return to this question in the last section of this article.

If all the above conditions are satisfied, the construction of the desired definition of truth presents no essential difficulties. Technically, however, it is too involved to be explained here in detail. For any given sentence of the object-language one can easily formulate the corresponding partial definition of form (3). Since, however, the set of all sentences in the object-language is as a rule infinite, whereas every sentence of the metalanguage is a finite string of signs, we cannot arrive at a general definition simply by forming the logical conjunction of all partial definitions. Nevertheless, what we eventually obtain is in some intuitive sense equivalent to the imaginary infinite conjunction. Very roughly speaking, we proceed as follows. First, we consider the simplest sentences, which do not include any other sentences as parts; for these simplest sentences we manage to define truth directly (using the same idea that leads to partial definitions). Then, making use of syntactical rules which concern the formation of more complicated sentences from simpler ones, we extend the definition to arbitrary compound sentences; we apply here the method known in mathematics as definition by recursion. (This is merely a rough approximation of the actual procedure. For some technical reasons the method of recursion is actually applied to define, not the notion of truth, but the related semantic notion of satisfaction. Truth is then easily defined in terms of satisfaction.)

On the basis of the definition thus constructed we can develop the entire theory of truth. In particular, we can derive from it, in addition to all equivalences of form (3), some consequences of a general nature, such as the famous laws of contradiction and of excluded middle. By the first of these laws, no two sentences one of which is the negation of the other can both be true; by the second law, no two such sentences can both be false.

2. THE NOTION OF PROOF

Whatever may be achieved by constructing an adequate definition of truth for a scientific language, one fact seems to be certain: the definition does not carry with it a workable criterion for deciding whether particular sentences in this language are true or false (and indeed it is not designed at all for this purpose). Consider, for example, a sentence in the language of elementary high school geometry, say "the three bisectors of every triangle meet in one point." If we are interested in the question whether this sentence is true and we turn to the definition of truth for an answer, we are in for a disappointment. The only bit of information we get is that the sentence is true if the three bisectors of a triangle always meet in one point, and is false if they do not always meet; but only a geometrical inquiry may enable us to decide which is actually the case. Analogous remarks apply to sentences from the domain of any other particular science; to decide whether or not any such sentence is true is a task of the science itself, and not of logic or the theory of truth.

Some philosophers and methodologists of science are inclined to reject every definition that does not provide a criterion for deciding whether any given particular object falls under the notion defined or not. In the methodology of empirical sciences such a tendency is represented by the doctrine of operationalism; philosophers of mathematics who belong to the constructivist school seem to exhibit a similar tendency. In both cases, however, the people who hold this opinion appear to be in a small minority. A consistent attempt to carry out the program in practice (that is, to develop a science without using undesirable definitions) has hardly ever been made. It seems clear that under this program much of contemporary mathematics would disappear, and theoretical parts of physics, chemistry, biology, and other empirical sciences would be severely mutilated. The definitions of such notions as atom or gene as well as most definitions in mathematics do not carry with them any criteria for deciding whether or not an object falls under the term that has been defined.

Since the definition of truth does not provide us with any such criterion and at the same time the search for truth is rightly considered the essence of scientific activities, it appears as an important problem to find at least partial criteria of truth and to develop procedures that may enable us to ascertain or negate the truth (or at least the likelihood of truth) of as many sentences as possible. Such procedures are known indeed; some of them are used exclusively in empirical science and some primarily in deductive science. The notion of proof—the second notion to be discussed in this paper—refers just to a procedure of ascertaining the truth of sentences which is employed primarily in deductive science. This procedure is an essential element of what is known as the axiomatic method, the only method now used to develop mathematical disciplines.

The axiomatic method and the notion of proof within its framework are products of a long historical development. Some rough knowledge of this development is probably essential for the understanding of the contemporary notion of proof.

Originally a mathematical discipline was an aggregate of sentences that concerned a certain class of objects or phenomena, were formulated by means of a certain stock of terms, and were accepted as true. This aggregate of sentences lacked any structural order. A sentence was accepted as true either because it seemed intuitively evident, or else because it was proved on the basis of some intuitively evident sentences, and thus was shown, by means of an intuitively certain argument, to be a consequence of these other sentences. The criterion of intuitive evidence (and intuitive certainty of arguments) was applied without any restrictions; every sentence recognized as true by means of this criterion was automatically included in the discipline. This description seems to fit, for instance, the science of geometry as it was known to ancient Egyptians and Greeks in its early, pre-Euclidean stage.

It was realized rather soon, however, that the criterion of intuitive evidence is far from being infallible, has no objective character, and often leads to serious errors. The entire subsequent development of the axiomatic method can be viewed as an expression of the tendency to restrict the recourse to intuitive evidence.

This tendency first revealed itself in the effort to prove as many sentences as possible, and hence to restrict as much as possible the number of sentences accepted as true merely on the basis of intuitive evidence. The ideal from this point of view would be to prove every sentence that is to be accepted as true. For obvious reasons this ideal cannot be realized. Indeed, we prove each sentence on the basis of other sentences, we prove these other sentences on the basis of some further sentences, and so on: if we are to avoid both a vicious circle and an infinite regress, the procedure must be discontinued somewhere. As a compromise between that unattainable ideal and the realizable possibilities, two principles emerged and were subsequently applied in constructing mathematical disciplines. By the first of these principles every discipline begins with a list of a small number of sentences, called axioms or primitive sentences, which seem to be intuitively evident and which are recognized as true without any further justification. According to the second principle, no other sentence is accepted in the discipline as true unless we are able to prove it with the exclusive help of axioms and those sentences that were previously proved. All the sentences that can be recognized as true by virtue of these two principles are called theorems, or provable sentences, of the given discipline. Two analogous principles concern the use of terms in constructing the discipline. By the first of them we list at the beginning a few terms, called undefined or primitive terms, which appear to be directly understandable and which we decide to use (in formulating and proving theorems) without explaining their meanings; by the second principle we agree not to use any further term unless we are able to explain its meaning by defining it with the help of undefined terms and terms previously defined. These four principles are cornerstones of the axiomatic method; theories developed in accordance with these principles are called axiomatic theories.

As is well known, the axiomatic method was applied to the development of geometry in the *Elements* of Euclid about 300 B.C. Thereafter it was used for over 2,000 years with practically no change in its main principles (which, by the way, were not even explicitly formulated for a long period of time) nor in the general approach to the subject. However, in the 19th and 20th centuries the concept of the axiomatic method did undergo a profound evolution. Those features of the evolution which concern the notion of proof are particularly significant for our discussion.

Until the last years of the 19th century the notion of proof was primarily of a psychological character. A proof was an intellectual activity that aimed at convincing oneself and others of the truth of a sentence discussed; more specifically, in developing a mathematical theory proofs were used to convince ourselves and others that a sentence discussed had to be accepted as true once some other sentences had been previously accepted as such. No restrictions were put on arguments used in proofs, except that they had to be intuitively convincing. At a certain period, however, a need began to be felt for submitting the notion of proof to a deeper analysis that would result in restricting the recourse to intuitive evidence in this context as well. This was probably related to some specific developments in mathematics, in particular to the discovery of non-Euclidean geometries.

The analysis was carried out by logicians, beginning with the German logician Gottlob Frege; it led to the introduction of a new notion, that of a *formal proof,* which turned out to be an adequate substitute and an essential improvement over the old psychological notion.

The first step toward supplying a mathematical theory with the notion of a formal proof is the formalization of the language of the theory, in the sense discussed previously in connection with the definition of truth. Thus formal syntactical rules are provided which in particular enable us simply by looking at shapes of expressions, to distinguish a sentence from an expression that is not a sentence. The next step consists in formulating a few rules of a different nature, the so-called rules of proof (or of inference). By these rules a sentence is regarded as directly derivable from given sentences if, generally speaking, its shape is related in a prescribed manner to the shapes of given sentences. The number of rules of proof is small, and their content is simple. Just like the syntactical rules, they all have a formal character, that is, they refer exclusively to shapes of sentences involved. Intuitively all the rules of derivation appear to be infallible, in the sense that a sentence which is directly derivable from true sentences by any of these rules must be true itself. Actually the infallibility of the rules of proof can be established on the basis of an adequate definition of truth. The best-known and most important example of a rule of proof is the rule of detachment known also as *modus ponens.* By this rule (which in some theories serves as the only rule of proof) a sentence "q" is directly derivable from two given sentences if one of them is the conditional sentence "if p, then q" while the other is "p"; here "p" and "q" are, as usual, abbreviations of any two sentences of our formalized language. We can now explain in what a formal proof of a given sentence consists. First, we apply the rules of proof to axioms and obtain new sentences that are directly derivable from axioms; next, we apply the same rules to new sentences, or jointly to new sentences and axioms, and obtain further sentences; and we continue this process. If after a finite number of steps we arrive at a given sentence, we say that the sentence has been formally proved. This can also be expressed more precisely in the following way: a formal proof of a given sentence consists in constructing a finite sequence of sentences such that (1) the first sentence in the sequence is an axiom, (2) each of the following sentences either is an axiom or is directly derivable from some of the sentences that precede it in the sequence, by virtue of one of the rules of proof, and (3) the last sentence in the sequence is the sentence to be proved. Changing somewhat the use of the term "proof," we can even say that a formal proof of a sentence is simply any finite sequence of sentences with the three properties just listed.

An axiomatic theory whose language has been formalized and for which the notion of a formal proof has been supplied is called a formalized theory. We stipulate that the only proofs which can be used in a formalized theory are formal proofs; no sentence can be accepted as a theorem unless it appears on the list of axioms or a formal proof can be found for it. The method of presenting a formalized theory at each stage of its development is in principle very elementary. We list first the axioms and then all the known theorems in such an order that every sentence on the list which is not an axiom can be directly recognized as a theorem, simply by comparing its shape with the shapes of sentences that precede it on the list; no complex processes of reasoning and convincing are involved. (I am not speaking here of psychological processes by means of which the theorems have actually been discovered.) The recourse to intuitive evidence has been indeed considerably restricted; doubts concerning the truth of theorems have not been entirely eliminated but have been reduced to possible doubts concerning the truth of the few sentences listed as axioms and the infallibility of the few simple rules of proof. It may be added that the process of introducing new terms in the language of a theory can also be formalized by supplying special formal rules of definitions.

It is now known that all the existing mathematical disciplines can be presented as formalized theories. Formal proofs can be provided for the deepest and most complicated mathematical theorems, which were originally established by intuitive arguments.

3. THE RELATIONSHIP OF TRUTH AND PROOF

It was undoubtedly a great achievement of modern logic to have replaced the old psychological notion of proof, which could hardly ever be made clear and precise, by a new simple notion of a purely formal character. But the triumph of the formal method carried with it the germ of a future setback. As we shall see, the very simplicity of the new notion turned out to be its Achilles heel.

To assess the notion of formal proof we have to clarify its relation to the notion of truth. After all, the formal proof, just like the old intuitive proof, is a procedure aimed at acquiring new true sentences. Such a procedure will be adequate only if all sentences acquired with its help prove to be true and all true sentences can be acquired with its help. Hence the problem naturally arises: is the formal proof actually an adequate procedure for acquiring truth? In other words: does the set of all (formally) provable sentences coincide with the set of all true sentences?

To be specific, we refer this problem to a particular, very elementary mathematical discipline, namely to the arithmetic of natural numbers (the elementary number theory). We assume that this discipline has been presented as a formalized theory. The vocabulary of the theory is meager. It consists, in fact, of variables such as "*m*," "*n*," "*p*," . . . representing arbitrary natural numbers; of numerals "0," "1," "2," . . . denoting particular numbers; of symbols denoting some familiar relations between numbers and operations on numbers such as "$=$," "$<$," "$+$," "$-$"; and, finally, of certain logical terms, namely sentential connectives ("and," "or," "if," "not") and quantifiers (expressions of the form "for every number *m*" and "for some number *m*"). The syntactical rules and the rules of proof are simple. When speaking of sentences in the subsequent discussion, we always have in mind sentences of the formalized language of arithmetic.

We know from the discussion of truth in the first section that, taking this language as the object-language, we can construct an appropriate metalanguage and formulate in it an adequate definition of truth. It proves convenient in this context to say that what we have thus defined is the set of true sentences; in fact, the definition of truth states that a certain condition formulated in the metalanguage is satisfied by all elements of this set (that is, all true sentences) and only by these elements. Even more readily we can define in the metalanguage the set of provable sentences; the definition conforms entirely with the explanation of the notion of formal proof that was given in the second section. Strictly speaking, the definitions of both truth and provability belong to a new theory formulated in the metalanguage and specifically designed for the study of our formalized arithmetic and its language. The new theory is called the metatheory or, more specifically, the meta-arithmetic. We shall not elaborate here on the way in which the metatheory is constructed—on its axioms, undefined terms, and so on. We only point out that it is within the framework of this metatheory that we formulate and solve the problem of whether the set of provable sentences coincides with that of true sentences.

The solution of the problem proves to be negative. We shall give here a very rough account of the method by which the solution has been reached. The main idea is closely related to the one used by the contemporary American logician (of Austrian origin) Kurt Gödel in his famous paper on the incompleteness of arithmetic.

It was pointed out in the first section that the metalanguage which enables us to define and discuss the notion of truth must be rich. It contains the entire object-language as a part, and therefore we can speak in it of natural numbers, sets of numbers, relations among numbers, and so forth. But it also contains terms needed for the discussion of the object-language and its components; consequently we can speak in the metalanguage of expressions and in particular of sentences, of sets of sentences, of relations among sentences, and so forth. Hence in the metatheory we can study properties of these various kinds of objects and establish connections between them.

In particular, using the description of sentences provided by the syntactical rules of the object-language, it is easy to arrange all sentences (from the simplest ones through the more and more complex) in an infinite sequence and to number them consecutively. We thus correlate with every sentence a natural number in such a way that two numbers correlated with two different sentences are always different; in other words, we establish a one-to-one correspondence between sentences and numbers. This in turn leads to a similar correspondence between sets of sentences and sets of numbers, or relations among sentences and relations among numbers. In particular, we can consider numbers of provable sentences and numbers of true sentences; we call them briefly provable* numbers and true* numbers. Our main problem is reduced then to the question: are the set of provable* numbers and the set of true* numbers identical?

To answer this question negatively, it suffices, of course, to indicate a single property that applies to one set but not to the other. The property we shall actually exhibit may seem rather unexpected, a kind of *deus ex machina*.

The intrinsic simplicity of the notions of formal proof and formal provability will play a basic role here. We have seen in the second section that the meaning of these notions is explained essentially in terms of certain simple relations among sentences prescribed by a few rules of proof; the reader may recall here the rule of *modus ponens*. The corresponding relations among numbers of sentences are equally simple; it turns out that they can be characterized in terms of the simplest arithmetical operations and relations, such as addition, multiplication, and equality—thus in terms occurring in our arithmetical theory. As a consequence the set of provable* numbers can also be characterized in such terms. One can describe briefly what has been achieved by saying that the definition of provability has been translated from the metalanguage into the object-language.

On the other hand, the discussion of the notion of truth in common languages strongly suggests the conjecture that no such translation can be obtained for the definition of truth; otherwise the object-language would prove to be in a sense semantically universal, and a reappearance of the antinomy of the liar would be imminent. We confirm this conjecture by showing that, if the set of true* numbers could be defined in the language of arithmetic, the antinomy of the liar could actually be reconstructed in this language. Since, however, we are dealing now with a restricted formalized language, the antinomy would assume a more involved and sophisticated form. In particular, no expressions with an empirical content such as "the sentence printed in such-and-such place," which played an essential part in the original formulation of the antinomy, would occur in the new formulation. We shall not go into any further details here.

Thus the set of provable* numbers does not coincide with the set of true* numbers, since the former is definable in the language of arithmetic while the latter is not. Consequently the sets of provable sentences and true sentences do not coincide either. On the other hand, using the definition of truth we easily show that all the axioms of arithmetic are true and all the rules of proof are infallible. Hence all the provable sentences are true; therefore the converse cannot hold. Thus our final conclusion is: there are sentences formulated in the language of arithmetic that are true but cannot be proved on the basis of the axioms and rules of proof accepted in arithmetic.

One might think that the conclusion essentially depends on specific axioms and rules of inference, chosen for our arithmetical theory, and that the final outcome of the discussion could be different if we appropriately enriched the theory by adjoining new axioms or new rules of inference. A closer analysis shows, however, that the argument depends very little on specific properties of the theory discussed, and that it actually extends to most other formalized theories. Assuming that a theory includes the arithmetic of natural numbers as a part (or that, at least, arithmetic can be reconstructed in it), we can repeat the essential portion of our argument in a practically unchanged form; we thus conclude again that the set of provable sentences of the theory is different from the set of its true sentences. If, moreover, we can show (as is frequently the case) that all the axioms of the theory are true and all the rules of inference are infallible, we further conclude that there are true sentences of the theory which are not provable. Apart from some fragmentary theories with restricted means of expression, the assumption concerning the relation of the theory to the arithmetic of natural numbers is generally satisfied, and hence our conclusions have a nearly universal character. (Regarding those fragmentary theories which do not include the arithmetic of natural numbers, their languages may not be provided with sufficient means for defining the notion of provability, and their provable sentences may in fact coincide with their true sentences. Elementary geometry and elementary algebra of real numbers are the best known, and perhaps most important, examples of theories in which these notions coincide.)

The dominant part played in the whole argument by the antinomy of the liar throws some interesting light on our earlier remarks concerning the role of antinomies in the history of human thought. The antinomy of the liar first appeared in our discussion as a kind of evil force with a great destructive power. It compelled us to abandon all attempts at clarifying the notion of truth for natural languages. We had to restrict our endeavors to formalized languages of scientific discourse. As a safeguard against a possible reappearance of the antinomy, we had to complicate considerably the discussion by distinguishing between a language and its metalanguage. Subsequently, however, in the new, restricted setting, we have managed to tame the destructive energy and harness it to peaceful, constructive purposes. The antinomy has not reappeared, but its basic idea has been used to establish a significant metalogical result with far-reaching implications.

Nothing is detracted from the significance of this result by the fact that its philosophical implications are essentially negative in character. The result shows indeed that in no domain of mathematics is the notion of provability a perfect substitute for the notion of truth. The belief that formal proof can serve as an adequate instrument for establishing truth of all mathematical statements has proved to be unfounded. The original triumph of formal methods has been followed by a serious setback.

Whatever can be said to conclude this discussion is bound to be an anticlimax. The notion of truth for formalized theories can now be introduced by means of a precise and adequate definition. It can therefore be used without any restrictions and reservations in metalogical discussion. It has actually become a basic metalogical notion involved in important problems and results. On the other hand, the notion of proof has not lost its significance either. Proof is still the only method used to ascertain the truth of sentences within any specific mathematical theory. We are now aware of the fact, however, that there are sentences formulated in the language of the theory which are true but not provable, and we cannot discount the possibility that some such sentences occur among those in which we are interested and which we attempt to prove. Hence in some situations we may wish to explore the possibility of widening the set of provable sentences. To this end we enrich the given theory by including new sentences in its axiom system or by providing it with new rules of proof. In doing so we use the notion of truth as a guide; for we do not wish to add a new axiom or a new rule of proof if we have reason to believe that the new axiom is not a true sentence, or that the new rule of proof when applied to true sentences may yield a false sentence. The process of extending a theory may of course be repeated arbitrarily many times. The notion of a true sentence functions thus as an ideal limit which can never be reached but which we try to approximate by gradually widening the set of provable sentences. (It seems likely, although for different reasons, that the notion of truth plays an analogous role in the realm of empirical knowledge.) There is no conflict between the notions of truth and proof in the development of mathematics; the two notions are not at war but live in peaceful coexistence.

Kant, Malcolm, and the
Ontological Argument

Jonathan Bennett

1. THE KANT-FREGE VIEW

The third and final chapter of Book II of the Dialectic of Kant's *Critique of Pure Reason* is on theology.[1] It treats three traditional arguments for God's existence, starting with the so-called *ontological* argument, which goes somewhat as follows.

If the word 'God' means, in part, 'being which is omnipotent, benevolent, omniscient . . .', then anyone who says 'God is not omnipotent' either contradicts himself or is not using 'God' with its normal meaning. Now, 'God' means, in part, 'being which is *existent, omnipotent, benevolent . . .*' That implies that anyone who says 'God is not existent' either contradicts himself or is not using 'God' in its normal meaning; whence it follows that 'God is existent', normally understood, is guaranteed as true just by the meaning of its subject-term.

Kant rejects this argument because, he says, 'existent' has no right to occur in a list of terms purporting to express what an item must be like in order to qualify for a certain label. Existent things are not things of a kind; existence is not a state or quality or process; 'existent' is not a predicate. '"Exist" . . . is a verb, but it does not describe something that things do all the time, like breathing, only quieter—ticking over, as it were, in a metaphysical sort of way'.[2]

Kant puts this by saying that 'existent' is not a 'real predicate' or a 'determining predicate'. It and its cognates can behave like predicates in a sentence, he admits, as when we say 'Unicorns don't exist', which

This essay first appeared as §§72–74 of Jonathan Bennett, *Kant's Dialectic*, © Cambridge University Press 1974. It is reprinted by permission of the author and Cambridge University Press.

1. Page references are to the second (B) edition of the *Critique*; these page numbers appear in the margin of Kant (1965).

2. J. L. Austin (1962, p. 68n).

may seem to report something that unicorns don't do. But that only qualifies it as a grammatical or 'logical' predicate:

> Anything . . . can . . . serve as a logical predicate; the subject can even be predicated of itself . . . But a *determining* predicate is a predicate which is added to the concept of the subject and enlarges it . . . *'Being'* is obviously not a real predicate; that is, it is not a concept of something which could be added to the concept of a thing. (B626)

Recall that a thing's 'determinations' are its properties or qualities. To 'determine' something is to discover or report detail about it.

This general view about the concept of existence was adumbrated, against Descartes, by Gassendi. Descartes argues that 'God' means '. . . existent . . .' because it means 'being with all perfections' and existence is a perfection:

> Existence can no more be separated from the essence of God than can its having three angles equal to two right angles be separated from the essence of a triangle . . .; and so it is just as impossible to conceive a God (that is, a supremely perfect being) who lacks existence (that is to say, who lacks a certain perfection), as to conceive of a mountain which has no valley.[3]

Gassendi denies that existence is a perfection or indeed a property or quality of any sort:

> Existence is a perfection neither in God nor in anything else; it is rather that in the absence of which there is no perfection. For that which does not exist has neither perfection nor imperfection, and that which exists and has various perfections does not have its existence as a particular perfection . . . but as that by means of which the thing itself equally with its perfections is in existence.

Descartes' reply to this is unsatisfactory:

> I do not see to what class of reality you wish to assign existence, nor do I see why it may not be said to be a property . . ., taking 'property' to cover any attribute or anything which can be predicated of a thing.

This amounts to saying that 'existent' must be a determining predicate because it is a logical or grammatical predicate.

3. *Fifth Meditation*, about one third of the way through. Next two quotations: Fifth Objections to the *Meditations*, Haldane and Ross (1911–12, v. 2, p. 186); Descartes's reply, *ibid.* p. 228.

One piece of evidence for the Kantian view is given by Moore (1959, pp. 117–20). He contrasts (a) 'Tame tigers exist' with (b) 'Tame tigers growl'. One might think that each of these reports something that tame tigers do, but there is a deep-lying dissimilarity which Moore displays by considering the question 'All of them or only some of them?' Asked of (b), this makes perfect sense: perhaps every tame tiger growls, perhaps some do and others do not. But the question cannot be applied to (a): we cannot suppose that perhaps some tame tigers exist while others do not.

Kant rests a good deal on a different line of argument.[4] He says that we entertain a possibility by considering some concept built out of determining predicates, and that to ask whether the possibility is realized is to ask whether that concept applies to any object. If 'existing' were a determining predicate, Kant argues, then a bare affirmative answer to the question could never be given. Suppose the question is 'Are there any tigers?' The answer that there are tigers means that some existing things are tigers; and that, if 'existing' is a determining predicate, asserts that something instantiates not merely the concept *tiger* but the richer concept *existing tiger*. An affirmative answer to our question is always over-informative, as though 'Are there tigers?' had to be answered by 'Yes, there are striped tigers' or 'Yes, there are fat tigers'. In Kant's words:

> By whatever and by however many predicates we may think a thing—even if we completely determine it—we do not make the least addition to the thing when we further declare that this thing *is*. Otherwise, it would not be exactly the same thing that exists, but something more than we had thought in the concept; and we could not, therefore, say that the exact object of my concept exists. (B628)

This argument is resistible. An opponent could reply that just as the answer 'Yes, there are tigers' means 'Yes, there are existent tigers', so the question 'Are there tigers?' means 'Are there existent tigers?'; in which case the answer does not say more than was asked.

The quoted passage also suggests that if 'existent' were a determining predicate then we could not entertain some concept and find that precisely *it* was instantiated: if instantiation involved existence, 'it would not be exactly the same thing that exists, but something more than we had thought in the concept.' But what exists is *always* 'more than we had thought in the concept'! Whatever one 'thinks in a concept' must be abstract, omitting answers to at least some questions

4. The paragraph on B626–7, and start of the following paragraph.

of detail, and so a reality corresponding to any such thought will always have some features with regard to which the thought was, as it were, silent. Kant implies that we might 'completely determine' a thing, but that is impossible. Anyway, if we could do so, i.e. could think the totality of a thing's determining predicates, perhaps that *would* involve us automatically in thinking of it as existing. In assuming the contrary, Kant is simply begging the question in favour of his view that 'existent' is not a determining predicate. So this argument of Kant's is, in two distinct ways, a complete failure.[5]

Yet I share the widespread belief that this discussion of Kant's contains something which is important and may be true. We should see him as presenting, in the garb of bad arguments, a considerable thesis or hypothesis about the logic of existence. It is at once an answer to Descartes' 'I do not see to what class of reality you wish to assign existence', and an amplification of Gassendi's sketchy remark that existence 'is that in the absence of which there is no perfection'.

Gassendi did well to avoid saying more than he knew. Lacking a positive theory about the concept of existence, he nevertheless saw clearly that an acceptable theory must not imply that existence is a property. Descartes' contemporary Clerselier, who translated the Objections to the *Meditations* and Descartes' Replies to them, must have found the sketchiness of Gassendi's treatment of existence intolerable. For he turned Gassendi's Latin 'It is that in the absence of which . . .' into his own French 'It is a *form or an act* in the absence of which . . .'! That is no good at all, of course, but some positive theory was needed, and more than a century later Kant provided it.

According to Kant, every existence-statement says about a concept that it is instantiated, rather than saying about an object that it exists. This is an important precursor of the view of Frege that any legitimate existential statement must be built out of propositional atoms of the form 'There is an *F*', where *F* stands for a determining predicate.[6] According to this Kant-Frege view, the real form of 'Tigers exist' is

5. I here follow J. Shaffer (1962).

6. "Existential propositions are ones which can be expressed in German with *es gibt* [in English with 'there is' or 'there are']. This expression is not followed immediately by a name in the singular or by a word with the definite article, but always by a concept-word [determining predicate] without a definite article. In such existential propositions something is said about a concept" (Frege 1969, v. 1, p. 274). I am indebted to Howard Jackson for showing me this passage. For a remark by Frege about the ontological argument, see Frege (1952), p. 38n.

not like that of 'Tigers growl', but rather like that of 'There are tigers', or 'The concept of tigerhood is instantiated'. Granted that Kant's arguments fall far short of proving this hypothesis, they do at least illustrate and elucidate it; and the hypothesis itself is a philosophical contribution which deserves attention and which may even be true.

The Fregean view about existence can be applied to philosophical problems, as follows. Suppose that a purported existence-statement S is somehow problematical. (1) If S remains problematical when it is quantified, i.e. translated into the form '. . . there is an F . . .', then this is a problem which the Fregean view does not solve. (2) If the problem disappears when S is quantified, then it has been solved by the Fregean view. (3) If S cannot be quantified, then the 'problem' it posed was illusory.

Because of (3), the ontological argument can be dissolved. It is based on a definition of the form: 'x is God' means 'x is omniscient and x is omnipotent and x is existent and x is benevolent and . . .', and there is no way that the component 'x is existent' can be quantified, i.e. expressed in the Fregean form '. . . there is an F. . .'.

There are difficulties in this position. For example, the statement 'I exist' seems to be legitimate and yet not quantifiable. There is also the problem that one cannot report an absolute existence-change in quantified form.[7] Here, however, I adopt the Kant–Frege view as a working hypothesis. The only live controversy I shall enter concerns its powers, not its truth.[8]

2. EXISTENCE AND NECESSARY EXISTENCE

Norman Malcolm has distinguished two ontological arguments, one of which he says is valid and does prove the existence of God.[9] The argument whose invalidity Malcolm concedes is the one I have been discussing. It is invalid, he says, 'because it rests on the false doctrine that existence is a perfection'; and he endorses Kant's handling of this matter, while rightly saying that Kant's position has not yet been conclusively established. The second argument involves a definiens which includes not just 'existent' but '*necessarily* existent'. That, Malcolm thinks, makes it safe from Kant's criticisms yet still adequate to prove the desired conclusion.

7. This problem is discussed in §21 of *Kant's Dialectic.*
8. For further discussion see Kneale (1936) and Alston (1960).
9. Malcolm (1960); the remark about Kant's position is on p. 44.

Malcolm is right to this extent: there is a form of argument which can be used to support the view that 'existent' is not a determining predicate, though it gives no support at all to the view that 'necessarily existent' is not a determining predicate. We have some ways of using 'existent' which can be rapidly and easily quantified: 'Tigers are existent' becomes 'There are tigers'. If we try to use the word as a determining predicate, by giving it a role in which it purports to mark off things of a kind, it always turns out to be vacuous. If I ask you to bring me a beer, and then add '. . . a cold one', that could make the request harder to comply with; but if I add '. . . an existent one', your task is not made harder, because an existent beer is just a beer. But it is not obvious that necessarily existent things are not things of a kind. If I ask you to bring me a beer, and add '. . . a necessarily existent one, please', you cannot now comply just by bringing me any old beer. The addition has made my order more difficult, and perhaps impossible, to fill. In short, 'existent' behaves vacuously when we pretend that it is a determining predicate, but 'necessarily existent' does not.

Malcolm even claims that necessary existence is a perfection, a property which it is good to have;[10] whereas the view that existence is a perfection involves such absurdities as that 'my future house . . . will be a better house if it exists than if it does not.'

He also argues convincingly that there is a theological-linguistic tradition in which 'necessarily existent' is part of what 'God' means.[11] Our reason for this connects with the preceding point: necessary existence is (analytically) a perfection, and God (analytically) has every perfection. There is also another reason: it does not 'make sense' to ask when God began, or whether God will cease to exist, or what causes God to exist—and such questions can fail to make sense only if God's existence is a logical truth, i.e. only if God has necessary existence. We shall see later that these two reasons clash.

Malcolm also hits back at two other lines of argument used by Kant.

Kant contends that, for any predicate *F*, from the necessity that God is *F* it follows only that *if* there is a God he is *F*:

> If, in an identical proposition, I reject the predicate while retaining the subject, contradiction results . . . But if we reject subject and predicate alike, there is no contradiction; for nothing is then left that can be contradicted. To posit a triangle, and yet to reject its three angles, is self-

10. *Ibid.* pp. 46–47; next quotation: *ibid.* p. 43.
11. References for this paragraph are all *ibid.* pp. 47–50.

contradictory; but there is no contradiction in rejecting the triangle together with its three angles. The same holds true of the concept of an absolutely necessary being. If its existence is rejected, we reject the thing itself with all its predicates; and no question of contradiction can then arise. (B622–3)

This implies that Malcolm's argument proves, at most, that if God exists then God necessarily exists.

Malcolm denies that his conclusion ought to be weakened in this way.[12] If Kant were right, Malcolm's premises would be consistent with 'God does not exist'. That would make them consistent with 'It is not necessary that God exists', and thus with 'God does not necessarily exist'. But one of Malcolm's premises is, precisely, that it is analytic that God *does* necessarily exist. So, Malcolm argues, Kant must be wrong.

This argument assumes that 'God exists necessarily' entails 'It is necessary that God exists', and this move is controversial. I have no quarrel with it if *logical* necessity is involved, as indeed it seems to be when Malcolm says that because God necessarily exists certain questions do not 'make sense'. As against this, however, when he says that necessary existence is a 'perfection', he seems to invoke causal rather than logical necessity, equating necessary existence with indestructibility. On that construal of Malcolm's position, the above argument of his collapses, for 'God is indestructible' is obviously not equivalent to 'It is necessary that God exists' in any sense of 'necessary' which is strong enough to license the further inference to 'God exists'. [13] On the causal construal, then, Malcolm ought to admit that all he has established is the conditional proposition that if there is a God then he is indestructible. So let us now set aside the causal reading of Malcolm's original argument. He needs to construe 'necessarily existent' in terms of logical necessity, for that is implied by his point about certain questions' not making sense, and—far more important—it is required if his conclusion is not to be reduced to a mere conditional.

Kant also attacks the ontological argument on the ground that 'All existential propositions are synthetic'.[14] That, if true, condemns Mal-

---

12. *Ibid.* pp. 56–58.

13. This point is well made by T. K. Swing (1969), pp. 307–9.

14. B626. Malcolm's refusal to defer: *op. cit.* pp. 52–53. Final sentence of this paragraph: *ibid.* pp. 53–56; see also Bennett (1971), §59.

colm's conclusion that it is analytically necessary that God exists. But Kant gives no clear reasons for this claim of his, and Malcolm refuses to defer to it. Malcolm also considers the related, contemporary view that all existential propositions are contingent and so cannot be proved by a priori argument, and he rightly says that this popular dogma is without visible support.

3. WHY MALCOLM'S ARGUMENT FAILS

Consider the form 'necessarily F', with the adverb being taken to express logical or a priori necessity and thus to express analytic necessity—according to my view and also to Malcolm's.[15] If something is necessarily F, it must be F by definition—the term standing for F must occur in its definiens. This implies that an object cannot be, in itself, necessarily F; because that would require that a certain expression occur in the object's definition, and objects don't have definitions. Cannibals are necessarily carnivores, but we cannot say of any cannibal that *he* is necessarily carnivorous—only that *qua* cannibal he is necessarily carnivorous. The classic source for this point is in Locke, who speaks of necessary properties as 'essences', and says this about them:

> *Essence,* in the ordinary use of the word, relates to sorts, and . . . is considered in particular beings no further than as they are ranked into sorts . . . Take but away the abstract ideas by which we sort individuals, and rank them under common names, and then the thought of anything essential to any of them instantly vanishes.[16]

Kant makes the same point, in very condensed form, when he says: 'The absolute necessity of the judgment is only a conditioned necessity of the thing' (B621). From this point of Locke's and Kant's, it follows that nothing of the form 'necessarily F' belongs in a definiens. A definiens sets a test that an object must pass if the definiendum is to fit it, but for no value of F could we test an object to discover whether *it* was necessarily F. If an object is F, then there will be some G and H such that *qua* G the object is necessarily F whereas *qua* H it is only contingently F.

That, I submit, destroys Malcolm's argument. But there is another

15. Malcolm, *op. cit.* p. 55: "I am inclined to hold the . . . view that logically necessary truth 'mainly reflects our use of words'."
16. Locke (1975), III.vi.4; see also the rest of 1–13.

point which also is fatal. In expressing it, I shall waive the first difficulty, and shall talk freely about objects as being *F*-by-definition and
so on.

Malcolm stresses certain facts about the Christian theological tra-
tion. In that tradition it has been widely accepted that something
couldn't count as 'God' if we could intelligibly ask about it 'Did it ever
not exist?' or 'Will it ever not exist?' or 'Under what conditions would
it not have existed?' or 'Because of what other facts does it exist?' or
the like. The semantics of the tradition do not allow such questions to
arise about God, properly so-called: anyone who asks them shows that
he has not grasped the *concept* of God. A being in respect of which
these questions cannot be asked must be necessarily existent, it seems.

The phrase 'necessarily existent' needs to be explained: we cannot
simply say that it has whatever meaning would turn those questions
into logical solecisms. Someone who thinks an expression can do that
kind of service owes us a positive account of its meaning which explains how it can do what he claims for it. Thus Kant:

> In all ages men have spoken of an *absolutely necessary* being . . . There is,
> of course, no difficulty in giving a verbal definition of the concept, namely,
> that it is something the non-existence of which is impossible. But this
> yields no insight into the conditions which make it necessary to regard the
> non-existence of a thing as utterly unthinkable. It is precisely these condi-
> tions that we desire to know, in order that we may determine whether or
> not, in resorting to this concept, we are thinking anything at all. (B620–1)

What sort of positive account can be given? Well, if we look for
guidance to easier cases, we find that where a question of the form
'Are *F*s *G*?' is clearly improper or unraisable or self-answering, this is
because the meaning of *F* somehow includes that of *G*. If that points to
how 'necessarily existent' has its question-blocking role, we get this:
'To say that something is necessarily existent is to say that its definition analytically involves existence'. A necessarily existent thing, then,
apparently has to be a thing which is existent by definition; but Malcolm has agreed that 'existent' is not a determining predicate, so that
it cannot legitimately occur in a definiens. I claim, in short, that
because 'existent' ought not to occur in a definiens, 'necessarily existent' ought not to occur anywhere.

That argument is Kant's. He considers not the concept of a most
perfect being but rather that of a most real thing, an *ens realissimum*.
He sees this as a traditional vehicle for the notion of necessary existence, and one which might be thought to escape his central attack:

> Notwithstanding all these general considerations . . ., we may be challenged with a case which is brought forward as proof that in actual fact . . . there is one concept, and indeed only one, in reference to which the not-being or rejection of its object is in itself contradictory, namely, the concept of the *ens realissimum* . . . My answer is as follows. There is already a contradiction in introducing the concept of existence—no matter under what title it may be disguised—into the concept of a thing which we profess to be thinking solely in reference to its possibility. (B624–5)

That is the core of my second argument against Malcolm: in claiming that God is necessarily existent he is 'introducing the concept of existence', in disguise, 'into the concept of a thing'.

To escape this argument, Malcolm must give a positive account of 'necessarily existent' such that (1) it does not mean anything like 'existent by definition', yet (2) God's being necessarily existent suffices both to block the forbidden questions and to entail that necessarily God exists. These two conditions cannot be satisfied by a single sense of 'necessarily existent'.

Malcolm may well be right when he says this:

> What Anselm has proved is that the notion of contingent existence or of contingent nonexistence cannot have any application to God. His existence must either be logically necessary or logically impossible. The only intelligible way of rejecting Anselm's claim that God's existence is necessary is to maintain that the concept of God, as a being a greater than which cannot be conceived [and thus as necessarily existing], is self-contradictory or nonsensical.[17]

I have tried to show that the concept of God, on the Anselm-Malcolm account of it, is logically defective; and so I contend that in that sense God's existence *is* self-contradictory or nonsensical. If that convicts a whole theological-linguistic tradition of talking nonsense, so be it. It can be argued that I must be wrong about this. The standards for what makes sense are set by actual meanings, and these are determined by actual uses. From this, some philosophers infer that there could not be a logical mistake made by a whole community. To reply to this line of argument would take me too far afield now.

Just to get it clear: I have argued, firstly, that there is no *F* such that 'necessarily *F*' can properly occur in a definiens, and, secondly, that 'necessarily existent' cannot properly occur anywhere at all.

17. Malcolm, *op. cit.* p. 49. The last point in this paragraph is discussed in Bennett (1961).

10

Quantifiers

Michael Dummett

The discovery by Frege, at the outset of his career, of the notation of quantifiers and variables for the expression of generality dominated his entire subsequent outlook upon logic (1972, §11).* By means of it, he resolved, for the first time in the whole history of logic, the problem which had foiled the most penetrating minds that had given their attention to the subject. It is not surprising that Frege's approach was ever afterwards governed by the lessons which he regarded as being taught by this discovery.

Aristotle and the Stoics had investigated only those inferences involving essentially sentences containing not more than one expression of generality. Scholastic logic had wrestled with the problems posed by inferences depending on sentences involving multiple generality—the occurrence of more than one expression of generality. In order to handle such inferences, they developed ever more complex theories of different types of *'suppositio'* (different manners in which an expression could stand for or apply to an object): but these theories, while subtle and complex, never succeeded in giving a universally applicable account, either from the standpoint of syntax (the characterization of valid inferences in formal terms) or from that of semantics (the explanation of the truth-conditions of sentences involving multiple generality). As a result of this increasing and never finally successful subtlety, the whole subject of logic fell into disrepute at the Renaissance, as part of the general rejection of the achievements of the scholastic era. Apart from Leibniz—whose work likewise failed to tackle the problem of multiple generality—no more serious work was done in logic by European mathematicians or philosophers until the nineteenth century. Indeed, what would otherwise have been the scan-

This essay first appeared as chapter 2 of Michael Dummett, *Frege: Philosophy of Language* (2nd ed., 1981). It is reprinted here by permission of the author, and of Gerald Duckworth Ltd. and Harvard University Press.

*Editor's note: The bibliographical references in this essay are to recent English translations of Frege's work. For major works the bibliography gives the date of original publication; thus the entry under "Frege (1972)" contains the information that the *Begriffschrift* was first published in 1879.

dal of the failure, over centuries, to resolve the problem of inferences involving multiple generality was for long concealed by doctrines entailing the non-existence of the problem. Any sentence expressed within first-order predicate logic and containing only one-place predicates is equivalent to some sentence in which no quantifier stands within the scope of any other quantifier. Hence the widely held opinion that relations are merely 'ideal', i.e. that any sentence involving predicates of more than one place can in principle be reduced to one involving only one-place predicates, implied that the study of multiple generality (nested expressions of generality) is unnecessary. That, blatantly, the logic which dealt only with simple generality was impotent to give any account of the simplest mathematical reasoning was a fact to which, almost universally, philosophers, who believed that essentially all the problems of logic had been solved by Aristotle, were simply blind.

It is necessary, if Frege is to be understood, to grasp the magnitude of the discovery of the quantifier-variable notation, as thus resolving an age-old problem the failure to solve which had blocked the progress of logic for centuries. Moore called Russell's theory of descriptions a 'paradigm of philosophy'. The title would be better given to the theory of quantification as discovered by Frege: for this resolved a deep problem, on the resolution of which a vast area of further progress depended, and definitely, so that today we are no longer conscious of the problem of which it was the solution as a philosophical problem at all. But, for the understanding of Frege, it is necessary to do more than apprehend the magnitude of the discovery: it is necessary to be able to understand its nature as it appeared to him. Much that seems too obvious to us to need saying, now that the quantifier-variable notation is simply a basic part of the received apparatus of logic, struck him forcefully as a penetrating insight; until we can think ourselves into the context in which he was writing, we shall often be baffled to comprehend why he argued as he did.

A sentence, or, in most symbolisms, a mathematical formula, is merely a linear ordering of words or signs. The most natural account of the structure of sentences or formulas would therefore consist of taking them as built by arranging the component words or signs in a linear order. Of course, in giving such an account, certain restrictions would have to be imposed on what sequences of words or signs were to be allowed as meaningful; and these restrictions would derive their rationale from the different roles which different words or signs played. For instance, in the expression '2 + 3', the sign '+' obviously functions in a quite different way from the signs '2' and '3': where they are numerals, '+' is an operator which serves to combine two numerals into a complex expression which is again a numerical term (i.e. one which functions just like a numeral, for example in being able to stand on either side of the '=' sign). But in the expression '(2 + 3) × 6', the parentheses, though again forming part of the linear ordering of the signs, evidently function in quite a different way again: they serve to show that, in relation to the operator '×', the whole expression '2 + 3' is to be treated as unitary. In making any attempt to give an account of the rules governing which expressions of this simple kind are well-formed, or what they mean, it is necessary to jettison the original natural idea that the linear ordering of symbols is a true guide to the process of formation of complex expressions. That is, although of course the final product is precisely a sequence of linearly ordered signs, the process by which it was constructed has to be conceived of, not as consisting of a simultaneous assembling of all the constituent signs, followed by a linear arrangement of them according to determinate rules, but rather as a process of construction which takes place in several stages. Thus the first stage in the construction of the above expression consists in joining '2' and '3' together by '+' to form '2 + 3', and the second stage in joining the expression formed by the first stage to the sign '6' by means of the operator '×'. In the resulting linear expression, the order of construction may be indicated by the use of parentheses, as in '(2 + 3) × 6'; or it may be determined by convention, as in '2 + 3 × 6'; or, as frequently in natural language, the expression may be simply ambiguous as to the order of construction, the ambiguity being left to be resolved by the probabilities conferred by the context.

One of the insights underlying Frege's discovery of the quantifier notation was precisely that this idea, that sentences are constructed in a series of stages, should be applied to the means whereby expressions of generality are incorporated into sentences. In the sentence, 'Everybody envies somebody', multiple generality is involved: it would be represented in quantificational symbolism in such a way that the existential quantifier would lie within the scope of the universal quantifier. It is easy enough to give an account of the truth-conditions of a statement containing a sign of existential generality when that is the only sign of generality occurring in the sentence: the complexities of the medieval theory of *suppositio* arose precisely when the theory attempted to account for an expression of generality governed by another. The difficulty arose out of trying to consider a sentence such as the above as being constructed simultaneously out of its three components, the relational expression here represented by the verb, and the two signs of generality.

Frege's insight consisted in considering the sentence as being constructed in stages, corresponding to the different signs of generality occurring in it. A sentence may be formed by combining a sign of generality with a one-place predicate (1964, v. 1, §§26, 30). The one-place predicate is itself to be thought of as having been formed from a sentence by removing one or more occurrences of some one singular term (proper name). Thus we begin with a sentence such as 'Peter envies John'. From this we form the one-place predicate 'Peter envies ξ' by removing the proper name 'John'—the Greek letter 'ξ' here serving merely to indicate where the gap occurs that is left by the removal of the proper name. This predicate can then be combined with the sign of generality 'somebody' to yield the sentence 'Peter envies somebody'. The resulting sentence may now be subjected to the same process: by removing the proper name 'Peter', we obtain the predicate 'ξ envies somebody', and this may then be combined with the sign of generality 'everybody' to yield the sentence 'Everybody envies somebody'.

Why is this conception, under which the sentence was constructed in stages, more illuminating than the more natural idea according to which it was formed simultaneously out of its three constituents, 'everybody', 'envies' and 'somebody', in exactly the same way that 'Peter envies John' is constructed out of its three components? The reason does not lie in syntax—at least, so far as this concerns only the determination of which sentences are well-formed—but in semantics. It allows the use only of the simple account of the truth-conditions of sentences containing signs of generality that is adequate for those involving only simple generality, as a general account applicable to all signs of generality, provided that the application is made only to the stage of construction at which the sign of generality in question is introduced. We may here evade questions relating to the range of generality, which, though extremely important, are not to the immediate point, by concerning ourselves only with generalization with respect to human beings. A one-place predicate is, then, true of a given individual just in case the sentence which results from inserting a name of that individual in the argument-place (gap) of the predicate is true. A sentence formed by means of this predicate and the sign of generality 'everybody' is true just in case the predicate is true of every individual, and one formed by means of the predicate and the sign of generality 'somebody' is true if the predicate is true of at least one individual. Once we know the constructional history of a sentence involving multiple generality, we can from these simple rules determine the truth-conditions of that sentence, provided only that we already know the truth-conditions of every sentence containing proper names in the places where the signs of generality stand. Thus, 'Everybody envies somebody' is true just in case each of the sentences, 'Peter envies somebody', 'James envies somebody', . . . , is true; and 'Peter envies somebody' is, in turn, true just in case at least one of the sentences, 'Peter envies John', 'Peter envies James', . . . , is true. We are blocked, however, from making the false assertion that 'Everybody envies somebody' is true just in case one of the sentences, 'Everybody envies John', 'Everybody envies James', . . . , is true, by the fact that the final sentence was not constructed by combining the sign of generality 'somebody' with the predicate 'Everybody envies ξ', but by combining the sign of generality 'everybody' and the predicate 'ξ envies somebody'.

In natural language, the form of the sentence does not reveal the order of construction: just as an ad hoc convention leads us to interpret '$2 + 3 \times 6$' as '$2 + (3 \times 6)$' and not as '$(2 + 3) \times 6$', so an ad hoc convention determines that we interpret the sentence 'Everybody envies somebody' as having been constructed in the order in which the sign of generality 'everybody' comes in at the second stage rather than as having been constructed in the alternative order. If we want to express the proposition which would result from taking it in the alternative order, we have to use the passive and say, 'Somebody is envied by everybody', or a form with a relative clause, 'There is somebody whom everybody envies'. This is because the ad hoc convention which we tacitly employ is that the order of construction corresponds to the inverse order of occurrence of the signs of generality in the sentence: when 'everybody' precedes 'somebody', it is taken as having been introduced later in the step-by-step construction, and conversely. Thus the expressive power of natural language depends upon a certain redundancy at a lower level: it is just because the active form 'Peter envies John' is fully equivalent to the passive form 'John is envied by Peter', and to the form with the relative clause, 'John is someone whom Peter envies', that it is possible to use the ad hoc convention to confer distinct and determinate senses on the corresponding forms when signs of generality are present.

Having gained this insight, Frege proceeded to replace the notation used to express generality in natural language with a new notation—that of quantifiers and variables. The point of this new notation was to enable the constructional history of any sentence to be determined unambiguously without the need for any ad hoc convention and therefore also without the need for any underlying redundancy at lower level. Aside from the convention which rules out this possibility, the sentence 'Everybody envies someone' might have been constructed by adjoining the sign of generality 'someone' to the predicate 'Everyone envies ξ'; but the form 'For every x, for some y, x envies y' could not have been constructed by attaching the quantifier 'for some y' to the predicate 'For every x, x envies ξ'. Whereas in natural language, the sign of generality is inserted in the argument-place of the predicate, so that, when two signs of generality occur, one cannot tell save by reference to a special convention which sign of generality was introduced last in the step-by-step construction of the sentence, and which therefore was the predicate to which it was attached, in Frege's notation the sign of generality was to precede the predicate, carrying with it a bound variable which should also occur in the argument-place of the predicate, thus displaying unambiguously how the sentence was formed.

We have seen that, for the convention according to which the signs of generality occurring in a sentence of natural language are to be regarded as having been introduced in the inverse order of their occurrence to be able to work, it is necessary that, for every sentence containing two proper names, there must be an equivalent sentence in which those two names occur in the opposite order. One way in which this is managed is by the use of the passive voice. Clearly this may be generalized: if natural language is to be able to express whatever may be expressed by means of any finite number of quantifiers occurring in any order, and ambiguity is to be avoided by appeal to the convention cited, then it is necessary that, for any sentence of natural language containing any number of distinct proper names, there be an equivalent sentence containing the same names in any permutation of the original order of occurrence. The redundancy that this demands within natural language at the level of sentences not containing signs of generality is very great indeed: but it does not exhaust the redundancy that is required for the means of expression of generality which natural language employs to be workable.

When the notation of quantifiers and variables is used, there is of course no difficulty about predicates which are formed by removing two or more occurrences of the same proper name from some sentence: the two or more gaps—which together constitute a single argument-place—will be filled by the same bound variable. There is no such simple solution when the notation of natural language is used, according to which the sign of generality has to occupy the argument-place of the predicate. Inserting the same sign of generality in each of the several gaps will not have the required effect: if the sentence 'Someone killed someone' were taken to have the sense of 'For some x, x killed x', then there would be no way of expressing 'For some x, for some y, x killed y'. The difficulty is overcome in natural language

by a further redundancy at lower level: for any sentence containing
two or more occurrences of some one proper name, there must be an
equivalent sentence containing only one occurrence of that name;
from this sentence the predicate can then be formed, and a sign of
generality inserted into the single gap representing its argument-
place. A well-known device for accomplishing this result is the use of
pronouns, of the reflexive pronoun in particular. Here it is essential,
for the recognition of valid inferences, that the equivalence between
the different forms be understood: for instance, the validity of the
syllogistic argument:

> Anyone who killed Brutus was a traitor;
> Brutus killed himself:
> Therefore, Brutus was a traitor.

depends upon the equivalence between 'Brutus killed himself' and
'Brutus killed Brutus'.

We can thus say that the ability of natural language to express all
that can be said by means of the notation of quantifiers and variables
depends upon the possibility of finding, for any sentence containing
any number of occurrences of each of any number of proper names,
an equivalent sentence containing only one occurrence of each of
those names, in any arbitrary specified order. Whether natural language actually has this power is not wholly clear: certainly it often
cannot be accomplished without considerable clumsiness.

The quantifier-variable notation thus permitted a single uniform
explanation for each universal quantifier and each existential quantifier. (Frege, observing the well-known equivalence of 'for some
$x, \ldots x \ldots$' with 'it is not the case that, for every x, not $\ldots x \ldots$',
did not in fact employ in his logical symbolism any special sign for the
existential quantifier—not even a defined one; but this point is of
little importance in the present context.) The scholastic logicians had
felt compelled, precisely because they had not hit on the idea of
regarding sentences as built up in a series of stages, to attribute a
different kind of *suppositio* to signs of generality according (as we
should say) to the number of other signs of generality in whose scope
they occurred: but Frege's notation enabled this complexity to be
avoided. An 'explanation' may here be taken either semantically, as a
stipulation of the truth-conditions of sentences containing expressions
of generality, or proof-theoretically, as a stipulation of the rules of
inference governing such sentences. Such explanations would apply
primarily to sentences formed directly by combining a quantifier with

a predicate—sentences in which, in modern terminology, the quantifier in question constitutes the principal logical constant. But it is of the essence of the conception of the step-by-step construction of sentences that such an explanation is adequate to account for all other occurrences of quantifiers. The rule which gives the truth-conditions of a sentence of the form '$(\exists y)A(y)$' does not directly apply to the sentence '$(\forall x)(\exists y)x$ envies y', because it is not of that form; but, as we have seen, provided that we know the truth-conditions of every sentence of the form 'a envies b', we can, using that rule, determine the truth-conditions of the doubly quantified sentence, since, in the process of its formation, a sentence such as '$(\exists y)$ Peter envies y' occurred, which was of that form.

The idea of the step-by-step construction of sentences of course applies more generally than just to the process whereby signs of generality are introduced into sentences: the combination of sentences by means of sentential operators has also to be regarded as part of the step-by-step construction, since evidently it makes a difference to the truth-conditions of a sentence whether a quantifier is regarded as occurring within, e.g., the antecedent of a conditional, or as governing the whole conditional sentence. In just the same way that a single explanation of each kind of quantifier was made possible, so it became possible, as a result of applying the idea of the step-by-step construction to sentential operators, to dispense with the idea of corresponding operators connecting expressions smaller than sentences. In 'Some people are charming and sincere', the connective 'and' does not join sentences together, nor is the sentence as a whole equivalent to any in which 'and' stands between two sentences; but the predicate 'ξ is charming and sincere', to which the sign of generality 'some people' has been attached to form the sentence in question, was derived from a sentence such as 'Peter is charming and sincere', which is equivalent to a sentence, 'Peter is charming and Peter is sincere', in which 'and' stands between two sentences. Thus the use of 'and' to conjoin adjectives can be regarded as another of the devices employed by natural language to convert a sentence containing two occurrences of a proper name into an equivalent one containing only one occurrence of it. Although it is not true that connectives such as 'and' stand only between whole sentences, still the truth-conditions of any sentence containing such a connective are determined once it is known what the truth-conditions are of a sentence in which it does conjoin subordinate sentences; since, in the step-by-step construction of the final sentence, the step at which the connective was originally introduced yielded precisely a sentence of this kind.

In the course of this account, a second fundamental idea, besides that of the step-by-step construction of sentences, has been introduced: that, namely, of the formation of complex predicates out of sentences by the omission of one or more occurrences of a single proper name (1979, pp. 204, 273). Here it is of great importance that the predicate itself is not thought of as having been built up out of its component parts: we do not need to invoke the conception of the conjunction of two predicates, 'ξ is charming' and 'ξ is sincere', to explain the formation of the predicate 'ξ is charming and sincere'; nor do we need to invoke the idea of the application of a quantifier to a two-place predicate, with respect to a specific argument-place, to explain the formation of the predicate '$(\exists y)\xi$ killed y'; nor, again, do we need the operation of identifying the argument-places of a two-place predicate to explain the formation of 'ξ killed ξ'. We do not, for present purposes, need to invoke the notion of a two-place predicate at all. Given a basic fund of atomic sentences, all other sentences can be regarded as being formed by means of a sequence of operations, which are of three kinds: the application of sentential operators to sentences to form new sentences; the omission from a sentence of one or more occurrences of a proper name to form a one-place predicate; and the application of a quantifier to a one-place predicate to form a sentence.

This account is not precisely the same as that given in a modern textbook of predicate logic: but it is essentially so. Modern symbolism usually differs from Frege's in allowing as well-formed expressions containing variables, known as 'free variables', not bound by any quantifier. Nothing exactly corresponding to a free variable appears in Frege's symbolism. A Greek letter, such as the 'ξ' we have been using, is not properly part of the symbolic language: it is merely a device for indicating where the argument-place of a predicate occurs. It is usual, in modern symbolism, to use the very same letters as 'free variables' as may be used as bound variables. In this case, the statement of the formation rules (rules for the construction of sentences) can be stated very simply, by describing first the formation of 'open sentences' (expressions like sentences save for possibly containing free variables): no separate operation of forming a predicate has to be stipulated, but only the operation of prefixing a quantifier to an open sentence, thus converting into a bound variable the free variable identical in form to the variable attached to the new quantifier. A sentence can then be specified as being an open sentence which contains no free variables. (In the present context the presence of schematic letters is being disregarded: for simplicity, we are considering only the case of a language for which there is a fixed interpretation for the individual constants and predicate- and function-symbols.) This simplification is, however, more or less illusory. When the truth-conditions of sentences are explained, this has to be done inductively, and, since sentences have to be constructed not only out of other sentences but out of open sentences, what in fact has to be defined is the truth or falsity of an open sentence relative to some assignment to the free variables of individuals from the domain of the bound variables. In regard to any given open sentence, such an assignment confers upon the free variables occurring in it the effective status of individual constants or proper names. Moreover, those clauses in the inductive stipulation of the truth-conditions of open sentences which relate to the quantifiers are stated in terms of the truth-conditions of the open sentence to which the quantifier is prefixed which result from holding fixed the assignments to the free variables other than the one which becomes bound by the new quantifier, and allowing the assignment to the latter free variable to run through all the individuals in the domain. This stipulation essentially corresponds to considering the predicate which results from removing every occurrence of the 'free variable' due to be bound by the new quantifier, and asking of which individuals it is true; the notion of a one-place predicate's being *true of* a given individual being explained in the same way as with Frege. Thus we can say that, in the standard form of explanation, a free variable is treated exactly as if it were a proper name at every stage in the step-by-step construction of a given sentence up to that at which a quantifier is to be prefixed which will bind that variable: at that stage, however, it is treated exactly as if it were one of the Greek letters Frege uses to indicate the argument-place in a predicate. Hence we have no real contrast with Frege's explanation of the matter at all, but essentially the very same explanation.

For Frege, the sentence resulting from attaching a universal quantifier to a predicate is true just in case the predicate is true of everything; and we understand, in turn, the notion of the predicate's being true of a given individual because we know this to be equivalent to the truth of a sentence formed by putting a name of that individual in the argument-place of the predicate. Frege did not take this form of explanation as presupposing that we have already a language which actually contains a name for every object: that would make it possible to quantify only over a finite or denumerable domain. Rather, he is making the assumption that, whenever we understand the truth-conditions for any sentence containing (one or more occurrences of) a proper name, we likewise understand what it is for any arbitrary object to satisfy the predicate which results from removing (those occurrences of) that proper name from the sentence, irrespective of whether we actually have, or can form, in our language a name of that object. Thus, where the predicate in question is 'A(ξ)', and 'c' is any proper name, then of course the predicate 'A(ξ)' could have been formed from the sentence 'A(c)' by removing (certain, perhaps all, occurrences of) the name 'c' from 'A(c)'; and Frege's assumption is that, if we understand 'A(c)', then we likewise understand, for any object whatever, what the truth-conditions would be of a sentence formed by putting a name of that object, rather than the name 'c', in the argument-place of 'A(ξ)'. And this, again, is precisely the assumption which underlies the explanation of the truth-conditions of quantified sentences which is framed in terms of 'free variables'. Under this explanation, we are supposed to be considering an open sentence 'A(x)' as having certain determinate truth-conditions relative to some particular assignment of an object in the domain of the variables to the free variable 'x': and now, in order to take the step necessary to grasp the truth-conditions of the quantified sentence '($\forall x$)A(x)', we have to consider the truth-conditions for 'A(x)' which result from assigning each object in the domain to the free variable 'x' in turn. Thus it is assumed that, simultaneously with our grasp of the truth-conditions of 'A(x)' under the assignment to 'x' with which we started out, we also understand its truth-conditions under every other assignment to that free variable which could be made. And this assumption is precisely the same as Frege's. Once again, if the domain of the individual variables is non-denumerable, then it is impossible that we should actually have in our language a name for every object in the domain, so that we cannot in such a case actually equate the truth of '($\forall x$)A(x)' with the conjoint truth of all the sentences 'A(a)', 'A(b)', 'A(c)', . . . , formed by putting each name that exists in the language in the argument-place of 'A(ξ)': nevertheless, the assumption which I have stated is made for this case also, just as Frege made the same assumption.

It would thus be quite wrong to oppose Frege's account of the formation of sentences containing signs of generality (quantifiers), and of the truth-conditions of such sentences, to that which is now standard: the difference is purely superficial. But, in order to understand Frege, and, indeed, to gain a correct understanding of the matter in general, it is preferable to consider the explanation as given in Frege's terms. 'Free variables' are merely a convenient notational device which simplifies the statement of the formation rules: they correspond to no type of expression for which there is any need in a language actually in functional use, but exist merely, as required, to serve the alternating roles of individual constant and indicator of the whereabouts of the argument-place in the predicate.

How plausible, then, is the assumption which underlies both Frege's and the now standard explanations of the quantifiers? It is very easy to express that assumption in a manner which makes it appear more plausible than it in fact is. We do this if we state the assumption by saying that, if we understand the truth-conditions of a sentence 'A(c)', then we likewise understand the conditions under which the predicate 'A(ξ)', formed from that sentence, is true of any given object. Such an assumption is indeed plausible: but that is precisely because we have smuggled in, by means of the word 'given', the presupposition that we have some quite determinate object in mind. For an object to be 'given' to us, we must have some means of referring to it or of indicating which object it is that is in question. Perhaps these means of referring to the object lie outside the circumscribed language which we happen currently to be treating of: but, in that case, it would be easy to imagine that language as being extended in such a way as to include a means of referring to the object in question.

It is, indeed, extremely plausible to say that, if 'c' and 'd' are two proper names within a language, and we understand a sentence 'A(c)', then we must also understand the sentence 'A(d)'—provided, of course, that we understand the name 'd'. It is true that the plausibility vanishes if we choose names of objects of quite different categories, e.g. a river and a political party; since, in such a case, the result of the substitution may be to convert a quite straightforward sentence into one about whose meaning, if there is one, we are in the dark: but that is not the sort of case with which we are at present concerned. We are, on the contrary, tacitly assuming that all the primitive predicates and functional expressions of the language are defined for all the objects in the domain of the variables: and, if this is so, then the same must be true for all the complex predicates as well. The assumption is plausible just because we understand the sentence by understanding the senses of its constituent expressions: since we understand the conditions under which 'A(c)' is true by understanding not only what object the name 'c' stands for but also by understanding the expressions which compose the predicate 'A(ξ)', we must in exactly the same way be able to determine the truth-conditions of 'A(d)', once we know for what object the name 'd' stands.

But, of course, this is not the nub of the question: the difficulty arose only because we may not assume that our language contains a name for every object, since, in particular, there may be too many objects for us to have names to go round. To imagine a situation in which we are considering whether or not the predicate is true of some 'given' object is to treat a case in which it is merely accidental that the language we have in mind lacks a name of the object in question. In such a case, the plausibility of the assumption that, from our understanding of 'A(c)', we can derive the conditions under which the predicate 'A(ξ)' is true of the given object, is virtually the same as that of the assumption that we can derive the truth-conditions of another sentence 'A(d)', given the sense of 'd'. But what is in question is not a case of this kind at all: what is in question is, rather, whether we can assume that, from a knowledge of the truth-conditions of 'A(c)', we can derive a knowledge of the conditions under which the predicate 'A(ξ)' will be true of all the objects in a domain, when we do not and could not have the means of referring to each of those objects.

This is evidently a difficult question, and, for the present, we shall not pursue it: for the time being it is enough to have isolated it. What we are at present concerned to understand is the perspective on the philosophical problems of logic and the analysis of language which Frege's discovery of quantification imposed upon him.

The most general lesson which Frege derived from his discovery was a certain disrespect for natural language. The intricate medieval theories of *suppositio* had failed to provide a solution, adequate for every case, of the problem of multiple generality with which the scholastic logicians wrestled for so long. As soon as Frege had hit upon his solution, the reason for the failure of the scholastics became at once apparent: they had followed too closely the leads provided by the forms of expression employed in natural language. As far as the sentence-structure of natural language is concerned, signs of generality such as 'someone' and 'anyone' behave exactly like proper names— they occupy the same positions in sentences and are governed by the same grammatical rules: it is only when the truth-conditions or the implicational powers of sentences containing them are considered that the difference appears. Likewise, as we have seen, the final form of the sentence gives no clue to the step-by-step construction of it in terms of which its sense has to be explained. Misled by these two superficial features of natural language, the scholastic logicians had attempted to explain signs of generality by theories which attributed to them the power of standing for objects, in a manner similar to, though more complicated than, that in which a proper name stands for its bearer, theories which, moreover, ignored the step-by-step construction of the sentences in which the signs of generality occurred, and depended merely on the varying kinds of *suppositio* attributed to those signs of generality. Frege, on the other hand, had solved the problem which had baffled logicians for millennia by ignoring natural language. He had made no attempt to give any systematic account of the truth-conditions or implicational powers of those sentences of natural language which involve multiple generality: instead, he had devised a wholly new means for the expression of generality, for which a sharp and straightforward explanation could be given. If the sentences of natural language had a precise and unambiguous sense, then anyone who understood such a sentence would be able to render it by means of the notation for generality which Frege had devised; if not, then so much the worse for natural language. In neither case was there any need either for a direct account of the means for expressing generality in natural language, or for a set of rules for translating sentences of natural language into Frege's improved language.

This state of affairs induced in Frege the attitude that natural language is a very imperfect instrument for the expression of thought (1979, pp. 6–7). At best, it works by means of principles which are buried deep beneath the surface, and are complex and to a large extent arbitrary (1979, p. 67); at worst, it allows the construction of sentences allowing of different interpretations, or possessing only an indeterminate sense (1979, p. 270). For reasons not connected with the expression of generality, Frege indeed came later to the conclusion that natural language is in principle incoherent: that is, it would be impossible to devise a set of rules determining the truth-conditions of sentences of natural language which would both agree with the way those sentences are used and avoid the assignment, under certain conditions, of different truth-values to the same sentence (1980, p. 68). This, of course, should not in itself be taken as a very paradoxical accusation against natural language: it must necessarily hold good if it be true—as it evidently is—that there are intrinsically ambiguous sentences of natural language, sentences, that is, for which no general rule, but only a common-sense appeal to probabilities, can remove the ambiguity. All that can be at issue is how deep this incoherence of natural language lies, that is, how fundamental are the principles governing its structure which would need to be modified if the incoherence were to be removed. Frege believed it to be very deep indeed (1977, p. 13). Undoubtedly, his predisposition to adopt such a belief was formed by the experience which the discovery of the quantifier-variable notation had given him.

Secondly, the conception of the step-by-step construction of sentences was deeply impressed upon Frege as a key to the analysis of language. Here it is perhaps worth while to interpose an observation which Frege did not make. There has been much inconclusive discussion by philosophers during the past few decades about where the boundary lies between logic and other branches of philosophy. Much of this discussion has resulted in the conclusion that the boundary is more or less arbitrary. Any branch of philosophy is, on this view, concerned with the analysis of the meanings of some range of words or forms of expression, with determining the truth-conditions and inferential powers of sentences containing those words or employing those forms of expression: since this is precisely what logicians do with respect to the so-called logical constants, no difference of principle appears, and the suggestion is made that the term 'logical constant' cannot be defined save by listing the expressions to which it is to apply. It is this view which forms the background to the vogue for phrases like 'the logic of achievement-verbs', 'the logic of colour-words' and even (God save us) 'the logic of God-talk'.

But, in fact, ever since Frege inaugurated the era of modern logic, there has been to hand a simple and precise principle of distinction. The basic idea of the step-by-step construction of sentences involves a distinction between two classes of sentences and, correspondingly, two types of expression. Sentences can be divided into atomic and complex ones: atomic sentences are formed out of basic constituents none of which are, or have been formed from, sentences, while complex sentences arise, through a step-by-step construction, from the application of certain sentence-forming devices to other sentences, or to 'incomplete' expressions such as predicates themselves formed from sentences, the whole construction of course beginning with operations on atomic sentences. The expressions which go to make up atomic sentences—proper names (individual constants), primitive predicates and relational expressions—form one type: sentence-forming operators, such as sentential operators and quantifiers, which induce the reiterable transformations which lead from atomic to complex sentences, form the other. (With the latter should also be grouped any term-forming operators, such as the description operator, which form singular terms from incomplete expressions such as predicates.) Logic properly so called may be thought of as concerned only with words and expressions of the second type, to which it is apparent that not only do quantifiers and sentential operators belong, but equally modal expressions such as 'possibly', 'necessarily', 'may', 'must', etc. With words and expressions of the first type, logic is, on this view, concerned only schematically: that is, it is concerned with the general rules governing the subdivision of words of the first type into different logical categories—proper names, one-place predicates, relational expressions, and so forth—and with the ways in which words of these various different types can be put together to form atomic sentences; but not with the senses of any particular words or expressions of these different categories. Thus, for instance, the question whether the sense of the word 'prefer' is such as to determine the relation for which 'John prefers ξ to ζ' stands as transitive is of no concern to the logician as such: by contrast, the phrase 'modal logic' is well taken. This principle of distinction has, indeed, the status only of a proposal: but it agrees so well with practice, and provides so clear a rationale for differentiating between logical constants and words of other kinds, that there can be little motive for rejecting it.*

We saw that, in applying the conception of the step-by-step construction of sentences to the expression of generality, it became necessary for Frege to invoke the general notion of a one-place predicate, thought of, not as synthesized from its components, but as formed by omission of a proper name from a sentence. Since this notion of a predicate is so crucial to Frege's whole understanding of philosophical logic, it is worth while to dwell a little more explicitly upon its character than Frege himself did. In order to give a complete account of the structure of the sentences of a language, it is necessary to describe the process whereby an atomic sentence is put together out of its parts as well as the various operations by means of which complex sentences may be constructed step by step from atomic ones. We have seen that, for Frege, these latter operations are of three kinds: first, the use of sentential operators, that is, either the attachment of the sign of negation to a sentence or the joining of two sentences by means of a

---

*The one expression normally treated as a logical constant which, on this principle, would be ruled out as belonging to the first type, is the sign of identity. The justification for this exception is quite different, and might be expressed as follows. Let us call a *second-level condition* any condition which, for some domain of objects, is defined, as being satisfied or otherwise, by every predicate which is in turn defined over that domain of objects. Among such second-level conditions, we may call a *quantifier condition* any which is invariant under each permutation of the domain of objects: i.e. for any predicate '$F(\xi)$' and any permutation φ, it satisfies '$F(\xi)$' just in case it satisfies that predicate which applies to just those objects $\varphi(a)$, where '$F(\xi)$' is true of a. Then we allow as also being a logical constant any expression which, with the help of the universal and existential quantifiers and the sentential operators, allows us to express a quantifier condition which could not be expressed by means of those two quantifiers and the sentential operators alone. Thus, the sign of identity is recognized, on this criterion, as a logical constant, since it allows us to express the condition that a predicate applies to at most one object, which cannot be expressed without it.

connective such as 'or' or 'and'; secondly, the formation of a one-place predicate from a sentence; and, thirdly, the attachment of a quantifier to a one-place predicate to form a sentence. If we were considering natural language, we should certainly have to add other operations to this list, for instance, the introduction of modal expressions; but Frege was, as we have noted, primarily concerned with the structure of a language adequate for the expression of mathematical propositions, to which many of such additional devices are irrelevant. As for atomic sentences, Frege considered them as constructed out of expressions of four kinds: logically simple proper names; functional expressions; predicates; and relational expressions. These categories of expression are, of course, precisely those which are treated of in ordinary first-order predicate logic, which is unsurprising, since the languages of which contemporary logic treats have been very little extended beyond Frege's symbolic language (save for the introduction of languages with infinitely long formulas): but, again, for an adequate treatment of the sentences which natural language permits us to form, further ingredients would have to be added—none of Frege's categories could comprise either adverbs or tense-inflections, for example. But, once more, these defects are not relevant to the analysis of the language of mathematics.

To characterize the general form of an atomic sentence, we have first to specify how a *singular term* is, in general, constructed. This specification is recursive, namely: a simple proper name constitutes a singular term; and a singular term can be formed by inserting singular terms into the argument-places of functional expressions. A one-place functional expression is here considered as an expression with a gap in it, indicating where a singular term is to be placed in order to form from it a more complex singular term. Normally, this gap will occur at the end of the expression, as in such instances as 'the capital of ξ' and 'the father of ξ': but there is no reason in principle why it should not occur at the beginning, as in 'ξ's father', or, for that matter, in the middle; all that is necessary is that it should be determinate where the term that represents the argument is to be inserted. On the other hand, there is no room, in this connection, for the admission of functional expressions containing two or more gaps, considered as having each to be filled by the same proper name or other term. Functional expressions with two gaps will have, indeed, to be considered, but these will be two-place ones, like 'the eldest child of ξ and ζ' or 'the mid-point between ξ and ζ' or 'the greatest common divisor of ξ and ζ': here the two gaps will be considered as being, in general, filled by two different terms. Since the specification of what constitutes a singular term is recursive—that is, certain expressions are recognized as singular terms outright, and instructions are then given for forming new singular terms out of already given ones—it could with reason be said that even the process of forming so-called atomic sentences is in fact a step-by-step one: but the important fact is that we are not here forming new sentences out of previously formed *sentences*, as is the case with the quantifiers and the sentential operators.

One place predicates and two- or more-placed relational expressions are then conceived in the same general way as one-, two- or more-placed functional expressions: namely simply as collocations of words or symbols with one or more gaps. The difference is, of course, that the process of filling the gaps cannot be reiterated: what results from inserting singular terms in the gap of a predicate or the gaps of a relational expression is an (atomic) sentence, out of which further sentences can be formed only by the different processes we have already reviewed. But the same observation holds good for predicates and relational expressions as for functional expressions: there is no place here for admitting, say, predicates with more than one gap representing distinct occurrences of the same singular term.

At this point some remarks become necessary about Frege's terminology. The distinction was made above between logically simple proper names and the complex singular terms that can be constructed out of them by means of functional expressions. Frege was perfectly well aware of this distinction: indeed, he was very insistent on the difference between a logically simple and a logically complex expression (1964, v. 2, §66; 1979, 207–9). A logically simple expression may be phonemically or typographically exceedingly complex: but what makes it logically simple is that there do not exist any general rules, the knowledge of which belongs to a speaker of the language, whereby its sense can be determined from the way it is made up out of its constituents. In the case of a predicate or relational expression, a logically simple expression may even be discontinuous, as, for example, 'ξ took ζ to task'. There is in fact complexity here, because of the tense-inflection, but we are here overlooking this factor: it is plain that an understanding of the words 'took', 'to' and 'task' will not suffice, or even help, to determine the meaning of 'took . . . to task'. But Frege made an eccentric use of the phrase 'proper name' to cover everything normally meant by (and everything defined above as) a 'singular term' (1952, p. 47n): 'proper name' did not for him imply 'logically simple', as it normally does. In what follows I shall frequently employ the expression 'singular term' or just the word 'term' where Frege would have written 'proper name': but I shall never use the expression 'proper name' specifically in its strict sense, to imply 'logically simple', without signalling the fact.

It would be an error to take the notion of logical simplicity, as conceived by Frege, as involving anything more than is implied by the definition given above. Many philosophical writers, for instance Russell, have taken it as a mark of a proper name—at least of what has a truly genuine claim to the title of 'proper name'—that it has an irreducible simplicity: it is not merely itself devoid of logical complexity, but no expression having the same meaning as it could be logically complex. There is no trace of this idea in Frege. A logically simple expression is, for him, merely one which is not composed of subordinate expressions each possessing its own sense and so contributing to determining the sense of the whole: there is no requirement that the sense which is borne by that expression *could* not be carried by one which was in this way logically complex. If a name or other expression is introduced by definition as a brief equivalent of some complex expression, then the expression so defined will itself be logically simple, even though its sense has been stipulated to be the same as that of the complex expression. Of course, we may distinguish between those expressions which are introduced by definition and those which are not; but, since Frege says very little about the senses of words not introduced by definition, this will help us little with the exegesis of Frege. Frege several times emphasized that it is impossible that every word of a language should be introduced by definition (1977, p. 42), because a definition presupposes a prior understanding of the words used in the defining expression, and the resulting circularity would make it impossible that anything should be learned from this system of explanations. He also clearly stated that the sense of a complex expression is to be regarded as made up out of the senses of the constituent words: it follows that a simple word, introduced by definition as the equivalent of a complex expression, has a complex sense (1979, p. 255). By contrast, however, Frege nowhere discussed under what conditions the sense of a word should be recognized as simple. While he stressed that it is impossible that every word should be defined, it is only very seldom that he stated, of any particular word, that it was impossible that it should be defined; examples for which he did hold this are the sign of identity, the word 'true' and the terms 'object' and 'function' (1894, p. 320; 1977, p. 13n; 1952, p. 42). Frege appears to have acknowledged that the sense of such an indefinable expression is simple in some more ultimate way than that of words which merely happen to have been introduced otherwise than by definition, but which might have been defined if a different choice of starting-point had been made. But the notion of unanalysability played no great part in his thought, and is in no way associated by him with proper names; in particular, he advanced no thesis to the effect that every sentence is analysable into one composed wholly of indefinable expressions.

A further feature of Frege's terminological usage needs mention. He normally used the word 'relation' to mean 'binary relation' only, and similarly in talking about expressions for relations. When he wanted to refer to ternary relations, or to expressions for them, he expressly mentioned the number of arguments (1979, p. 249): he never referred to relations of higher degree at all, nor used the word 'relation' independently of how many arguments there were. He seldom used the word 'predicate', preferring his own neologism 'concept-word': but I shall rarely follow this example.

Properly speaking, in discussing the formation of atomic sentences, another kind of functional expression ought to have been mentioned, namely a functional expression of second level, which carries a bound variable with it, and which, in order to form a singular term, is attached to a predicate (the argument-place of which is filled with a bound variable corresponding to that carried by the functional expression or operator). This kind of expression in fact plays a role of the utmost importance in Frege's construction of the foundations of arithmetic: the most familiar example is the definite description operator (whose role in natural language is effected by the definite article). Many accounts of the foundations of logic in fact assume that the only candidates in natural language for the position of complex singular terms are what Russell called 'definite descriptions', i.e. expressions formed by prefixing the definite article to a (grammatically singular) predicative expression. Whether such accounts do or do not accord to such expressions that status of complex singular terms depends upon whether they reject or accept Russell's Theory of Descriptions. If they reject it, then such expressions are to be represented in symbolic notation as singular terms formed exactly in the way described above: that is, 'the founder of Rome' is to be construed as having the form 'the x such that x founded Rome'. On such accounts, first-level functional expressions such as those described above do not occur in natural language. Of course, it would be possible to employ a language which possessed a description operator but no first-level functional expressions: but it would become exceedingly cumbersome to do this in mathematics, as a little experimentation with a formalization of arithmetic in such a language—involving the replacement of the symbols for addition, multiplication and exponentiation by symbols for the corresponding ternary relations—will readily show. That is why neither Frege nor modern accounts of predicate logic dispense with such first-level operators. As to whether natural language contains such operators, or gets on, by means of the description operator, without them, the question has no sharp sense. The means for forming definite descriptions in natural language are certainly far more complex and varied than the simple type of construction carried out by means of first-level functional expressions as described above; at the same time, they are far from identical with the use of the device of a description operator, which involves the employment of bound variables, which do not occur in natural language. Most of the complex singular terms of natural language, therefore, are, properly speaking, neither terms formed by functional expressions nor ones formed with the description operator. Still, if it is a matter of convenience of representation, it is surely more cumbersome and unnatural to take 'the capital of France' as a concealed form for 'the x such that x is a capital of France' than to take it, as Frege does, as analogous to (say) '4!' (1952, p. 31).

Nevertheless, Frege did admit, and make essential use of, second-level operators of the same category as the description operator, and, to that extent, the characterization of atomic sentences given above is incomplete. Of course, once such operators are included, then the processes of forming singular terms, preparatory to forming atomic sentences, cannot be cleanly severed from the processes of forming complex sentences: for the sentence from which the predicate was formed, to which the term-forming operator is to be attached, may itself have been highly complex, involving quantifiers and sentential operators. The omission of such second-level operators in the above account was intended to avoid this complication, the better to focus attention on the important point.

This point is the necessity for distinguishing clearly—as Frege himself was at no great pains to do—between the notion of a predicate as it is required for Frege's account of the expression of generality, and the notion of a predicate as required in explaining the structure of atomic sentences. These two notions are, in fact, needed to fulfil roles of quite different kinds. The only kind of predicate or relational expression we need consider when we are concerned with the structure of atomic sentences is one which is logically simple (1979, p. 17). In order to explain how we grasp the sense of such a sentence as 'Brutus killed Caesar', for example, we need only consider it as composed of its three constituent expressions, the two (simple) proper names 'Brutus' and 'Caesar' and the (simple) relational expression 'killed' (here I am, as in all cases, once more prescinding from the actual complexity of root and tense-inflection within the word 'killed'). The relational expression may here be regarded as a simple unitary expression, as much a linguistic entity capable of standing on its own as are the two proper names. Like them, it cannot form a sentence standing on its own (unless the rest of the sentence is understood from the context); but, like them, it constitutes a word that is physically capable of being detached from the sentence. If we represent it by means of Greek letters to show its argument-places, namely as 'ξ killed ζ', this is only in order to show where the proper names (or other singular terms) have to be put in relation to it in order to form a sentence: contrast, for example, 'ξ is married to ζ' with 'ξ and ζ are man and wife'. These indications how the link between relational expression and proper names is to be made have to be attached to the relational expression, and not to the proper names, since how the link is made depends upon it and not upon the proper names: there is no general rule determining that, e.g., 'Brutus' has to come at the beginning, or at the end, or in the middle, of an atomic sentence. But there is no sense whatever in which 'ξ killed ζ' is to be thought of as formed from the sentence 'Brutus killed Caesar', or any other like it: on the contrary, that sentence was formed from it, together with the two proper names.

The notion of a complex predicate, thought of as formed from a sentence by omission of one or more occurrences of a proper name, is required, by contrast, only in order to explain sentences formed by attaching a quantifier to it (or, more generally, expressions formed by attaching to it some variable-binding operator, for instance the description operator). This notion is needed at this stage because it is required to give an account of the sense of the quantifier and this involves an account of the truth-conditions of the most general form of sentence that can be constructed by applying that quantifier: the only correct characterization of this general form of sentence is 'A sentence formed by attaching the quantifier to a complex predicate'. Once the notion of a complex predicate has had to be introduced for this purpose, then it also becomes necessary to recognize the complex predicate as occurring in the sort of sentence from which it was formed: it is this which gives rise to what people have in mind when they speak about different, equally legitimate, logical analyses of one and the same sentence. But it is important to notice for what purpose this sort of 'analysis' is needed. The representation of 'Brutus killed Caesar' as composed of a (complex) one-place predicate 'ξ killed Caesar' and, in its argument-place, the name 'Brutus', is required only in order to state the general principle to which we are appealing when we recognize an inference from this sentence, together with, say, 'Anyone who killed Caesar is an honourable man', to the conclusion, 'Brutus is an honourable man'. We need this representation of the sentence, that is to say, in giving an account of inferences in which it and also some sentence involving the attachment of a sign of generality to the complex predicate in question both figure. The representation of the sentence as consisting of 'Brutus' and 'ξ killed Caesar' is quite irrelevant to any explanation of the way in which the sense of the atomic sentence is determined from that of its constituents. An inference may easily arise in which it is necessary, in order to explain the general scheme of inference appealed to, to consider the sentence, 'If Brutus killed Caesar, then Brutus's wife hated Brutus', as composed of the name 'Brutus' and the predicate, 'If ξ killed Caesar, then Brutus's wife hated ξ'. But the possibility of giving such an 'analysis' of the sentence has no bearing on the process by which we form the sentence, or on that by which we come to grasp its sense. We understand the sentence by reference to the process by which it was formed, namely as being put together out of two atomic sentences joined by the connective 'if', those atomic sentences having in turn been constructed by linking singular terms and relational expressions; the thought that one might recognize the complex predicate cited above as occurring within that sentence could be utterly remote from the mind of someone who had the firmest grasp upon its meaning.

In the same way, the notion of a complex relational expression, considered as formed from a sentence by the omission of one or more occurrences of each of two proper names, is strictly needed only when it is desired to introduce, or required to explain, some operator carrying with it two bound variables: for instance, if one wanted to introduce an operator 'Tx,y:' which, attached to a relational expression '$A(\xi,\zeta)$', yielded a sentence '$T\ x,y$: $A(x,y)$' having the sense of 'For all x and y, if $A(x,y)$, then not $A(y,x)$'. It is true that, although not strictly needed, the notion of a complex relational expression may be very useful in connection with what are known within formalized logical systems as 'derived rules of inference'. Thus, for instance, from any particular sentence of the form '$(\exists x)(\forall y)A(x,y)$' it is possible to infer—if desired, by a series of very simple steps—the conclusion '$(\forall y)(\exists x)A(x,y)$'. In any particular instance, there would be no occasion to invoke the notion of a complex relational expression. But once someone has carried out this chain of reasoning in several particular instances, he may notice the general pattern, and wish to record it mentally (or otherwise) to be appealed to in the course of subsequent chains of reasoning, without having on each occasion to go through all the individual steps. To express the general form of the inference, it is necessary to employ a schematic representation—such as the '$A(\xi,\ \zeta)$' used above—for an arbitrary complex relational expression; and the recognition of the general pattern thus constitutes an implicit appeal to the general notion of a complex relational expression.

Thus a simple predicate or relational expression must be recognized as occurring in any sentence in which it does occur, if we are to understand the sense of that sentence, or even recognize it as well-formed; whereas the notion of a complex predicate has to be invoked only when we have to deal with quantifiers or other expressions of generality; and, when the argument-place of a complex predicate is filled, not by a bound variable, but by a singular term, then it is unnecessary, in order to understand the sentence in which that predicate occurs, to recognize the predicate as occurring in it. Indeed, so much is implicit in saying that the complex predicate is formed, not directly out of its constituent expressions, but from a sentence in which it occurs. When the argument-place of the predicate is filled by a term, then it is only for a different purpose and in special circumstances that it becomes necessary to recognize the predicate as occurring in a sentence: namely in order to recognize the validity of certain arguments of which that sentence may form premiss or conclusion.

Unless this radical difference between the roles of the notions of simple and complex predicates is clearly apprehended, it will be easy to become confused about Frege's notion of an incomplete expression. Frege himself did not draw attention to this difference of role: having demonstrated the need for appealing to the notion of a complex predicate, if expressions of generality are to be explained, he tacitly assimilated simple predicates to complex ones. And, indeed, in one sense such an assimilation represents an economy. Once we have acquired the notion of a complex predicate, we cannot refuse to allow, as a degenerate case, the 'complex' predicate 'ξ snores', considered as formed from such a sentence as 'Herbert snores' by omission of the name 'Herbert'; it would then seem quite redundant to insist on considering, as a separate linguistic entity, the simple predicate '. . . snores'. Nevertheless, it remains the case that, strictly speaking, if 'ξ snores' is treated as a complex predicate, on all fours with, say, 'If anyone snores, then ξ snores', we do need to recognize the separate existence of the simple predicate '. . . snores' as well: for, precisely because the 'complex' predicate 'ξ snores' has to be regarded as formed from such a sentence as 'Herbert snores', it cannot itself be one of the ingredients from which 'Herbert snores' was formed, and thus cannot be that whose sense, on Frege's own account, contributes to composing the sense of 'Herbert snores'. Rather, if there is to be economy, it is the degenerate 'complex' predicate that should be dispensed with, with the sign of generality, in 'Everyone snores', being regarded as in this special case attached directly to the simple predicate.

Now complex predicates form the prototype for Frege's general notion of an 'incomplete' expression (1979, pp. 228, 243). Such expressions are said by him to contain gaps, and, further, to be *unselb-*

ständig: they cannot subsist—they cannot stand up, one might say—on their own (1960, §60; 1979, pp. 177, 201). If one considers complex predicates formed by the omission of more than one occurrence of the same proper name from a sentence, the purport of this is immediately clear. The complex predicate 'ξ killed ξ' cannot be regarded as literally *part* of the sentences in which it occurs (1964, v. 1, §1): it is not a word or a string of words, not even a discontinuous string. There is no part in common to the sentences 'Brutus killed Brutus' and 'Cassius killed Cassius' which is not also part of the sentence 'Brutus killed Caesar': yet the predicate 'ξ killed ξ' is said to occur in the first two and not in the third. Such a complex predicate is, rather, to be regarded as a *feature* in common to the two sentences, the feature, namely, that in both the simple relational expression '. . . killed . . .' occurs with the same name in both of its argument-places. (Not all sentences in which the complex predicate is said to occur will be of that simple structure: but all will have such a sentence as one of their ancestors in their constructional history.) It is precisely in this sense that an expression is said by Frege to be 'incomplete': it does not consist merely of some sequence of words or symbols, but in the occurrence within sentences of such a sequence standing in a certain uniform relation to terms occurring in those sentences. It is for this reason that it cannot liberally be removed from a sentence in which it occurs and displayed on its own: we can only indicate the common feature of various sentences which we have in mind by the use, together with words or symbols belonging to the language, of the Greek letters which represent argument-places. And it is, in turn, just because the complex predicate is thus not really an expression—a bit of language—in its own right, that we are compelled to regard it as formed from a sentence rather than as built up of its components.

When we consider this doctrine in terms of complex predicates, as we have seen these are needed to explain the formation of quantified sentences, the notion of incomplete expressions appears quite unperplexing. The reason why people have found it difficult to understand Frege's doctrine of incomplete expressions is largely that they have concentrated on the degenerate case in which there is a simple predicate corresponding to the complex one: or rather, failing to observe the difference in kind between simple and complex predicates, they apply Frege's doctrine to simple ones, and then, not unnaturally, find themselves unable to see its point. This is precisely one of the cases in which Frege, by looking at things from the perspective induced by his discovery of quantification, obtained a very different view of them from the familiar one. Philosophers tackling the notions of subject and predicate naturally incline to scrutinize very simple examples—atomic sentences, proper names (strictly so called) and simple predicates. But for Frege, *the* important notion of a predicate was just that notion of a complex predicate which his discovery of quantification had shown to be required. It is therefore unsurprising that he finds quite different things to say about predicates in general from those which philosophers adopting a more conventional approach find it natural to say. In contrasting Frege's approach with the traditional one, I am not merely opposing what Frege did to what used to happen in earlier times: on the contrary, even so recent a work as Strawson's *Individuals* resolutely holds to what I have described as the traditional approach to the topic of subject and predicate.

If one applies Frege's doctrine that predicates are incomplete in a sense in which proper names and other singular terms are not to simple predicates, and considers only them, then one will, rightly, be at a loss to understand Frege's thesis. Simple predicates are *selbständig* in the way that complex ones are not: they are merely words or strings of words which can quite straightforwardly be written down. In one sense, of course, they are incomplete—they do not constitute a sentence, a 'complete utterance': but, in *that* sense, proper names are equally incomplete. It is true that, in order to give an account of the rules governing the formation of atomic sentences, we must explain the 'valencies' belonging to different words—which expressions can, and which cannot, be juxtaposed, and when we have a whole sentence and when only a fragment of one. It is also true, as we have seen, that, in stating these rules, it is to the simple predicates and relational expressions that we must assign slots into which singular terms have to be fitted, rather than ascribing to the singular terms slots into which the predicates and relational expressions have to be fitted. But this does not make the simple predicates incomplete in the sense that Frege intended when he spoke of incomplete expressions. We might say that, in the case of simple predicates, the slots are external to them, whereas in the case of complex predicates, they are internal. That is, we can know what linguistic entity, considered just as a sequence of phonemes or of printed letters, a simple predicate is, without knowing anything about the slot it carries with it: the slot consists merely in the predicate's being subject to a certain rule about how it can be put together with a term to form a sentence. But the complex predicate cannot be so much as recognized unless we know what slots it carries: they are integral to its very being.

11

Existence and Quantification

W. V. Quine

The question whether there are numbers, or qualities, or classes, is a metaphysical question, such as the logical positivists have regarded as meaningless. On the other hand the question whether there are rabbits, or unicorns, is as meaningful as can be. A conspicuous difference is that bodies can be perceived. Still, this is not all that matters; for we can evidently say also, meaningfully and without metaphysics, that there are prime numbers between 10 and 20.

What typifies the metaphysical cases is rather, according to an early doctrine of Carnap's (1937, p. 292), the use of category words, or *Allwörter*. It is meaningful to ask whether there are prime numbers between 10 and 20, but meaningless to ask in general whether there are numbers; and likewise it is meaningful to ask whether there are rabbits, or unicorns, but meaningless to ask in general whether there are bodies.

But this ruling is unsatisfactory in two ways. The first difficulty is that there is no evident standard of what to count as a category, or category word. Typically, in terms of formalized quantification theory, each category comprises the range of some distinctive style of variables. But the style of variable is an arbitrary matter, and surely of no help in distinguishing between meaningful questions of existence and metaphysical questions of existence. For there are no external constraints on styles of variables; we can use distinctive styles for different sorts of number, or a single style for all sorts of numbers and everything else as well. Notations with one style of variables and notations with many are intertranslatable.

There is another idea of category that may superficially seem more profound. It is the idea of semantic category, as Leśniewski called it (1929), or what linguists call a substitution class. Expressions belong to the same substitution class if, whenever you put one for the other in a meaningful sentence, you get a meaningful sentence. The question

---

This essay first appeared in Joseph Margolis (ed.) *Fact and Existence*, (Oxford: Blackwell, and Toronto: University of Toronto Press, 1969). It is reprinted here by permission of the author and Blackwell Publishers.

whether numbers constitute a category gives way, in these terms, to a question of the meaningfulness of the sentences that we obtain by supplanting number words by other words. However, what to count as meaningful is not at all clear. The empirical linguist manages the point after a fashion by considering what sentences could be elicited by reasonable means from naive native speakers. But such a criterion is of little value to a philosopher with a reform programme. In fact, the question what existence sentences to count as meaningless was where we came in.

Existence questions were ruled meaningless by Carnap when they turned on category words. This was, I said, an unsatisfactory ruling in two respects. We have seen one of the respects: the tenuousness of the idea of category word. Now the other respect is that anyway sense needs to be made of categorial existence questions, however you choose your categories. For it can happen in the austerest circles that some one will try to rework a mathematical system in such a way as to avoid assuming certain sorts of objects. He may try to get by with the assumption of just numbers and not sets of numbers; or he may try to get by with classes to the exclusion of properties; or he may try, like Whitehead, to avoid points and make do with extended regions and sets of regions. Clearly the system-maker in such cases is trying for something, and there is some distinction to be drawn between his getting it and not.

When we want to check on existence, bodies have it over other objects on the score of their perceptibility. But we have moved now to the question of checking not on existence, but on imputations of existence: on what a theory says exists. The question is when to maintain that a theory assumes a given object, or objects of a given sort—numbers, say, or sets of numbers, or properties, or points. To show that a theory assumes a given object, or objects of a given class, we have to show that the theory would be false if that object did not exist, or if that class were empty; hence that the theory requires that object, or members of that class, in order to be true. How are such requirements revealed?

Perhaps we find proper names of the objects. Still, this is no evidence that the objects are required, except as we can show that these proper names of the objects are used in the theory *as* proper names of the objects. The word 'dog' may be used as a proper name of an animal species, but it may also be used merely as a general term true of each of various individuals and naming no one object at all; so the presence of the word is of itself no evidence that species are being assumed as objects. Again even 'Pegasus', which is inflexibly a proper name grammatically speaking, can be used by persons who deny existence of its object. It is even used in denying that existence.

What would count then as evidence that an expression is used in a theory as a name of an object? Let us represent the expression as 'a'. Now if the theory affirms the existentially quantified identity '$(\exists x)$ $(x = a)$', certainly we have our answer: 'a' is being used to name an object. In general we may say that an expression is used in a theory as naming if and only if the existentially quantified identity built on that expression is true according to the theory.

Of course we could also say, more simply, that 'a' is used to name an object if and only if the statement 'a exists' is true for the theory. This is less satisfactory only insofar as the meaning of 'exists' may have seemed less settled than quantifiers and identity. We may indeed take '$(\exists x)$ $(x = a)$' as explicating 'a exists'. John Bacon (1966) has noted a nice parallel here: just as 'a eats' is short for 'a eats something', so 'a is' is short for 'a is something'.

An expression 'a' may occur in a theory, we saw, with or without purporting to name an object. What clinches matters is rather the quantification '$(\exists x)$ $(x = a)$'. It is the existential quantifier, not the 'a' itself, that carries existential import. This is just what existential quantification is for, of course. It is a logically regimented rendering of the 'there is' idiom. The bound variable 'x' ranges over the universe, and the existential quantification says that at least one of the objects in the universe satisfies the appended condition—in this case the condition of being the object a. To show that some given object is required in a theory, what we have to show is no more nor less than that that object is required, for the truth of the theory, to be among the values over which the bound variables range.

Appreciation of this point affords us more than an explication of 'a exists', since the existentially quantified identity '$(\exists x)$ $(x = a)$' is one case of existential quantification among many. It is a case where the value of the variable that is said to exist is an object with a name; the name is 'a'. This is the way with singular existence sentences generally, sentences of the form 'a exists' or 'There is such a thing as a', but it is not the way with existence sentences generally. For instance, under classical set theory there are, given any interpreted notation, some real numbers that are not separately specifiable in that notation. The existence sentence 'There are unspecifiable real numbers' is true, and expressible as an existential quantification; but the values of the variable that account for the truth of this quantification are emphatically not objects with names. Here then is another reason why quantified variables, not names, are what to look to for the existential force of a theory.

Another way of saying what objects a theory requires is to say that they are the objects that some of the predicates of the theory have to be true of, in order for the theory to be true. But this is the same as saying that they are the objects that have to be values of the variables in order for the theory to be true. It is the same, anyway, if the notation of the theory includes for each predicate a complementary predicate, its negation. For then, given any value of a variable, some predicate is true of it; viz., any predicate or its complement. And conversely, of course, whatever a predicate is true of is a value of variables. Predication and quantification, indeed, are intimately linked; for a predicate is simply any expression that yields a sentence, an open sentence, when adjoined to one or more quantifiable variables. When we schematize a sentence in the predicative way '*Fa*', or '*a* is an *F*', our recognition of an '*a*' part and an '*F*' part turns strictly on our use of variables of quantification; the '*a*' represents a part of the sentence that stands where a quantifiable variable could stand, and the '*F*' represents the rest.

Our question was: what objects does a theory require? Our answer is: those objects that have to be values of variables for the theory to be true. Of course a theory may, in this sense, require no objects in particular, and still not tolerate an empty universe of discourse either, for the theory might be fulfilled equally by either of two mutually exclusive universes. If for example the theory implies '$(\exists x)$ (*x* is a dog)', it will not tolerate an empty universe; still the theory might be fulfilled by a universe that contained collies to the exclusion of spaniels, and also vice versa. So there is more to be said of a theory, ontologically, than just saying what objects, if any, the theory requires; we can also ask what various universes would be severally sufficient. The specific objects required, if any, are the objects common to all those universes.

I think mainly of single-sorted quantification; i.e., a single style of variables. As remarked, the many-sorted is translatable into one-sorted. Generally such translation has the side effect of admitting as meaningful some erstwhile meaningless predications. E.g., if the predicate 'divisible by 3' is henceforth to be trained on general variables instead of number variables, we must make sense of calling things other than numbers divisible by 3. But this is easy; we may count such attributions false instead of meaningless. In general, thus, the reduction of many-sorted quantification to one-sorted has the effect of merging some substitution classes; more words become meaningfully interchangeable.

Carnap's reservations over *Allwörter* now cease to apply, and so his special strictures against philosophical questions of existence lapse as well. To what extent have we meanwhile become clearer on such questions of existence? On the higher-order question, what things a theory assumes there to be, we have gained a pointer: look to the behavior of quantified variables and don't cavil about names. Regarding the meaning of existence itself our progress is less clear.

Existence is what existential quantification expresses. There are things of kind F if and only if $(\exists x)Fx$. This is as unhelpful as it is undebatable, since it is how one explains the symbolic notation of quantification to begin with. The fact is that it is unreasonable to ask for an explication of existence in simpler terms. We found an explication of singular existence, 'a exists', as '$(\exists x)(x = a)$'; but explication in turn of the existential quantifier itself, 'there is', 'there are', explication of general existence, is a forlorn cause. Further understanding we may still seek even here, but not in the form of explication. We may still ask what counts as evidence for existential quantifications.

To this question there is no simple, general answer. If the open sentence under the quantifier is something like 'x is a rabbit' or 'x is a unicorn', then the evidence, if any, is largely the testimony of the senses. If the open sentence is 'x is a prime number between 10 and 20', the evidence lies in computation. If the open sentence is merely 'x is a number', or 'x is a class', or the like, the evidence is much harder to pinpoint. But I think the positivists were mistaken when they despaired of evidence in such cases and accordingly tried to draw up boundaries that would exclude such sentences as meaningless. Existence statements in this philosophical vein do admit of evidence, in the sense that we can have reasons, and essentially scientific reasons, for including numbers or classes or the like in the range of values of our variables. And other existence statements in this metaphysical vein can be subject to counter-evidence; we can have essentially scientific reasons for excluding propositions, perhaps, or attributes, or unactualized bodies, from the range of our variables. Numbers and classes are favoured by the power and facility which they contribute to theoretical physics and other systematic discourse about nature. Propositions and attributes are disfavoured by some irregular behaviour in connection with identity and substitution. Considerations for and against existence are more broadly systematic, in these philosophical examples, than in the case of rabbits or unicorns or prime numbers between 10 and 20; but I am persuaded that the difference is a matter of degree. Our theory of nature grades off from the most concrete fact to speculations about the curvature of space-time, or the continuous creation of hydrogen atoms in an expanding universe; and our evidence grades off correspondingly, from specific observation to broadly systematic considerations. Existential quantifications of the philosophical sort belong to the same inclusive theory and are situated way out at the end, farthest from observable fact.

Thus far I have been playing down the difference between commonsense existence statements, as of rabbits and unicorns, and philosophical existence statements, as of numbers and attributes. But there is also a curious difference between commonsense existence statements and philosophical ones that needs to be played up, and it is one that can be appreciated already right in among the rabbits. For let us reflect that a theory might accommodate all rabbit data and yet admit as values of its variables no rabbits or other bodies but only qualities, times, and places. The adherents of that theory, or *immaterialists*, would have a sentence which, as a whole, had the same stimulus meaning as our sentence 'There is a rabbit in the yard'; yet in the quantificational sense of the words they would have to deny that there is a rabbit in the yard or anywhere else. Here, then, prima facie, are two senses of existence of rabbits, a common sense and a philosophical sense.

A similar distinction can be drawn in the case of the prime numbers between 10 and 20. Suppose someone has for reasons of nominalism renounced most of mathematics and settled for bodies as sole values of his variables. He can still do such part of arithmetic as requires no variables. In particular he can still subscribe to the nine-clause alternation '11 is prime or 12 is prime or 13 is prime or . . . or 19 is prime'. In this sense he agrees with us that there are primes between 10 and 20, but in the quantificational sense he denies that there are primes or numbers at all.

Shall we say: so much the worse for a quantificational version of existence? Hardly; we already found this version trivial but undebatable. Are there then two senses of existence? Only in a derivative way. For us common men who believe in bodies and prime numbers, the statements 'There is a rabbit in the yard' and 'There are prime numbers between 10 and 20' are free from double talk. Quantification does them justice. When we come to the immaterialist, and we tell him there is a rabbit in the yard, he will know better than to demur on account of his theory; he will acquiesce on account of a known holophrastic relation of stimulus synonymy between our sentence and some sentence geared to his different universe. In practice he will even stoop to our idiom himself, both to facilitate communication and because of speech habits lingering from his own benighted youth. This he will do when the theoretical question is not at issue, just as we speak of the sun as rising. Insofar we may say, I grant, that there are for him two senses of existence; but there is no confusion, and the theoretical use is rather to be respected as literal and basic than deplored as a philosophical disorder.

Similar remarks apply to our nominalist. He will agree that there are primes between 10 and 20, when we are talking arithmetic and not philosophy. When we turn to philosophy he will condone that usage as a mere manner of speaking, and offer the paraphrase. Similar remarks apply to us; many of our casual remarks in the 'there are' form would want dusting up when our thoughts turn seriously ontological. Each time, if a point is made of it, the burden is of course on us to paraphrase or retract.

It has been fairly common in philosophy early and late to distinguish between being, as the broadest concept, and existence, as narrower. This is no distinction of mine; I mean 'exists' to cover all there is, and such of course is the force of the quantifier. For those who do make the distinction, the existent tends to be on the concrete or temporal side. Now there was perhaps a reminder of the distinction in the case of the rabbit and the immaterialist. At that point two senses of 'there is', a common and a philosophical, threatened to diverge. Perhaps the divergence which that sort of case suggests has been one factor in making philosophers receptive to a distinction between existence and being. Anyway, it ought not to. For the point there was that the rabbit was not a value of the immaterialist's variables; thus existence, if this were the analogy, would not be a species of being. Moreover, we saw that the sensible materiality of the rabbit was inessential to the example, since the prime numbers between 10 and 20 sustained much the same point.

Along with the annoying practice of restricting the term 'existence' to a mere species of what there is, there is Meinong's bizarre deviation of an opposite kind. *Gegenstände* or objects, for him, comprised more even than what there was; an object might or might not be. His notion of object was, as Chisholm puts it (1961), *jenseits von Sein und Nichtsein.* Oddly enough, I find this idea a good one, provided that we bolster it with Bentham's theory of fictions. Contextual definition, or what Bentham called paraphrasis, can enable us to talk very considerably and conveniently about putative objects without footing an ontological bill. It is a strictly legitimate way of making theories in which there is less than meets the eye.

Bentham's idea of paraphrasis flowered late, in Russell's theory of descriptions. Russell's theory affords a rigorous and important example of how expressions can be made to parade as names and then be explained away as a mere manner of speaking, by explicit paraphrase of the context into an innocent notation. However, Russell's theory of descriptions was less a way of simulating objects than of contextually defining terms to designate real objects. When the description fails to specify anything, Russell accommodates it grudgingly: he makes its immediate sentential contexts uniformly false.

Where we find Russell exploiting paraphrasis for simulation of objects is not in his theory of descriptions but rather in his contextual theory of classes. There are really no such things as classes, according to him, but he simulates discourse about classes by contextual definition, and not grudgingly; not just by making all immediate contexts false.

There is a well-known catch to Russell's theory of classes. The theory depends on an unheralded but irreducible assumption of attributes as values of bound variables. Russell only reduces classes to attributes, and this can scarcely be viewed as a reduction in the right direction unless for wrong reasons.

But it is possible by paraphrasis to introduce a certain amount of class talk, less than Russell's, without really assuming attributes or any other objects beyond the ones wanted as members of the simulated classes. I developed this line somewhat under the head of virtual classes, long ago, and Richard Martin was at it independently at that time (Martin, 1943). Lately I made much use of it in *Set Theory and Its Logic*. What it yields is substantial enough to implant new hopes, in many breasts, of making do with a nominalist ontology. Unfortunately these would have to be breasts unmindful of the needs of mathematics. For of itself the virtual theory of classes affords no adequate foundation for the classical mathematics even of the positive integers. However, it is handy still as a supplementary technique after we have bowed to the need of assuming real classes too; for it enables us to simulate further classes beyond those assumed. For that reason, and also because I think it good strategy in all subjects to postpone assumptions until needed, I am in favour of exploiting the virtual theory for all it is worth.

Virtual classes do not figure as values of bound variables. They owe their utility partly to a conventional use of schematic letters, which, though not quantifiable, behave like free variables. The simulated names of the virtual classes are substitutable for such letters. We could even call these letters free variables, if we resist the temptation to bind them. Virtual classes can then be seen as simulated values of these simulated variables. Hintikka has presented a logic, not specifically of classes but of entities and non-entities generally, in which the non-entities figure thus as values only of free variables.[1] Or, to speak

1. Hintikka (1959). For a bigger venture in this direction see Leonard (1964).

less figuratively, the singular terms which fail to designate can be substituted only for free variables, whereas singular terms which do designate can be used also in instantiating quantification.

So much for simulated objects. I want now to go back and pick up a loose end where we were considering the immaterialist. I said he would fall in with our statement 'There is a rabbit in the yard' just to convey agreement on the stimulus content, or even out of habit carried over from youth. But what about the alternative situation where the immaterialist is not a deviant Western intellectual, but a speaker of an unknown language which we are bent on construing? Suddenly the conditions themselves become problematical. In principle there is no difficulty in equating a sentence of his holophrastically, by stimulus meaning, with our sentence 'There is a rabbit in the yard'. But how could it ever be determined, even in probabilistic terms, that his ontology includes qualities, times, and places and excludes bodies? I argued in *Word and Object* that such ontological questions regarding a radically alien language make no objective sense. In principle we could devise any of various sets of analytical hypotheses for translating the language into ours; many such sets can conform fully to all evidence and even be behaviourally equivalent to one another, and yet disagree with one another as to the native's equivalents of our predicates and quantifiers. For practical translation we fix on one of the adequate sets of analytical hypotheses, and in the light of it we report even on the native's ontology; but what to report is uniquely determined neither by evidence nor by fact. There is no fact of the matter.

Consider, in contrast, the truth functions. We can state substantial behavioural conditions for interpreting a native sentence connective as, say, alternation. The requirement is that the natives be disposed to dissent from any compound statement, formed by the connective in question, when and only when disposed to dissent from each of the component statements, and that they be disposed to assent to the compound whenever disposed to assent to a component. These conditions remain indeed less than definitive on one point: on the question of a native's assenting to the compound but to neither component. For instance we may affirm of two horses that one or the other will win, and still not be prepared to affirm of either one that he will win.[2] Still, the two conditions do much toward identifying alternation; more than any behavioural conditions can do for quantification. And it is easy to do as well for the other truth functions as for alternation.

---

2. In *Word and Object* (1960 p. 58), I gave only the condition on dissent and so overlooked this limitation on the assent side. Conjunction suffered in equal and opposite fashion.

There is indeed a variant of quantification, favoured by Leśniewski (1929) and by Ruth Marcus (1961), which does admit behavioural criteria of translation as substantial as those for the truth functions. I shall call it *substitutional* quantification. An existential substitutional quantification is counted as true if and only if there is an expression which, when substituted for the variable, makes the open sentence after the quantifier come out true. A universal quantification is counted as true if no substitution makes the open sentence come out false. Behavioural conditions for interpreting a native construction as existential substitional quantification, then, are readily formulated. We fix on parts of the construction as candidates for the roles of quantifier and variable; then a condition of their fitness is that the natives be disposed to dissent from a whole quantified sentence when and only when disposed to dissent from each of the sentences obtainable by dropping the quantifier and substituting for the variable. A second condition is that the natives be disposed to assent to the whole whenever disposed to assent to one of the sentences obtainable by dropping the quantifier and substituting for the variable. As in the case of alternation, the behavioural conditions do not wholly settle assent; but they go far. Analogous criteria for universal substitutional quantification are equally evident.

Naturally we never expect mathematical certainty as to whether such a behavioural criterion is fulfilled by a given construction in the native language. For any one choice of native locutions as candidates for the role of quantifier and variable, an infinite lot of quantified sentences and substitution instances would have to be tested. The behavioural criteria for the truth functions are similar in this respect. Empirical induction is all we have to go on, and all we would ask.

Substitutional quantification and the truth functions are, in brief, far and away more recognizable behaviourally than classical quantification, or what we may call *objectual* quantification. We can locate objectual quantification in our own language because we grow up using those very words: if not the actual quantifiers, then words like 'exists' and 'there is' by which they come to be explained to us. We can locate it in other languages only relative to chosen or inherited codes of translation which are in a sense arbitrary. They are arbitrary in the sense that they could be materially different and still conform to all the same behaviour apart from the behaviour of translation itself. Objectual quantification is in this sense more parochial than substitutional quantification and the truth functions.

In his substitutional quantification Leśniewski used different styles of variables for different substitution classes. Substitutional quantification in the substitution class of singular terms, or names, is the sort that comes closest to objectual quantification. But it is clearly not equivalent to it—not unless each of our objects is specifiable by some singular term or other in our language, and no term of that substitution class fails to specify an object. For this reason substitutional quantification gives no acceptable version of existence properly so-called, not if objectual quantification does. Moreover, substitutional quantification makes good sense, explicable in terms of truth and substitution, no matter what substitution class we take—even that whose sole member is the left-hand parenthesis.[3] To conclude that entities are being assumed that trivially, and that far out, is simply to drop ontological questions. Nor can we introduce any control by saying that only substitutional quantification in the substitution class of singular terms is to count as a version of existence. We just now saw one reason for this, and there is another: the very notion of singular term appeals implicitly to classical or objectual quantification. This is the point that I made earlier about analyzing sentences according to the scheme '*Fa*'. Leśniewski did not himself relate his kind of quantification to ontological commitments.

This does not mean that theories using substitutional quantification and no objectual quantification can get on *without* objects. I hold rather that the question of the ontological commitment of a theory does not properly arise except as that theory is expressed in classical quantificational form, or insofar as one has in mind how to translate it into that form. I hold this for the simple reason that the existential quantifier, in the objectual sense, is given precisely the existential interpretation and no other: there are things which are thus and so.

It is easy to see how substitutional quantification might be translated into a theory of standard form. Consider a substitutional quantification whose quantifier is existential and contains the variable v and governs the open sentence S. We can paraphrase it in syntactical and semantical terms, with objectual quantification, thus: there is an expression which, put for v in S, yields a truth. Universal quantification can be handled similarly. For this method the theory into which we translate is one that talks about expressions of the original theory, and assumes them among its objects—as values of its variables of objectual quantification. By arithmetized syntax, natural numbers would do as well. Thus we may look upon substitutional quantification not as avoiding all ontological commitment, but as getting by with, in effect, a universe of natural numbers.

Substitutional quantification has its points. If I could see my way to getting by with an all-purpose universe whose objects were denumer-

3. Leśniewski's example, from a conversation of 1933 in Warsaw.

able and indeed enumerated, I would name each object numerically and settle for substitutional quantification. I would consider this an advance epistemologically, since substitutional quantification is behaviourally better determined than objectual quantification. Here then is a new reason, if one were needed, for aspiring to a denumerable universe.

In switching at that point to substitutional quantification we would not, as already stressed, reduce our denumerable universe to a null universe. We would, however, turn our backs on ontological questions. Where substitutional quantification serves, ontology lacks point. The ontology of such a theory is worth trying to elicit only when we are making translations or other comparisons between that theory and a theory which, because of an indenumerable or indefinite universe, is irreducibly committed to something like objectual quantification. Indenumerable and indefinite universes are what, in the end, give point to objectual quantification and ontology.[4]

I urged that objectual quantification, more than substitutional quantification, is in a sense parochial. Then so is the idea of being; for objectual existential quantification was devised outright for 'there is'. But still one may ask, and Hao Wang has asked, whether we do not represent being in an unduly parochial way when we equate it strictly with our own particular quantification theory to the exclusion of somewhat deviant quantification theories. Substitutional quantification indeed would not serve as an account of being, for reasons already noted; but what of intuitionistic quantification theory, or other deviations?[5] Now one answer is that it would indeed be a reasonable use of words to say that the intuitionist has a different doctrine of being from mine, as he has a different quantification theory; and that I am simply at odds with the intuitionist on the one as on the other. When I try to determine the universe of someone else's theory, I use 'being' my way. In particular thus I might come out with a different inventory of an intuitionist's universe then the intuitionist, with his deviant sense of being, would come out with. Or I might simply see no satisfactory translation of his notation into mine, and so conclude that the question of his ontology cannot be raised in terms acceptable to me.

But this answer misses an important element in Wang's question.

4. The foregoing reflections on substitutional quantification were elicited largely by discussion with Burton Dreben. On the pointlessness of ontology at the denumerable level see also my *The Ways of Paradox* (1966, p. 203).

5. One such, propounded by Leonard (1964, p. 39), combines substitutional and objectual quantification.

Namely, how much better than arbitrary is our particular quantification theory, seen as one in some possible spectrum of quantification
theories? Misgivings in this direction can be fostered by noting the
following form of sentence, due essentially to Henkin (1961):

(1) Each thing bears P to something y and each thing bears Q to something
    w such that Ryw.

The best we can do for this in ordinary quantificational terms is:

(2) $(\forall x)(\exists y)(Pxy \ \& \ (\forall z)(\exists w)(Qzw \ \& \ Ryw))$.

or equally:

(3) $(\forall z)(\exists w)(Qzw \ \& \ (\forall x)(\exists y)(Pxy \ \& \ Ryw))$.

These are not equivalent. (2) represents the choice of y as independent of z; (3) does not. (3) represents the choice of w as independent
of x; (2) does not. Moreover there are interpretations of 'P', 'Q', and
'R' in (1) that make both dependences gratuitous; for instance, interpretation of 'P' as 'is part of', 'Q' as 'contains', and 'R' as 'is bigger
than'.

(4) Each thing is part of something y and each thing contains something z
    such that y is bigger than z.

One may suspect that the notation of quantification is at fault in
forcing a choice between (2) and (3) in a case like this.

By admitting functions as values of our bound variables, Henkin
observes, we can escape the limitations of (2) and (3) as follows:

(5) $(\exists f)(\exists g)(\forall x)(\forall z)(Pxf_x \ \& \ Qzg_z \ \& \ Rf_x g_z)$.

But this move assumes higher-order objects, which may seem out of
keeping with the elementary character of (1). Henkin then points out
a liberalization of the classical quantification notation which does the
work of (5) without quantifying over functions. Just allow branching
quantifiers, thus:

$$(\forall x)(\exists y)$$
(6) $\qquad (Pxy \ \& \ Qzw \ \& \ Ryw)$.
$$(\forall z)(\exists w)$$

One may feel, therefore, that an ontological standard geared to classical quantification theory is over-critical. It would interpret (4) as assuming functions, by interpreting it as (5), whereas the deviant quantification theory with its branching quantifiers would interpret (4) more plausibly as not talking of any functions. And it would do so without slipping into the inappropriate bias of (2), or that of (3).

One is tempted farther by the following considerations. The second-order formula (5) is of a kind that I shall call *functionally existential*, meaning that all its function quantifiers are out in front and existential. Now there is a well-known complete proof procedure of Skolem's for classical quantification theory, which consists in showing a formula inconsistent by taking what I call its functional normal form and deriving a truth-functional contradiction from it.[6] Anyone familiar with the procedure can quickly see that it works not only for all first-order formulas, that is, all formulas in the notation of classical quantification theory, but all these functionally existential formulas as well. Any inconsistent formula not only of classical quantification theory, but of this functionally existential annex, can be shown inconsistent by one and the same method of functional normal forms. This makes the annex seem pretty integral. One is tempted to seek further notational departures, in the first-orderish spirit of the branching quantifiers, which would suffice to accommodate all the functionally existential formulas the way (6) accommodates (5). Henkin has in fact devised a general notation of this kind.

By considerations of duality, moreover, these reflections upon functionally existential formulas can be paralleled with regard to functionally universal formulas—those whose function quantifiers are out in front and universal. Skolem's method of proving inconsistency has as its dual a method of proving validity, and it works not only for all first-order formulas but for all these functionally universal formulas as well. Thus this still further annex would be every bit as integral as the functionally existential one. We seem to see our way, then, to so enlarging classical quantification theory as to gain all the extra power that would have been afforded by assuming functions, so long as the function quantifiers were out in front and all existential or all universal. It would mean a grateful slackening of our ontological accountability.

These reflections encourage the idea that our classical logic of quantification is arbitrarily restrictive. However, I shall now explain what I think to be a still weightier counter-consideration. The classi-

6. See my *Selected Logic Papers* (1966, pp. 196 ff.)

cal logic of quantification has a complete proof procedure for validity and a complete proof procedure for inconsistency; indeed each procedure serves both purposes, since a formula is valid if and only if its negation is inconsistent. The most we can say for the functionally existential annex, on the other hand, is that it has a complete proof procedure for inconsistency; and the most we can say for the functionally universal annex is that it has a complete proof procedure for validity. The trick of proving a formula valid by proving its negation inconsistent, or vice versa, is not applicable in the annexes, since in general the negation of a functionally existential formula is not equivalent to a functionally existential formula (but only to a functionally universal one), and conversely. In fact there is a theorem due to Craig (1956, p. 281) which shows that the negation of a functionally existential formula is never equivalent to a functionally existential formula, unless the functions were superfluous and the formula was equivalent to a first-order formula; and correspondingly for functionally universal formulas. Thus classical, unsupplemented quantification theory is on this score maximal: it is as far out as you can go and still have complete coverage of validity and inconsistency by the Skolem proof procedure.

Henkin even shows that the valid formulas which are quantified merely in the fourfold fashion shown in (5), or (6), are already more than can be covered by any proof procedure, at any rate when identity is included.[7]

Here then is a reason to draw boundaries in such a way as to regard (6) as talking covertly of functions after all, and as receiving a just analysis in (5). On this view (1) is not the proper business of pure quantification theory after all, but treats of functions. That is, if the form (1) is not to be read with the bias (2) or the bias (3), it is to be explained as (5).

We may be somewhat reconciled to this conclusion by an observation of Jean van Heijenoort, to the effect that (1) is not after all very ordinary language; its grammar is doubtful. Can the 'such that' reach back across the 'and' to cover the 'y'? If assignment of meaning to extraordinary language is what we are about, we may indeed assign (5) and not wonder at its being irreducibly of second order.

Since introducing (1), I have proved nothing. I have explained two sorts of considerations, one to illustrate how we might be led to see the classical state of quantification theory as arbitrary, and the other to

7. Henkin (1961, p. 182 and footnote). Henkin derives this conclusion from a theorem of Mostowski by an argument which he credits to Ehrenfeucht.

illustrate how it is better than arbitrary. Classical quantification theory enjoys an extraordinary combination of depth and simplicity, beauty and utility. It is bright within and bold in its boundaries. Deviations from it are likely, in contrast, to look rather arbitrary. But insofar as they exist it seems clearest and simplest to say that deviant concepts of existence exist along with them.[8]

8. I am indebted to Peter Geach for first bringing the question of (1) to my attention, in January 1960; and I am indebted to my colleagues Burton Dreben and Saul Kripke and my pupil Christopher Hill for steering me to pertinent papers. Dreben's advice has been helpful also everywhere.

The Significance of "On Denoting"

Peter Hylton

No one doubts that "On Denoting" marks a significant change in Russell's philosophical views.[1] My main aim in this essay is to see exactly what the significance of the article is in the development of Russell's philosophy, and thus of twentieth-century analytic philosophy more generally. My interest is thus in the consequences of the view set forth in OD, not in Russell's reasons for coming to hold that view. The two issues, however, cannot be completely separated, partly because the general issue of the significance of OD is confused by some of Russell's statements of his reasons for adopting the views of that article. One such statement is as follows:

> [Meinong] argued, if you say that the golden mountain does not exist, it is obvious that there is something that you are saying does not exist—namely the golden mountain; therefore the golden mountain must subsist in some shadowy Platonic world of being, for otherwise your statement that the golden mountain does not exist would have no meaning. I confess that, until I hit upon the theory of descriptions, this argument seemed to me convincing.[2]

This sort of statement suggests the following account of Russell's reasons for adopting the view of OD. According to Russell's views before OD, the meaningfulness of a sentence such as "The golden mountain does not exist" or "The present king of France is bald" demanded that there be a golden mountain or a present king of France. Russell's theory of meaning thus committed him to accepting the being (or the subsistence, as it is sometimes put) of nonexistent golden mountains, kings of France, and even worse ontological excesses involving round squares, even primes other than 2, and what

This essay first appeared in C. Wade Savage and C. Anthony Anderson (eds.) *Rereading Russell* (Minneapolis: University of Minnesota Press, 1989). It is reprinted here by permission of the author and publisher.

1. Russell (1905), and repr. in Russell (1973). I shall abbreviate the title of the article as OD, and cite it, as here, by page number in Russell (1973).

2. Russell (1959, p. 84). See also Schilpp (1946, pp. 13–14).

not. The significance of OD, according to this account, is that it reformed Russell's theory of meaning in such a way that he could accept the meaningfulness of the sentence "The king of France is bald" without having to accept that there is, in any sense, a king of France; similarly, the existence of meaningful sentences that purport to be about golden mountains, round squares and so on is shown not to imply that these expressions correspond to objects that have being.

This account is misleading both in its implications about Russell's views before OD and, consequently, in its claim about Russell's reasons for abandoning those views in favor of the OD view. An understanding of exactly how the account is misleading will put us in a better position to assess the significance of OD. I shall, therefore, adopt the following strategy. In section 1, I shall set out the relevant views of Russell from the period before OD. In section 2 I shall draw upon these views to argue that the preceding account of Russell's reasons for adopting the OD view is incorrect. This section will be largely negative in its immediate aim. I shall not attempt to give Russell's actual reasons for adopting the OD view, though I shall indicate the direction in which I think those reasons lie. In section 3, finally, I shall discuss the significance of OD for Russell's philosophy. I shall argue, in particular, that a number of fundamental ideas of twentieth-century analytic philosophy, ideas that we take for granted, can be seen as coming into Russell's philosophy through that article. My claim will be that it is hard for us fully to assess the significance of that article precisely because we do take those ideas for granted.

1. PROPOSITIONS AND DENOTING CONCEPTS

Two general doctrines of Russell's from the period before OD are directly relevant. The first, to which I shall return in the last section, is that Russell's concern in this period is never with words and sentences, but with propositions and their constituents.[3] On one of the rare occasions when he talks explicitly about words he says:

3. G. E. Moore, who was closely associated with Russell in this period, manifests a similar lack of interest in words. He makes, for example, the following remark about what he means by a "definition of good" (1903, p. 6): "A definition does indeed often mean the expressing of one word's meaning in other words. But this is not the sort of definition I am asking for. Such a definition can never be of ultimate importance in any study except lexicography. . . . My business is solely with that object or idea, which I hold, rightly or wrongly, that word is generally used to stand for. What I want to discuss is the nature of that object or idea."

Words all have meaning, in the simple sense that they are symbols which stand for something other than themselves. But a proposition, unless it happens to be linguistic, does not itself contain words: it contains the entities indicated by words. Thus *meaning in the sense in which words have meaning is irrelevant to logic.*[4]

By a proposition's being "linguistic" Russell here means that it is *about* words, in which case it would (as we shall see in a moment) *contain* words. But in general a proposition is not made up of words, or of ideas; propositions are objective nonmental entities that are, as Russell puts it, "independen[t] of any knowing mind" (1937, p. xvii). Although Russell does talk about meaning in the sense in which words have meaning, he does so only to dismiss this sense as philosophically irrelevant: he is certainly not concerned to advance any theory of meaning in this sense. Thus his statement that words are all "symbols which stand for something other than themselves" is not to be taken as a philosophical theory of meaning,[5] and when Russell speaks of "the entities indicated by words" he is not using "indicate" as a technical term.

The second general doctrine that will be relevant is one that we have already anticipated. This is that a proposition, in the standard case, *contains* the entities that it is about (and thus the entities indicated by the words that express it). Thus the proposition expressed by the sentence "Socrates is mortal" contains Socrates, or Socrates is a *constituent* of the proposition (as is mortality and, it seems, a relation between them—though this last point is problematic). It may seem obscure and paradoxical to claim that anything so concrete as a human being could be a constituent of anything so abstract as a proposition, but this is Russell's claim.[6] Some of the air of paradox may be dispelled by remarking that the distinction between abstract objects and

4. *Principles of Mathematics* (1903, 2nd ed. 1937), section 51; second emphasis mine. The second edition of the book is identical with the first, except for a new introduction and the corresponding renumbering of the pages of the preface. When I quote from the preface I cite the numbering in Russell (1937), i.e., the 2nd edition; other citations are by section number, not page number, in Russell (1903).

5. Contrast Sainsbury (1979, p. 16).

6. Compare Moore, "The Nature of Judgement" (*Mind*, 1899). Moore argues that propositions are made up of what he calls "concepts," which are objective, nonmental entities. He then claims that these concepts also make up the world: "It seems necessary, then, to regard the world as formed of concepts" (p. 182).

concrete objects is not a fundamental one for Russell. Human beings and propositions, numbers and mountains, all *are*, or have being, in exactly the same sense. Human beings happen to have the additional property of *existing* at some moments of time and points of space (and not at others), but it is being, not existence, that is Russell's fundamental (and in a sense his only) ontological category. Thus for Russell human beings and propositions are not so heterogeneous as to make it absurd that a proposition should contain a human being. It is Russell's view, then, that the constituents of a proposition in general include the things which that proposition is about. This doctrine is clearly stated in his correspondence with Frege. Taking as an example perhaps the most concrete object that he could think of, Frege had said, "Mont Blanc with its snowfields is not itself a component part of the thought that Mont Blanc is more than 4,000 meters high" (letter of November 13, 1904). Russell's reply, in a letter dated the December 12, 1904, is as follows:

> I believe that in spite of all its snowfields Mont Blanc itself is a component part of what is actually asserted in the *Satz* "Mont Blanc is more than 4,000 meters high." We do not assert the thought, for this is a private, psychological matter: we assert the object of the thought, and this is, to my mind, a certain complex (an *objectiver Satz*, one might say) in which Mont Blanc is itself a component part.[7]

(I leave the German *Satz* untranslated here. In its first use one might substitute "sentence" or "statement." In the second use, Russell seems to use *objectiver Satz* as German for "proposition." His claim is that the object of thought is objective, neither psychological nor made up of words, and can have things as concrete as mountains among its components.)

I turn now to *denoting*, understood as a technical term of Russell's view in (1903).[8] The Russellian doctrine that the things that are the

7. Frege (1976, pp. 250–51). I have followed the translation of Hans Kaal (Frege 1980, p. 169).

8. It is important to note that "denoting" and its cognates are technical terms in Russell's early philosophy. But even in that period he sometimes uses these words in a looser sense, and this becomes more common in OD and after, when there is no longer a use for "denoting" in the technical sense. I shall always use these words with their technical sense. The only serious ambiguity that arises is that Russell constantly speaks of the "theory of denoting" in OD and afterward, meaning the later theory, whereas this name would more naturally be used for the earlier theory. I shall call the earlier view "the theory of denoting concepts" to avoid this ambiguity.

subject matter of the proposition are also, in the ordinary case, constituents of the proposition is crucial to an understanding of denoting.
That notion is to be understood as a mechanism for bringing about
exceptions to this general rule. The proposition expressed by "Socrates is mortal" *contains* Socrates and is *about* Socrates. The proposition expressed by "The teacher of Plato is mortal," however, contains
the denoting concept *The teacher of Plato*, but it is not *about* that
denoting concept—it is about Socrates. Denoting is Russell's explanation of—or at least his label for—this kind of (supposed) phenomenon. Thus he says:

> A concept *denotes* when, if it occurs in a proposition, the proposition is not
> *about* the concept, but about a term connected in a peculiar way with the
> concept. (1903, 56)

"Term" here is used simply to mean "thing" or "object," in the widest
possible sense—everything, Russell says, is a term (see, e.g., 1903,
47). "Denoting" is Russell's name for the "peculiar way" in which a
concept may be connected with a term or combination of terms; in the
technical sense it is not a relation between words and things but a
relation between things of a particular kind (denoting concepts) and
things in general. It is in virtue of this relation that a proposition may
be *about* things which it does not contain: if a proposition contains a
denoting concept it is about the things which that concept denotes,
and not about the denoting concept itself. Denoting is a relation
between a denoting concept and the object (or objects) it denotes. It is
in no sense a psychological or linguistic relation, as Russell makes
quite clear:

> The notion of denoting, like most of the notions of logic, has been ob-
> scured hitherto by an undue admixture of psychology. There is a sense in
> which *we* denote, when we point to or describe, or employ words as sym-
> bols for concepts; this, however, is not the sense that I wish to discuss. But
> the fact that description is possible . . . is due to a logical relation between
> some concepts and some terms, in virtue of which such concepts inher-
> ently and logically *denote* such terms. It is this sense of denoting which is
> here in question. (1903, 56)

The presence of a denoting concept in a proposition is indicated by
the fact that a denoting phrase occurs in sentences expressing the
proposition. Denoting phrases are, typically, phrases formed with "a,"
"any," "all," "every," "some," or "the." (I shall call phrases formed

with "the" definite descriptions, and phrases formed with one of the other wirds indefinite descriptions.) As an example of the use of the theory of denoting concepts, consider the proposition expressed by the sentence "I met a man." What constituent of this proposition corresponds to the words "a man"? One might be tempted to say that, if Jones is the man I met, then Jones is the corresponding constituent of the proposition. A moment's thought, however, shows that this sort of answer will not do. To begin with, it seems to have the consequence that the two sentences, "I met a man" and "I met Jones," express the same proposition in the case where it is in fact Jones whom I met. This is most implausible. Worse, the suggested answer seems to leave us with no account at all of the proposition expressed by "I met a man" if this sentence occurs in a hypothetical context or is negated or is simply false. If, in fact, I met no one then I can still *say* "I met a man" and express a proposition thereby, and this proposition is presumably the same one I would have expressed by the same words if I had in fact met Jones. It is, after all, the same proposition that would be false in the one case and true in the other. Russell's answer to this sort of difficulty is to say that the proposition in question contains the denoting concept, *a man.* Similarly, we have also the denoting concepts *some man, every man, any man,* and *all men.* Each of these denoting concepts, Russell says, denotes a different combination of men. Thus he says that *all men* denotes all men taken together, whereas *every man* denotes all men taken severally rather than collectively; *a man* denotes the constant disjunction of men; and so on (see 1903, 59–61). Russell devotes considerable subtlety to discussing the exact nature of each of these combinations of objects.

It is important to realize that Russell's reasons for developing the theory of denoting concepts go right to the heart of his philosophy at this period. He does not hold the theory because it enables him to solve some puzzles that he just happens to come across. On the contrary, the theory of denoting is directly connected with the attempt to reduce mathematics to logic that is the overarching aim of *Principles.* The most important link here is the variable. The propositions of logic and mathematics, according to Russell, are wholly general in nature. They contain no constants except logical constants; all their other constituents are variable (1903, 8). The variable, according to Russell, is "*the* characteristic notion of Mathematics" (1903, 87), and an understanding of the nature of the variable, he says, is "absolutely essential to any theory of Mathematics" (ibid.). It is in terms of denoting that Russell attempts to give an explanation of the variable, and

thus of generality. The denoting concept *any term* is closely connected
with the variable; the variable is explained by means of this denoting
concept, and thus also by means of the theory of denoting. Thus it is
that Russell can say that "*any* is presupposed in mathematical formalism" (89). Because the theory of denoting concepts explains the nature of generality, it also explains how we can talk about the infinite:

> With regard to infinite classes, say the class of numbers, it is to be observed
> that the concept *all numbers*, though not itself infinitely complex, yet de-
> notes an infinitely complex object. *This is the inmost secret of our power to
> deal with infinity.* An infinitely complex concept, though there may be such,
> certainly cannot be manipulated by the human intelligence; but infinite
> collections, owing to the notion of denoting, can be manipulated without
> introducing any concepts of infinite complexity. (1903, 72; emphasis added)

Further indication of the importance to Russell of the problems
that he attempted to solve by the theory of denoting comes in a
passage of the preface of *Principles.* Russell is writing of the development of his intellectual concerns that led him to write the book: "I
was led to a re-examination of the principles of Geometry, thence to
the philosophy of continuity and infinity, and thence, with a view to
discovering the meaning of *any,* to Symbolic Logic" (1937, p. xvii).
Russell introduces the theory of denoting primarily in the hope of
explaining the variable, and thus the nature of generality, which he
holds to be essential to logic and mathematics.

The reasons that we have so far discussed for the introduction of
denoting apply to indefinite descriptions; rather different considerations apply to definite descriptions. Such phrases, according to Russell, indicate denoting concepts that in turn denote the individual
uniquely described by the definite description (if such there be). Here
again there is a connection with the reduction of mathematics to logic.
The application of denoting to definite descriptions is crucial to Russell's account of the role of definition in mathematics: to define an
object (or a class), we find a class or a class of classes) of which it is
the sole member; we can then define it as *the* member of that class (cf.
1903, 31, 63). More generally, denoting explains how a statement of
identity can ever be informative. If a proposition corresponding to
such a statement simply contained the same object twice over, then it
is hard to see how it could be other than trivial. But on Russell's
account an ordinary statement of identity (i.e., one that is *not* trivial)
corresponds to a proposition that contains on the one hand an indi-

vidual and, on the other hand, a denoting concept that, it is claimed, uniquely denotes the given individual; or it contains two distinct denoting concepts that it is claimed, uniquely denote the same individual. I shall quote Russell at some length on this point:

> But the question arises: Why is it ever worthwhile to affirm identity? This question is answered by the theory of denoting. If we say "Edward VII is the King," we assert an identity; the reason why this assertion is worth making is that, in the one case the actual term occurs, while in the other a denoting concept takes its place. . . . Often two denoting concepts occur, and the term itself is not mentioned, as in the proposition "the present Pope is the last survivor of his generation." When a term is given, the assertion of its identity with itself, though true, is perfectly futile, and is never made outside the logic-books; but where denoting concepts are introduced, identity is at once seen to be significant. (1903, 64)

2. DENOTING CONCEPTS AS A SOLUTION TO MEINONG'S PROBLEM

The theory of denoting concepts is rejected in OD—later uses of the word "denotes" by Russell are not in the technical sense but as synonyms for "indicates" or "refers." We have now seen enough of the theory to discuss what changes in Russell's philosophical views are effected by this rejection. I shall, to begin with, argue that the theory of OD—the theory of nondenoting, if you like—is not required to free Russell from a commitment to the being of the present king of France and his like. This is not to say that Russell in *Principles* does not accept the being of entities that seem to be no more respectable than the king of France. In a notorious passage he admits chimeras and Homeric gods as among the things that *are* (427). What I do wish to claim is that the theory of denoting concepts gives Russell a way of avoiding such ontological commitments, so that it cannot be held that such avoidance is possible only after OD. The supposed ontological commitment arises from the old problem: unless something *is,* in some sense, how can we say anything about it? How can we even deny that it is? The influence of this problem on Russell is clear. The passage about Homeric gods continues: ". . . if they were not entities of a kind, we could make no propositions about them" (1903, 427). This argument is straightforward only so long as you hold it to be true, without exception, that the entities which a proposition is about— or purports to be about—must occur in the proposition. For then an entity must indeed be, in some sense, if there is to be a proposition that purports to be about it. But the theory of denoting concepts is, as I emphasized, a means of allowing exceptions to the general rule that the things a proposition is about must occur in the proposition. According to the theory of denoting concepts, the proposition expressed by the sentence "The present king of France is bald" does not contain the present king of France; it contains a denoting concept, *the present king of France,* and this is not an actual or possible human being of any kind, bald or not; it is a denoting concept. But then, given the theory of denoting concepts, it is far from obvious that the possibility of propositions that purport to be about the present king of France is enough to show that there *is* a present king of France. The question turns on whether there can be denoting concepts that do not denote anything. Russell's view, even in *Principles,* is that there can be such denotationless denoting concepts. He says this explicitly in section 73: "It is necessary to realize, in the first place, that a concept may denote although it does not denote anything." This admission raises certain problems for Russell, some of which have to do with the null-class, which he changed his mind about in the course of writing *Principles.* But in spite of these problems his view is clear: there can be denoting concepts that do not in fact denote anything.

Russell in *Principles* thus has resources at his disposal that would enable him to deny being to the present king of France. He can do this while still accepting that the sentence "The present king of France is bald" expresses a proposition. According to the theory of denoting concepts, this proposition does not contain the present king of France (as the corresponding proposition about Socrates would contain Socrates); it contains instead the denoting concept *the present king of France.* Given that a denoting concept may lack a denotation, nothing in Russell's account of the proposition demands that there be a present king of France, in any sense of "be." If Russell did not explicitly draw this conclusion in *Principles* it is perhaps because at that stage he saw no reason to deny being to the present king of France, but also because the sort of puzzles that are associated with the alleged king were simply not on his mind when he wrote the book. It was, I think, Russell's renewed study of Meinong between 1903 and 1905 that led him to consider these issues seriously.[9] When he does consider them seriously, he uses the theory of denoting in just the way that I suggested to deny being to the present king of France. He also

9. See "Meinong's Theory of Complexes and Assumptions" (*Mind,* 1904), and Russell's review of *Untersuchungen zur Gegenstandstheorie und Psychologie* (*Mind,* 1905). Both are reprinted in Russell (1973).

treats at least some proper names in the same way that he treats definite descriptions. I quote from "The Existential Import of Propositions," written before OD:[10]

> "The present king of England" is a denoting concept denoting an individual; "The present king of France" is a similar complex concept denoting nothing. The phrase intends to point out an individual, but fails to do so: it does not point out an unreal individual, but no individual at all. The same explanation applies to mythical personages, Apollo, Priam, etc. These words have a meaning, which can be found by looking them up in a classical dictionary; but they have not a *denotation;* there is no individual, real or imaginary, which they point out. (Russell 1973, p. 100)

The theory of denoting concepts—the theory that is rejected in OD—thus allows Russell to claim that there need be no object corresponding to a definite description or a proper name, even though that description or that name has a use in sentences that express propositions. Before he wrote OD Russell had come to recognize this and to exploit the theory of denoting concepts to show that there need be no king of France, even though we can meaningfully say "The king of France is bald." Getting rid of the present king of France and his like cannot, therefore, have been the reason for rejecting the theory he held before OD.

Russell's later statements about OD, as we have seen, stress the ontological economy which that article effected. One might therefore think that reasons for rejecting the pre-OD theory had to do with a desire to avoid the need for denoting concepts. The relevant ontological economy, on this view, would have to do not with the king of France but with the denoting concept *the king of France.* This view is perhaps encouraged by Russell's own insistence on the need for a "robust sense of reality" in logic.[11] Denoting concepts, mysterious and unexplained entities, might seem to offend a robust sense of reality just as much as nonexistent kings of France; and for Russell to talk about the latter when he means the former is perhaps an understandable piece of carelessness. There thus seems to be some reason to think that Russell adopted the OD theory for the sake of the ontological economy that it effected by eliminating the need for denoting concepts. In fact, however, this view is also seriously misleading. The issues here are extremely complex, and I shall not discuss them

10. First published in *Mind* (July, 1905), and reprinted in Russell (1973).
11. Russell (1919, p. 170). Compare Russell (1956, p. 223).

in any detail. I shall instead simply make two rather dogmatic remarks. First, there is no sign that Russell in 1905 was much concerned with ontological economy for its own sake. The rejection of the theory of denoting concepts was based not on a desire to eliminate entities but on difficulties that arise within that theory when it is thought through. Some of these difficulties come to the surface in the notorious "Gray's *Elegy*" passage of OD (pp. 111–113); other difficulties are discussed by Russell in works that are still unpublished.[12] Second, OD did have crucial ontological consequences for Russell's philosophy, but these consequences are quite different in kind from the elimination of denoting concepts (see pp. 193–96, below). One can thus explain the connection that Russell makes between OD and ontological economy without supposing that this economy consisted in the elimination either of the king of France or of the corresponding denoting concept.

3. 'ON DENOTING' AND PHILOSOPHICAL ANALYSIS

I turn now to the issue of the general significance of OD for Russell's philosophy. Besides the ontological consequences of the article, this significance consists chiefly in the effects it has on Russell's view of the nature of propositions, of their relation to sentences, of philosophical analysis, and thus of the aim and nature of philosophy itself. These changes contribute to the development of a conception of logical form, and to the idea that words and sentences might themselves be of philosophical interest. In *Principles*, as we have seen, Russell's view is that propositions and their constituents are what is philosophically important, and that words and sentences are more or less irrelevant. Russell continues, after OD, to hold that words are not philosophically important for their own sake, but he is subject to pressures that force him to make them the subject of explicit attention.

Let us now turn to the details of OD to see why it should have the consequences I have attributed to it. "The principle" of the new theory of OD, Russell says, is "that denoting phrases never have any meaning in themselves, but that every proposition in whose verbal expression they occur has a meaning" (OD, Russell 1973, p. 105). I shall explain this. Consider the sentence "All numbers are prime."

---

12. See especially "Points about Denoting," "On the Meaning and Denotation of Phrases," "On Meaning and Denotation," and "On Fundamentals," all in the Russell Archives at McMaster University. I am grateful to the Archives for allowing me access to these and other unpublished works of Russell.

This is a meaningful sentence; for Russell it is thus the verbal expression of a proposition. The *Principles* theory of denoting took it for granted that this proposition would contain a constituent corresponding to the words "all numbers"; since this phrase is a denoting phrase, that constituent is not all the numbers but rather the denoting concept *all numbers*. Whether there actually is anything that this denoting concept denotes is, as we have seen, a further question. The words "all numbers," according to the *Principles* view, thus indicate or stand for a constituent of the proposition that is expressed by the sentence in which those words occur. In the sense of "meaning" in which it is words that have meaning, those words have a meaning; their meaning is the denoting concept for which they stand. The new theory advanced in OD also has to account for the fact that a sentence such as "All numbers are prime" expresses a proposition. The new theory, however, does not presuppose that this proposition contains a constituent corresponding to or indicated by the words "all numbers." In fact, the theory claims that there is no such constituent: this is what Russell means in OD and later by saying that denoting phrases are "incomplete symbols" or have "no meaning in themselves" or "no meaning in isolation." The theory then goes on to explain how sentences containing denoting phrases can express propositions, even though denoting phrases have no meaning in themselves.

I shall put the point of the previous paragraph in a slightly different way. Meinong, according to Russell's account, seems to have been willing to argue as follows:

1. "The king of France is bald" expresses a proposition.
hence: 2. "The king of France" is a meaningful expression, which therefore corresponds to a constituent of the proposition.
hence: 3. the king of France is, in some sense.

The *Principles* theory of denoting concepts enables one to block this argument by denying the step from (2) to (3). "The king of France" corresponds to a constituent of the proposition, but this constituent is a denoting concept, not an actual or possible king.[13] The OD theory,

---

13. If one equates a Fregean thought (*Gedanke*) with a Russellian proposition—as Russell is inclined to do—then Frege's view here is analogous to the *Principles* view. The sense (*Sinn*) of "the king of France" is a constituent of that thought expressed by a sentence containing those words, but the king of France himself is not a constituent of that thought. The thought thus contains an entity (a Fregean sense) corresponding to the definite description. The two views are different in ways I shall not attempt to discuss, but the analogy that I have given explains why Russell speaks of his view as "very nearly the same as Frege's." (OD, p. 104; see also (1903), 476.)

by contrast, blocks the argument by denying the step from (1) to (2). The phrase "The king of France," according to that theory, corresponds to no constituent of the proposition that is expressed by a sentence containing those words; we are misled into thinking that there is such a constituent because we take the form of the sentence closely to resemble the form of the proposition that it expresses. The theory is then left with the task of explaining the true form of the propositions expressed by "The king of France is bald" or "All numbers are prime" in such a way as to make it clear that the propositions contain no constituents corresponding to the denoting phrases "the king of France" and "all numbers." The details of the way in which the theory accomplishes this task are familiar enough to require only a very brief explanation. Russell takes as fundamental and indefinable the variable and the notion of a proposition containing a variable and the notion of a proposition containing a variable being "always true," or true for all values of the variable, as we might put it (OD, Russell 1973, p. 104). The proposition corresponding to "All numbers are prime" is then said to contain, beside these notions, the properties or propositional functions . . . *is a number* and . . . *is prime.* Spelled out, the proposition has this form:

"If x is a number, then x is prime" is always true.

Or, in quantificational notation:

$(\forall x)\,(Nx \supset Px).$

If this is the true form of the proposition, then it is clear that the proposition contains no constituent corresponding to "all numbers." "$(\forall x)\,(Nx$" is patent nonsense, while "$(\forall x)\,(Nx)$" is a sentence saying that all objects are numbers, and this is certainly not what "all numbers" stands for. Definite descriptions are treated in a way that is slightly more complicated, but with the same results. Denoting concepts disappear in favor of the variable, the notion of a proposition containing a variable being "always true," and propositional functions; with the denoting concept eliminated there is no constituent of the proposition that could be held to correspond to, or to be indicated by, the definite description.

A general consequence of the new theory put forward in OD is that the grammatical arrangement of words in a sentence will in most cases be a poor guide to the logical arrangement of constituents in the proposition that the sentence expresses. Grammatically, the sentence

"The king of France is bald" is a subject-predicate sentence, as is "Socrates is bald." We have seen that the theory of denoting concepts gives a complex account of the corresponding proposition, but this account preserves the segmentation of the sentence. According to the theory of denoting concepts, the proposition contains one constituent corresponding to the subject-phrase ("the king of France") and one constituent corresponding to the predicate-phrase ("is bald"). That the constituent corresponding to the subject-phrase is a denoting concept does not alter the fact that the proposition is segmented into subject-constituent and predicate-constituent. For all its complexity, the theory of denoting concepts does not call this segmentation into question. The form of the proposition, and the way in which it divides into logical units, is taken to be identical with the superficial form of the sentence and the way in which it divides into grammatical units. (Similar remarks apply to sentences that contain indefinite descriptions, provided that one holds that such sentences also have a subject-predicate form—and it is the most superficial form that is in question here.) Now Russell in *Principles* had assumed that the superficial grammatical form of a sentence is in general a good guide to the form of the proposition it expresses:

> Although a grammatical distinction cannot be uncritically assumed to correspond to a genuine philosophical difference, yet the one is prima facie evidence of the other, and may often be most usefully employed as a source of discovery. Moreover, it must be admitted, I think, that every word occurring in a sentence must have *some* meaning; a perfectly meaningless sound could not be employed in the more or less fixed way in which language employs words. The correctness of our philosophical analysis of a proposition may therefore be usefully checked by the exercise of assigning the meaning of each word in the sentence expressing the proposition. (1903, 46)

OD does away with the idea of a congruence between sentences and propositions. There comes to be a sharp break between the grammatical form of the sentence and the form of the proposition it expresses— logical form, to anticipate a later terminology. This is perhaps clearest in the case of definite descriptions. The proposition expressed by "The king of France is bald" has a structure that is most accurately reflected by the sentence:

$$(\exists x)(Fx \ \& \ Gx \ \& \ (\forall x)(Fy \supset y = x))$$

or, in prose (following Russell's example in OD):

It is not always false of *x* that *x* is the king of France and that *x* is bald and that "if *y* is the king of France then *y* is identical with *x*" is always true of *y*.

There is a fundamental difference between the structure of the subject-predicate sentence that would normally be used to express the proposition and the sentence (whether in symbols or in prose) that is said to express the proposition in a way that accurately reflects its structure. There is no similarity of form between them. The gap here is so marked that the form of the sentence cannot be taken as even an approximate guide to the form of the proposition it expresses.

This contrast between grammatical form and logical form has crucial consequences for Russell's view of philosophical analysis and of philosophy itself.[14] According to *Principles*, the process of philosophical analysis does not affect the way a proposition divides into units. This segmentation was assumed to be the same as that of the sentence; the form or structure of a proposition was not a primary concern in analysis. Philosophical analysis was chiefly concerned with the entities making up the proposition, not with the form of the proposition. We have already seen that Russell's account, in *Principles*, of the proposition expressed by "All numbers are prime" would take it for granted that this proposition contained one constituent corresponding to "all numbers" and another corresponding to "is prime." The philosophical work, on this account, is to analyze these constituents (or, in the case of simple constituents, to perceive them clearly). This is, in fact, what most of the philosophical analysis in *Principles* does. It analyzes particular concepts, such as *is prime*, or *is a number*. This sort of philosophical analysis takes the form of a proposition and its segmentation into units for granted, and is primarily concerned to analyze those units.

The conception of philosophical analysis that comes to dominate Russell's work after OD is crucially different. Here the main work of analysis concerns the form of propositions, or logical forms; the chief problem is to find the logical form that is masked by the grammatical form of a given sentence or kind of sentence. The analysis of a particular expression comes to be, generally, a matter of analyzing the sentences in which the expression occurs to find the logical form of the propositions that such sentences express. Alongside these specific

---

14. Compare Wittgenstein: "It was Russell who performed the service of showing that the apparent logical form of a proposition need not be its real one" (1961, 4.0031). For the view that the crucial point of OD has to do with the notion of logical form, see also David Kaplan (1972).

results about particular concepts there are also general results about all propositions of a given form, or about what logical forms a proposition can have. Russell comes to see philosophy as consisting largely, at least, of discovering, investigating, and cataloguing logical forms. The study of logical forms is, Russell claims, a part of logic, and it is this part of logic that he has in mind when he speaks of logic as the essence of philosophy[15] or when he says that "philosophy . . . becomes indistinguishable from logic."[16] Contrasting philosophy with the synthetic method of the special sciences, Russell says:

> . . . in philosophy we follow the inverse direction: from the complex and relatively concrete we proceed towards the simple and abstract by means of analysis, seeking in the process, to eliminate the particularity of the original subject-matter, and to confine our attention entirely to the logical *form* of the facts concerned. (1926, pp. 189–90; emphasis in the original)

I turn now to what I take to be the ontological significance of the conception of philosophical analysis that is introduced in OD. This significance is that sentences that appear to be about entities of one kind are shown by the analysis to be really about entities of a different kind. As an example, consider the definition that forms the basis of Russell's mature theory of types. Russell assumes that there are propositional functions, i.e., intensional entities that yield propositions when applied to objects. I shall follow Russell in using expressions of the form "$\psi\hat{z}$" or "$\phi!\hat{z}$" to refer to these entities. Where f is any property of propositional functions, we can introduce symbols of the form "$f\{\hat{z}(\psi z)\}$" by means of the following definition:[17]

$$f\{\hat{z}(\psi z)\} =_{df} (\exists\phi)[(\forall x)(\phi!x \equiv \psi x) \& f(\phi!\hat{z})].$$

15. Russell (1926, ch. 2, esp. p. 67).

16. "Scientific Method in Philosophy," reprinted in Russell (1963, p. 84).

17. See "Mathematical Logic as Based on the Theory of Types," in Russell (1956, p. 89), and also *Principia Mathematica*, proposition *20.01, vol. 1, p. 190. Russell uses "!" in symbols of the form "$\phi!x$" to indicate that the propositional function ϕ is *predicative*. The precise significance of this term depends upon the intricacies of his type theory; roughly, it means that the function is of the lowest type compatible with its having the argument that it has. The definition as a whole then equates a symbol that appears to ascribe a property to a class defined by a given propositional function with the assertion that there is a predicative propositional function coextensive with the given propositional function, and that the predicative propositional function has the given property.

In virtue of this definition, the truth-value of "$f\{\hat{z}(\psi z)\}$" depends only upon the extension of the propositional function $\psi\hat{z}$. The symbol "$\hat{z}(\psi z)$" thus operates (in the context "$f\{\hat{z}(\psi z)\}$") as if it stood for an extensional entity—the class of objects of which the propositional function $\psi\hat{z}$ is true. But in fact the symbol "$\hat{z}(\psi z)$" does not stand for any kind of entity: it is an incomplete symbol. The definition gives a sense to expressions of the form "$f\{\hat{z}(\psi z)\}$," and shows that some such expressions can be true, without implying that there is an entity for which "$\hat{z}(\psi z)$" stands. Sentences that appear to be about classes are shown to be in fact about propositional functions, so that the truth of such sentences is shown not to imply the existence of classes. Analyzing sentences (which appear to be) about classes shows that the truth of these sentences does not require that there be classes. In such a case analysis is elimination.

It is important to realize that the use made of the notion of an incomplete symbol in the theory of descriptions does not have the sort of ontological consequences I emphasized in the previous paragraph. What is crucial to those consequences is the idea that we can have a body of *true* sentences (which purport to be) about classes without supposing that there are classes. The analogue of this does not hold for definite descriptions. There is no body of truths (which purport to be) about the present king of France, and there could be no body of truths about the present queen of England if there were no such woman.[18] The theory of descriptions claims that propositions expressed by sentences that contain definite descriptions do not themselves contain entities for which the definite descriptions stand. But if such sentences are true then there must be such entities, even though they are not in the corresponding propositions. If it is true to say "The *F* is *G*," then there must be a unique entity that is *F*. When we are dealing with a body of true sentences (of the ordinary kind), e.g., when we are analyzing a theory we hold to be true, the significance of

---

18. Taken literally, the claim is false. According to the theory of descriptions there is a body of truths (purportedly about the present king of France [or at least containing the words "the present king of France" in subject position]), e.g., "The present King of France does not exist," "It is not the case that the present king of France is bald," "Either grass is green or the present king of France is bald," and so on. But there can be no true sentences that purport to ascribe an intuitively simple property to the present king of France, i.e., no true atomic sentences containing "the present king of France" in subject position. When I wish to make this qualification I shall speak of sentences *of the ordinary kind* that purport to be about something.

the theory of definite descriptions is not ontological but, in the broad sense, epistemological. The theory changes the account of the entities that must be in the propositions corresponding to the sentences (and thus of the entities with which we must be acquainted in order to understand the sentences), but it does not change the account of the entities that there must be in the world in order for the sentences to be true.

The notion of an incomplete symbol thus has an ontological significance that is not exploited in the theory of descriptions. This sort of ontological significance, unlike the elimination of the king of France, is something that could not readily be duplicated by the theory of denoting concepts. The idea that analysis is elimination is not explicitly contained in OD, but it is a natural consequence of the conception of analysis that this article introduces. For Russell the paradigm of eliminative analysis was the definition I gave earlier as an example, i.e., the definition of statements that purport to be about classes in terms of propositional functions. In spite of its simplicity, this definition was of crucial importance to Russell. By showing that there need be no classes, the analysis seemed to enable him to find an escape from the class paradox.[19] This is why he frequently links the theory of descriptions with the paradox, although the connection is by no means obvious on the face of it. He says, for example:

> When the *Principles of Mathematics* was finished, I settled down to a resolute attempt to find a solution to the paradoxes. . . . Throughout 1903 and 1904, my work was almost wholly devoted to this matter, but without a vestige of success. My first success was the theory of descriptions. . . . This was, apparently, not connected with the contradictions, but in time an unsuspected connection emerged. (1959, p. 79)

Strictly speaking, the connection here is not directly with the theory of descriptions but rather with the notion of an incomplete symbol. But Russell introduced the notion of an incomplete symbol in the

---

19. Russell always speaks as if the elimination of classes by defining them in terms of propositional functions were crucial to the solution of the paradox. Unfortunately, it is unclear why he should hold this, for one can state a direct analogue of the class paradox for propositional functions, provided one makes sufficiently strong assumptions about propositional functions. I suspect that Russell's view is that the restrictions that enable one to avoid the paradoxes are completely arbitrary and untenable if stated as restrictions on classes, but are somehow natural as restrictions on propositional functions. See Warren Goldfarb (1989).

context of the theory of descriptions, and once introduced the notion rather obviously lends itself to the sort of ontological use that makes the elimination of classes possible.

Although the analysis of sentences containing class expressions was, for Russell, the paradigm of eliminative analysis, the idea of analysis as elimination came to be central to other parts of his philosophy. This can be clearly seen in two areas that were among his major concerns in the period (roughly) 1905–18. The first is his theory of judgment. The basis of this theory is that judgment is not a two-place relation, between a person and a proposition, but a many-place relation between a person and the various entities that (according to the old view) are constituents of the proposition. (This theory is usually known as the "multiple-relation theory," for this reason.) A corollary of this is that there are no propositions. Phrases that appear to refer to or express propositions are said to be incomplete symbols;[20] such phrases can occur meaningfully in various contexts even though there are no propositions.

The second major concern of Russell's is his epistemology. This is both more complicated and more interesting from the present point of view, for it shows the contrast between the two uses of incomplete symbols that I have distinguished. Before 1913 or 1914 Russell only employs the nonontological use of incomplete symbols in his discussion of sentences that appear to refer to physical objects. He thus holds that if our ordinary and scientific beliefs are correct then there really are physical objects quite independent of sense-data. We cannot grasp propositions containing physical objects, but our real interest is in the truth or falsity of these propositions. There is thus a problem about what principles of inference it is legitimate to use in deriving these propositions from propositions about sense-data. There is also a more subtle issue about how we understand such propositions at all. Russell's answer is that in a sense we do not. The propositions that we are really interested in are *described* by propositions that we *do* grasp

---

20. This is importantly distinct from the idea that the propositions are themselves symbols, but the distinction is easy to blur. Russell often says that classes (for example) are incomplete symbols, meaning that symbols that appear to refer to classes are incomplete symbols, and that in fact there are no classes (or no classes are being assumed in his theory). This is simply shorthand and does not indicate any confusion on Russell's part. The same shorthand used about propositions, however, is less innocent. Russell does come to hold that propositions are just symbols, and the shorthand both eases and disguises the transition.

(see "Knowledge by Acquaintance and Knowledge by Description," 1963, p. 158).

This curious position results from the fact that Russell uses the theory of descriptions to eliminate physical objects from the propositions expressed by certain sentences that might appear to be about physical objects, without taking the further step of eliminating physical objects from the world. So while physical objects do not occur in any proposition that we can directly grasp, still there must be physical objects if those propositions are to be true. In 1913 or 1914 he takes the further step and analyzes sentences that appear to be about physical objects in such a way that the existence of physical objects is not required for the truth of those sentences. Such sentences now appear to express propositions that neither contain nor describe physical objects; the sentences are true provided that sense-data occur in the right patterns. This is the view that physical objects are "logical constructions" or "logical fictions." With this view there are no longer ungraspable propositions that are merely described by the propositions we do grasp. The problem of inference to the unknown disappears and is replaced by the problem of showing that it is possible to analyze or translate sentences about physical objects into sentences about sense-data. Russell was sufficiently impressed by this new technique to say, "The supreme maxim in scientific philosophizing" is "Wherever possible, logical constructions are to be substituted for inferred entities" ("The Relation of Sense-Data to Physics," 1963, p. 115).[21]

A further important feature of the new conception of analysis is that nothing in the process of analysis itself enables us to tell when analysis is complete.[22] Analysis is complete when the true form of the proposition has been attained, but Russell has no clear criterion for when this has happened. When we have substituted a definite or indefinite description for each denoting phrase, we may well find that our descriptions contain proper names that may in turn need to be analyzed as definite descriptions. Russell's examples, "The king of France" and "the author of *Waverley*" make this clear, since both "France" and "*Waverley*" are themselves names. It is also true that we cannot think of successive stages in the analysis as closer and closer approximations to the true form of the proposition. The reason for this is that carry-

21. Russell attributes the use of this technique in physics to Whitehead (see Russell, 1963, pp. 88, 116). These applications demand considerable logical and mathematical sophistication, but the fundamental technique is the one that Russell had already used in the philosophy of mathematics.

22. I owe this insight to Warren Goldfarb.

ing the analysis a stage further, analyzing something previously left unanalyzed, may yield a sentence of completely different form. There is no reason to think that every stage of analysis yields a form that is closer to the true form of the proposition than are all previous stages, so the picture of closer and closer approximations to the real form of the proposition cannot be applied. What this suggests is that there is a need for external constraints on the process of analysis that are not intrinsic to the process but are imposed upon it. There is no explicit sign that Russell is aware of this need, but it may have affected him nevertheless. In particular, one of the reasons for the importance of the notion of acquaintance may be that it provides an external constraint on the process of analysis. The notion of acquaintance is present in Russell's philosophy from *Principles* onward, but its role becomes much more important in OD and after. One reason for this may be that the notion of acquaintance tells you what the ultimate entities of analysis are: they are the entities with which you are acquainted. The process of analysis is complete—and the true form of the proposition discovered—when all entities with which you are not acquainted have been eliminated. The new conception of analysis thus demands that the notion of acquaintance should bear much more weight than it had done before OD. On the other hand, it is also true that this conception of analysis makes possible a more realistic notion of acquaintance, i.e., one more closely tied to actual sensory experience.[23] Because analysis is indefinitely extendable, any putative object with which it is implausible to say that we are acquainted can be thought of as analyzable, and thus as not being an object of acquaintance. (Strictly one should say: expressions that might appear to refer to objects with which we not acquainted can be thought of as analyzable.)

The contrast between grammatical form and logical form, together with the conception of analysis that accompanies it, forces Russell to pay explicit attention to words and sentences. Language begins to become a subject of philosophical interest in its own right. In part this is something of which Russell is aware and explicitly accepts; in part it is a matter of pressures that force him in a direction his explicit doctrines do not acknowledge. The change in Russell's overt view is to be understood in terms of the break between grammatical form and

---

23. One cannot, of course, both have a realistic (in this sense) notion of acquaintance and hold that we are acquainted with abstract objects. Russell continues to hold this belief in an unequivocal form until at least 1912—see Russell (1912, ch. 5).

logical form. The assumption of congruence between sentences and propositions had served, before OD, to make it easy for Russell to ignore words (see, for example, *Principles* 46, quoted earlier, p. 191). That assumption makes words and sentences a transparent medium through which propositions and their constituents may be grasped. The medium may be essential, but just because of its transparency nothing more need be said about it. Words themselves need never be the subject of explicit attention. This sort of attitude is in sharp contrast with Russell's later emphasis on the dangers of being misled by grammar. His later attitude is that the grammatical form of the sentence will usually be quite different from the logical form of the proposition, and that many philosophical mistakes arise precisely from the neglect of this distinction. Thus in Lecture One of "The Philosophy of Logical Atomism" he says:

> Some of the notions that have been thought absolutely fundamental in philosophy have arisen, I think, entirely through mistakes as to symbolism. (1956, pp. 185–86)

Because Russell comes to believe that symbols are fundamentally misleading, he also comes to think that symbolism is of great philosophical importance—not because it is really the thing we mean to talk about in philosophy but because it will mislead us if we do not pay attention to it. This is quite explicit in a well-known passage, also from Lecture One of "The Philosophy of Logical Atomism":

> There is a good deal of importance to philosophy in the theory of symbolism, a good deal more than at one time I thought. I think the importance is almost entirely negative, i.e. the importance lies in the fact that unless you are fairly self-conscious about symbols, unless you're fairly aware of the relation of the symbol to what it symbolizes, you will find yourself attributing to the thing properties which only belong to the symbol. That, of course, is especially likely in very abstract subjects such as philosophical logic, because the subject-matter that you are supposed to be thinking about is so exceedingly difficult and elusive that . . . you do not think about it except perhaps once in six months for a half a minute. (1956, p. 185)

Perhaps more important than this somewhat grudging overt admission of the importance of language is the pressure that Russell is under, contrary to his explicit doctrines, to take language as the real subject with which he is dealing. One way in which this arises is from the fact, which we have already examined, that the new conception of analysis makes it hard to tell when an analysis is complete. The propo-

sition itself, whose form is given by the final stage of analysis, becomes
inaccessible, and our attention is focused on stages of analysis that
may be short of the final stage. But all that we have at these stages are
sentences. A single proposition, after all, is expressed equally by the
unanalyzed sentence and by the fully analyzed sentence and by all the
sentences that constitute the various stages of analysis between the
two. So philosophical progress may consist in the transition from one
sentence to another. Russell may say that this is progress only because
the second sentence more nearly reflects the form of the proposition,
but nothing in the process of analysis itself gives these words any
force. Once the relation between sentences and the propositions that
they express becomes problematic, the idea that one sentence can
"reflect" the form of a proposition more accurately than another has
to carry more weight than it can bear. As Russell becomes more
conscious of symbols—of words and sentences—it becomes clear that
analysis essentially concerns sentences; the references to propositions
become *pro forma*.

I have argued that the significance of OD is *not* that it shows that
there can be names or definite descriptions that occur in meaningful
sentences without referring to anything. The significance of the article has to do rather, I have claimed, with the idea of analysis as
elimination, and with the development of certain conceptions of logical form and of philosophical analysis. Perhaps most important, the
article is a crucial step on the way to the idea that language is a
primary philosophical concern. These ideas are so fundamental to
analytic philosophy as it has developed since 1905 that it is hard to put
them in a historical perspective. Those who are, even in a remote
sense, the heirs of Russell, tend to take absolutely for granted the
notion of logical form, the corresponding view of philosophical analysis, and the idea of elimination by analysis. I do not mean that we all
accept the philosophical views embodied in these ideas. I mean,
rather, that we all take it for granted that there are such ideas, that the
philosophical views that they embody are available options—even if we
think that these views need to be revised in some way. Such an attitude
makes it difficult to appreciate an article whose significance lies largely
in its contribution to the development of these ideas. For this requires
that we see those ideas as the product of a historical process, that we
realize that they were not always philosophical commonplaces but
came to be so over a particular period of time and for traceable
reasons. In short, we have to cease taking those ideas for granted. This
is even more clearly true of the view that language is an important
subject of philosophical study. It is hard to detach oneself enough

from this idea to ask where it came from, and why it came to have such a hold over so many philosophers. Yet if one takes this idea for granted, it is hard fully to appreciate not only the significance but also the substance of OD. That article was written against the background of a view according to which the question, what are the constituents of the proposition expressed by a given sentence, is a real question with a right answer that is independent of how we choose to analyze the sentence—a fact of the matter that is independent of us. This assumption, I claimed, is one that OD itself helped to undermine, but OD cannot be fully understood unless one realizes that this was Russell's assumption.[24]

POSTSCRIPT

This essay left my hands in 1982. There is much in it that I would now put quite differently, but to attempt to do so would be to write a wholly new piece. There is, however, one implication that now seems definitely wrong. I strongly suggest that Russell's elimination of classes was made possible only by the theory of incomplete symbols introduced in OD, i.e., that no analogue of the definition of (symbols for) classes in terms of propositional functions is possible in the theory of denoting concepts. This now seems wrong; given sufficient ingenuity in manipulating the theory of denoting concepts, I think it can be made to serve this purpose. I also think, however, that it remains true that Russell thought that the theory of incomplete symbols was required for the elimination of classes. My more recent views are set out in detail in my *Russell, Idealism, and the Emergence of Analytic Philosophy* (1990).

---

24. I thank Burton Dreben and Warren D. Goldfarb for their helpful conversations about the subject of this essay, and for their criticisms of an earlier draft. Comments by Thomas G. Ricketts and Catherine Elgin and a question from Wade Savage also resulted in changes I am glad to have made.

QUANTIFICATIONAL

LOGIC:

PROOF

THEORY

13a

Gentzen's Analysis of

First-Order Proofs

Dag Prawitz

A basic question in general proof theory is of course the question how the notion of logical proof within first order languages is to be analysed. The work by Gentzen (1935) may be viewed as an answer to this question. The answer was given in two steps: In a first analysis, Gentzen showed how the notion could be defined in terms of certain formal systems constructed by him. Then, by a deeper analysis of the structure of these proofs, he showed that they could be written in a very special form, which altogether gave a very satisfactory understanding of these proofs.

The first step was carried out for the so-called systems of natural deduction, while the second step was carried out for the so-called calculi of sequents. There are certain advantages (which will soon become apparent) in carrying out both steps for the systems of natural deduction and I shall briefly do this here.[1]

1. GENTZEN'S SYSTEMS
OF NATURAL DEDUCTION

1.1. *Main idea*

Gentzen's systems of natural deduction arise from a particular analysis of deductive inferences by which the deductive role of the different logical constants are separated. The inferences are broken down into atomic steps in such a way that each step involves only one logical constant. The steps are of two kinds, and for each logical constant

This essay first appeared as sections II.1 and II.2 of "Ideas and Results in Proof Theory," in J. E. Fenstad (ed.), *Proceedings of the Second Scandinavian Logic Symposium* (1971). It is reprinted with minor changes by permission of the author and Elsevier Science Publishers.

1. [*editor's note*] In this essay the first step is shown in detail, but only a brief sketch is given of the second (2.2.3). For a full treatment of the latter, see "Ideas and Results in Proof Theory," from which this extract is taken.

there are inferences of both kinds: steps that allow the *introduction* of the logical constant (i.e., the conclusion of the inference has the constant as outermost symbol) and steps that allow the *elimination* of the logical constant (i.e., the premiss or one of the premisses of the inference has the constant as outermost symbol).

The proofs start from *assumptions,* which at certain steps in the proof may be discharged or *closed;* typically, an assumption A is closed at an introduction of an implication $A \supset B$.

1.2. *Inference rules*

It is suitable to represent the proofs as *derivations* written in tree form. The top formulas of the tree are then the assumptions, and the other formulas of the tree are to follow from the one(s) immediately above by one of the *inference rules* that formalizes the atomic inferences mentioned above. A formula A in the tree is said to *depend* on the assumptions standing above A that have not been closed by some inference preceding A. The *open assumptions* of a derivation are the assumptions on which the last formula depends.

I state the inference rules in the form of schemata in the usual way. A formula written within square brackets above a premiss is to indicate that assumptions of this form occurring above the premiss are discharged at this inference. An inference rule is labelled with the logical constant that it deals with followed by "I" when it is an introduction and "E" when it is an elimination.

$$\&\text{I)} \quad \frac{A \quad B}{A \,\&\, B} \qquad\qquad \&\text{E)} \quad \frac{A \,\&\, B}{A} \quad \frac{A \,\&\, B}{B}$$

$$\vee\text{I)} \quad \frac{A}{A \vee B} \quad \frac{B}{A \vee B} \qquad \vee\text{E)} \quad \frac{A \vee B \quad \overset{[A]}{C} \quad \overset{[B]}{C}}{C}$$

$$\supset\text{I)} \quad \frac{\overset{[A]}{B}}{A \supset B} \qquad\qquad \supset\text{E)} \quad \frac{A \quad A \supset B}{B}$$

$$\forall\text{I)} \quad \frac{A(a)}{(\forall x)A(x)} \qquad\qquad \forall\text{E)} \quad \frac{(\forall x)A(x)}{A(t)}$$

$$\exists\text{I)} \quad \frac{A(t)}{(\exists x)A(x)} \qquad\qquad \exists\text{E)} \quad \frac{(\exists x)A(x) \quad \overset{[A(a)]}{B}}{B}$$

1.2.1. *Restrictions.*   Obvious conventions about substitution are to be understood. The rules ∀I and ∃E contain the following further restrictions concerning the parameter *a*, called the *proper parameter* (or Eigenparameter) of the inference: In ∀I, *a* is not to occur in the assumptions that $A(a)$ depends on; in ∃E, *a* is not to occur in *B* nor in the assumptions that the premiss *B* depends on except those of the form $A(a)$ (closed by the inference).

1.2.2. *Negation.*   We assume that the first order languages contain a constant Λ for absurdity (or falsehood) and that $\sim A$ is understood as shorthand for $A \supset \Lambda$. The obvious introduction and elimination rules for negation

$$\sim\text{I)}\quad \frac{\begin{array}{c}[A]\\ \Lambda\end{array}}{\sim A} \qquad\qquad\qquad \sim\text{E)}\ \frac{A \quad \sim A}{\Lambda}$$

are then special cases of ⊃I and ⊃E, respectively.

1.2.3. *Major and minor premisses.*   In an inference by an application of an E-rule, the premiss in which the constant in question is exhibited (in the figures above) is called the *major premiss* of the inference and the other premiss(es) if any, we call the *minor premiss(es)*.

1.2.4. *Convention about proper parameters.*   To simplify certain formal details in the sequel, it will tacitly be assumed that a parameter in a derivation is the proper parameter of at most one inference, that the proper parameter of an ∀I-inference occurs only above the conclusion of the inference, and that the proper parameter of an ∃E-inference occurs only above the minor premiss of the inference.

1.3. *The systems* **M, I, C**

1.3.1. *Minimal logic.*   The rules given above determine the system of natural deduction for (first order) *minimal logic*, abbreviated **M**.

1.3.2. *Intuitionistic logic.*   By adding the rule Λ_I (intuitionistic absurdity rule)

$$\frac{\Lambda}{A}$$

where A is to be atomic and different from Λ, we get the system of natural deduction for (*first order*) *intuitionistic logic* (**I**).

1.3.3. *Classical logic.* The system of natural deduction for (first order) *classical logic* (**C**) is obtained by

(i) considering languages without the constants $\vee$ and $\exists$ and leaving out the rules for these constants (they become derived rules when $\vee$ and $\exists$ are defined in the usual way) and

(ii) adding to the rules of **M** the rule Λ_C (classical absurdity rule)

$$\frac{\begin{array}{c} [\sim\!A] \\ \Lambda \end{array}}{A}$$

where A is atomic and different from Λ.

1.4. *Derivations and derivability*

We say that Π is a *derivation* in **M** (**I** or **C**) of A from a set of formulas Γ when Π is a tree formed according to the above explanations using the rules of **M** (**I** or **C**) with an end formula A depending on formulas all belonging to Γ. If there is such a derivation, we say that A is *derivable* in the system in question from Γ; in short: $\Gamma \vdash A$. When A is derivable from the empty set of assumptions, we may say simply that A is *derivable*.

1.5. *Extensions by the additions of atomic systems*

It is also of interest to consider extensions of the three systems defined above by adding further rules for atomic formulas. There may also be reason to specify the languages of the systems exactly. By an *atomic system*, I shall understand a system determined by a set of *descriptive constants*, (i.e. individual, operational, and predicate constants) and a set of *inference rules* for atomic sentences with these constants (i.e. both the premisses and the conclusion are to be atomic formulas of this kind). A rule may lack premisses and is then called an *axiom*. Let **S** be an (atomic) system of this kind. By a *formula over* **S**, we shall understand a formula whose descriptive constants are those of **S**. By **M(S)**, we shall understand the system of natural deduction whose language is the first order language determined by the descriptive constants of **S** and whose rules are the rules of **S** and **M**. We define the systems $I(S)$ and $C(S)$ similarly. Note that $I(S)$ is the same as $M(S^+)$ where S^+ is obtained from S by adding the rule Λ_I.

In many contexts, it is not essential how the rules of a system S are specified and we make no restriction of that kind. Of special interest, however, are the *Post systems* where the inference rules are determined as the instances of a finite number of schemata of the form

$$\frac{A_1 \; A_2 \ldots A_n}{B}$$

where A_1, A_2, A_n, and B are atomic formulas. One may also require that B contains no parameter that does not occur in some A_i.

1.6. *Remark*

A trivial reformulation of the systems described above is obtained if we make explicit the assumptions that a formula in a derivation depends on by writing these assumptions in a sequence followed by an arrow in front of the formula. The tree of formulas is then replaced by a tree of so-called *sequents* of the form $\Gamma \rightarrow A$ where Γ is a sequence of formulas. If the inference rules are now formulated with these sequents as the basic objects, they get a somewhat different look. For instance, $\supset$I and $\supset$E now become

$$\frac{\Gamma, A \rightarrow B}{\Gamma \rightarrow A \supset B} \qquad \frac{\Gamma \rightarrow A \quad \Delta \rightarrow A \supset B}{\Gamma, \Delta \rightarrow B}$$

and the derivations now start not from assumptions but from axioms of the form $A \rightarrow A$. Clearly, there is only an inessential notational difference between the first formulation and this reformulation; and the new formulation is not to be confused (as is sometimes done) with the calculus of sequents, which differs more essentially by having, instead of elimination rules, rules for operating on the formulas to the left of the arrow (cf. for instance, the new formulation of $\supset$E with the rule for introducing $\supset$ in the antecedent in the calculus of sequents).

2. THE SIGNIFICANCE OF GENTZEN'S SYSTEMS

The most noteworthy properties of Gentzen's systems of natural deduction seem to be (2.1) the analysis of deductive inferences into atomic steps, by which the deductive role of the different logical constants is separated and (2.2) the discovery that these atomic steps are of two kinds, viz. introductions and eliminations, standing in a certain symmetrical relation to each other.

2.1. This analysis may be understood as an attempt to characterize the notion of proof, not only provability as first done by Frege, in the sense that it is an attempt (2.1.1) to isolate the essential deductive operations and (2.1.2) to break them down as far as possible.[2]

2.1.1. The deductive operations that are isolated are to begin with constructive (or intuitionistic) ones. There is a close correspondence between the constructive meaning of a logical constant and its introduction rule. For instance, an implication $A \supset B$ is constructively understood as the assertion of the existence of a construction of B from A, and in accordance with this meaning $\supset$I allows the inference of $A \supset B$ given a proof of B from A. Of course, a proof of B from A is not the same as a construction of B from A; it is rather a special kind of such a construction (cf. section 2.2.2). There is thus not a complete agreement but a close correspondence between the constructive meaning of the constants and the introduction rules; sometimes the correspondence is very close: some of Heyting's explanations, see e.g. Heyting (1956, pp. 97–99 and 102), may almost be taken as a reading of Gentzen's introduction rules.

This correspondence between the introduction rules and the constructive interpretation of the logical constants is a strong indication that the essential *constructive* deductive operations have been isolated. By a (first order) *positive proof,* I shall in this paper understand a (first order) proof that uses intuitionistically valid deductive operations but no operation assuming any special properties of Λ; an *intuitionistic proof* is then simply a proof using intuitionistically valid deductive operations. The claim is thus that **M** constitutes an analysis of first order positive proofs and **I** an analysis of first order intuitionistic proofs.

The *classical* deductive operations are then analysed as consisting of the constructive ones plus a principle of indirect proof for atomic sentences, which may be understood as stating as a special assumption that the atomic sentences are decidable.[3] One may doubt that this is the proper way of analysing classical inferences, and it is true that the rules of the classical calculus of sequents or some variants of it (like the one by Schütte (1951) or the one by Tait (1968)) are closer to the

---

2. Frege's formal definition of derivability is perhaps the first investigation in general proof theory; see section I.4.1 of "Ideas and Results."

3. In the formulation by Gentzen (1935), one adds the axiom of the excluded middle instead of the rule Λ_C to get classical logic from intuitionistic logic.

classical meaning of the logical constants. But this possibility of analysing classical inferences as a special case of constructive ones (applicable to decidable sentences) provides a way of constructively understanding classical reasoning (which is the essential fact behind Kolmogoroff's (1925) and Gödel's (1933) interpretation of classical logic in intuitionistic logic; see also Prawitz and Malmnäs (1968)) and also explains the success in carrying over to classical logic the deeper results concerning the structure of proofs, which at first sight are evident only for constructive proofs (cf. sec. 2.2.3).

The claim that the essential deductive operations have been isolated is not to be understood as a claim that these operations mirror all informal deductive practices, which would be an unreasonable demand in view of the fact that informal practices may sometimes contain logically insignificant irregularities. What is claimed is that the essential logical content of intuitive logical operations that can be formulated in the languages considered can be understood as composed of the atomic inferences isolated by Gentzen. It is in this sense that we may understand the terminology *natural* deduction.

Nevertheless, Gentzen's systems are also natural in the more superficial sense of corresponding rather well to informal practices; in other words, the structures of informal proofs are often preserved rather well when formalized within the systems of natural deduction. This may seem surprising in view of what was said about the correspondence between the inference rules and the *constructive* meaning of the logical constants. But it is a fact that actual reasoning often makes use of a mixture of constructive and non-constructive principles with predominance of constructive principles, the non-constructive ones typically amounting to an occasional use of the principle of indirect proof. For instance, it is a fact that an implication $A \supset B$ most often is proved by deducing B from A, a procedure that is not singled out by the classical truth functional meaning of $\supset$ as the most natural one.

2.1.2. It seems fair to say that a proof built up from Gentzen's atomic inference is *completely analysed* in the sense that one can hardly imagine the possibility of breaking down his atomic inferences into some simpler inferences.

The separation of the deductive role of the different logical constants was partly achieved already by Hilbert in some of his axiomatic formulations of sentential logic. Gentzen is able to complete this separation by separating also the role of implication from that of the other constants.

We may note in passing that the derivations in Gentzen's systems are completely analysed also in the less important sense that for each formula in the derivation, it is uniquely determined from what premisses and by which inference rule it is inferred; these are properties that Gentzen's systems share also with certain other logical calculi.

2.1.3. From what has been said above, it should be clear that Gentzen's systems of natural deduction are not arbitrary formalizations of first order logic but constitute a significant analysis of the proofs in this logic..[4]

The situation may be compared to the attempts to characterize the notion of computation where e.g. the formalism of μ-recursive functions or even the general recursive functions may be regarded as an extensional characterization of this notion while Turing's analysis is such that one may reasonably assert the thesis that every computation when sufficiently analysed can be broken down in the operations described by Turing.

2.2. What makes Gentzen's systems especially interesting is the discovery of a certain symmetry between the atomic inferences, which may be indicated by saying that the corresponding introductions and eliminations are *inverses* of each other. The sense in which an elimination, say, is the inverse of the corresponding introduction is roughly this: the conclusion obtained by an elimination does not state anything more than what must have already been obtained if the major premiss of the elimination was inferred by an introduction. For instance, if the premiss of an &E was inferred by introduction, then the conclusion of the &E must already occur as one of the premisses of this introduction. Similarly, if the major premiss $A \supset B$ of an $\supset$E was inferred by an introduction, then a proof of the conclusion B of the $\supset$E is obtained from the proof of the major premiss of the $\supset$E by simply replacing its assumption A by the proof of the minor premiss.

2.2.1. In other words, a proof of the conclusion of an elimination is already "contained" in the proofs of the premisses when the major premiss is inferred by introduction. We shall refer to this by saying

---

4. It seems fair to say that no other system is more convincing in this respect. The axiomatic systems introduced by Frege and continued by Russell, Hilbert, and others clearly do not usually have this aim at all. There exist other systems, often proposed for didactical purposes, that have been called systems of natural deduction. To the extent that they are not to be considered as mere notational variants of Gentzen's systems, it must be said that they do not even approximately match Gentzen's analysis. (Their alleged pedagogical merits also seem doubtful; see Prawitz (1965, pp. 103–5, and 1967).) Gentzen's calculi of sequents may be considered as (and were historically) derived from his systems of natural deduction.

that the pairs of corresponding introductions and eliminations satisfy the *inversion principle*. We shall see very soon how to make this principle more precise, but let us first consider another aspect of the principle.

2.2.2. The inversion principle seems to allow a *reinterpretation* of the logical symbols. With Gentzen, we may say that the introductions represent, as it were, the "definitions" of the logical constants. An introduction rule states a sufficient condition for introducing a formula with this constant as outermost symbol (which, as we saw, was in very close agreement with the constructive meaning of the constant but did not express this meaning completely), and this condition may now be taken as the "meaning" of the logical constant. For instance, $A \supset B$ is now to mean that there is a deduction of B from A. The eliminations, on the other hand, are "justified" by this very meaning given to the constants by the introductions. As guaranteed by the inversion principle, the conclusion of an elimination only states what must hold in view of the meaning of the major premiss of the elimination. The examples with &E and $\supset$E given above already illustrate this. As a further illustration, consider the inference

$$\frac{\sim(\forall x)A(x)}{(\exists x) \sim A(x)}$$

This inference is clearly not justified by the meaning given to the constants by the introductions: The sufficient condition for introducing $\sim(\forall x)A$ i.e. a proof of Λ from the assumption $(\forall x)A$, in no way guarantees that $(\exists x) \sim A$ holds (in the sense of the introduction rules) since such a proof may not at all contain a proof of $\sim A(t)$ for some term t.

These ideas of Gentzen's are of course quite vague since it is not meant that the introductions are literally to be understood as "definitions."

2.2.3. One way of making the inversion principle precise is the following.[5] Since the principle says that nothing new is obtained by an elimination immediately following an introduction (of the major premiss of the elimination), it suggests that such sequences of inferences can be dispensed with. From this observation, it is possible to obtain quite simply Gentzen's results about the structure of proofs, the sec-

5. Another way of doing so is considered in Appendix A of "Ideas and Results."

ond step in his analysis. Indeed, the whole idea of this analysis is contained in the observations made above. Note, however, that only the rules of minimal logic are governed by the inversion principle; both the rule Λ_I and the rule Λ_C clearly fall outside the pattern of introductions and eliminations. Note in particular that the principle of indirect proof when not restricted to atomic formulas constitutes quite a new principle for inferring compound formulas (which is not at all justified in the terminology of sec. 2.2.2 by the meaning given to the constants by the introduction rules). Our restriction that the conclusions of applications of the rules Λ_I and Λ_C are to be atomic (1.3.2 and 1.3.3) are motivated by these considerations. This restriction ensures that these extra rules do not disturb the pattern of introduction and elimination rules, and enables us to prove that every derivation in **M**, **I**, or **C** can be converted into one in "normal form."[6] A "normal form" derivation is *direct* in the sense that it proceeds from the assumptions to the conclusion by first only using the meaning of the assumptions by breaking them down into their components (the analytic part), and then establishing the meaning of the conclusion by building it up from its components (the synthetic part). With Gentzen, we may say that the proof represented by a normal derivation makes no detours (*"es macht keine Umwege"*).

6. [*editor's note*] A precise specification of what it is for a derivation to be in normal form, and a proof of this theorem, are contained in Section II.3 of "Ideas and Results."

On the Idea of a
General Proof Theory

Dag Prawitz

I have been asked to speak about 'the main lines of thought of a general proof theory', and I shall divide my paper into three parts:

(I) *Historical introduction,* where I shall outline some aspects of the historical development of proof theory and try to describe the general character of the subject.

(II) *Logical consequence and the validity of derivations,* where I shall contrast some different theories about logical consequence and try to indicate how proof theory may contribute to the understanding of this notion via the notion of validity of arguments.

(III) *Interpretation of formal derivations,* where I shall briefly consider how Gentzen's system of natural deduction is to be interpreted in the light of Section II and point out how some traditional proof theoretical results are related to this interpretation.

1. HISTORICAL INTRODUCTION

As is well-known, proof theory originated with Hilbert at the beginning of the century. Hilbert did not really create a theory, however; rather he introduced a certain research project which he named proof theory. The goal of the project as it was first formulated by Hilbert (1900) and (1905) was to prove the consistency of mathematics, or more precisely, of the arithmetic needed for mathematical analysis. To prove the consistency of a mathematical theory is of course not a very precise undertaking. It was first to be made precise by formalizing the mathematical theory. The goal was then to be attained, Hilbert suggested, by a detailed study of the proofs of the formalized theory; hence the name proof theory.

A moment's reflection shows however that even after the step of formalization, the project is not a very precise one. There can be no

This essay first appeared in *Synthese* 27 (1974). It is reprinted by permission of the author and Kluwer Academic Publishers. Copyright ©1974 by D. Reidel Publishing Company, Dordrecht, Holland.

absolute consistency proof. The consistency of a theory is made credible only to the extent that the principles used in the consistency proof are trustworthy. If we want to strengthen the belief in the consistency of a given theory, which presumably already has some plausibility, the principles we use on the meta-level, i.e. in the proof theory in which the consistency is proved, must be more convincing than the principles occurring in the given theory.

Hilbert never stated precisely what principles he wanted to use in his proof theory, but it is clear that the ones he had in mind—he called them finitary—were of a very elementary kind and would form a proper part of the set of principles occurring in (first order) arithmetic.

Thus, the most one can hope for by a consistency proof is a reduction of the consistency of certain principles to the consistency of some other principles. The reduction obtained in this way may be formulated in a more interesting way, which Hilbert was aware of in later publications (see e.g. Hilbert, 1926). To use Hilbert's own terminology, we may talk about the *real* and *ideal* part of arithmetic. The real part of a theory consists of the finitary reasoning that Hilbert wanted to use in the consistency proof, the rest of the theory constitutes the ideal part. Hilbert's project can now also be formulated in the following equivalent way: To prove in the real part of arithmetic that each proof of a real sentence (i.e., a sentence in the real part) which uses also the ideal part of arithmetic, can be replaced by a proof using only the real part. From a real point of view, so to say, the ideal part would thus be shown in this way to be only a convenient auxiliary extension of the real part, which could never conflict with the real part. To take an example, consider the real sentence $2^5 \times 2^4 = 2^9$. The most expedient proof of this real sentence may use the ideal part of arithmetic establishing the general result that $n^p \cdot n^q = n^{p+q}$. But the sentence has also a real proof, the somewhat tedious calculation that both $2^5 \times 2^4$ and 2^9 are identical to 512. We require of course that the more abstract, ideal proofs do not come into conflict with such calculations, the real proofs. By establishing this fact in the real part, one would obtain what could be called a reduction of the ideal part to the real part. Using another terminology, we may also describe Hilbert's project as an attempt to prove in the real part of arithmetic that arithmetic is a conservative extension of its real part.

As we know today by Gödel's result, it is impossible to carry out Hilbert's program in the way he intended. According to Gödel's first incompleteness theorem, there can be no complete formalization of arithmetic. And according to his second incompleteness theorem, every consistency proof of an arithmetical theory requires the use of some principles that do not belong to the theory in question.

These results do not rule out, however, the possibility of carrying out a somewhat modified program. The necessary modifications are of two kinds: Firstly, one has to be satisfied with proving the consistency of some proper part of arithmetic codified in a formal theory. Secondly, one has to find elementary (real) principles which happen not to occur in the theory and which have a sufficient strength to allow the consistency to be proved on the meta-level with the help of these principles but with the exclusion of the seemingly more dubious ideal principles that occur in the formal theory. This possibility was utilized by Gentzen in his proof of the consistency of first-order arithmetic (a proper part of arithmetic) where he used transfinite induction up to a certain constructive ordinal, epsilon-zero (which principle does not occur in first order arithmetic) but did not use any induction over quantified formulas (which principle occurs in first order arithmetic).

Gentzen thus obtains a reduction of first order arithmetic including the principle of (ordinary) induction over first order formulas to an arithmetic that contains instead of that principle the principle of transfinite induction (up to epsilon-zero) over quantifier-free formulas. Results of the same general kind were later obtained for more comprehensive systems of arithmetic; all of them were essentially weaker than second order arithmetic, however.

In the terminology used above, we can formulate these results by saying that the arithmetical systems in question are conservative extensions of their real parts—but these results are now proved not in the real part but in a certain constructive extension of it. Often, these results can be somewhat strengthened by showing that the whole system (and not only its real part) can be interpreted in this constructive extension of the real part.

In principle, results of this kind can of course be obtained in many ways, e.g., by model-theoretical ones. Characteristic of proof theory is the method by which the results are obtained, namely by a study of the proofs of the systems.

I have suggested that this kind of proof theory where one theory T_1 is reduced to another theory T_2 either by proving in T_2 that T_1 is consistent or more generally by interpreting T_1 in T_2 be called *reductive proof theory*. The interest of the results depends on the extent to which the principles of the reducing theory T_2 are epistemologically more fundamental than the reduced theory T_1.

However, it is often felt that these results or rather the work which is summarized in these results shows something about the proofs of the reduced theory T_1 and that in this way, they are of interest in themselves independent of questions about epistemological reductions. Indeed, Gentzen's consistency proofs (especially in his second formulation) were obtained by applying some general insights about the structure of first-order proofs that he had obtained in earlier work. It must be admitted, however, that such insights have seldom been formulated in a way which clearly shows their independent interest. Thus, it seems reasonable to try to isolate these general results about proofs from their applications to problems of reductive proof theory. I have suggested that such a study of proofs in their own right where one is interested in general questions about the nature and structure of proofs be named *general proof theory*.

One may contrast a general proof theory of this kind with model theory, which has been a rather dominant branch of logic for the last decades. In model theory, one concentrates on questions like what sentences are logically valid and what sentences follow logically from other sentences. But one disregards questions concerning how we know that a sentence is logically valid or follows logically from another sentence. General proof theory would thus be an attempt to supplement model theory by studying also the evidence or the process—i.e., in other words, the proofs—by which we come to know logical validities and logical consequences.

2. LOGICAL CONSEQUENCE AND THE VALIDITY OF DERIVATION

I have elsewhere (Prawitz, 1965 and 1973) tried to develop some notions and ideas of a general proof theory and have summarized some of the main things known about proofs using these notions. Here, I should like to dwell upon how the theory may give us some better understanding of the notion of a logical consequence. For comparison, I shall first discuss briefly some traditional theories about logical consequence.

(1) After Frege's development of a logical calculus, the identification of logical consequence and derivability in such a given calculus became common. It is easy to criticize this identification, as e.g. Tarski (1936b) did, but before we turn to the criticism, let us consider the merits. Frege was aware of a difficulty in dealing with logical matters, which e.g. Boole was not aware of, namely the difficulty of avoiding circularity. If we simply axiomatize or define the notion of logical consequence with the understanding that a logical consequence holds when this follows logically (!) from the axioms or the definition, then one may rightly ask whether anything really is achieved. Since the logic that is needed to handle Frege's calculus is of such a rudimentary

kind, it is clear that Frege really did obtain a significant reduction by the introduction of logical calculi. And no doubt, his contribution constituted a major step forward in our understanding of the notion of logical consequence.

Today, we are certainly (and perhaps too much) aware of the short-comings of the idea of identifying logical consequence and derivability in a given calculus: Clearly, there is something arbitrary in Frege's calculus as in most other logical calculi that have been proposed. Why should logical consequence be identified with derivability in exactly that calculus and not some other? Furthermore, to construct a logical calculus does not ordinarily seem to be the same as to analyze the meaning of the notion of logical consequence. Thus, one may argue, the most one can hope for by constructing such a calculus would be an extensional agreement between the logical consequence relation and the relation of derivability in the calculus, which would fall short of an intensional analysis of the consequence relation. Finally, we know that when we go above first order logic, the calculi will be incomplete and thus, we cannot even obtain an extensional analysis in that case.

(2) Pointing out some of these shortcomings in the then common conception of logical consequence, Tarski made the well-known sug-gestion that a sentence B should be defined as a logical consequence of a sentence A when in effect, B is true in each model in which A is true. While Tarski's definition avoids the shortcomings discussed above, it involves exactly the kind of circularity that the Frege-inspired idea avoided. Whether e.g. a sentence $(\exists x)\neg P(x)$ follows logically from a sentence $\neg(\forall x)P(x)$ depends according to this definition on whether $(\exists x)\neg P(x)$ is true in each model (D, S) in which $\neg(\forall x)P(x)$ is true. And this again is the same as to ask whether there is an element e in D that does not belong to S whenever it is not the case that every e in D belongs to S, i.e. we are essentially back to the question whether $(\exists x)\neg A(x)$ follows from $\neg(\forall x)A(x)$.

I do not claim that Tarski's definition is methodologically defective. It is of course not circular in the strict sense of using the *definiens* in the *definiendum*. But it is clear that Tarski's semantical theory of truth with this definition of logical consequence does not constitute any reduction of this notion. And what is more serious, it seems to give very little information about the notion. It may be too much to de-mand a real reduction. But if we cannot define the notion of logical consequence without implicitly assuming that we already know when a sentence follows logically from other sentences we should at least demand that a theory about the notion relates the notion to other interesting notions.

One such notion to which one may expect the theory to establish a connection is the notion of a valid argument. Logic was sometimes traditionally described as the study of arguments, viz., as the theory that distinguished valid arguments from invalid ones. The only thing Tarski's semantical theory can say about the valid arguments is that an argument is valid when its conclusion follows logically from its premisses. This is surely a rather meager result when logical consequence is defined in the way Tarski does: it is to treat an argument as a black box, to observe only the input and output, i.e. the premisses and the conclusion, while completely disregarding the inner structure of the argument. It seems to me that the validity of an argument should also depend on its inner structure. It may be more promising to define the notion of a logical consequence on the basis of such a notion of valid arguments instead of attempting the other way around.

(3) A theory which does take the notion of proof seriously is the intuitionistic one. In an intuitionistic spirit, we may define a sentence B as a logical consequence of a sentence A when (for any systems of proofs of atomic sentences) there is a function which applied to any proof of A (relative to S) gives a proof of B (relative to S).

The key concept in this definition is the one of proof, which plays here about the same role as the notion of truth does in Tarski's definition of logical consequence. The intuitionistic definition has thus to be supplemented by a definition of the notion of proof. A proof is here understood as an abstract entity, as the thing represented by a derivation, in about the same way as propositions are abstract entities represented by sentences. There are some disagreements concerning the exact definition of the notion of proof. It is unproblematic that a proof of a conjunction, e.g., consists of a pair of proofs of the conjuncts. But a proof of an implication $A \rightarrow B$ is by some understood as a function which applied to any proof of A yields a proof of B (Prawitz 1971 and Martin-Löf 1973) while others understand it as a pair whose first element is such a function and whose second element is a proof of the fact that the function has the property mentioned (Kreisel 1962). In both cases, iterated implications will give rise to a hierarchy of functions where functions higher up in the hierarchy operate on those further down.

These intuitionistic notions have by no means been studied as much or as systematically as the corresponding semantical ones and seem to deserve a much greater attention.

(4) While the intuitionistic ideas bring the notion of logical consequence in contact with the notion of an abstract proof, they do not establish a connection with the notion of valid arguments as suggested

at the end of Section 1. Let me therefore finally outline some proof theoretical conceptions which do establish such a connection. This approach may be open to more criticism than any of the other approaches discussed above. And even if some of the ideas turn out to be sound, the exact details may have to be revised considerably. In the following presentation, I shall concentrate on the main ideas of this approach and shall not very much discuss its weaknesses. But it will be kept in mind that the outline is to be understood as a tentative proposal.

The basic notion of this approach is thus that of a valid argument. What are we to understand by an argument? Clearly, an argument is an argument *for* some sentence *A*. Normally, one can further distinguish one or several sentences in the argument which are claimed to support *A*. These sentences are either claimed to hold outright or they are again supported by other sentences in the argument, and so on. We can thus distinguish a tree structure of sentences in an argument, and I shall call such a structure an *argument skeleton.*

When only sentences are involved and the sentences in the top of the tree are asserted as holding, I shall say that the argument is *closed.* I shall also consider *open* arguments that are like closed ones but may contain open sentences instead of sentences and unsupported assumptions in the top of the tree instead of assertions. By replacing the free variables by names and the assumptions by arguments for the assumptions, we turn an open argument into a closed one. This closed argument is said to be an *instance* of the open one.

A closed argument may contain an open argument as a part as e.g. when we argue for $A \rightarrow B$ by giving an open argument for *B* with the assumption *A*. When this open argument for *B* from *A* is used to support $A \rightarrow B$, the assumption *A* is said to become *closed;* in the open argument for *B* from *A* taken separately, the assumption *A* is said to be *open.* In a similar way, a free variable in an open argument may become closed when the open argument occurs as a part of another (open or closed) argument, e.g. when we argue for $(\forall x)A(x)$ by giving an open argument for $A(a)$. I shall assume that the way assumptions and variables are closed in an argument is indicated in the skeleton. As exemplified above, a skeleton can be divided into inferences but the 'premisses' of the inferences may sometimes be whole arguments instead of single sentences.[1]

---

1. In Prawitz (1973) these notions are defined in more detail. There is a slight change in terminology, however. What is here called an argument skeleton was there called an argument.

Does an argument consist of anything more than its skeleton? Before answering this question, I shall consider what will be required of a valid argument. From a constructive point of view, it seems reasonable to require that a valid argument for (i) $A \wedge B$, (ii) $A \vee B$, (iii) $A \rightarrow B$, (iv) $(\forall x)A(x)$, (v) $(\exists x)A(x)$, respectively, shall be built up of (i') valid arguments for A and for B, (ii') a valid argument for A or for B, (iii') a valid (open) argument for B from A, (iv') a valid (open) argument for $A(a)$, (v') a valid argument for $A(t)$ for some term t, respectively. (Classically, we should liberalize the requirements on $A \vee B$ and $(\exists x)A(x)$ by understanding them as synonomous with $\neg(\neg A \wedge \neg B)$ and $\neg(\forall x)\neg A(x)$.)

The arguments obtained from a given argument when its last step is deleted, i.e. what remains when the conclusion of the last inference is taken away, I shall call the *strict immediate subarguments* of the given argument. To say that the requirements listed above are sufficient conditions of validity is thus to say that an argument for a sentence of one of the forms (i)–(v) is valid when its strict immediate subarguments are as described in (i')–(v') respectively. The form of the skeleton of the argument may then be indicated by the figures ($i = 1$ or 2)

$$
(1) \quad \frac{\begin{array}{cc} \vdots & \vdots \\ A_1 & A_2 \end{array}}{A_1 \wedge B_2}
\qquad
(2) \quad \frac{\begin{array}{c} \vdots \\ A_i \end{array}}{A_1 \vee A_2}
\qquad
(3) \quad \frac{\begin{array}{c} A \\ \vdots \\ B \end{array}}{A \rightarrow B}
$$

$$
(4) \quad \frac{\begin{array}{c} \vdots\,(a) \\ A(a) \end{array}}{(\forall x)A(x)}
\qquad
(5) \quad \frac{\begin{array}{c} \vdots \\ A(t) \end{array}}{(\exists x)A(x)}
$$

I shall say that an argument whose skeleton has one of the forms (1)–(5) is in *canonical form* and that the last inferences in (1)–(5) are *canonical inferences*.

With this terminology, we can say that an argument in canonical form whose strict immediate subarguments are valid is itself valid. Conversely, I assume from a constructive point of view that a valid closed argument can be written in canonical form with valid strict immediate subarguments. Of a valid open argument it seems reasonable to require that all its closed substitution instances are valid when they are obtained by replacing open assumptions by closed valid arguments for the assumptions. Whether this condition is also sufficient for validity of open arguments, I shall discuss later.

We may summarize the above in the following:

Principle concerning the validity of arguments. A closed argument is valid if and only if it can be written in canonical form where the strict immediate subarguments are valid. An open argument is valid only if its closed substitution instances obtained by replacing open assumptions by valid arguments is valid.

One could perhaps think that all inferences of a valid argument should be of this canonical kind, but this idea is clearly mistaken since we often argue validly in a quite different way from an assumption (about the existence of a valid argument). Consider e.g. arguments whose skeleton has one of the following forms where in (c) x is not free in B.

$$
(a) \quad \frac{\overset{\vdots}{A \wedge B}}{A} \qquad\qquad (b) \quad \frac{\overset{\vdots}{A} \quad \overset{\vdots}{A \to B}}{B} \qquad\qquad (c) \quad \frac{\overset{\vdots}{(\exists x)A(x)} \quad \overset{\vdots}{(\forall x)(A(x) \to B)}}{B}
$$

Why are the last inferences here so trivially correct? From our present point of view, we may say that since it is possible to write a valid argument for $A \wedge B$ in the form (1), we can extract from it a valid argument for A, and hence, we are certainly justified in inferring A from $A \wedge B$. Similarly, it is possible to write a valid argument for $A \to B$ in the form (3). We can then extract a valid open argument for B from A and (by the second half of the principle above) we then obtain a valid argument for B by replacing the open assumption A in the open argument by the given argument for A provided this argument is valid. We thus see that on the assumption that we are given valid arguments for A and for $A \to B$, we can form a valid argument for B. In other words, there exists an operation which allows us to bring the argument (b) into a valid canonical form provided the strict immediate subarguments are valid. The operation in question which in this way justifies (b), call it φ_b, may be indicated by saying that it transforms arguments whose skeleton is of the form shown to the left below into an argument whose skeleton is of the form shown to the right below.

$$
(\varphi_b) \qquad
\begin{array}{c}
A \\
\vdots \\
\vdots \quad B \\
\hline
A \quad A \to B \\
\hline
B
\end{array}
\qquad
\begin{array}{c}
\vdots \\
A \\
\vdots \\
B
\end{array}
$$

Similarly, we can justify the inference (c) by an operation φ_c defined on arguments whose skeleton is of the form to the left below and which then takes as value an argument with the skeleton to the right below.

(φ_c)

$$
\begin{array}{ccc}
 & \begin{array}{c} A(a) \\ \vdots\,(a) \\ B \end{array} & \vdots \\
\vdots & & A(t) \\
\cfrac{A(t) \qquad \overline{A(a) \to B}}{\cfrac{(\exists x)A(x) \quad (\forall x)(A(x) \to B)}{B}} & & \begin{array}{c} \vdots\,(t) \\ B \end{array}
\end{array}
$$

As already suggested by the terminology, I do not regard the argument skeleton as constituting the whole argument but shall consider the justifying operations of the kind exemplified above as a part of the argument. By an argument, I shall thus understand an argument skeleton together with an assignment of justifying operations to each non-canonical inference in the skeleton.[2]

The justifying operations are to tell us how we shall find a closed valid argument in canonical form for the conclusion when (after possible substitutions for free variables and open assumptions) the strict immediate subarguments are given in valid canonical form. The argument constitutes the claim that the justifying operations have this required property. Hence, in the definition of an argument, we do not impose any special requirements on the operations that are assigned to the various inferences in the argument except for the obvious one that when the operation is defined for an argument for a formula A, then its value is also an argument for A;[3] the essential requirements on the operations will then enter into the definition of valid arguments.

An open argument, e.g. the one step argument

$$
\frac{A \quad A \to B}{B}
$$

2. What is here called an argument is in Prawitz (1973) called a justified argument.

3. A requirement about uniformity with respect to substitutions is also reasonable and is important in some connections. It can be stated: the result of substitutions (for free variables and open assumptions) in the value of the operation carried out on a certain argument is the same as the value of the operation carried out on the result of the same substitution on the given argument, or in symbols: $\varphi(\alpha)^\sigma = \varphi(\alpha^\sigma)$ where φ is the operation, α is the argument and σ the substitution.

(with open assumptions A and $A \rightarrow B$), to which the operation φ_b defined above is assigned is to be understood as a schema for finding a closed argument for the conclusion: if we replace the open assumptions A and $A \rightarrow B$ by closed arguments for A and $A \rightarrow B$ and write the second one in canonical form, then the argument for B is the one indicated to the right in the definition of φ_b. I shall use the word *reduce* for the kind of rewriting of arguments allowed by the operations. Thus, the left argument in the definition of the operation φ_b or φ_c reduces to the argument to the right in respective definition. An argument that contains these left arguments as parts is also said to reduce to the argument obtained by replacing these parts with their right counterparts. Generally, an argument α reduces to another argument β, if β can be obtained from α by successively replacing parts γ of the argument by the value assumed by the operation assigned to the last inference in γ when carried out on the argument γ.

If we now replace the unprecise 'it can be rewritten' by 'reduces' in the principle concerning the validity of arguments formulated above and read 'if and only if' in the second clause of the principle, then we obtain a recursive definition of the notion of valid argument relative to a choice of valid closed arguments for atomic sentences.

If we accept this notion of a valid argument relative to some choice $\mathscr{C}$ of valid closed arguments for atomic sentences, it seems reasonable to define a sentence B as a logical consequence of sentences A_1, $A_2, \ldots, A_n$ by the existence of an operation φ which for every choice $\mathscr{C}$ transforms any closed arguments for $A_1, A_2, \ldots, A_n$ valid relative to $\mathscr{C}$ to a closed argument for B valid relative to $\mathscr{C}$. This means again according to our definition that B is a logical consequence of A_1, $A_2, \ldots, A_n$ if and only if there exists an argument for B from A_1, $A_2, \ldots, A_n$ that is valid relative to any such choice $\mathscr{C}$.

As a final remark concerning the validity of arguments, I want to point out that the condition of validity of open arguments used above is rather weak: it is vacuously satisfied if there is no valid closed argument of the open assumptions of the argument. From the point of view that the operations assigned to the various inferences of the argument should be well-defined in the sense of not allowing infinite series of reductions, a stronger requirement would be reasonable. I have called it strong validity and it is again relative to some choice $\mathscr{C}$ of strongly valid closed arguments for atomic sentences. Let us by an *immediate subargument* of α over S understand a result of substituting arguments in a set S and terms for those open assumptions and open variables, respectively, in a strict immediate subargument of an argument α which are closed in α. (Compare the definition of subformula where $A(t)$ is defined as an immediate subformula of $(\forall x)A(x)$; in analogy with the terminology above, $A(x)$ would be the only *strict* immediate subformula.) We can then define strong validity relative to $\mathscr{C}$ for both open and closed arguments by the following recursion:

(1) An argument in canonical form is strongly valid relative to $\mathscr{C}$ if and only if its immediate subarguments over the set of strongly valid arguments relative to $\mathscr{C}$ are strongly valid relative to $\mathscr{C}$.

(2) An irreducible argument not in canonical form is strongly valid relative to $\mathscr{C}$ if and only if it either belongs to $\mathscr{C}$ or is open.

(3) A reducible argument not in canonical form is strongly valid relative to $\mathscr{C}$ if and only if by each way of reducing it, it reduces to an argument that is valid relative to $\mathscr{C}$ according to (1) or (2).

3. INTERPRETATION OF FORMAL DEFINITIONS

Note that the notion of argument developed above is not tied to any particular formal system (although, of course it depends on certain formal languages, viz., those of first order). This is the reason that I have spoken here about arguments and not derivations, which I conceive of as proceeding according to the fixed rules of a given formal system. The derivations of correct formal systems, however, give rise to valid and even strongly valid arguments.

The notion of strongly valid argument that I have developed above is a generalization of a notion which has been defined for the derivations of certain formal systems and which have played a major role in some recent proof theoretical investigations, and in particular in attempts towards a general proof theory. Let me end by briefly describing this connection.

Gentzen (1935) summed up his general result about derivations, which were later applied to obtain results in reductive proof theory, in what he called his *Hauptsatz.* It states, as you know, that the use of a certain rule, the so-called cut rule, can be eliminated from derivations in the calculus of sequents constructed by him; in English, the result is accordingly often called the cut-elimination theorem. Although the cut-rule has a different character than that of the other rules in Gentzen's calculus of sequents, it is not immediately obvious from Gentzen's formulation what the significance of his result is. In an attempt to show the significance of this result more clearly, I have reformulated it for Gentzen's system of natural deduction where one then obtains the result that each deduction can be transformed in a normal form with certain characteristic properties (Prawitz 1965 and 1971). In this formulation, the result has been extended to several more comprehensive systems such as the theory of iterated inductive definitions, second order logic and more general, the theory of finite types (see e.g. Girard 1971, Martin-Löf 1973, and Prawitz 1971).

The way formal derivations give rise to valid arguments is especially evident for Gentzen's system of natural deduction. The inferences of this system are of two kinds, so-called introduction and elimination inferences. The introduction inferences are exactly identical to the ones that I have called the canonical inferences and which were basic for the notion of (strong) validity. The elimination inferences are what can be described as the inverses of the corresponding introduction inferences. According to Gentzen, they could be justified on the basis of the meaning given to the logical constants by the rules of introduction. In our present terminology, we can say that they can be justified by operations which allow us to find a valid canonical derivation of the conclusion given valid canonical derivations of the premisses. Furthermore, they seem to constitute a maximum set of inferences that can be justified in this way, i.e., it seems reasonable to conjecture that the system of introduction and elimination inferences is complete with respect to logical consequence defined above (see further Prawitz 1973). While e.g. (a) and (b) above are examples of elimination inferences, (c) can be analysed as composed of several elimination inferences; I leave it to you to construct the corresponding valid argument containing only elimination inferences.

The result that each derivation in the system of natural deduction can be transformed to normal form, the normalization theorem, can in our present terminology be expressed by saying that some way of reducing the argument whose skeleton consists of the derivation in question and where each elimination inference is assigned its justifying operation terminates in a finite number of steps in an irreducible argument. The strong normalization theorem says that the same holds for each way of reducing the argument. This result is slightly weaker than the result that each such derivation is strongly valid relative to any choice of strongly valid closed arguments for atomic sentences. The significance of the strong normalization theorem is very clear from the present point of view. To carry out a reduction is essentially to replace a definiendum by its definiens: the meaning of the unreduced argument is defined by the assigned operations as the result obtained by carrying out these operations when defined on the subarguments in question. The strong normalization theorem then says that the arguments in question are well-defined in the sense that each way of successively replacing definiendum by definiens will finally terminate.

What Is Logic?

Ian Hacking

What follows is a general theory about classical logic. It is not to be expected that logic can be or should be characterized to everyone's satisfaction, for the subject is too ancient, its workers too active, and its scope too vast for that. Instead this paper falls within one lively and enduring tradition, the one called "logicist." It is an organization and development of some of the thoughts of Leibniz, Bolzano, Frege, Russell, and Wittgenstein. The main technical device is due to Gentzen. The chief philosophical idea that has not already been widely used by many writers is taken from the *Tractatus*. The general thrust of the inquiry goes back to Frege and to Leibniz, but although I shall allude to origins I shall not trace them in any detailed way.

A theory is prompted by problems, and it is well to begin by stating some longstanding questions that this one tries to answer. My focus will be the demarcation of logic: What distinguishes logic from the extralogical? The question has been important because it is closely connected with something deeper. What has been achieved by the program, now in disarray, of trying to show that parts of mathematics are analytic? There is a third question that I hope to take up in later work: Which, if any, of the nonstandard logics can in some strict sense be regarded as alternatives to classical logic? Only two at present have sufficiently serious and far-reaching motivations to have anything in their favor. It is an important question, why intuitionist and quantum logic are at least candidates for being called "logic." But I shall not address that question now, and shall instead consider only the nature of classical logic. We should start by recalling the fate of Frege's project of reducing arithmetic to logic. That is what gave bite to my question, What is logic?

1. THE ANALYTIC PROGRAM

Frege tried to prove that arithmetic is analytic. "The problem," he wrote at the beginning of his *Grundlagen*, "becomes, in fact, that of

This essay first appeared in *The Journal of Philosophy* LXXVI, 6 (1979). It is reprinted by permission of the author and of *The Journal of Philosophy*.

finding the proof of the proposition, and of following it up right back to the primitive truths. If in carrying out this process we come only on general logical laws and on definitions, then the truth is an analytic one." (1960a, p. 4) General logical laws and definitions are the crux. The idea is older than Frege, and the very word 'analytic' recalls Leibniz's doctrine that all necessary truths can be traced back to logical identities by finite analysis. Frege first cast this idea into a form precise enough for it to be established or refuted. Hence I speak of the *analytic* program of showing, for example, that arithmetic can be obtained from logic and definitions.

The analytic program is not primarily epistemological. It is not trying to make mathematics certain, nor to provide foundations for a shaky edifice, although some latter-day logicists had that in mind. Nor, as I understand the tradition stemming from Leibniz, is the chief interest in "what there is." There are ontological spinoffs to be sure, like the proposed answer to the question, What is a number? But remarks on certainty and on the existence of objects are by the way. The chief point is to explain the nature of at least some kinds of necessary truth.

Logicists have not agreed on whether the analytic program would work for all necessity. Leibniz argued that the necessary truths are just those which can be proved from identities by pure logic in a finite number of steps. Frege, in contrast, maintained that, although Euclidean geometry is necessarily true, it is synthetic, and founded on what Kant called intuition. Whatever we may think about such infighting, it seems that the analytic program as a whole has run into sand. Russell's paradox shook Frege's confidence that we know the basic laws of logic. Diverging set theories made it seem that propositions about sets lack the universality and apodictic certainty claimed for logic. *Principia Mathematica* was a poor tool for research in higher mathematics. Then Gödel showed that no such system is able even to analyze computable arithmetic completely.

Despite such discoveries, a philosopher might draw in his horns and admit that even though not all mathematics is analytic, analyticity remains a valuable concept. Drilling at mathematics with Frege's tools, we hit impermeable matter, but that, one might feel, is no reflection on the tools. If mathematics cannot be fully embedded in logic, that is an important discovery showing that analyticity was indeed a good investigative idea. We cannot, however, rest there. Even in 1936 Quine was launching his critique. Thirty years later most philosophers had concluded that Frege's drill would hardly make it through a bar of soap. His general laws of logic and definitions: where are they now? A whole system of philosophy has arisen around Quine's demolition of definition, synonymy, analyticity, and meaning. His comments on logic were briefer but as effective, and lead to the chief question of this paper.

2. THE DEMARCATION OF LOGIC

A logical truth, said Quine, is a truth in which only logical constants occur essentially. But, as Tarski had earlier implied, there is no delineation of the logical constants (1936b, esp. p. 420). We can at best list them. It is as if we could characterize the concept *planet of the sun* only by reciting Mars, Venus, Earth, etc., and could not tell by any general principle whether the heavenly body epsilon is a planet or not. We have a laundry list of logical constants, but no characterization of what a logical constant is—except the circular one, that logical constants are those which occur essentially in analytic truths.

The question, What is a logical constant? would be unimportant were it not for the analytic program. There is no point in trying to separate logic from other science, except for that profound speculation about the nature and origin of necessary truth. But, because of that speculation, a fruitful definition of 'logical constant' is called for. This paper to some extent revives the analytic program by providing such a demarcation. Doubtless it is not the only definition that is both rigorous in application and rich in consequences, but it is curiously appropriate to the logistic tradition. It does not go as far as Frege had hoped, but it does include the ramified theory of types. This is just what the authors of *Principia* expected; for in their opinion the ramified theory is logic, but the simplified theory obtained by adding the axiom of reducibility is not logic.

The theory also seems able to resolve a difference between Leibniz and Kant. Leibniz held that all necessary truth is analytic, whereas Kant thought that even $5 + 7 = 12$ is synthetic. Kant is wrong in particular, but right in general. On my theory, truths about individual integers, such as $5 + 7 = 12$, are analytic, but arithmetic as a whole is synthetic. The concept *number* is not explicable by logical constants alone. Hence, even sentences of the form, "For every natural number x, then . . .," are not in general analytic, for the numerical quantifier is not a logical one. The concept *number* must be given by what Kant called intuition, or at least by some extralogical practice. This is despite the fact that any particular natural number can be characterized analytically. I must add at once that this rather trivial resolution of an issue between Leibniz and Kant is only an historical oddity. For anyone interested in arithmetic it is, of course, a mere scratching of the surface.

3. WITTGENSTEIN'S "BY-PRODUCT"
THEORY OF LOGIC

The interrogative, 'What is logic?' can be used to express two questions. I have just asked how to identify logic, but, having identified something, one can still ask after its essential nature. Had Frege been right, we should have reduced arithmetic to logic and shown that its truth conditions lie in logic itself. But what then is the nature of logical truth? Frege said that laws of logic are laws of thought, not in the sense that they are laws about what men do in fact take for true but because they are "the most general laws, which prescribe universally the way in which one ought to think if one is to think at all." (1964, p. 12) He prefers to call them laws of truth, "boundary stones set in an eternal foundation, which our thought can overflow, but never displace" (13). So it seems not to make sense to ask what makes them true, for they help constitute the nature of true thought itself.

In the *Tractatus* we find what seems to be an entirely different idea. Wittgenstein tried to explain how some classes of logical truth are a "by-product" of facts about the use of logical constants. Imagine a language of independent elementary sentences whose meanings are understood. In order to form complex sentences, let logical constants be implanted in this language, and let certain rules determine the truth conditions of such complexes as functions of their components. Then some compound sentences take the value true regardless of their components. This fact is a by-product of rules for the introduction of the logical constants. "[W]ithout bothering about sense or meaning, we construct the logical proposition out of others using only *rules that deal with signs.*"[1] The fact that these logical truths are a by-product of rules for signs is taken to explain the necessary, apodictic, and a priori character of some of the truths that we call logically necessary.

Recall the positivist slogan that "mathematical truths are true in virtue of the meanings of the words that express them." This came to be used in what one can only call a lighthearted way by some writers who seemed not to reflect on the complexities of mathematical reasoning. But when first propounded the slogan had real force, thanks to Frege's analytic program taken together with Wittgenstein's by-product theory. First, the meanings of mathematical expressions are to be analyzed into purely logical terminology. Secondly, the meanings of

---

1. Wittgenstein (1961, 6.126). For an alternative translation see the text for fn. 15.

the logical constants are conveyed by their introduction rules, and these rules have as a by-product the class of logical truths. The meanings of the mathematical terms are given in terms of logic. The meanings of logical constants are conveyed by the introduction rules. Hence, if *both* Frege *and* Wittgenstein had been right, then meanings, in some imprecise sense of that word, would have been responsible for a good deal of mathematical truth. I know of no other plausible motivation for the crisp positivist slogans about "true in virtue of the meanings" or even "true by convention."

Wittgenstein tried to extend his theory of tautology in a natural way to first-order language, anticipating the theory of countable conjunction and disjunction. He had another meaning-oriented—or at least name-oriented—theory for arithmetical identities. Aside from the account of tautology, no one except Ramsey took much of this seriously. However, my demarcation of logic turns out to confirm Wittgenstein's hunch about the logical constants, using Gentzen's devices to take in the first-order quantifiers and even identity. Although Wittgenstein often alluded to the importance of rules and notational conventions of a "deep" sort, he was never able to say which ones are specifically logical. We are now able to specify a precise class of rules that fits his descriptions, yet includes the whole "logical" part of *Principia Mathematica.*

I must emphasize at once that the resulting *Tractatus*-like theory is not incompatible with the Fregean doctrine that logic constitutes the laws of truth. Nor is it incompatible with Wittgenstein's later reflections on following a rule, stated in *Remarks on the Foundations of Mathematics.* It is a matter of some delicacy to get straight the relations among these different insights. I attempt it in the concluding section of this paper, but first we require the demarcation of logic.

4. DEDUCIBILITY NOT LOGICAL TRUTH

What distinguishes logic from the other branches of knowledge? Quine starts his elementary textbook by implying that logic is a science of truths.[2] That is where I part company. If we must have a one-word answer, logic is the science of deduction. The point is made by Michael Dummett, who accuses Frege himself. Frege's approach was "retrograde," he says, in that it formalized "logical systems on the quite misleading analogy of an axiomatized theory." "The representation of logic as concerned with a characteristic of sentences, truth, rather than of transitions from sentences to sentences, had highly

2. Essay 1 in this volume.

deleterious effects both in logic and in philosophy" (1981, pp. 432–3). He implies that we owe the first corrective to Gerhard Gentzen.

I am less sure than Dummett that this is a corrective to *Frege*, although it is certainly a corrective to the early twentieth-century tradition in mathematical logic. When Frege speaks of logical axioms he commonly does so with some hint of qualification, and when we go back to *Begriffsschrift* we find passages such as the following:

> We have already introduced in the first chapter several principles of [pure] thought in order to transform them into rules for the application of our symbols. The rules and laws to which they correspond cannot be expressed in our "conceptual notation" because they form its basis (1972, p. 136).

Tractatus 5.132 says that "Laws of inference which—as in Frege and Russell—are to justify the conclusions, are senseless and would be superfluous." This may be a legitimate objection to the primitive propositions *1.1 and *1.11 of *Principia Mathematica*. But if one had the view that anything not expressible in concept-writing is *sinnlos* and can at best be elucidated, one would find less of a difference between *Begriffsschrift* and *Tractatus* than Wittgenstein asserts.

Disregarding this historical issue, I agree entirely with Dummett that the right way to answer the question, What is logic? is to consider transitions between sentences. It is now natural to present rules for such transitions in a metalanguage. To avoid Wittgenstein's strictures, we must insist that such rules are not justifications of transitions. They are descriptions, or, perhaps, codifications of what one knows when one knows how to make certain transitions that we call logical. In one respect this talk of metalanguage is like doing the grammar of English in English. There is evidently a distinction between two uses of the word 'justify'. On the one hand, should an author challenge an editor who has corrected a grammatical solecism, the editor may reply by citing a rule to justify the emendation. It is not to be inferred that in general the rules of grammar "justify" standard usage. They merely codify it, and are often couched in the very forms that they describe. Yet this is only an analogy; for although English grammar will alter in time and varies a little in different communities, it is an open question whether there is any real alternative to classical logic.

Deducibility comes first, I have said, and not logical truth. Today we sharply distinguish between syntactic and semantic aspects of transitions between sentences. The opening parts of my discussion will proceed by considerations about deducibility which are intended to be almost neutral between a syntactic and a semantic treatment of the idea. This is not a quirk of the exposition but a feature of the theory, which is quite in the spirit of the older logicists.

The details of my delineation of logic are so indebted to Gentzen as to make that aspect of this paper only a footnote to his work, although what I do is to turn him upside down. He took a given axiomatized entity, first-order logic, and characterized it by rules of inference. (Gentzen, 1935) I proceed in the opposite way, using rules of a certain kind to define an entity, namely "logic." I give reasons for saying that anything defined by a rule of inference like Gentzen's is a logical constant. Of course, the exact boundary depends entirely on what shall count as "like" Gentzen's rules. I shall present and defend some general propositions about deducibility and the definition of constants, all of which are in fact true of Gentzen's work, and which, in my opinion, capture its essence. I do not claim this is the only delineation; only that it is remarkably instructive.

5. THE SEQUENT CALCULUS

Gentzen invented two kinds of logical calculi, called "natural deduction" and "sequent calculus." He thought that the former gets at the heart of logical reasoning, and used the sequent calculus only as a convenient tool for proving his chief results. Dag Prawitz (1965) was able to obtain many of these results directly for the systems of natural deduction. Per Martin-Löf and other workers have found them the best vehicle for investigations of higher mathematics.[3] W. W. Tait has suggested to me that the sequent calculus is right for classical logic, whereas natural deduction best fits a constructive approach. Despite all this, my exposition will without discussion employ only the sequent calculus.

In the present work the sequent calculus is regarded as a meta-theory about an object language. We suppose that an object language is given, and that the class of formulas of this language is determinate. Finite (possibly empty) sets of formulas are represented by Greek capitals such as Γ and Θ. Individual formulas are represented by Roman capitals, A and B. For brevity we write, e.g., 'A,B' to stand for the set whose members are the formulas A and B, and 'Γ, A,B' for the set whose members are A,B and the members of Γ. In the meta-language we make statements about deducibility relations in the object language, such as 'A is deducible from Γ'. The turnstile abbreviates

---

3. See, e.g., papers by Girard, Jervell, Kreisel, Martin-Löf, Prawitz, and Tait in Fenstad (1971).

the converse of this relation: '$\Gamma \vdash A$'. It is to be emphasized that the
turnstile ($\vdash$) is a symbol of the metalanguage, and not a constant of the
object language.

There is of course an intended connection between deducibility
and logical consequence, so that at least $\Gamma \vdash A$ only if A is a consequence of Γ. But I shall proceed in as syntactic a way as possible,
stating certain constraints that will hold on any relation that can be
accounted a deducibility relation. Some readers will feel this gets the
cart before the horse: we know that my constraints are appropriate to
deducibility only because of our understanding of logical consequence. In my opinion, such questions of priority are a red herring. It
is not necessary to define deducibility to discover that we have some
constraints on this notion. Even the very simple constraints that I cull
out are sufficient for a good deal of work, and, wherever they come
from, it is a virtue that they can be stated in terms of '$\vdash$' alone.

The notion of deducibility is, however, extended in one slightly
loaded way. Gentzen noticed that it is convenient to make statements
of the form $\Gamma \vdash \Theta$, where Θ may have several members.[4] On the
intended reading, this will be valid only if *some* member of Θ is
assigned the value true whenever *each* member of Γ is assigned the
value true. It is well known that in Gentzen's calculi, with his rules,
intuitionist logic results from insisting that Θ have at most one member. I shall not discuss this seemingly magical fact here.

6. THREE FACTS ABOUT
CLASSICAL DEDUCIBILITY

When is a relation between formulas a deducibility relation? Without
aiming at necessary conditions, three sufficient conditions will be
readily assented to.

1. *Reflexivity.* $A \vdash A$. Leibniz believed that every logical truth is
derived from identity statements by definitions. He did not work this
out, because he did not have the distinction between object and metalanguage. But, with the distinction, the sequent calculus curiously
confirms his hunch. The top statements in any derivation of a theorem
are always instances of reflexivity. Reflexivity might be called *the deducibility of identicals.* Moreover, as we shall see in §§10 and 16, the
substantive steps in the derivation may always be regarded as the
application of definitions. So Leibniz's claim about the nature of
logical truth is vindicated by the sequent calculus.

4. A general theory is provided in Shoesmith and Smiley (1978).

2. *Dilution.* If $\Gamma \vdash \Theta$, then $\Gamma, A \vdash \Theta$ and $\Gamma \vdash A, \Theta$. Adding a possibly irrelevant premise or consequent does not affect the deducibility relation. This is clear for a classical notion of deducibility and consequence. In a nonclassical language, such as might be suggested by quantum mechanics, the joint assertion of arbitrary sentences might not make sense; so this rule is here asserted only for the classical case. We may call this the *stability of classical deducibility* under the addition of arbitrary sentences. Note that it provides an essential contrast between deductive and inductive reasoning; for the introduction of a new premise may spoil an inductive inference.

3. *Transitivity.* If $A \vdash B$ and $B \vdash C$, then $A \vdash C$. In the context of our other facts about deducibility, this is naturally generalized to the form: If $\Gamma \vdash A, \Theta$ and $\Gamma, A \vdash \Theta$, then $\Gamma \vdash \Theta$. Gentzen called this *cut,* and it will occupy us a good deal.

These three facts about deducibility do not depend on the presence of any logical constants. The elementary sentences of the *Tractatus* were all independent, so there were no relations of deducibility between different sentences. A less ideal primitive language, even if it had no recognized logical constants, might have some relations of deducibility: "Rachel is a sister $\vdash$ Rachel is a sibling." An unanalyzed language of elementary arithmetic is rich in statements of deducibility. And even if all sentences were independent, identical sentences would be interdeducible. So the class of statements of deducibility about a "prelogical" language will never be entirely vacuous.

7. BUILDING RULES

A sequent calculus is a device for deriving statements of deducibility and is thus a metalinguistic instrument. The top statements are all instances of $A \vdash A$, the deducibility of identicals. All nodes in the tree are to be instances of the application of rules of derivation. These rules are of two sorts. Gentzen called one lot *structural.* Since his formulation used sequences rather than finite sets of formulas, these included rules for permutation and for contraction of identical formulas, which we may ignore. The other structural rules are precisely those which correspond to my basic facts about deducibility, namely dilution and transitivity. Thus he had rules for dilution on the left and right of the turnstile, and a rule for cut:

$$\frac{\Gamma \vdash \Theta}{\Gamma, A \vdash \Theta} \qquad \frac{\Gamma \vdash \Theta}{\Gamma \vdash A, \Theta} \qquad \frac{\Gamma \vdash A, \Theta \quad \Gamma, A \vdash \Theta}{\Gamma \vdash \Theta}$$

These rules are to be understood as instructions: having derived the statements of the form shown above the line, one may derive the statement of the corresponding form below the line. Γ and Θ are called *side formulas* and may be empty. For brevity I shall include the deducibility of identicals as a structural rule. It allows one to start a derivation with a statement of the form $A \vdash A$. *The structural rules embody basic facts about deducibility and obtain even in a language with no logical constants at all.*

Gentzen called his other class of rules *operational.* Each of these characterizes a particular logical constant. In the case of conjunction we have, for example:

$$\frac{\Gamma, A \vdash \Theta}{\Gamma, A \& B \vdash \Theta} \qquad \frac{\Gamma, B \vdash \Theta}{\Gamma, A \& B \vdash \Theta} \qquad \frac{\Gamma \vdash A, \Theta \quad \Gamma, \vdash B, \Theta}{\Gamma \vdash A \& B, \Theta}$$

The formulas that occur in the top line but not in the bottom line are *components.* The new formula in the bottom line is the *principal formula.* We shall consider only rules with a single principal formula. Statements of deducibility occurring in the top line of a rule of derivation will be called the *premises* of that rule. Gentzen considered only rules with one or two premises, but we allow more and can even generalize to rules with countably many premises.

I shall not repeat Gentzen's calculi here. All his operational rules build up complex formulas from less complex ones. In the case of the sentential connectives, the components are literally subformulas of the principal formula. This is not the case, for example, with the rules for the universal quantifier:

$$\frac{\Gamma, Fa \vdash \Theta}{\Gamma, (\forall x) \, Fx \vdash \Theta} \qquad \frac{\Gamma \vdash Fa, \Theta}{\Gamma \vdash (\forall x) \, Fx, \Theta} \qquad \text{where } a \text{ does not occur free in the bottom line}$$

Even so, the principal formula is built up out of a part of the component. A generalization of this property is called the *subformula property,* and is defined elsewhere. It has the effect that principal formulas are, according to a certain complexity ordering, more complex than their components, and that they are built up out of parts of their components. *Gentzen's operational rules are all building rules:* according to a natural ordering in terms of complexity, they always pass from less complex to more complex formulas.

8. CUT-ELIMINATION

Only the cut rule can have a conclusion that is less complex than its premises. Hence, when cut is not used, a derivation is quite literally constructive, building up more complex formulas from their components. The theorem known as Gentzen's *Hauptsatz* shows that derivations in first-order logic can always have this property, for any statement derived using the cut rule can be obtained without it. If there are derivations of both $\Gamma \vdash A$, Θ and $\Gamma, A \vdash \Theta$, then a finite induction on the length and complexity of the derivations shows that they may be rearranged and combined so as to derive $\Gamma \vdash \Theta$ without cut. Haskell Curry called this the *elimination theorem*, for it shows how to eliminate A. Other writers call this result "cut-elimination" because it shows that the cut rule itself is eliminable. I shall speak of *eliminating rules* in the latter sense, and not in Curry's.

Cut-elimination is useful in proof theory. For an elementary example, we see at once why first-order logic is consistent. If it is inconsistent, there must be some formula A for which both $\vdash A$ and $A \vdash$ are derivable (the latter being interderivable with $\vdash \sim A$). Then, by cut, plain $\vdash$ is derivable. Hence $\vdash$ must be derivable without cut. That is impossible, for none of the other rules decreases complexity.

Gentzen's proof of the consistency of arithmetic uses this sort of consideration, but requires a transfinite induction up to ϵ_0. In systems of natural deduction, cut-elimination corresponds to the result that every proof can be put into a normal form in which one first analyzes certain formulas, and then synthesizes new formulas out of bits and pieces that have been obtained. During the 1960s cut-elimination and normal-form theorems yielded many valuable results in proof-theoretic investigations. The ordinal of the transfinite induction required indicates the degree of constructivity of the proofs. Here, however, we shall be concerned only with finitistic proofs of cut-elimination.

9. ELIMINATION THEOREMS AND DEFINITION

Gentzen's proof-theoretic work is rich in philosophical asides. For example, he had the idea that his operational rules actually define the logical constants that they introduce. This needs qualification, but first notice where it leads. We commonly require that definitions should be noncreative. Roughly speaking, if the expression *w* does not occur in a language fragment and is added to that fragment by means of a definition, we require that this not change what can be said in the fragment without the use of *w* and its definition. No more should be assertible in the fragment after defining *w* than could be asserted before. Nothing less should be assertible either. One is usually afraid of creating truths by definition, but one also ought not to destroy any. Wanting to guard against both possibilities, I shall say simply that definitions must be *conservative.*

Now suppose that operational rules are to be regarded as defining logical constants. Then they must be conservative. *Proving cut-elimination is one ingredient in showing that the operational rules are conservative definitions.*

How does this come about? Gentzen's rules are peculiar definitions. We start with an object language possibly but not necessarily lacking logical constants, and for which various statements of deducibility may be made in the metalanguage. Then some operational rules are added, together with syntactic rules for the logical constants thus introduced. Now what should these definitions conserve? Among other things, they should not affect the facts about deducibility that obtain for the original language fragment.

We can put this another way. We add rules for disjunction, the universal quantifier, and so forth, all couched in terms of a deducibility relation denoted by '⊢'. We should ensure that adding these rules does not muck up the basic facts about the deducibility relation noted in §6. If those facts no longer obtained, then our rules would have been destructive, and we would have no reason to think that '⊢' still denotes a relation of deducibility.

I take this to be the chief moral of Arthur Prior's logical connective "tonk." (Prior, 1960) Prior stated inferential rules that introduced a new connective, but these rules led to absurdity. He intended this as a criticism of the very idea of introducing or defining logical connectives by rules of inference. I draw a more familiar moral. All definitions, including Gentzen-like ones, should be conservative. One may state a sequent calculus for Prior's tonk from which one can derive $A \vdash A\text{-tonk-}B$ and $A\text{-tonk-}B \vdash B$; yet there is no way to get $A \vdash B$. So cut-elimination does not hold. If we were to postulate Prior's rules, '⊢' would no longer be transitive. That is, it would no longer be a deducibility relation. Cut-elimination assures that the operational rules, regarded as definitions of the logical constants, still leave '⊢' denoting a deducibility relation.

I listed two other facts about deducibility: the deducibility of identicals, and dilution. These also must be conserved. For purposes of proof theory they are either trivial or irrelevant, but if one is to develop

Gentzen's suggestion that operational rules provide definitions, then we must check them out.

Gentzen himself stated the deducibility of identicals as "$A \vdash A$ for arbitrary formulas." But a second elimination theorem is that any derivation starting from $A \vdash A$, where 'A' is complex, may be replaced by a derivation starting from the deducibility of identicals for elementary formulas. For example, if we start with $B \vee C \vdash B \vee C$, we could instead start with $B \vdash B$ and $C \vdash C$ and use the operational rules for disjunction. The requirement is, then, that the deducibility of identicals for arbitrary formulas should be eliminable. It is in fact eliminable for first-order logic.

That is a trivial fact but not a vacuous one. Consider the compound quantifier '$(\forall\exists xy)$', short for '$(\forall x)(\exists y)$'. This can be introduced by the rules:

$$\frac{\Gamma, Fab \vdash \Theta}{\Gamma, (\forall\exists xy)\, Fxy \vdash \Theta} \qquad \frac{\Gamma \vdash Fab,\, \Theta}{\Gamma \vdash (\forall\exists xy)\, Fxy,\, \Theta}$$

In the rule on the left, b does not occur free on the bottom line; for the rule on the right, a does not occur free on the bottom line. Although, assuming the deducibility of identicals, cut-elimination can be proved for this rule, there is no way to derive $(\forall\exists xy)\, Fxy \vdash (\forall\exists xy)\, Fxy$ itself. So this is a rule that does not conserve the deducibility of identicals.

Likewise, although it is a trivial constraint that dilution should be conserved, the elimination of dilution for complex formulas is not vacuous. Consider these rules for S4:

$$\frac{\Gamma, A \vdash \Theta}{\Gamma, \Box A \vdash \Theta} \qquad \frac{\Box\Gamma \vdash A}{\Box\Gamma \vdash \Box A}$$

In the second rule the side formulas must all start with a box, as indicated. One cannot eliminate the dilution rule for arbitrary formulas even though, when the rule is added, cut-elimination is provable. In general one cannot eliminate the dilution rule (for arbitrary formulas) from systems of modal logic. Since our concern is with object-level logic rather than metalogic, dilution-elimination is a convenient way of excluding metalogic and modal logic from our immediate considerations.

I shall presently qualify the suggestion that Gentzen's operational rules can be regarded as definitions. I claim here only that if we are to pursue that idea, we shall require that the definitions be conservative. Cut-elimination, dilution-elimination, and identicals-elimination (all for complex formulas) are necessary conditions for this. Thus we use elimination theorems for purposes quite different from those of the student of proof theory.

I can here forestall an objection raised by Christopher Peacocke against an earlier and more obscure draft of this paper (1976).[5] Crudely put, it amounts to "What's so great about cut-elimination?" More precisely, if we want to define logical constants, why not just give the operational rules, plus the cut rule and any other structural rules we want? The immediate answer is that then the operational rules are certainly not, in themselves, the definitions of the logical constants. But what is wrong with just adding the operational rules and the structural rules stated for arbitrary formulas built up out of the logical constants? Nothing, except that one is not then defining logical constants in connection with some previous language fragment. Rather one is creating, as a totality, a new system of logistic. Moreover, to foreshadow one use I shall make of these ideas, this system could not have added to it rules for yet another logical constant, without then changing the structural rules once again, asserting that they are to hold for yet more complex formulas. When we add only conservative operational rules, however, we never add any structural postulates. They hold for elementary "prelogical" formulas, and are proved to hold for arbitrary complex formulas.

For a rough analogy to textbook cases of creative definition, take a system of first-order logic with identity and an operation '$\bigcirc$' for which there is only an associative axiom: $x \bigcirc (y \bigcirc z) = (x \bigcirc y) \bigcirc z$. Try defining '$e$' by the formula $x \bigcirc e = x$. This is not conservative, for we can now prove $(\exists y)(\forall x)(x \bigcirc y = x)$. To caricature Peacocke's question, why not add this last sentence along with the sentence defining 'e'? There is nothing wrong with that. But it leads to a new theory of '$\bigcirc$' which is substantively different from the old one. One has not defined 'e' for the original system with simply associative '$\bigcirc$'.

I hasten to add that Peacocke's chief objection was that purely syntactic rules could not possibly be expected to be what is fundamental in characterizing logical constants. Logic is concerned with the preservation of truth, and hence with logical consequence and a semantics, so a syntactic approach ought not be basic. My doctrine is, however, that the peculiarity of the logical constants resides precisely in this: that, given a certain pure notion of truth and consequence, all

5. Hacking (1976, esp. p. 231).

the desirable semantic properties of the constants are determined, as in §16, by their syntactic properties. Peacocke is more favorably disposed to the subformula property (which he seems to imply is associated with cut-elimination), but I can give no defense of it as a requirement that the definitions should be conservative.

10. DEFINING LOGICAL CONSTANTS

If operational rules could be regarded as definitions, then they would have to be conservative. But can they be so regarded? Several quite different kinds of objection arise.

First, it is clear that these rules could not define the constants for a being that lacked all logical concepts. One must understand something like conjunction to apply the conjunction rule, and one must have some surrogate for some sort of quantifier to apply the rule for universal quantification. This kind of consideration particularly influences workers trying to find predicative or other constructive foundations for branches of mathematics. They look for definitions that genuinely reduce seemingly nonconstructive concepts or reasonings to ideas that are better understood. I shall not argue that the operational rules serve any such purpose.

On the contrary, the operational rules at most *characterize* the logical constants in a certain way for a person that already has some logical ideas. In fact of course there is a legitimate sense of "definition" in which a definition characterizes what one already understands. To avoid confusion, however, I shall often speak of the operational rules not as defining but only as characterizing the logical constants. This in no way weakens the demand that the rules be conservative. If they are not, the operational rules of themselves fail to characterize the logical constants.

A quite different objection arises from the fact that Gentzen wrote only at the dawn of semantic theory. Today we expect that anything worth calling a definition should imply a semantics. Since the operational rules are syntactic, they must, it will be urged, fall short of definitions. This objection is partially met by the "do-it-yourself semantics" of §16 below. Let there be assumed a notion of classical truth and falsity for elementary sentences lacking logical constants, and let the deducibility relation be complete for classical logical consequence among the class of such sentences. Then one is in a certain sense able to read off the semantics of the logical constants from the operational rules. Given the underlying notions of truth and logical consequence, the syntactic rules determine a semantics.

The operational rules do not themselves determine this semantics. It is not as if one could somehow fix what truth and logical consequence are, just by stating the operational rules. This bears on a useful observation of Hilary Putnam's. He recalls Gödel's mapping of classical sentential logic into intuitionist logic, in which, for example, classical conjunction is identified with intuitionist conjunction but classical disjunction is identified with intuitionist $\neg(\neg p \& \neg q)$. Then he writes, in italics: *"Contrary to what a number of philosophers— including recently Hacking—have asserted,* [the operational rules] *do not fix the 'meanings' of the logical connectives. Someone could accept all of those rules (and all classical tautologies, as well) and still be using the logical connectives in the nonclassical sense just described."* (Putnam, 1978, p. 27) Putnam makes this observation in the course of urging that if the logical connectives are given a "quasi-intuitionist" interpretation one can then go on to define 'true', as he puts it, *"exactly à la Tarski.* Only 'truth' becomes provability . . ." (p. 28). On this point my theory does not seem to diverge much from Putnam's ideas. He is avoiding the following maneuver: someone says, "I'll first fix the meaning of the logical constants by giving rules of inference; then I'll define 'true' à la Tarski, so any indeterminacy in truth itself will be entirely avoided." I claim, on the contrary, that the operational rules "fix the meanings of the logical connectives" in the sense of giving a semantics, only if classical notions of truth and logical consequence are already assumed. So any avoidance of Putnam's indeterminacy would be circular. The minimum classical assumptions on truth and consequence are stated in §15 below.

11. CATEGORICAL GRAMMAR

This discussion of definition may suggest that I want to characterize conjunction or universal quantification or some other specific constant—as if logicians did not already know what they mean! Quite the contrary. I am concerned with a general *form* of definition. Now Gentzen studied a given class of first-order constants. He proceeded in the standard way, first stating the elements of his object language, then giving rules for well-formedness, and finally giving rules of inference. That is good practice for a preassigned set of logical constants, but we shall be concerned with *any* constant that can be introduced in a certain way. Hence we should think of the inferential rules introducing a constant as accompanied by syntactical rules for the grammar of the constant.

These grammatical rules should be effective. The symbol w is to be added to some well-understood language *L*. Suppose that not only is there an effective test for determining which strings of symbols from *L* are well-formed, but also that there is an effective procedure for uniquely parsing well-formed formulas of *L*. Then there should be grammatical rules for *w*, ensuring that *L* + *w* has the same properties. It is well known that Russell introduced the definite-description operator so as to make its scope ambiguous; our definitions should avoid that defect.

It would be nice to state the general form for introducing a constant into any language of sufficient complexity. That would require a knowledge of the general form of language itself, and there is no such thing. But we can achieve a remarkably high degree of generality by using the categorical grammar invented by Kasimirz Ajdukiewicz (1935). He intended it as the grammar for the theory of types, but it has recently been generalized and enriched by Richard Montague.[6] We need have no views on how suitable it is for the analysis of English: categorical grammar is plainly adequate for any of the more formal languages used in logic.

This grammar assigns a category to each expression of the language. The notation for the categories indicates how new expressions are to be formed from old and also indicates the category of the resulting expression. If the primitive categories are s (for formula) and t (for term), then a singulary predicate is of category $(t)/s$, because when applied to a term it yields a sentence. Binary predicates are $(t, t)/s$. Binary sentential connectives are of category $(s, s)/s$, adjectives are $(t)/t$, and so forth. The existential and universal quantifiers of first-order logic are of category $((t)/s)/s$. Such a notation rapidly takes in some of the more complex structures even of ordinary speech. It allows, by indexing, for different kinds of nouns, of adjectives that apply to them, and so forth. By systems of indexing it is well adapted to the theory of types, which was the point for which Ajdukiewicz designed it. I shall not elaborate the cumbersome details of this syntax, relying on the fortunate fact that there is now a reservoir of categorical grammar on which to draw. In practice we consider only language fragments of the sort familiar to logicians, the functional calculi. But I emphasize that this is an altogether general theory. We can investigate the possibility of conservative Gentzen-like rules as far as others can develop precise and unambiguous categorical grammars. Although I shall not proceed to the discussion of adverbs, for example, the road to

6. "The Proper Treatment of Quantification in Ordinary English," and other papers in Montague (1974).

a logic of adverbs, such as it is, lies open before us. Similarly for the logic of those second-order quantifiers, such as 'every man', retrieved by Montague from scholastic logic.

Suppose, then, that we have a language fragment and wish to introduce a constant by means of a Gentzen-like rule. It is not enough, in general, to write down some inference schemes. Take the simplest case, a fragment L with no logical constants whatsoever, and whose expressions are all of category s. Let us add a binary connective '$*$' to this language. The steps are as follows. The grammar of L must be augmented by a category $(s,s)/s$, together with rules for sentence formation with this category. Then it is stated that '$*$' is of this category. Then operational rules are stated. Using our intuitive (but grammatically formalizable) scheme for representing the rules, we have, say:

$$\frac{\Gamma \vdash A, \Theta \quad \Gamma \vdash B, \Theta}{\Gamma, A * B \vdash \Theta} \qquad \frac{\Gamma, A, B \vdash \Theta}{\Gamma \vdash A * B, \Theta}$$

That completes the characterization of '$*$'. Next one must check that it is conservative. Yes, the deducibility of identicals, dilution, and cut are all eliminable for formulas with '$*$'.

Perhaps no one has written down this "definition" before. What does '$*$' mean? That is the best way to put the demand that Gentzen-style definitions ought to provide a semantics. In fact the do-it-yourself semantics of §16 does automatically provide a semantics for the above constant. One sees at once that $A * B$ is true in a model if and only if at least one of A or B is false in that model. This '$*$' is Sheffer's stroke.

The requirement that operational rules be conservative can make unexpected demands. Let us start with a language L of terms and monadic predicates. Its nonempty categories are at least s, t and $(t)/s$. To bring in a universal quantifier we must add the category $((t)/s)/s$. It is stated that the universal quantifier is of this category, and one gives the usual Gentzen rules. But proof of cut-elimination is not yet possible. In the course of restructuring the derivations of Γ, $(\forall x)Fx \vdash \Theta$ and $\Gamma \vdash (\forall x)Fx, \Theta$, one will in general require at least one item of category t that does not occur in Γ, Θ. Since there is no upper bound on the number of terms that can occur in Γ, Θ, we shall require a stock of items of category t that cannot be exhausted. In more familiar terms, to add the universal quantifier to a language of monadic predicates, one must also add a countable class of variables. For some purposes it is doubtless true that the variables of first-order logic can be regarded as prepositions and place-holders that could in principle be dispensed with, say by a system of arrows indicating what places fall in the scope of which quantifier. The above remarks are yet another way of making the point that this is not the whole story about variables in logic.

Henceforth it will be assumed that rules for introducing a logical constant have two parts. There is the syntactic part determining the rules of well-formedness for the constant. This may include adding stocks of parameters of various categories, required to prove cut-elimination. Then there is the inferential part, giving the rules of derivability of statements in which the constant occurs.

12. WHAT IS A LOGICAL CONSTANT?

Gentzen's rules are built around a deducibility relation. Deduction has seemed, to some, to be the essence of logic. Hence philosophers have long suggested that systems of natural deduction or the sequent calculus precisely capture "the province of logic." The phrase is that of William Kneale. Similar ideas were propounded by Karl Popper, independently of Gentzen. Paul Lorenzen's operational logic is a related syntactic development of logic which is also supposed to lead to the semantics of logical constants.[7] One basic idea of all these workers may be that *a logical constant is a constant that can be introduced, characterized, or defined in a certain way.*

What way? My answer is about the same as Kneale's: a logical constant is a constant that can be introduced by operational rules like those of Gentzen. The question becomes, "like" in what respects? Different answers will mark off different conceptions of logic. My answer is that the operational rules introducing a constant should (i) have the subformula property, and (ii) be conservative with respect to the basic facts of deducibility. The second clause means (finitistic) provability of the elimination theorems.

Why should rules for "pure logic" have the subformula property and be conservative? There are several kinds of answers. They correspond to criteria of adequacy like the following. (A) The demarcation should give the "right" logicist class of logical constants and theorems. That is, it should include the traditional (and consistent) core of what logicists said was logic and should exclude what they denied to be logic. (B) Since the demarcation is couched in terms of how logical constants are characterized, it should provide the semantics for the constants called "logical." (C) It should explicate why logic is important to the analytic program. Although (A) and (B) are impor-

7. Kneale (1956); Popper (1947), and other papers referred to in note 1 to Lejewski (1976), p. 669; Stegmüller (1964).

tant, (C) is essential. A demarcation of logic that leaves the analytic program unintelligible is of little philosophical interest (unless the point is to show that the analytic program *is* unintelligible).

I shall briefly explain how my demarcation satisfies (A)–(C), then develop these themes more fully. As regard (A), the most coherent conclusion to logicist investigations is *Principia Mathematica*. Its authors held that all of the ramified theory of types (including identity relations for various ramified types) is logic. But they regretfully concluded that the simplified theory of types is not logic. That is exactly our result. Conservative rules having the subformula property can be used to introduce the ramified quantifiers and identity, but they do not go as far as full second-order logic.[8] So criterion (A) is satisfied. In §13 I shall discuss whether this is really desirable: is it now known that Russell excluded something truly logical or included something that is not? I don't think so.

As for criterion (B), I have already mentioned that "do-it-yourself semantics" is generated from Gentzen's operational rules for first-order logic. Indeed, what makes it work is precisely the subformula property and the elimination theorems. §15 gives some indication of how criterion (B) is satisfied.

Criterion (C) is fundamental. To delineate logic without explicating the intuitions underlying the analytic program is to forget the point of the whole exercise. Without the idea of analyticity, who cares exactly what logic *is*? Quine, in contending that logic coincides with first-order logic, is as usual entirely germane. He thinks that the intuitions underlying the analytic program are fundamentally mistaken. Hence his answer to the question, "What is logic?" does indeed satisfy criterion (C), albeit vacuously—he thinks there are few ultimately coherent intuitions to explicate. In the concluding sections of the paper I argue that the present demarcation of logic, in terms of a form of definition, does elucidate some of these intuitions in a more positive way.

13. FIRST- AND SECOND-ORDER

Russell said that the ramified theory of types is logic. The axiom of reducibility, the simplified theory of types, and even full second-order logic are not, then, logic. By my criterion (A), I took it as a virtue of my demarcation that it agrees with the logicist answer. But it would be no virtue if the logicists were just wrong. I now wish to examine a few

8. For the ramified theory of types and second-order logic, see Prawitz (1965, note 10, pp. 62–73). For identity, see my (1978).

putative counterexamples to show that the logicist thesis is at least not manifestly absurd.

To stop halfway between first- and second-order logic is to leave oneself in the middle of an uncomfortable slanging match. On the one hand is the position favored by Quine. He once denied that we can stake out a separate preserve for logic. Now he says that if logic is a special kind of entity, it can only be first-order logic.[9] That is not much of a shift of position. Part of the original argument was that nothing distinguishes the peculiarly logical. Now we relax: there is after all one firm distinction, namely, the distinction between first-order logic and everything else. This is buttressed by ontological considerations. Quine does not want to quantify over predicates, and so excludes second-order quantification. Then there are powerful formal results: for example, first-order logic is the strongest complete compact theory with a Löwenheim-Skolem theorem.[10]

It is well known that Richard Montague, in contrast, urged that second-order logic is the very tool for mathematical inquiries and that it is also the foundation of the categorical grammar of English. George Boolos (1975) has recently vigorously defended second-order reasoning. He stands up to the ontological threats and he asks, for example, why on earth compactness, whatever its virtues, should be definitive of logic itself. My theory of logic goes between these two extremes. It appears to have some of the advantages that each party claims for its own side, while lacking some of the faults that each party finds in the other. Logic, on my account, includes the ramified theory of types, but goes no further toward a higher-order logic. This may seen an inauspicious claim, for the ramified theory is now generally held to have been a mistake. But that is because of the historical accident that the authors of *Principia* tried to find a foundation for all mathematics. They thought that logic stopped at the ramified theory, which is too weak for much set theory. Hence they added an extralogical postulate, the axiom of reducibility. As Ramsey noticed, this makes ramification redundant; since then, no one has been much interested in the ramified theory. But if we accept the fact that logic is not going to provide a

---

9. Essay 11, this volume; also Quine (1970), chs. 5, 6.

10. Lindström (1969). I refer of course to a countable Löwenheim-Skolem theorem and not to generalizations such as are found in Barwise et al. (1978). Note that their Stationary Logic also falls between first- and second-order logic. There are numerous other investigations showing either that first-order logic has all of certain desirable properties or else is the strongest logic with certain desirable properties; e.g. Zucker (1979).

foundation for mathematics and if we do not add an extralogical axiom of reducibility, then the ramified structure is untouched, and has, I believe, certain merits.

Consider, for example, the fact that second-order logic has no chance of a completeness theorem unless one ventures into intensional entities and possible worlds. I sympathize with the extensionalist object to these devices, and am glad that the completeness proof for ramified theory is entirely extensional. One does not need to posit any class of entities larger than the class of inscriptions demanded by the theory itself, although the intensionalist may, if he so wishes, suppose that one is quantifying over certain well-circumscribed classes of properties.[11]

Ramified theory is not adequate even for the analysis of recursive arithmetic, and the second-order theorist will object to this fact. In my opinion, this is, on the contrary, something that we have learned: arithmetic is not logic. There are many ways to do arithmetic, and not all demand second-order theorizing, but there is one new and prospering discipline that has thus far been conducted only in a second-order way. This is Montague's grammar.

Montague was of course a champion of second-order theory in mathematical investigations as well as in the sphere of grammar. Let us keep these separate. Although second-order theory provides a powerful grammar for all sorts of fragments of English, we should not at once jump to conclusions. We should consider whether we need the full force of second-order logic to effect Montague's analysis of bits of ordinary language that we well understand. I tentatively propose that there is nothing in the more accessible parts of the analysis which cannot also be provided by a ramified theory.

A Löwenheim-Skolem theorem holds for anything which, on my delineation, is logic. It follows from Per Lindström's result that logic is not compact. Defending second-order theory, Boolos asks why logic should be compact? Compactness is a handy property, but there is no argument that it is of the essence of logic. On my account, however, classical logic has a property that we might call *proof-compactness*. I allow countably many premises. The question then arises whether we could obtain additional theorems by allowing proofs with more than finitely many steps, using an ω-rule. The answer is that no new theorems arise in this way. This property of proof-compactness has a venerable tradition behind it. It was Leibniz's original demarcation of the logically necessary: that which can be proved in finitely many steps.

11. There is an unpublished extensional semantics for ramified theory, due to David Kaplan.

The second-order logician has one telling objection against his first-order antagonist. Leon Henkin (1961) proved that there is no first-order treatment of branching quantifiers such as

(1)
$$
\begin{array}{c}
(\forall x)(\exists y) \\
\quad\quad (Pxy \ \& \ Qzw \ \& \ Ryw) \\
(\forall z)(\exists w)
\end{array}
$$

Branching quantifiers do not seem to involve any idea that is fundamentally different from ordinary quantification; so why, it is asked, should we exclude them from the province of logic? We understand them, it is said, in just the way that we understand ordinary universal quantification. The second-order logician does have a rendering of branching quantifiers, namely:

(2) $(\exists f)(\exists g)(P(x, fx) \ \& \ Q(z, gz) \ \& \ R(fx, gz))$

The question of branching quantifiers leads also to another rival theory on the nature of logic, the game-theoretic semantics being developed by Jaakko Hintikka and his students.[12] Hintikka claims it as a virtue of his theory that it provides an analysis of real sentences of English. To use an example due to Janet Beehner,

(3) Some melody of every big band from the forties is copied in some hit song of every rock'n roll star.

Students of English grammar are by no means agreed on whether such sentences do bear the branching quantifier reading.[13] Such current issues will take a number of years to settle down, and here I wish only to warn against too speedy a slide: "If you look at these sentences, you see they involve no idea basically different from the sort of thing we do in first-order logic; we can indeed explain everything in terms of individuals. So you must count branching quantifiers as much a part of 'logic' as first-order logic." Then comes: "The natural abstraction of the idea of branching quantifiers produces a theory formally as strong as full second-order logic." I would interject that there is nothing that we understand in (3) that cannot be understood by (2) where f and g are restricted to very low-grade ramified functions. I

12. Hintikka (1973), ch. III, and (1974).

13. For some relevant considerations on these tentative matters I am indebted to Laurie Carlsen and Alice ter Meulen (1979) and to an unpublished paper by Jon Barwise.

don't know whether (3) has to have a branching reading in English syntax. But, if it does, then it can be represented in a way that stops short of full second-order logic. To express matters in a modest way, the ramified theory once again shows itself to be a buffer between first- and second-order logic.

14. OTHER LOGICS

A demarcation can be bad in two distinct ways. It can be too strait, denying the existence of borderline cases, or it can be too vague, muttering that there will always be a messy border. A good criterion is one which is sharp but which can also be relaxed in various ways. For example, a good criterion of "grammatical sentence" is one that provides a natural measure of degrees of being grammatical. Likewise, we should allow that a core definition of "logic" can forge out in various directions. Here are some examples of how my demarcation does this.

I say that a Gentzen-like rule should have the subformula property. Now a number of workers have prepared Gentzen versions of Hilbert's ϵ-calculus, where cut-elimination does not hold. Linda Wessells (1977) has recently offered a cut-free sequent calculus for Hilbert's ϵ, but her rules do not, strictly speaking, have a subformula property.[14] (It may be possible to find a more encompassing but not merely *ad hoc* property that they do have.) On present evidence we should say not that Hilbert's ϵ is not logical but that it fails to fall under the logicist conception of logic in an entirely specific and well defined way.

A much better understood extension of the logicist conception of logic concerns the power of proofs of cut-elimination. I have considered only finitistically provable cut-elimination. Transfinite induction up to limit ordinals provides more and more generous classifications of logic. Many readers will say that is how we ought to go, for the restriction to finitistic proofs is provincial or old-fashioned. There are many things to say on that score. One logicist defense might recall Leibniz's idea that a proof of a necessary proposition must have a finite number of steps. Now take a theory like arithmetic for which one proves an elimination theorem using transfinite induction. That does not imply that cut-free proofs in the object-level theory itself have to be infinite in length; for any particular use of the cut rule can be dealt with in a finite number of steps. So Gentzen's object-level theory of arithmetic is not to be faulted on that Leibnizian score. But there is

---

14. Wessels (1977). For a debate on whether Hilbert's 'ϵ' is a logical constant see Bjurlöf (1978) and Peacocke (1978).

also a logicist conception that logic is the very canon of consistency. If, for Leibnizian reasons, proofs in logic are things that stop, then only when logic is construed in terms of finitistically provable elimination theorems do we have a theory whose consistency can be established by logic itself.

Modal logics provide yet another direction in which to extend logic. Obviously the principles underlying this extension must be quite different from those which lead on to arithmetic. Our demarcation displays this very nicely. It is not provability of cut-elimination that excludes modal logic, but dilution-elimination, as was shown in §9. The serious modal logics such as *T*, *S4*, and *S5* have cut-free sequent-calculus formalizations, but the rules place restrictions on side formulas. Gentzen's rules for sentential connections are all "local" in that they concern only the components from which the principal formula is built up, and place no restrictions on the side formulas. Gentzen's own first-order rules, though not strictly local, are equivalent to local ones. That is why dilution-elimination goes through for first-order logic but not for modal logics. What does this formal difference amount to? The meaning is clearer when one thinks of natural-deduction formulations. To place a restriction on side formulas is to insist that whether a step in a proof is valid depends on the history of the proof and on the forms of the sentences that occur higher up in the proof. Modal logic is in this sense metalogical, and our criterion picks out object-level classical logic. This is not to deny that modal logic is in some general sense logic, but rather to specify precisely a formal respect in which it differs from first-order and ramified logic. Thus the subformula property, finitistic cut-elimination, and dilution-elimination may all be relaxed to provide different kinds of extension of my core logicist demarcation of logic. That is as it should be.

The difference between first-order and modal logic shows up in a more familiar way at the semantic level. Models for modal logic use domains of possible worlds. The seriously motivated nonclassical logics, such as are inspired by intuitionist mathematics or quantum physics, also have different semantics. I believe that the difference between such nonclassical logics and classical logics lies in the deducibility relation itself and in the corresponding semantic relation of logical consequence. The nonclassical logics assume a different underlying semantic framework. I shall develop this idea in the next two sections.

15. SEMANTIC FRAMEWORKS

Suppose that Gentzen-like operational rules are to be added to a language fragment. If the initial bit of language is something one can understand, then it ought to be possible to understand this fragment augmented by the constants introduced by the rules. If not, the rules are not definitions.

We must, then, provide a semantics for the new logical constants, presupposing a semantics for the original language fragment. That assumes some substantive and precise analysis of the fragment. The assumption has two parts: first, a general assumption about the form that the semantics should take, and, second, a specific account of the language fragment to hand.

By the form of the semantics I mean an initial abstraction about the nature of truth and logical consequence. What I have to say in detail about this abstraction does not depend on any philosophy, but it is well to offer one philosophical setting, which the reader need not accept. I do not believe that English is by its nature classical or intuitionistic or whatever. Classical and intuitionistic truth are both abstractions made by logicians. We all know that logicians attend to numerous different objects that might be served by uttering 'if . . . then . . .' sentences. The abstractions that result include the material conditional, several kinds of strict implication, and a panoply of stronger connectives of which relevant implication is the current favorite. In a more ambitious way classical and some serious nonclassical logics abstract from the very point of making statements. Classical logic is one of several interesting abstractions. If the point of uttering sentences (perhaps only with some selected topics of conversation) were to say what can be established, or to say what makes sense in microphysics, then one is drawn to non-classical abstractions.

These remarks about abstraction are intended chiefly as a flag, posting quicksand. It might well be the case that there are decisive arguments in favor of classical, intuitionist, or quantum logic (to mention only views that are widely attributed to Kripke, Dummett, and Putnam in turn). I here contend only that none of these is the logic of English. When I speak of a semantic framework for a language fragment, I mean an abstraction from the point of uttering declarative sentences. It is art, not nature, that determines the semantics of natural languages.

A semantic framework is to be the general form of the semantics of a language. It may well be that I include too little in the framework, and then smuggle in more assumptions as part of the semantics of specific languages. Perhaps I focus too much on what has been the subject of recent discussion. But I shall make two assumptions only, one about truth, and the other about logical consequence. The strongest version of the assumption about truth is that every sentence of the language fragment should be assigned the value true or false but not both. The second assumption is that a set of sentences Θ is a logical consequence of the set of sentences Γ if no matter what values are assigned to the members of Γ, Θ, some member of Θ is true when every member of Γ is true. We make only these two assumptions. The language fragment might have a rich field of logical consequence, or it might be a "prelogical" language of independent elementary sentences like that envisaged by the *Tractatus*, in which there are no nontrivial consequences.

There is an important connection between the structural rules and this classical semantic framework. Let us say that a set of rules of deducibility is *complete* with respect to a language with a classical semantic framework, when $\Gamma \vdash \Theta$ is derivable if and only if Θ is a logical consequence of Γ. *Then the structural rules are complete with respect to a prelogical classical language.* Or to put it differently, Θ is a logical consequence of Γ in any classical language whatsoever, if and only if $\Gamma \vdash \Theta$ is derivable by the structural rules alone.

I began in §6 writing out general constraints on anything that could count as a relation of deducibility. These constraints had already been recognized by Gentzen as the structural rules of his sequent calculus. They also pick out the minimum facts of logical consequence that obtain from a classical point of view. Thus the structural rules formalize the "pure" theory of classical logical consequence. It is my contention, not developed here, that a nonclassical logic has a right to be called logic (and not merely another logical algebra) just if there is a different semantic framework, with respect to which some nonclassical structural rules are complete.

16. DO-IT-YOURSELF SEMANTICS

The rules for logical constants always take the following form. Since the requirement of dilution-elimination means that all rules are local in the sense of placing no restrictions on side formulas, side formulas may be disregarded. Omitting side formulas, the form of the rules is:

$$\frac{\{\Pi_i \vdash \Sigma_i\}}{A \vdash} \qquad \frac{\{\Pi_j \vdash \Sigma_j\}}{\vdash A}$$

The formulas in Π and Σ are components of A. A set of statements $\{\Pi_j \vdash \Sigma_j\}$ from which one may derive $\vdash A$ is called a *right protopremise*; $\{\Pi_i \vdash \Sigma_i\}$ above is a *left protopremise*. Consider a Gentzen-like rule which is to add a constant to a language fragment. A semantics and a class of models for the language is assumed. A model assigns every sentence of this language the values T or F. We are concerned with how to assign values to complex sentences in terms of a model for the original language. Thanks to the subformula property an inductive definition may be used.

> *A* takes the value T in a model iff there is a right protopremise for *A*, $\{\Pi_j \vdash \Sigma_j\}$, such that for each *j* some member of Σ_j takes T or some member of Π_j takes F.

Thanks to the elimination theorems, it is possible to establish a matching assertion,

> *A* takes the value *F* iff there is a left protopremise for *A*, $\{\Pi_i \vdash \Sigma_i\}$ such that for each *i* some member of Σ_i takes T or some member of Π_i takes F.

There is nothing more to be said about sentential logic. More complicated languages have more structured models. In §11 it was pointed out that provability of cut-elimination for first-order logic might require the addition of countably many items of category *t*, i.e., an infinite stock of variables. This applies only to languages which already have some terms and predicates and for which we assume models with a nonempty domain of individuals. For each model *M* of the original language, we now need all models obtained by assigning the new variables to individuals in the domain of *M*. This indicates a general technique for ramified logic, and is possible because variables of a given category are added only to a language that already has items of that category and, hence, whose models already have a nonempty class of objects for items of that category.

This semantics is not directly applicable to Gentzen's quantifier rules. His rule for the universal quantifier is stated on the left below. Instead we use the equivalent ω-rule on the right, which is local in the sense of §14, i.e., places no restrictions on the side formulas. (That such a rule is equivalent is implied already by Gentzen's Lemma 3.10 "redesignating of free object variables.")

$$\frac{\Gamma \vdash Fa,\ \Theta}{\Gamma \vdash (\forall x)Fx,\ \Theta} \quad \begin{array}{l}\text{where } a \text{ does not occur}\\ \text{in the bottom line}\end{array} \qquad \frac{\{\Gamma \vdash Ft_i,\ \Theta\}_i}{\Gamma \vdash (\forall x)Fx,\ \Theta} \quad \begin{array}{l}\text{where } t_i \text{ runs}\\ \text{over all terms}\end{array}$$

Such devices may be immediately generalized to ramified logic. Charles Parsons points out that such ω-rules precisely parallel the *Tractatus* account of the first-order quantifiers.

The completeness theorem states that, under the above semantics, $\Gamma \vdash \Theta$ is derivable if and only if Θ is a logical consequence of Γ. I have elsewhere (1977) stated some details of the proof. This do-it-yourself semantics is of course a fraud. It purports to be a mechanical way of providing the semantics of the logical constants. But in fact it needs a thoroughly hand-crafted semantics for the original language fragment in order for the whole thing to work. In the case of the quantifiers with the ω-rule above, one would have to understand something like arithmetic, or at least counting, to deploy the semantics. This is not a problem for the present paper, for I have tried only to find a demarcation of the logical constants. The claim is that the constants are those which can be introduced into a language in a certain way. They can be introduced by rules of a certain form. The rules are syntactic in character. Yet they are such that if strong semantic assumptions of a general kind are made, then the specific semantics of the individual logical constants is thereby determined. The rule for '$*$' in §11 will illustrate this. What are the truth conditions for '$A * B$'? The rules stated above show that $A * B$ takes the value T if and only if at least one of A or B is F. So the do-it-yourself semantics is not vacuous; for one could well have failed to understand what the '$*$' meant, and then found it out by these semantics.

17. PRELOGICAL LANGUAGE

The *Tractatus* imagines a language of elementary sentences that lack logical constants, which has in addition sentential connectives for forming compound sentences. The truth tables exhibit the character of these connectives and show how the truth conditions for complex sentences may be explained in terms of simpler sentences. One could carry this myth one step further, and consider the fragment of the language consisting just of elementary sentences. Then one could imagine the logical connectives being added to that language, and their use being conveyed by syntactic rules and the truth tables. The point of this extra myth would not be to show how the connectives are in fact learned, but rather to display something about the logical connectives—"they are words of this peculiar sort, that one can imagine them being planted in the language in this way."

There is no part of the *Tractatus* of which Wittgenstein became more scornful than the myth of elementary sentences. But having been taught some of the lessons of later philosophy, one can still usefully deploy the myth. It is an instructive myth because it is the purest form of the idea of a purely descriptive part of language.

This myth, and the task of distinguishing nondescriptive logical constants, is foreshadowed by the schoolmen. The signs of quantity, 'some', 'all', and 'no', were central examples of syncategorematical terms. But what, it was asked, distinguishes them from descriptive terms? It was natural to contrast *velus* (meaning 'veil') and *vel* (meaning something like inclusive disjunction) but there was never an agreed basis to the distinction. In general one tried to say as much, or more, about what it is to be descriptive as about what it is to be syncategorematical. Much the same holds for similar dichotomies in judgments, say between the empirical and the a priori, or in faculties, say between sensibility and the understanding. It is a virtue of my demarcation that it enables one to characterize the logical constants without being forced to say what is on the other side of the dichotomy. One does not have to say what pure descriptive constants are. A logical constant is a constant that can be added to any language of a certain sort.

Yet the myth of the prelogical or entirely descriptive language still has some force. It enables us to ask, What are the minimum conditions on a language, in order that logical constants should be added by means of operational rules? If the rules are to be regarded as something like definitions, then we suppose the formulas of a prelogical language are themselves intelligible. Such understanding might be achieved by providing a theory of truth for the language, or a formal semantics, or: the language is simply understood. A number of philosophers have recently been reinforcing the point that the stating of meanings comes to an end, and languages are in the end just understood.

A fact about the terminology of the *Tractatus* has been widely overlooked. Wittgenstein speaks of *truth conditions* for compound sentences. He shows how truth conditions of compounds are determined by their components. But he does not speak of truth conditions for elementary sentences. He does speak of their truth possibilities, but not of their truth conditions.[15] This thought could be combined with a recent doctrine of Putnam's. He urges that the theory of understanding a language is not to be couched in terms of truth conditions and correspondence, although those ideas are important for explaining the success of discourse. Without taking a stand on such matters, one could urge that understanding the prelogical language is indeed

---

15. For *Wahrheitsbedingungen*, see 4.431, 4.442, 4.45, 4.46, 4.461, 4.463; for *Wahrheitsmöglichkeiten*, see 4.3, 4.31, 4.4, 4.41, 4.42, 4.43, 4.431, 4.44, 4.442, 4.45, 4.46, 5.101. Note that in 4.063 (b) the word sometimes translated as "conditions" is *Umständen*.

not to be explained in terms of truth conditions. Complex sentences, obtained by adding logical constants, however, may have their truth conditions explained in terms of more elementary sentences.

It may well be asked whether a prelogical language could be understood by a being that had no logical concepts. I doubt that there are any compelling arguments one way or the other, and the question is idle because prelogical language is a myth. Beneath any "elementary" sentence—be it "this is black," said pointing at this letter '*r*'—there is a swarming underworld of logically germane sentences that bear on the sentence in more than a merely empirical or inductive way. The best metaphor may be that of an hourglass, of endless constructions which converge on a collection of what are at one level simple sentences, but which, when they pass through the narrow point of the hourglass, open up again in endless complexity. The elementary sentences of the *Tractatus* are merely the elements that occur at a narrowing in an hourglass, and are not ultimate. Logic, depth grammar, structuralism, and the like should postulate points of convergence or condensation, not atoms.

18. LOGICAL TRUTH

My criterion (C) insists that a demarcation of logical constants should connect with the analytic program. The immediate Fregean aim had been to reduce arithmetic to logic, proving thereby that arithmetic is not synthetic. The results are negative. Recursive arithmetic cannot be reduced to logic, strictly construed. If, however, one were to extend the definition of logic to allow for transfinite proofs of cut-elimination, then arithmetic does get included as "logic." In §14 I have expressed some reservations about this strategy.

The strict demarcation of logic provides some vindication for both Leibniz and Kant. In the ramified hierarchy cumbersome definitions enable one to prove that $5 + 7 = 12$. So, on my explication, Kant's immediate claim about arithmetic is wrong. *That* sum is not synthetic. But although Leibniz may win this battle he loses the war, for the concept *natural number* cannot itself be categorically characterized in pure logic. We can say only that the natural numbers are those which come in the sequence 1, 2, 3, ⋯. We do have an intuition of this sequence. Perhaps, as Kant supposed, it is connected to the intuition of succession in time.

Arithmetic was a special project for the analytic program. More generally, it aimed at understanding the nature of logical truth. A. J. Ayer could say, in the great days of enthusiasm, that "there is nothing mysterious about the apodictic certainty of logic and mathematics. Our knowledge that no observation can ever confute the proposition '7 + 5 = 12' depends simply on the fact that the symbolic expression '7 + 5' is synonymous with '12', just as our knowledge that every oculist is an eye doctor depends on the fact that the symbol 'eye-doctor' is synonymous with 'oculist'. And the same explanation holds good for every other a priori truth." (Ayer 1946, p. 85) No one would dare say this sort of thing any more, but there is a lingering belief in the maxim, "Necessary truths are true in virtue of the meanings of the words used to express them."

The by-product theory of logical truth, which in §3 I attributed to the *Tractatus*, gives some credibility to that idea. Intended originally for the truth-functional connectives, it is readily extended to any constant introduced by Gentzen-like rules satisfying my criteria. "Without troubling ourselves about a sense and a reference, we form the logical theorems out of others by rules that deal with signs alone." That fits the operational rules rather well. Rules for a notation are provided, in consequence of which certain complex sentences come out as theorems. As the *Tractatus* continues, "All theorems of logic are of equal status; there are not some that are essentially primitive and others deduced from these." "Logic can always be conceived so that every theorem is its own proof."[16] In the sequent calculus every theorem has, indeed, its own analysis, and no theorems are primitive. Moreover this analysis answers rather exactly to Leibniz's idea of the finitely long analysis of necessary propositions.

This way of thinking makes the existence of theorems in logic look like a by-product of the rules that convey the use of logical constants. It guards against the supposition that theorems represent constraints on how the world must be. The only constraints arise from the system for forming complex sentences. Some complexes that are built up using logical constants describe complex possibilities, but theorems and contradictions are only limiting cases that arise from the rules for the notation itself. As Leibniz well understood, the concept *logically necessary proposition* is to be explained in terms of proof, and not in terms of truth in all possible worlds (as if necessity represented some constraint on what worlds can be created).

It is not to be inferred that logical truths are in any instructive sense true by convention. Imagine that notational conventions in the

16. Wittgenstein (1961, 6.126, 6.127, 6.1265); for this discussion one must translate *Satz* as 'theorem'.

form of operational rules were added to a "prelogical" language. Even in that mythical case convention would not completely account for logical truth. There would remain the question prompted by Lewis Carroll's Achilles and the Tortoise, and elaborated by Quine long ago.[17] By what conventions, it would be asked, do we apply the rules as we do when we derive theorems in the calculus? Even when we deliberately adopt a convention (say with the rule that turned out to introduce Sheffer's stroke in §11) that convention is not the *complete* account of the logical theorems that result.

To reject truth by convention is not to reject truth in virtue of meaning. The operational rules display certain features of logical constants. These constants do have a "meaning," aspects of which are displayed by these rules. The rules do not produce or create or justify logical truths, but set out what it is about their meaning that is connected with logical truth. Note that a particular objection to "truth in virtue of meaning" is irrelevant here. It is rightly observed that 'It is raining or it is not raining' cannot be true in virtue of the meaning of the words, because the proposition expressed would be true even if we used quite different words. Yet this tautology is still a product of meanings, not (except adventitiously) of the English signs 'or' and 'not', but of the abstract "meaning" that is conveyed by the operational rules that we happen to label as disjunction and negation. Whatever be the signs we associate with those rules, there will be a tautology corresponding.

These considerations are all of a negative sort: logical truth has no source outside language and whatever makes language possible. There still remain the familiar questions as to what it is to grasp the meaning. Undoubtedly we understand some constants before formulating any rules, and, even if we did not, there would be questions about following the rules. It may be, however, that certain positive conclusions are to be drawn from the theory of operational rules. For it is not as if they justify talk of logical *truth.* All we get from applying the rules are some sentences with the deducibility sign in front. To construe these as truths we require a semantics.

I have contended that the semantic framework has nothing to do with particular logical constants. Given a semantic framework for a language, one may use operational rules to characterize logical constants; the do-it-yourself semantics shows how the semantics for the

17. Carroll (1895), and "Truth by Convention" (1936) in Quine (1966, pp. 70–99).

language works out for the constants that are thus introduced. This leads one to recall some remarks of Frege quoted earlier.[18] Analytic truths are those whose proofs may be traced back to "general logical laws." But these general laws were not to be primitive propositions written down in the object language. What are these "most general laws, which prescribe universally the way in which one ought to think if one is to think at all"? I believe that in the end they are not about particular logical ideas, such as the quantifier or the conditional. They must be what Frege calls "laws of truth." A law of truth would concern the nature of the semantic framework itself.

The analytic program has come full circle. In an attempt to understand the idea of analyticity, one considered the logical truths. A logical truth is a truth in which only logical constants occur essentially. So one searched for a demarcation of the logical constants. Having used the theory of deducibility to find it, we then see that although the existence of particular theorems of logic may be explained in terms of rules that define individual constants, the notion of logical truth depends on the notion of truth for a language. If a nonstandard logic is possible, in a way that is not parasitic upon classical logic, then a nonclassical notion of truth and consequence is possible. But if a nonstandard logic must ultimately be explained using classical logic, then indeed we would have found something that "our thought can overflow, but never displace."[19]

18. See the first six pages of this essay. Frege himself seems to have abandoned the analytic program late in life; see his "Neuer Versuch der Grundlegung der Arithmetik," in Frege (1969, p. 298).

19. A first version of this paper was duplicated for a seminar in Cambridge University, November 1970, and a second version for seminars at the London School of Economics, February 1971. I owe many debts of gratitude to people who have helped me with this project since then. I particularly wish to thank T. J. Smiley for his patient encouragement and advice.

15

On First-Order Logic

R. I. G. Hughes

1. INTRODUCTION

The second edition of the *Critique of Pure Reason* was published in 1787. In his preface Kant wrote, "Logic . . . is . . . to all appearances a closed and completed body of doctrine" (Kant 1965, Bviii).

Appearances were deceptive. A century later, the publication of Frege's *Begriffschrift* opened a door to fresh thoughts on an ancient subject.[1] This work, Bochenski suggests, "can only be compared with one other work in the whole history of logic, the *Prior Analytics* of Aristotle" (1970, p. 268). For van Heijenoort (1967, p. 1), "It is perhaps the most important work ever written in logic." Yet its importance was not at first widely recognized; Frege's ideas became known largely through the work of Bertrand Russell in the first decade of this century.[2] When Carnap writes in 1930 about "The Old Logic and the New Logic," the work he cites as "the great basis work of the new logic" is not the *Begriffschrift* but Whitehead and Russell's *Principia Mathematica.*[3]

Frege's innovations were many and various, but the core of "the new logic" came to be first-order quantificational logic.[4] This logic is *first*

---

1. T. W. Bynum translates *Begriffschrift* as "Conceptual Notation." See Frege (1972).

2. Dummett writes, "Three great figures—Edmund Husserl, Bertrand Russell and Ludwig Wittgenstein—studied Frege and were influenced by him, but the general philosophical public was largely unaware of him." (Michael Dummett 1978, p. 87)

3. Rudolf Carnap (1959, pp. 134–5). This essay first appeared in *Erkenntnis* 1 (1930–31). Alfred North Whitehead and Bertrand Russell, *Principia Mathematica to *56,* (1962). The full three-volume work was originally published from 1910 to 1913.

4. Frege also makes significant use of second-order quantification, as do Russell and Whitehead. For a list of Frege's innovations, see either Bochenski (1970, p. 268) or van Heijenoort (1967, p. 1).

order in that it allows quantification over individuals, but not over predicates; a first-order language that treats "is defective" as a predicate cannot express the second quantification in the sentence, "Every one of these light bulbs is defective in some way or other." First-order logic contains Aristotelian categorical logic and the Stoic logic of propositions as proper parts; it deals, however, not only with monadic predicates, like ". . . is red" or ". . . is a mammal," but with relations, like ". . . is descended from . . .," and, more generally still, with polyadic predicates. It also treats multiple quantification over individuals, of the kind exemplified by the English sentence "Everyone detests somebody." As Dummett shows (essay 10, this volume) these innovations alone would mark the new logic as a revolutionary advance on the old.

The study of first-order logic is now part of the professional training of virtually every graduate student in philosophy. In this essay I will address two related questions. What exactly did the articulation of first-order logic involve? And what was achieved thereby? I will locate much of my answer to the first question by reference to four historical landmarks. Two of them I have already mentioned: Frege's *Begriffsschrift*, published in 1879, and Whitehead and Russell's *Principia Mathematica* of 1910–13. A third is a pair of papers by Tarski, "The Concept of Truth in Formalized Languages" (1933) and "The Establishment of Scientific Semantics" (1936), and the fourth, Gentzen's "Investigations into Logical Deduction," which appeared in 1935.[5] As a point of comparison I take Kant's lectures on logic.[6] This may seem an odd choice, since Kant's aim was not Frege's, and to the twentieth-century historian of logic the lectures present "a peculiarly confused version of the traditional mixture of Aristotelian and Stoic elements."[7] That is part of the point. By the end of the eighteenth century the study of logic had been stagnant for several hundred years; indeed, Kant was one of the few Enlightenment philosophers to pay serious attention to it.[8] Against this background the achievements of modern logic stand out the more clearly.

5. See Alfred Tarski (1983, chs. 8 and 15); and Gerhard Gentzen (1969, ch. 3).

6. Kant gave these lectures for forty years, and there are various versions of them extant. My references will be to the *Jäsche Logic*, published as Immanuel Kant, *Logic*, (1974).

7. Kneale and Kneale (1962, p. 355).

8. Another, of course was Leibniz, but his work largely went unheeded; see fn. 11, below.

2. SYNTAX

A logic is typically presented by specifying (a) the syntax of a formal language, (b) a semantics for that language, and (c) a system of deduction, or proof, for the logic. In the next three sections of this essay I will follow this order of presentation.

Consider the English sentence:

(a) George congratulated the woman.

We can modify (a) by adding a relative clause, thereby producing another sentence:

(b) George congratulated the woman who drove the dogsled.

The same operation can be performed on the second sentence to yield a third:

(c) George congratulated the woman who drove the dogsled that won the race.

We could, if we wished, continue this procedure indefinitely, in the manner of nursery rhymes like "The House That Jack Built." It is a simple example of a recursive process, whereby an operation is performed on an object, in this case a sentence, to produce another object of the same kind, and repeated on the second object to form a third, and so on.[9]

The formal languages used in modern logic are recursively defined. We are given lists of symbols falling under various headings; in this essay I use predicate letters ("P," "Q," "R," . . .), individual constants, which function as names ("a," "b," "c," . . .), variables ("x," "y," "z," . . .), connectives ("$\sim$," "$\&$," "$\vee$," "$\supset$"), quantifier symbols ("$\forall$," "$\exists$"), and parentheses to act as punctuation marks ("(", ")"). A recursive definition specifies how these symbols may be concatenated to yield well-formed (i.e. grammatical) sentences; we are first told what is to count as an atomic sentence, and then given a rule of recursion for constructing complex sentences out of simpler ones. The rule has a number of clauses, each one corresponding to a specific connective or quantifier (more generally, to a specific sentential operator). The clause for "$\&$," for instance, allows that any two sen-

---

9. For an instructive and entertaining discussion of recursive processes, see Hofstadter (1980, ch. 5).

tences can be conjoined to form a conjunction. Other clauses permit that conjunction to be negated, or to be used as the consequent of a conditional; the negation or the conditional can then be used as a component of a larger sentence, and so on. A final rule stipulates that no string of symbols is a sentence unless it is built up in accordance with this procedure. A language generated in this way contains infinitely many sentences, each of them of finite length.

If we look at Kant's lectures on logic with this procedure in mind, two significant differences emerge. In the first place, Kant talks of judgements, rather than sentences, and his specification of a judgement is in psychological terms; he writes (1974, p. 106), "A judgement is the presentation of the unity of the consciousness of several presentations, or the presentation of their relation as far as they make up one concept."[10] Frege, in the *Begriffschrift*, also talks of judgements; he thinks of judgements, however, not as mental acts but as elements in a language, to be asserted or denied. Indeed the subtitle of the work is "A Formalized Language of Pure Thought Modelled upon the Language of Arithmetic." The second difference is that Kant never considers judgements of a high degree of complexity. In discussing dilemmas he mentions conditionals with disjunctive consequents (1974, p. 134), but that is as far as he goes.

As we have seen, natural languages, like formal languages, allow the formation of complex sentences from simpler ones. In a natural language, however, multiple reiteration may lead to unintelligibility. Consider, for instance, what the simple use of parentheses achieves in the symbolic representation of Peirce's Law:

$$((A \supset B) \supset A) \supset A$$

Whatever sentences were substituted for A and B, it is not obvious how this might be rendered into comprehensible English.

Furthermore, natural languages can be syntactically ambiguous. Confronted by the sentence "Flying kites can be dangerous," we cannot be sure whether the first word is a gerund or a participle.

For an example of a syntactically unambiguous language with a recursive grammar, Frege looked to arithmetic. In this he followed earlier nineteenth-century mathematical logicians like Boole and McColl.[11] Since the invention of algebra, mathematicians have been

10. Arnulf Zweig tells me that in the *Critique* Kant occasionally uses "*Satz*" ("sentence") rather than "*Urteil*."

11. The ancestor of these languages is Leibniz's proposed Characteristica Universalis; see the essay, "Preface to a Universal Characteristic" in Leibniz,

used to dealing with complex formulae constructed from simple ones by successive reiterations of basic operations. Boole extended this process to logic; he formed the logical product (the conjunction, as we would say) of three expressions, two of them negations, by writing "$z\,(1-x)\,(1-y)$" to represent the proposition "It freezes, but neither hails nor rains."[12]

In passing, we may contrast Boole's attitude to complex propositions with that of J. S. Mill. Writing in the same decade as Boole, Mill declared (1843, v. 1, p. 109),

> What is called a complex proposition is often not a proposition at all, but several propositions held together by a conjunction. Such, for example, is this, Caesar is dead and Brutus is alive. . . . There are here two distinct assertions; and we might as well call a street a complex house, as these two propositions a complex proposition.

Although Mill talks of "propositions," within this passage we find an echo of Kant's emphasis on the (psychological) unity of a judgement. Apparently Mill did not heed his predecessor Bentham in this matter; Quine tells us (1966b, p. 659), "Bentham was perhaps the first to see the sentence as the primary vehicle of meaning. Frege took up the tale." It would have been hard for Mill to argue that, because it contained two smaller sentences as parts, "Caesar is dead and Brutus is alive" was not a sentence.

Frege tells us that his formal language is modelled on that of arithmetic, but his notation is very different from Boole's.[13] He represents a judgement by an expression of the form,

(1) $$\vdash\!\!\!-\!\!-\!\!- A$$

The *content* of this judgement, which we might express by the phrase "The proposition that A," is represented by

(2) $$-\!\!-\!\!- A$$

(1989, pp. 5–10). And in the eighteenth century Lambert too used algebraic notation to show the distributivity of "and" over "or", and vice versa; see Weyl (1949, p. 5).

12. Boole, (1952, p. 90). See also Bochenski (1970, p. 308).

13. In a letter to Schröder Frege says that he avoided Boole's symbolism because he wanted a notation which would enable him to analyse mathematical reasoning, rather than engage in a particular (algebraic) variety of it; see Kneale and Kneale (1962, p. 478).

The horizontal line in figure (2) Frege calls the "content-stroke," and the vertical line in figure (1), which serves to affirm the judgement, he calls the "judgement-stroke." Complex propositions, or, in his terms, the content of complex judgements, are set out in diagrammatic form. The figures

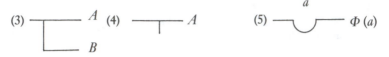

represent, respectively, the conditional we would write as "$B \supset A$," the negation "$\sim A$," and the universally quantified sentence, "$(\forall x)\Phi(x)$." More complex figures can be built up using these devices. Thus the figure

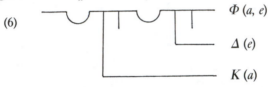

would appear in a more familiar notation (with Greek letters replaced by Roman) as

$$(\forall x)(Cx \supset \sim(\forall y)(Dy \supset \sim Fxy))$$

This is equivalent to

$$(\forall x)(Cx \supset (\exists y)(Dy \& Fxy))$$

which would be the standard rendering of "Every cat fears some dog."[14] Note that Frege calls figures like (3)–(6) "expressions," thus emphasizing their kinship with elements of more orthodox written languages.

Effectively, Frege uses two sentential connectives, representing negation and the conditional, and the universal quantifier. Disjunction, conjunction, and existential quantification are expressed in terms of these; thus Frege's language is rich enough to express all of first-order quantificational logic. One of the notational devices which enabled Frege to do this has survived; the other has not. His use of the functional notation "$\Phi(a)$" to represent a sentence containing a variable letter "a" was followed by Russell and Whitehead and is now standard. In the same way that the mathematical expression "$f(x, y)$"

14. The example is the Kneales'. (1962, p. 486).

represents a function with two arguments, in Frege's logic the expression "$\Phi(a, b)$" is used to represent a relation between two objects.[15]

No one, however, has followed Frege in his use of two-dimensional diagrams to represent complex sentences. Venn, for one, dismissed the notation as "cumbrous and inconvenient." "It does not seem to me," he wrote, "that Dr. Frege's scheme can for a moment compare with that of Boole."[16] Yet these diagrams are worth examining in more detail, since they offer immediate and graphic representations of the logical relations and procedures that Frege was concerned with.

To start with a trivial example: the inference figure *modus ponens*, also known as detachment, is represented in Frege's symbolism by the move from

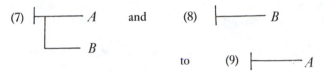

The lower arm of expression (7) has, quite literally, been detached to yield the conclusion (9).

More significant are the ways in which the elements of these expressions can be stacked together. In specifying the three typographical operations that yield complex expressions from simpler ones, Frege gives what is essentially a recursive definition of a logical expression. Since all expressions represent judgements, all these operations correspond to logical operations. The operations that yield the expressions (3), (4), and (5), above, correspond to the logical operations of weakening, negation, and universal generalization, respectively. Note in passing that weakening appears as the reverse of detachment. It "attaches" another well-formed expression to A in a way that preserves truth.

These diagrams, together with his functional notation, allowed Frege to represent his insights into quantification with admirable clarity. The diagrams display the fact that, like negation, quantification is to be regarded as an operation on an already existing proposition; since a sequence of operations can be performed one after the other, multiple quantification is possible. The use of variables and functional notation

15. The importance of this innovation is brought out by Dummett (essay 10, this volume).

16. John Venn, review of Frege's *Begriffschrift*, *Mind*, 5 (1880), p. 297; also in Frege (1972).

shows precisely which variables are to be governed by which quantifier, and the scope of a quantifier can be read off immediately and
unambiguously from the diagram. This last fact is true of all three
operations. Typographically, each operation attaches to a particular
point on a content-stroke, and its scope is the expression to the right
of that point. All these virtues are nicely illustrated by the Kneales'
cat-and-dog example in figure (6), above.

A defect is that the asymmetry in its treatment of binary connectives, though appropriate in the case of the conditional, makes the
notation inapt for the representation of "&" and "∨." For these connectives the algebraic, Boolean representation is more perspicuous.[17]
There are also pragmatic reasons for choosing another notation. Frege's
diagrams are not only rather bulky, permitting no more than three or
four middle-sized expressions to be printed on the same page, but also
difficult for the typesetter.

For these reasons the notation has not survived. Nowadays the
standard notation for first-order logic is essentially that of *Principia
Mathematica*, through which Frege's ideas gained currency. This notation in turn was an adaptation of one devised by Peano. In this essay I
use a variant of *Principia* notation; the major difference is that I rely
exclusively on parentheses for punctuation, rather than on the system
of dots favoured by Russell.[18]

I also employ sentence schemata; to talk, for example, about condi-
tionals in general, I use the sentence schema $\ulcorner A \supset B \urcorner$. A and B
appear in this schema as metalinguistic variables. They stand for any
sentences (not necessarily distinct) of the formal language, but they
are not themselves sentences of that language. For example, if "P,"
"Q," and "R" are all atomic sentences of the language, then, by
substituting "$P \& Q$" for A and "$Q \vee R$" for B, we obtain, as an
instance of $\ulcorner A \supset B \urcorner$, the sentence "$(P \& Q) \supset (Q \vee R)$."

Where sentences of the formal language appear in the text, they are
placed within quotation marks. The schema $\ulcorner A \supset B \urcorner$, however, is a
curious hybrid; although it contains the symbol "$\supset$" of the formal
language, it is not a sentence of that language but a recipe for generating such sentences. To mark that distinction I follow Quine's practice
of placing schemata within corners, or *quasiquotation marks*.[19] Where

---

17. But note fn. 13, above.

18. See Whitehead and Russell (1962, p. 10). Bochenski (1970, p. 319) and
the Kneales (1962, p. 521) both give tables of notational variants. Bochenski
illustrates Polish notation more perspicuously, but gives no variants for quantifiers.

19. See Quine (1951, ch. 1, §6). Various different strategies for treating the

sentences of the formal language and sentence schemata are displayed, rather than embedded in the text, I omit quotation and quasi-quotation marks. Sentential variables will be represented by italicized capital letters from the beginning of the alphabet.

3. SEMANTICS

When the syntax of a formal language has been specified, the language can be given an interpretation. This involves giving the truth-conditions for the sentences of the language. As an elementary example, consider the propositional fragment L_p of a first-order language. The sentences of L_p are those containing only zero-place predicates, connectives, and parentheses. (A zero-place predicate, like the English sentence, "It is raining," is itself an atomic sentence.) L_p is standardly given a *bivalent truth-functional semantics*. Sentences are either true or false, and to each sentential connective there corresponds a truth-function. A sentence of the form $\ulcorner A \supset B \urcorner$, for example, is false if and only if A is true and B is false. Recall that A and B stand for any sentences of the language; "$(P \mathbin{\&} Q) \supset (Q \vee R)$" is an instance of $\ulcorner A \supset B \urcorner$, false when "$P \mathbin{\&} Q$" is true and "$Q \vee R$" false, and true otherwise. Given the truth-functions for "&" and "$\vee$," the truth-values of these components are determined in turn by the truth-values of "P," "Q" and "R." The truth-functional interpretation of the connectives, and the fact that the set of sentences of L_p is recursively defined, together guarantee that the truth value of any sentence of L_p is uniquely determined by the truth values of its atomic components.[20]

The rudiments of truth-functional analysis can be found in Stoic logic; indeed the material conditional, expressed by $\ulcorner A \supset B \urcorner$, is sometimes called the *Philonian conditional*, after Philo of Megara.[21] Curiously, although §§5 and 7 of the *Begriffschrift* give essentially truth-functional accounts of conditionals and negations, Frege never uses the terms "true" and "false" (or their German equivalents) in those sections; instead he uses "affirmed" and "denied," which to us suggest speech acts rather than truth values; by 1891, however, he was

---

use/mention distinction in the presentation of logic are discussed in Thomason (1970, pp. 56–60).

20. Since there are infinitely many sentences in the language, we need to prove this theorem by induction. See sections 1.1–1.3 of Wilfred Hodges, "Elementary Predicate Logic," ch. 1 of Gabbay and Guenther (1983), v. 1.

21. See Kneale and Kneale (1962, p. 128).

talking in terms of "The True" and "The False."[22] When Russell and Whitehead talk of a proposition being "asserted," they mean that it is a theorem of their system (i.e. a logical truth), like "$P \supset P$."[23] A vestigial use of Frege's notation appears when they express this by writing,

$$\vdash P \supset P$$

Truth-tables first appear as a means of displaying truth-functions in 1921, in Wittgenstein's *Tractatus*.[24] The truth-table approach to, say, negation is markedly more precise than Whitehead and Russell's informal statement that "$\sim P$ means not-P, which means the negation of P." In a sense, however, it is also less ambitious. It moves discussion away from meaning, and confines it to questions of truth. The two topics are not the same; the meaning of a sentence cannot be identified with its truth-conditions, as the following sentences show:

(1) Next year is a leap year.

(2) Next year is a leap year and π is irrational.

Since π is (necessarily) irrational, the truth-conditions for (1) and (2) are the same; however, we would not normally say that the two sentences had the same meaning.[25]

Semantics, the study of the interpretation of languages, traditionally dealt with questions of meaning. As it became more formal it abandoned these questions, and concerned itself entirely with the relation of language to the world. In Tarski's work this move becomes explicit. He writes,

> The word "semantics" is used here in a narrower sense than usual. We shall understand by semantics the totality of considerations concerning the concepts which, roughly speaking, express connections between the expressions of a language and the objects and states of affairs referred to by those expressions.[26]

22. Gottlob Frege, "Function and Concept", in Frege (1970, pp. 21–41).

23. When I quote *Principia*, I adjust the notation slightly, so that it conforms with that used in the rest of this essay.

24. Wittgenstein (1961, p. 67, 4.442).

25. The example is essentially due to Dummett.

26. Tarski, "Scientific Semantics," (1983, p. 401).

As examples of such concepts he gives *denotation, satisfaction,* and *definition,* as they appear in the statements:

> The expression "the victor of Jena" denotes Napoleon; snow satisfies the condition "*x* is white"; the equation "$x^3 = 2$" defines (determines uniquely) the cube root of the number 2.[27]

Note the use of quotation marks within these statements. They mark off expressions of the language under investigation (the *object language*) from those of the language in which the investigation is being carried out (the *metalanguage*). Semantic concepts appear in the metalanguage.

I drew attention to the distinction between object language and metalanguage in the previous section. The distinction is crucial if, like Tarski, we regard *truth* as a semantic concept. If it is allowed to collapse—more precisely, if the concept of truth is expressible in the object language—then we can always generate antinomies within that language.[28] The Liar Paradox can be generated in English, for instance, because English contains the predicate "is true" and applies it to sentences of English. In Tarski's terms, English, like other natural languages, is *semantically universal.* A formally correct account of truth, he says, cannot be given for such languages, and he restricts the scope of his semantic theory to formal languages.

A theory of truth for a first-order language gives a systematic account of the truth-conditions of all the sentences of that language. For Tarski, such a theory of truth, or of any other semantic concept, must be not only formally correct but materially adequate. To see what the second condition involves, consider these two examples:

(a) John and Peter satisfy the sentential function "X and Y are brothers" if and only if John and Peter are brothers.

(b) The sentence "snow is white" is true if and only if snow is white.

Tarski calls statements of equivalence like these "partial definitions" of satisfaction and truth, respectively. There are as many partial definitions of truth as there are sentences of the language, i.e., infinitely many. In themselves these partial definitions may seem obvious, even

---

27. Ibid.

28. For amplification of this paragraph and the next, see the essay by Tarski in this volume.

trivial. But, by their very obviousness, they give us a yardstick by which to gauge the adequacy of a theory of truth. A materially adequate theory of truth would be able to prove all partial definitions like (b), and a materially adequate theory of satisfaction would be able to prove all partial definitions like (a).

Again, the obviousness of partial definitions like (b), coupled with the requirement that a theory of truth be materially adequate, gives added emphasis to the problem of the Liar Paradox. For if the language for which we are giving a theory of truth contains a truth-predicate, then we can be confronted with the partial definition:

(c) The sentence "The sentence (d) on p. 270 is not true" is true if and only if the sentence (d) on p. 270 is not true.

This would seem unexceptionable, until we read the following sentence:

(d) The sentence (d) on p. 270 is not true.

With the specification of (d), (c) becomes paradoxical, as we can see by writing the sentence itself in place of the phrase describing it on the righthand side of the biconditional. It follows that a theory of truth for a semantically universal language must either outlaw this partial definition and so fail to be materially adequate, or include it and be inconsistent.

On this reading, Tarski's achievement in "The Concept of Truth in Formalized Languages" is twofold. He first makes explicit what an adequate theory of truth for a formal language has to do: it must satisfy the criteria of formal correctness and material adequacy. He then presents a theory for first-order languages that does so.[29]

The set of sentences of the language is recursively defined. Hence, as Tarski suggests, an obvious strategy in formulating such a theory consists in "giving all the operations by which simple sentences are combined into composite ones, and then determining the ways in which the truth or falsity of complex sentences depends on the truth or falsity of the simpler ones."[30] This is, of course, exactly what the

29. In the same paper he also deals with languages of higher order, but these are not my concern here.
30. Tarski, "Concept of Truth," (1983, p. 189). In describing this as "an obvious strategy" I speak with hindsight. It was Tarski who first made explicit the recursive nature of the syntax of formal languages.

truth-table method achieves in the case of the propositional fragment of first-order logic. Every sentence of this language contains a finite number of atomic sentences as proper parts, and, as we saw, the truth-values of these components determine the truth-value of the whole sentence. The truth-conditions for atomic sentences can be given by partial definitions, and the result will be a materially adequate theory of truth for the language.

Quantified sentences, however, pose more of a problem. We may regard the sentence "$(\forall x)\,(Px \supset Qx)$" as generated by a recursive step from the sentence "$Pa \supset Qa$," where "a" is a name, an expression, that is, whose semantic role is to denote an individual in the domain of interpretation. Thus it is tempting to think of the truth-value of "$(\forall x)$ $(Px \supset Qx)$" as determined by the truth-values of the sentences "$Pa \supset Qa$," "$Pb \supset Qb$," "$Pc \supset Qc$," and so on, and to propose as the truth-condition for "$(\forall x)\,(Px \supset Qx)$,"

> (U_s) "$(\forall x)\,(Px \supset Qx)$" is true iff the sentences "$Pa \supset Qa$," "$Pb \supset Qb$," "$Pc \supset Qc$," . . . are all true.

In general, however, this way of specifying the truth-condition for a universal generalization will not be adequate. The reason is that we may not have enough names to go round.[31] Consider the case where the intended domain of interpretation is the set of real numbers, and the intended reading of "$(\forall x)\,(Px \supset Qx)$" is that every P-number is a Q-number. Since the set of real numbers is nondenumerable, there are inevitably more numbers than we have names to attach to them. It follows that, on this interpretation, U_s fails the material-adequacy condition, since its righthand side is not equivalent to the condition that every P-number is a Q-number, as material adequacy requires.

While keeping to the same basic approach, however, we can modify U_s to meet this difficulty;[32] the result is the *substitutional interpretation* of quantification, outlined but not endorsed by Quine in essay 11 of this volume. Tarski's response is more radical. He considers a language without names; on his account (the *objectual interpretation*, as Quine calls it) the truth-condition for the quantified sentence "$(\forall x)$ $(Px \supset Qx)$" is expressed in terms of the satisfaction of the sentential function "$Px \supset Qx$" by objects in the domain of interpretation. And satisfaction, rather than truth, is the semantic concept appearing at

31. On this topic, see the essay by Dummett in this volume.
32. For an example, see Benson Mates (1965, ch. 4.1, especially p. 54). See also Leblanc (1983); on pp. 262–63 he gives a brief history of the substitutional interpretation.

each step of the recursion before the last. Effectively, Tarski's truth condition can be unpacked as follows:

> The sentence "$(\forall x) (Px \supset Qx)$" is true
>   iff
> the sentential function "$Px \supset Qx$" is satisfied by every object a in the domain of interpretation
>   iff
> for every object a in the domain, either a fails to satisfy "Px" or a satisfies "Qx"

The last condition is in terms of partial definitions of satisfaction for atomic sentential functions. These partial definitions ground the interpretation.

Tarski extends the analysis to sentential functions with an arbitrary number of variables, as he must if he is to deal with polyadic predicates; he does so by talking of the satisfaction of a sentential function by a *sequence* of objects. The extension, while technically ingenious, does not involve a significant change of strategy.

Formal semantics as we know it begins with Tarski.[33] I will close this section with a note on the concept of a *model*. While others before Tarski had talked in terms of models, he made the concept precise and showed how valuable it could be in semantic theory. Rather than give a definition, I will illustrate what a model is by means of the three sentences, all characterizing a relation R:

$$(\forall x) (\forall y) (\forall z) (Ryz \supset (Rxy \supset Rxz))$$
$$(\forall x) \sim Rxx$$
$$(\forall x) (\exists y) Rxy$$

The set of natural numbers ordered by the relation $<$ (*is strictly less than*) is a model for this class of sentences; on the other hand, the set $\{1, 2, 3, 4\}$ ordered by the same relation is not, since in the latter case the third sentence fails to hold, there being no member of the set which is greater than 4.

More generally, a model of a sentence, or of a class of sentences, consists of a set of objects (the domain of discourse) on which are defined subsets, relations, and so on. To each monadic predicate letter "P" occurring in the sentences is associated the subset containing just those objects with the property that we want "P" to denote. Likewise, to each diadic predicate letter "R" is associated the relation consisting

33. For a brief but comprehensive assessment of his work, see Andrzej Mostowski, "Tarski," in Edwards (1967), v. 8, pp. 77–81.

of the set of R-related pairs of objects in the domain. (In the example above, this was the set of pairs $<a, b>$ of numbers such that $a < b$.) Polyadic predicate letters are treated similarly. Then each member of the class of sentences will be "true in the model," true, that is, under the interpretation that assigns to each predicate letter the associated subset, relation, or whatever. More briefly, we can say that the model is "a model for that class of sentences." Other semantic concepts can then be defined in terms of models.[34] Famously, Tarski himself defined logical consequence (sometimes called "semantic entailment") in that way:

> The sentence X *follows logically* from the sentences of the class K if and only if every model of the class K is also a model of the sentence X.[35]

The use of models represents a further move in the formalization of semantics. Since models are defined in terms of sets, a semantic theory expressed in terms of models can avail itself of all the mathematical resources that set theory provides.

4. DEDUCTION

In his *Elements,* written around 300 B.C., Euclid assumed a remarkably small number of propositions as axioms, and from them derived the theorems of the geometry that bears his name. For twenty-two hundred years Euclidean geometry remained the paradigm of a deductive science. Yet until the end of the nineteenth century no analysis of the logic underlying Euclid's proofs had been undertaken, nor had his methods been applied to any branch of mathematics other than geometry.[36] Kant, indeed, believed that arithmetic could not be axiomatized,[37] and in his lectures on logic he makes only one reference to mathematical reasoning. Of indirect argument he says (1974, p. 58), "This procedure, of which frequent use is made in geometry, has the advantage that I need derive only one false consequence from a cognition to prove its falsity." In saying this Kant is not analyzing geometrical reasoning; rather, he is appealing to it to illustrate a claim about valid inference.

34. See, e.g., Bas C. van Fraassen, (1971, especially pp. 107–9).

35. Alfred Tarski, "On the Concept of Logical Consequence" (1983, ch. 16). See also the essay by Corcoran in this volume.

36. They were applied to physics, for example by Newton, who laid out both his *Principia* and his *Opticks* according to the "synthetic method."

37. Kant (1965, A164).

In the last two decades of the nineteenth century the situation changed. In 1889 Peano produced an axiomatization of arithmetic,[38] and in the next decade Hilbert (1899) applied the method of abstract axiomatics to geometry. The method is abstract in that it seeks to eliminate reliance on pretheoretic, intuitive conceptions of geometrical terms like "point" and "line" and to treat these terms as implicitly defined by the axioms in which they appear. Clearly this aim is rendered easier by the adoption of a formal notation; for instance, if we write,

(*) $(\forall x)\ (\forall y)\ [(Px\ \&\ Py) \supset (\exists z)\ (Lz\ \&\ (Czx\ \&\ Czy))]$

for, "Given any two points, there is a straight line that contains them both," we can then "deinterpret" the predicates "P," "L," and "C" so that the only relations between them are those implicit in (*) and whatever other axioms we employ. One result of this is that we cannot, as Euclid did, smuggle in unacknowledged assumptions into our proofs.[39] The derivation of theorems becomes purely syntactic, a matter of performing permissible transformations on uninterpreted axioms. Having generated the theorems, we are then free to reinterpret the predicate letters, not only in the original way, but in other ways as well. We can, for example, interpret "Px" as "x is a line," "Lx" as "x is a point," and "Cxy" as "y contains x." The theorems will be true in any interpretation in which the axioms are true. In Tarski's terms, any model of the axioms will be a model of the theorems.

In the *Begriffschrift*, logic itself was organized as an axiomatic system, with explicitly defined rules of inference, and over the next fifty years various equivalent axiomatizations were suggested.[40] Whitehead and Russell's axioms for propositional logic are these:

(A1) $\vdash (P \lor P) \supset P$
(A2) $\vdash Q \supset (P \lor Q)$
(A3) $\vdash (P \lor Q) \supset (Q \lor P)$
(A4) $\vdash (P \lor (Q \lor R)) \supset (Q \lor (P \lor R))$
(A5) $\vdash (Q \supset R) \supset ((P \lor Q) \supset (P \lor R))$

There are two rules of inference, *modus ponens* (from $\vdash A$ and $\vdash \ulcorner A \supset B \urcorner$ to infer $\vdash B$), and a rule of substitution. The latter permits the re-

38. See Blanché (1962, section 11).

39. In Proposition 1, for example, Euclid assumes something not guaranteed by his axioms, namely that if two circles are drawn whose centres are the two ends of a given line, and the radius of each circle is equal to the length of that line, then the circles have a point in common.

40. See Kneale and Kneale (1962, ch. 9.2, pp. 524–38).

placement of each occurrence of a specific atomic sentence in an axiom by another sentence. Thus we may replace "Q" in (A2) by "$Q \supset R$" to obtain,

$$\vdash (Q \supset R) \supset (P \lor (Q \supset R))$$

A *proof* is a sequence of sentences, each of them either an axiom or obtained from earlier sentences by one of the rules of inference.

In 1927 von Neumann suggested (though with Hilbert in mind rather than Whitehead and Russell) that a rule of substitution could be dispensed with if *axiom schemata* were used instead of axioms. Axiom schemata contain sentential variables in place of atomic sentences. This practice is now widely adopted.

There are formal oddities in Whitehead and Russell's presentation. Although the connective "$\supset$" plays the central role in inference, it appears in the system as a defined connective. Only the logical signs for negation and disjunction are taken as primitive, and "$P \supset Q$" is simply an abbreviation for "$\sim P \lor Q$." Furthermore, (A4) is redundant; as Bernays showed in 1926, it may be derived from the other four axioms. Quantificational logic is also treated with less elegance in *Principia* than in Frege's *Begriffschrift*. The *Principia* system was, however, very fully developed, so that a specific theorem, like "$((P \ \& \ Q) \supset R) \supset (P \supset (Q \supset R))$," can be referred to either as "Exportation," the name used by Whitehead and Russell, or as "*Principia* 3.3." Largely for this reason, the system remained for thirty years probably the best known of the available axiom systems.

Its deficiencies were remedied by later writers. We now have, on the one hand, axiom systems which employ in a perspicuous way all the connectives and quantifiers we customarily use, and, on the other, highly economical systems free of its clumsiness and redundancies.[41] Nonetheless, one might object, not just to the details of the *Principia* program, but to its basic strategy. This strategy is common to all axiomatic systems of deduction; the theorems of logic are to be deduced from indubitable axioms. But why, one may ask, is the generation of logical theorems, all of them equivalent to "$P \supset P$," a philosophically significant activity?

For Russell, at least, its significance can be traced to his philosophy of mathematics. He was a logicist, and for the logicist, "The theorems of mathematics can be derived from logical axioms through purely

---

41. Examples are, respectively, S. C. Kleene (1967, p. 387) and Elliott Mendelson (1964, p. 57).

logical deduction."[42] But logicism faces both ways. Not only is mathematics reducible to logic, but logic is the fundamental mathematical enterprise. For Russell, the twenty-seven logical truths printed opposite the Introduction to *Principia* are the deepest mathematical theorems of all.

Thus the logicist has good reasons for setting out logic *more geometrico*. But if one is not a logicist and nevertheless believes that one of the aims of formalizing logic is to make explicit the inner workings of mathematical reasoning, then it seems inappropriate to borrow the customary form of that reasoning to do so. Yet this is precisely what the axiomatic approach does; it presents logic in Euclidean clothing. To put this another way, if we are interested in the logic underlying Euclid's reasoning, then, instead of providing him with more axioms, we should look at the way he gets from one line to the next. To quote Hacking (essay 14 in this volume), we should think of logic, not as the science of truths, but as the science of deduction.

Like Prawitz in essays 13a and 13b, Hacking traces this view to the work of Gerhardt Gentzen, who turned away from the axiomatic approach used by Frege, Russell, and Hilbert. "In contrast," he wrote (1969, p. 68), "I intended to set up a formal system which came as close as possible to actual reasoning. The result was a *calculus of natural deduction*" (his emphasis).

Gentzen reminds us that, even in propositional logic, *modus ponens* is not the only recognizable way in which one line of a proof can follow logically from others. In his system there are no axioms; there are only rules of inference.[43] Associated with each connective and each quantifier there is an introduction rule (or pair of rules) and an elimination rule (or pair of rules). Thus the introduction rule(s) for "&" are:

$$(\&\text{-I}) \qquad
\begin{array}{cc}
\bullet & \bullet \\
A & B \\
\bullet & \bullet \\
B & A \\
\bullet & \bullet \\
A \,\&\, B & A \,\&\, B
\end{array}$$

42. Rudolf Carnap, "The Logicist Foundations of Mathematics," tr. E. Putnam and J. G. Massey, Benacerraf and Putnam (1983, p. 41). A view close to logicism is presented by W. V. Quine in essay 1 of this volume, especially in the last paragraph.

43. I discuss here Gentzen's natural deduction system, not his calculus of sequents.

The elimination rules for "&" are:

$$(\&\text{-E}) \quad \begin{array}{c} \bullet \\ A \,\&\, B \\ \bullet \\ A \end{array} \qquad \begin{array}{c} \bullet \\ A \,\&\, B \\ \bullet \\ B \end{array}$$

These rules are displayed here, not as Gentzen presented them, but in the neater format devised by Fitch (1952). A Fitch-style derivation consists of a sequence of sentences; each sentence is either an assumption (and listed as such at the head of the sequence) or obtained from one or more earlier sentences of the sequence by one of the rules of inference. The rule &-I, for instance, tells us that the appearance of both A and B in the sequence licenses the inference to $\ulcorner A \,\&\, B \urcorner$.

Every derivation must start from some assumptions to give the rules of inference something to work on. Some of the rules, however, allow assumptions to be *discharged,* so that they are no longer operative. The $\supset$-introduction rule, for example, often called "the method of conditional proof," has this form:

$$(\supset\text{-I}) \quad \begin{array}{|l} A \\ \hline \bullet \\ B \end{array}$$

$$A \supset B$$

It licenses the assertion of $\ulcorner A \supset B \urcorner$ provided that the assumption of A has led to a derivation of B. Application of the rule then discharges the assumption A. That is to say, on the line where $\ulcorner A \supset B \urcorner$ appears, and thereafter, the assumption is no longer in force. In this way the system allows us to prove theorems, statements that rely on no assumptions at all. The last line of any proof in which every assumptions has been discharged is a theorem of the system.

In essay 13a of this volume Prawitz sets out Gentzen's systems in their original format. He first presents minimal first-order logic (M), and then shows how the successive addition of rules relating to negation yields, first, intuitionist first-order logic (I), and then classical first-order logic (C). Clearly, provided they are independent of one another, the more rules a system contains, the more powerful the system will be, i.e. the more theorems will be provable within it. In terms of the inferences it permits and the theorems it generates, the system C is exactly equivalent to the *Principia* system.

Generally speaking, it is easier to generate derivations within a natural deduction system than within an axiomatic system; on the other hand, proofs of metatheorems about natural deduction systems are comparatively laborious. More significant, however, than the pragmatic differences between the two types of system are the philosophical differences between them. If, as I have suggested, a logicist would turn to an axiomatic system, then an intuitionist would naturally choose a system of natural deduction.[44]

The philosophical differences between the two approaches emerge when we consider the question of justification.[45] An axiomatic system is successful provided it allows all and only logical truths to be derived from the axioms; deductive theory is to be assessed entirely in terms of truth. To justify the rule of *modus ponens*, for example, we need to show that, for any sentences *A* and *B*, whenever *A* and ⌜*A* ⊃ *B*⌝ are both true, so is *B*. We show that this is the case by means of an informal argument based on the truth table for "⊃." But, as Haack points out in essay 6, this leads us, if not in a circle, at least along a helix. Inferential moves in the object language are justified by arguments using similar moves in the metalanguage; to justify these we would presumably move to a metametalanguage, and so on. Justification is thus deferred, rather than achieved. And if, as Horwich suggests in essay 5, our customary truth tables are no more than summaries of relations of deducibility, then the justification of rules of inference by appeal to these truth tables would be viciously circular.

In contrast, the use of a natural deduction system like Gentzen's allows us to interpret each connective in terms of its role within the system. On this interpretation, variously called "constructivist" or "intuitionist," the introduction rules require no justification; they are simply descriptive. When we apply the &-I rule to write ⌜*A* & *B*⌝, we do no more, according to the intuitionist, than assert within our formal language that we have already constructed derivations of *A* and of *B*. Again, the use of the ⊃-I rule to write ⌜*A* ⊃ *B*⌝ just records the fact that the assumption of *A* enables us to construct a derivation of *B*. Complex sentences thus become repositories of information about derivations. This information can then be retrieved by using the elimination rules, by inferring *A* from ⌜*A* & *B*⌝, for example.

The classical rule for ∼-elimination, however, cannot be justified in this way, and the intuitionist rejects it. The result, as I noted earlier, is

44. This is not a historical claim. Brouwer, early in the century, regarded any formalization of logic with suspicion, and Heyting (1956) has produced an axiomatization of intuitionist logic. See Ruitenberg (1991, pp. 134-160).

45. The ideas in this paragraph and the next receive fuller treatment in Prawitz's essays in this volume.

a logic that permits fewer inferences than the logic of Frege and Russell. The rule in question is actually a rule of "double-negation elimination":

$(\sim\text{-}E_c)$
$$\begin{array}{c} \bullet \\ \sim\sim A \\ \bullet \\ A \end{array}$$

From the classical perspective this rule is justified by the truth-functional reading of "$\sim$" within a bivalent semantics. For the intuitionist, however, who interprets negation deductively, the move is impermissible. He includes in his language a sentential constant "Λ," the *absurd sentence,* and for him $\lceil\sim A\rceil$ is equivalent to $\lceil A \supset \Lambda\rceil$; to the statement, that is, that A leads to absurdity. The introduction rule for "$\sim$" makes this explicit:

$(\sim\text{-}I)$

$$\sim A$$

Likewise, on this reading the introduction rule for "Λ" is just $\supset$-elimination, i.e. *modus ponens:*

$(\Lambda\text{-}I)$
$$\begin{array}{c} \bullet \\ A \\ \bullet \\ \sim A \\ \bullet \\ \Lambda \end{array}$$

The intuitionist agrees that any sentence whatever is derivable from the absurd sentence. He denies, however, that when a sentence A is derived in this way this licenses the discharging of an assumption $\lceil\sim A\rceil$. In other words, he rules out the use of the inference pattern:

$(\sim\text{-}E_c^*)$
$$\begin{array}{|c} \sim A \\ \bullet \\ \Lambda \\ \hline A \end{array}$$

Given the rules for "Λ" and "$\supset$," $\sim\text{-}E_c^*$ is equivalent to the inference to A from $\lceil(A \supset \Lambda) \supset \Lambda\rceil$, i.e. to double-negation elimination.[46]

46. There are various equivalent ways to strengthen the system I to produce a system equivalent to C. (See Prawitz, essay 13a.) I have chosen the rule $\sim\text{-}E_c$ for expository purposes.

The rules $\sim$-E_c and $\sim$-$E_c{}^*$ can both be justified on a truth-functional account of negation, if we regard "Λ" as the sentence which is always false. This, however, is precisely the kind of analysis that an intuitionist rejects. The derivability of a contradiction from the assertion that a contradiction is derivable from A, he maintains, provides no warrant for asserting A.

In the absence of a rule equivalent to $\sim$-E_c or $\sim$-$E_c{}^*$, $\ulcorner A \lor \sim A \urcorner$ is not provable in the intuitionist's system. Reasonably enough, we may think, he denies that an arbitrary sentence A must either be provable or provably lead to a contradiction.

The rejection of a truth-functional semantics for the connectives in favour of an interpretation in terms of their role in deduction may seem a radical move to make. But it cannot be lightly dismissed. In mathematics in particular, it is not clear what meaning we can attach to the claim that a given statement holds, other than that a proof of it is available.[47] The intuitionist sounds less plausible, however, when talking (as he does) in terms of truth. Intuitionistic logic permits the derivation of $\ulcorner \sim\sim(A \lor \sim A) \urcorner$ as a theorem-schema, but not of $\ulcorner A \lor \sim A \urcorner$; correspondingly the intuitionist is led to agree that, "It is inconsistent to assert of any statement that it is neither true nor false," but to withhold assent from the principle that every statement is either true or false.[48] This combination of agreement and dissent seems more paradoxical than the simple rejection of the law of excluded middle in Maimonides' negative theology, for example, or in the Pali *Pitakas*. The paradox arises because, in unpacking the quoted sentence to see exactly what it means, our habits lead us to eliminate the double negation within it, and thus to obtain the very principle we are told to reject, the principle of excluded middle. If we seek a rationale for these habits, we find implicit in them a principle of bivalence, and a truth-functional account of negation. Our habits, in other words, are thoroughly classical, which is not to say they are good.

5. METALOGIC

How far logic had developed in the half century following the publication of the *Begriffschrift* can be measured by the number of questions that could be answered at the end of that period which would not have been meaningful at its beginning. Questions about a whole

47. This line of thought is pursued by Dummett in "The Philosophical Basis of Intuitionistic Logic," included in Dummett (1978; see especially p. 225 ff.)
48. Dummett (1978, p. 233).

system of quantificational logic make sense, obviously, only if such a system exists. They are the questions dealt with by formal metalogic.

The questions that most concern logicians fall into three groups: (1) those which deal just with semantic issues, (2) those which deal just with proof-theoretic features of a system, and (3) those which deal with the relations between semantics and proof theory. Metalogical theorems that deal only with syntactic matters, like the theorem which tells us that any well-formed sentence contains exactly as many right parentheses as left parentheses, are not, in general, very interesting. (Here, as before, I distinguish between the syntax of a formal language and the specification of axioms and/or rules of inference of a deductive system. Some writers [e.g. Carnap, 1938] bring the proof-theoretic features of a system under the heading of syntax.)

An example from group (1) is the theorem that the set of connectives $\{\&, \sim\}$ is functionally adequate for propositional logic; that is to say, any truth function of a finite number of atomic sentences can be expressed by a sentence whose only connectives are "&" and "$\sim$" (see Hunter 1971, §21). Bernays's proof that the fourth of the *Principia* axioms for propositional logic is redundant (i.e. that all the *Principia* theorems are derivable from the remaining axioms) is an example of a theorem from group (2).[49] Another is Gentzen's *Hauptsatz* for his calculus of sequents, whose significance Hacking discusses in essay 14 of this volume.

Some of the most significant metalogical results, however, are in the third category. A natural criterion of adequacy for a deductive system, we may think, is that it meshes properly with the semantics of the language. The idea of "meshing properly" can be cashed out in terms of two conditions: soundness and completeness. A deductive system is *sound* provided that, if a sentence A is derivable in the system from a set Γ of sentences, then Γ semantically entails A (in Tarski's vocabulary, then A is a logical consequence of Γ). In the usual notation, the system is sound provided that

(M1) If $\Gamma \vdash A$, then $\Gamma \Vdash A$.

The deductive system is *complete*, provided that to every instance of a semantic entailment there is a corresponding derivation; i.e., provided that

49. In this case the distinction between a theorem *of* the system and a metatheorem *about* the system is quite subtle. The sentence $(A1 \& A2 \& A3 \& A5) \supset A4$ is a theorem of the system, but general considerations about (e.g.) the transitivity of deducibility have to be brought into play to prove the metatheorem, that $A4$ is redundant.

(M2) If $\Gamma \Vdash A$, then $\Gamma \vdash A$.

The completeness condition requires that the system licenses as many derivations as it ought; the soundness condition that it licenses no more than it should.

For some systems of logic only a weaker version of (M2) is provable:

(M2*) If $\Vdash A$, then $\vdash A$.

Systems for which (M2*) holds, but not (M2), are said to be *weakly complete* (with respect to the relevant semantics); those for which (M2) holds are said to be *strongly complete*. First-order logic, for example, is not strongly complete with respect to the substitutional interpretation of the quantifiers, unless a very strong assumption is made about the number of names available in the language.[50] No such problem exists, however, with respect to the objectual interpretation.

The converse of (M2*) gives us the condition for semantic consistency: A system S of axioms and rules of inference is *semantically consistent* provided that every theorem of S is a logical truth.

In 1920 the propositional fragment of the *Principia* system was shown to be consistent and weakly complete by Emil Post in his doctoral dissertation. This dissertation has some claim to being the first systematic work in formal metalogic. In 1928 Hilbert and Ackermann showed that their system of first-order logic was sound, and in 1930 Gödel showed the *Principia* system to be weakly complete. The strong completeness of first-order logic was shown by Henkin in 1947.[51]

To regard soundness and completeness as criteria of adequacy for a deductive system is to give priority to the semantic approach; a deductive system is thought adequate insofar as it reproduces semantic relations without transgressing them. One radical feature of Horwich's deflationary account of truth (essay 5, this volume) is that it inverts this priority; semantic relations are seen as codifications of

50. The language has to be *infinitely extendible*; that is, given any (possibly infinite) set Γ of sentences, we require that there exist a denumerably infinite number of names in the language which do not appear in the sentences of Γ. The problem was first pointed out by Thomason (1965), and is discussed in Leblanc (1983, p. 204), where a proof of strong completeness is given.

51. See Post (1921), Hilbert and Ackermann (1950, pp. 88–89), Gödel (1930), and Henkin (1949), respectively; a Henkin-style proof of strong completeness for propositional logic appears in Hunter (1971, §32).

deductive ones. *A propos* of this suggestion, we may observe, first, that a definition of consistency is available that makes no reference to semantics; we may say that a system S is *syntactically,* or *proof-theoretically, consistent* if there is no sentence A such that both A and $\ulcorner\sim A\urcorner$ are provable in the system. (See Church 1956, §§17 and 18, for a detailed discussion.) A demonstration of the proof-theoretic consistency of S would then fall into group (2) of metalogical results. Secondly, a minor metatheorem, readily provable for Gentzen's system C (see Prawitz, essay 13a), is the following.

Assume that
    (1) every sentence of the formal language is either true or false on a given interpretation, but not both;
    (2) under each interpretation there is at least one sentence that is false;
    (3) derivations in accordance with C preserve truth, in that (i) if $\Gamma \vdash A$, then there is no interpretation under which all members of Γ are true but A is false, and (ii) if $\vdash A$, then A is true on all interpretations;
    (4) the connectives "&," "∨," "⊃," "∼" are all truth-functional;
    (5) the truth of the quantified sentences $\ulcorner(\forall x)A(x)\urcorner$, $\ulcorner(\exists x)A(x)\urcorner$ on a particular interpretation in a given domain is determined by the satisfaction or otherwise of $\ulcorner A(x)\urcorner$ by the members of that domain under that interpretation.

Then (a) the sentential constant "Λ" is always false;
    (b) the customary truth-tables hold for the connectives;
    (c) the truth-conditions for quantified sentences are those given by Tarski.

The proof of this, which is essentially an exercise in the do-it-yourself semantics proposed by Hacking (essay 14), is left as an exercise for the reader. It turns out that the resources of the corresponding intuitionist system I are sufficient to generate all these results except two: the fact that, when A is false, $\ulcorner\sim A\urcorner$ takes the value true, and the fact that $\ulcorner(\forall x)A(x)\urcorner$ receives the value true when $\ulcorner A(x)\urcorner$ is satisfied by all members of the domain under the relevant interpretation. The second fact is a bit more surprising than the first.[52]

52. The approach to truth tables taken by Horwich, and also by Tennant (1978), is not exactly the one taken here. Their account gives a *reductio ad trivialissimum* of the second line of the truth table for negation, telling us merely that, for any sentence A, $\sim A \vdash \sim A$. As Tennant points out, even an intuitionist can subscribe to that. The philosophical commitments underlying Tennant's account of logic, which is deeply influenced by Dummett and Prawitz, are spelled out in Tennant (1987).

To conclude this brief overview of metalogic, I will quote and comment on two important group (1) theorems for first-order logic, the compactness theorem and the Löwenheim-Skolem theorem. The compactness theorem can be stated in various equivalent ways. The version proved by Gödel (1930, p. 119), restated in Tarski's vocabulary, is:

> If Γ is an infinite set of sentences in a first-order language, then Γ has a model provided that every finite subset of Γ has a model.

An equivalent version is:

> If A is semantically entailed by a set Γ of sentences, then A is semantically entailed by a finite subset of Γ.

Given the soundness and completeness of first-order logic, the proof is trivial. Assume $\Gamma \Vdash A$; then, by completeness, $\Gamma \vdash A$. But, by definition, any derivation contains only a finite number of sentences, hence there is a finite subset Γ_f of Γ such that $\Gamma_f \vdash A$, and so $\Gamma_f \Vdash A$, by soundness.

One might object to the manner, as opposed to the validity of this proof, on the grounds that a group (1) theorem, whose content is purely semantic, should be provable without appeal to proof theory. A proof of this kind appears in van Fraassen (1975).

This theorem has an odd corollary, that any first-order axiomatization of arithmetic has a finite model, despite the fact that the intended model of the axioms contains an infinite set of natural numbers. Consider, for example, Peano's axiomatization of arithmetic, which uses a first-order language containing one individual constant "O" and a successor function "S." (The number 2, for instance, is denoted by "SSO.") Now suppose that we add another constant "q" to the language, along with a denumerable list of axioms of the form

$$0 < q, \; SO < q, \; SSO < q, \; SSSO < q, \; \ldots$$

Any finite subset of these axioms, together with the Peano axioms, has a model. Since we are using a first-order language, the compactness theorem then tells us that the whole list (together with the Peano axioms) also has a model. In other words, we can obtain a model of arithmetic in which there is a "natural number" that is "greater than" any "natural number" in the series 0, 1, 2, . . . —or rather, to be more precise, in the series denoted in this interpretation by "O," "SO," "SSO," . . . (See Mac Lane 1986, p. 376).

The Löwenheim-Skolem theorem tells us that any set of sentences of a first-order language has a denumerably infinite model if and only if it has a model of any arbitrary infinite cardinality (Hunter 1971, pp. 201–2).

Between them, these two theorems show a severe limitation on the expressive power of first-order languages: No such language can capture the concept of the denumerably infinite. For that we would have to go to languages of second order. On the other hand, "Nonstandard models for analysis have turned out quite useful for their own sake, and countable models of set theory are at the base of the independence proofs: first-order logic's loss thus can often be the mathematician's or philosopher's gain." (Van Benthem and Doets, 1983, p. 277)

6. SIGNIFICANCE AND INFLUENCE

In this final section I will look first at the significance of modern logic for mathematics, and then at its influence on philosophy.

The articulation of first-order logic was achieved by professional mathematicians like Frege, Russell, and Hilbert, and it should be recognized, above all, as a remarkable mathematical achievement, no less remarkable for the fact that the hopes of those involved were never fully realized. Frege, for example, hoped to show that all truths of mathematics were truths of logic. This hope, however, was dashed when Russell pointed out that his set theory was inconsistent. The problem derived from Frege's unrestricted use of a principle of comprehension; given any description of an object that was expressible in the formal language, the principle asserted the existence of a set of such objects. As Russell pointed out, this entailed the existence of the set N of those sets which were not members of themselves, like the set of all left shoes (which is not itself a left shoe). But then "$N \varepsilon N$" entails "$\sim(N \varepsilon N)$," and conversely.

Russell, pursuing the same logicist program, avoided this antinomy by introducing a theory of types. Very roughly, only sets of a lower type than S could be members of S.[53] But, in the first place, the intricacies of his type theory made the claim that all its axioms were logical truths implausible. (But see §§12, 13 of Hacking's essay, this volume.)

---

53. In *Principia* the hierarchy is not of sets but of propositional functions (open sentences). A propositional function of order n may not include in its argument propositional functions of order n or higher; see Wang (1974), ch. III.3, and also fns. 17 and 19 of Hylton's essay in this volume. For an overview of the theory, see Copi (1971).

In the second, as Gödel noted later, any adequate axiomatization of arithmetic will include some version of the axiom of infinity, asserting the existence of an infinite set of numbers.[54] But, at least since Hume did so, it has been customary to distinguish "Matters of Fact and Existence" from "Relations of Ideas," i.e. from analytic truths.

Hilbert's formalist program likewise could not be implemented. Hilbert—whose contribution to logic has not been sufficiently emphasized in this essay—divided arithmetic into two parts, the concrete and the ideal (see Prawitz, essay 13b). Finitary arithmetic belonged to the concrete, Cantor's transfinitary set theory to the ideal. Hilbert hoped that the (syntactic) consistency of the whole, the concrete plus the ideal, could be proved by purely finitary methods; in this way the foundations of mathematics would be rendered secure. But Gödel's Incompletenesss Theorem (Gödel 1931), showed that, on the contrary, no axiomatization could capture the truths even of elementary arithmetic, on pain of inconsistency.[55]

Gödel's theorem was published in 1931. "Since then," Weyl wrote in 1949 (p. 219), "the prevailing attitude has been one of resignation." He went on, nevertheless, "Yet I find little to change in what I said about [Hilbert's enterprise] in 1926, although I should probably now set my words a little more cautiously."

In other words, the apparent failure of the program was accompanied by very real successes. Indeed, Tarski points out (essay 8, this volume) that Gödel's result can be regarded, not as the death-knell of a particular program, but as a profound mathematical result in its own right. In the same way, though the philosophical aims of the logicists were never realized, the paradox-free axiomatization of set theory achieved by Zermelo and Fraenkel is expressible in a first-order language (with equality) that contains just one primitive relational symbol "ε," for set membership. (For an exposition, see Monk 1969.) Since all mathematics is expressible in terms of set theory, it could be argued that first order logic furnishes a canonical language for the whole of mathematics. Furthermore, the inferences used by mathematicians can be codified in this language, and shown to involve the application of a finite set of intuitively appealing rules. To say, as does Mac Lane (1986, p. 375), that an examination of a few proofs laid out in this way

54. See Gödel (1944), p. 139; I have given the page number as it appears in Gödel (1990), v. 2, where the article is prefaced by a valuable commentary by Charles Parsons.

55. For extended discusisons of the logicist and the formalist programs, and of the problems they encountered, see Körner (1960).

"may support the conviction that such formal proofs are always possible and always pedantic" is to miss the point.[56] The conviction of their possibility would be baseless were it not for the work of Whitehead and Russell.

The history of mathematics, however, is replete with successes, and mathematicians do not linger on them. In the years since 1931 logic has been absorbed into the larger discipline. Alternative approaches to the foundations of mathematics have appeared, notably the structuralist approach suggested by the Bourbaki group, while logic itself, pursued as a formal enterprise, is now one branch of mathematics among many. And while any arithmetical statement can be transcribed into set-theoretical language, no mathematician would recommend doing so as a means of achieving insights into number theory.

Philosophy, on the other hand, is unused to success. More often than not, the insights of one generation are presented as awful warning to the next. The articulation of first-order logic offered an exception to this rule, and was greeted accordingly.[57] An indisputable advance had been made, in a subject, moreover, that had been central to philosophy since antiquity, but had long seemed to be "a closed and complete body of doctrine."

The stimulus it provided was manifested in two ways. Philosophers, sometimes alongside but more often independently of mathematicians, investigated other systems of logic of philosophical interest. The most notable achievement of this kind was the analysis of modal logic, the logic of possibility and necessity, provided by Kripke and others during the 1960s, but the range of these investigations was broad enough to warrant the publication in 1983 of a four-volume *Handbook of Philosophical Logic* (Gabbay and Guenther 1983), in which only the first entry in the first volume was devoted to standard first-order logic.[58]

Secondly, analytic philosophy became the dominant philosophical

---

56. It is also at odds with his advocacy, three pages later, of a standard of rigor in mathematics, and the approving mention of Frege, Whitehead, and Russell that accompanies it.

57. In *Loving Little Egypt*, the novelist Thomas McMahon recounts how the illegal activities of his blind hero brought the telephone system of the United States to a halt. He adds (I quote from memory), "Because blind people ordinarily achieve little in the way of criminality, this was thought to be marvelous."

58. Modal logic occupies the first five hundred pages of vol. 2 of the *Handbook*.

movement in the English-speaking world, to such an extent that it was often referred to as "Anglo-American philosophy." Central to the analytic program was the investigation of language. Whereas in England, through the work of Austin, Wittgenstein, and Strawson, emphasis was placed on the analysis of ordinary language, in the United States, whither a number of leading positivists had emigrated after Hitler's rise to power in Germany and Austria, formal methods were preferred. For two decades after its publication in 1949, the *vade mecum* of the American analytic philosopher was Feigl and Sellars's anthology *Readings in Philosophical Analysis.* In his Introduction Feigl characterizes philosophical analysis as follows (Feigl and Sellars 1949, p. 8).

> Philosophical or logical analysis, in the sense of a clarification of the meaning of language, differs from *philological* analysis in a least three important respects. First, logical analysis concentrates on terms of basic importance for the representation of knowledge. The more general these terms the greater is the danger of various confusions due either to unclarity in type of meaning or simply to vagueness or ambiguity of meaning. Hence the necessity and the value of such an analysis as a therapeutic measure. Second, the logical reconstruction is independent of the grammatical (and *a fortiori* the emotive) peculiarities of the specific language, living or dead, in question. Inasmuch as it is the cognitive meanings that we are interested in, idealized models, or in the extreme limit, an ideal language (something in the direction of Leibniz' Mathesis Universalis) may be used. The tools developed in modern symbolic logic prove of utmost value for this purpose. Third, logical analysis is usually *directed* analysis. That is to say, it is either *postulational codification* (as in the mathematical and the exact empirical sciences) or *epistemo-logical reduction* (the reconstruction of factual terms and propositions on a basis of observational evidence).

In brief, the task of philosophical analysis is to undo the work of Nimrod, who built the Tower of Babel.

The second of the features Feigl mentions, the use of "the tools developed in modern symbolic logic," is displayed in paradigmatic fashion by Russell's theory of descriptions—not surprisingly, "On Denoting" is included in the anthology—and the whole paragraph amply confirms Hylton's estimate (essay 12) of the historical significance of Russell's paper.

The anthology also contains Frege's "On Sense and Nominatum."[59] As far as I can discover, this is the first published English

59. The translation is by Herbert Feigl. Max Black subsequently translated "Über Sinn und Bedeutung" as "On Sense and Reference" (Frege 1952), and this is the English title by which the essay is now usually known.

translation of an essay by Frege. A collection of his philosophical writings (Frege 1952), edited by Geach and Black, followed three years later. This collection, which included a translation of part of the *Begriffschrift*, brought Frege's work to the attention of English-speaking philosophers, and during the next twenty years its full importance came to be widely, if belatedly, recognized.[60] Thus in 1967 the very title of van Heijenoort's source book *From Frege to Gödel* proclaimed Frege as the father of mathematical logic; then in 1973, after a long gestation period, Michael Dummett's *Frege, Philosophy of Language* appeared, providing a comprehensive account of Frege's achievement in that area. Chapter 2 of that book is reprinted in this volume (essay 10).

During these years the stimulus provided by the rediscovery of Frege's writings was coupled with the immediate influence of the work of Davidson and, especially, Quine. A retrospective essay by Tyler Burge, "Philosophy of Language and Mind: 1950–90" (1992), gives a detailed, sympathetic, yet properly critical account of this period in analytic philosophy, and of the major issues discussed. We may note here Davidson's thesis that Tarski's theory of truth need not be divorced from a theory of meaning, as Tarski himself had suggested, but instead could form the basis of such a theory,[61] and Quine's insistence that first-order logic not only codifies our inferential practices but also determines our ontological commitments (see essay 11 in this volume).

Not all philosophers, however, were enthusiastic about the "linguistic turn" that philosophy had taken, or about the priority given to formal methods. J. N. Findlay, for example, wrote of the philosophical scene in 1976, "Plainly the Aristotelian warnings against misapplied accuracy have been forgotten, as well as the Baconian criticisms of the syllogism, which apply without exception to its more resplendent successors" (1976, p. 59). In retrospect we can see the justice of this criticism. And increasingly we may feel that the philosophical analogue of a Mies van der Rohe building is no place to dwell. For, even if we enrich first-order logic by the use of sundry modal operators and speak of many worlds rather than one, their only inhabitants, logically speaking, will be bare particulars, whose life consists in forming the extensions of different predicates in different worlds. By barring or

60. With one exception, I have indexed Frege's work in the bibliography by the dates of publication of English translations; revealingly, these run from 1952 to 1980, and include two complete translations of the *Begriffschrift* (see the entry for Frege 1972).

61. The relevant essays are collected in Davidson (1984).

permitting quantification over these predicates, the logic may or may not formally adhere to a strict nominalism, but in either case the net effect is the same. We are presented with a universe of Platonic concepts, all of them devoid of cultural, historical, and pragmatic connotations. Seen in this light, the therapeutic measure advocated by Feigl begins to look like the nineteenth-century practice of bleeding the patient, which did so much for Queen Victoria's father.

What critics of analytic philosophy often neglect, however, is its capacity to renew itself from within.[62] The 1980s saw analytic philosophers forsaking tough-mindedness for tender-heartedness, and emphasizing the importance of moral psychology within a theory of ethics, of the history and practices of science within the philosophy of science, and of the context of production and reception of works of art within aesthetics. This return to the real world betrayed no disrespect for the achievements of modern logic; nor was it accompanied by faint praise of Frege as "a symbolic technician of surpassing virtuosity rather than a genuine philosopher" (Findlay 1976, p. 62).[63] The question was simply one of emphasis: "Gradually, but unmistakably, in the latter part of the 1970s, the philosophy of language lost its place as the dominant starting point for philosophical activity" (Burge 1992, p. 27). Like mathematicians some decades earlier, philosophers had learned to accord logic its proper place in the practice of philosophy, a place not unlike the one allotted to it by Aristotle two millennia ago.

62. The centenary issue of *The Philosophical Review* (vol. 101, no. 1, 1992), in which the editors set out "to take stock of the current state of philosophy and reflect on its recent history" (p. 1), bears witness to this.

63. Did Findlay ever read *The Foundations of Arithmetic,* one wonders, or Frege's 1894 review of Husserl?

Bibliography

Adams, E. (1975), *The Logic of Conditionals*, Dordrecht: Reidel

Ajdukiewicz, K. (1935), "Die syntaktische Konnexität," *Studia Philosophica*, 1, 1–27; tr. H. Weber as "Syntactic Connection" in McCall (1967), 207–31

Alston, W. P. (1960), "The Ontological Argument Revisited," *Philosophical Review*, 69, 452–74

Austin, J. L. (1950), "Truth," *Proceedings of the Aristotelian Society*, suppl. vol. 24, 111–28

Austin, J. L. (1962), *Sense and Sensibilia*, Oxford: Oxford University Press

Ayer A. J. (1946), *Language, Truth and Logic*, 2nd ed., London: Gollancz

Ayer, A. J. (ed.) (1959), *Logical Positivism*, New York: Free Press

Bacon, J. B. (1966), *Being and Existence*, dissertation, Yale University

Barker, S. F. (1965), "Must Every Inference Be Either Inductive or Deductive?," in Black (1965), 58–73

Barwise, J., M. Kaufmann, and M. Makkai, "Stationary Logic," *Annals of Mathematical Logic*, 13, 171–224

Belnap, N. D. (1961), "Tonk, Plonk, and Plink," *Analysis*, 22, 130–34, repr. in Strawson (1967), 132–37

Benacerraf, P. and H. Putnam (1983), *Philosophy of Mathematics, Selected Readings*, 2nd ed., Cambridge: Cambridge University Press

Bennett, J. (1961), "On Being Forced to a Conclusion," *Proceedings of the Aristotelian Society*, supp. vol. 35, 15–34

Bennett, J. (1971), *Locke, Berkeley, Hume: Central Themes*, Oxford: Oxford University Press

Bernays, P. (1926), "Axiomatische Untersuchung des Aussagen-Kalkuls der 'Principia mathematica'," *Mathematische Zeitschrift*, 25, 305–20

Birkhoff, G. and S. Mac Lane (1953), *A Survey of Modern Algebra*, rev. ed., New York: Macmillan

Bjürlof, T. (1978), "A Note on Logical Constants," *Analysis*, 38, 119–21

Black, M. (1954), *Problems of Analysis*, Ithaca: Cornell University Press

Black, M. (ed.) (1965), *Philosophy in America*, London: Allen and Unwin

Blanché, R. (1962), *Axiomatics*, tr. G. B. Keene, London: Routledge and Kegan Paul

Bochenski, I. M. (1970), *A History of Formal Logic*, tr. and ed. I. Thomas, New York: Chelsea

Bolzano, B. (1972), *Theory of Science*, tr. R. George, Berkeley: University of California Press

Boole, G. (1952), *Studies in Logic and Probability*, ed. R. Rhees, London: Watts

Boolos, J. (1975), "On Second Order Logic," *Journal of Philosophy*, 72, 508–26

Bradley, F. H. (1914), *Essays on Truth and Reality*, Oxford: Clarendon Press

Brouwer, L. E. J. (1952), "Historical Background, Principles and Methods of Intuitionism," *South African Journal of Science*, 49, 139–46

Burge, T. (1992), "Philosophy of Language and Mind: 1950–90," *Philosophical Review*, 101, 3–51

Butts, R. and J. Hintikka (eds.) (1977), *Logic, Foundations of Mathematics, and Computability Theory*, Boston: Reidel

Carlsen, L. and A. ter Meulen (1979), "Informational Independence in Intensional Contexts," in Saarinen (1979), 61–72

Carnap, R. (1930), "Die alte und die neue Logik," *Erkenntnis* 1, tr. I. Levi as "The Old and the New Logic" in Ayer (1959), 133–46

Carnap, R. (1937), *The Logical Syntax of Language*, tr. A. Smeaton, London: Kegan Paul (orig. pub. as *Die logische Syntax der Sprache*, Vienna, 1934)

Carnap, R. (1968), "Inductive Logic and Inductive Intuition," in Lakatos (1968), 258–314

Carnap, R. (1983), "The Logicist Foundations of Mathematics," tr. E. Putnam and J. G. Massey, in Benacerraf and Putnam (1983), 41–52

Carroll, Lewis (1895), "What the Tortoise Said to Achilles," *Mind*, 4, 278–80

Chisholm, R. (1961), "Jenseits von Sein und Nichtsein," in K. S. Guthke (ed.), *Dichtung und Deutung*, Bern: Francke, 23–31

Church, A. (1950), "The Need for Abstract Entities in Semantic Analysis," *Proceedings of the American Academy of Arts and Sciences*, 80, no. 1, 100–112

Church, A. (1956), *Introduction to Mathematical Logic*, Princeton: Princeton University Press

Copi, I. M. (1971), *The Theory of Logical Types*, London: Routledge and Kegan Paul

Corcoran, J. (1972), "Conceptual Structure of Classical Logic," *Philosophy and Phenomenological Research*, 33, 25–47; Portuguese translation by E. T. Gasparim, *Boletim da Sociedade Paranaense de Matematica* 9 (1988) 77–118.

Craig, W. (1956), "Three Uses of the Herbrand-Gentzen Theorem," *Journal of Symbolic Logic*, 22, 269–85

Craig, W. and B. Mates (1970), "Review of Encyclopedia of Philosophy," *Journal of Symbolic Logic*, 35, 295–310

Davidson, D. (1967), "Truth and Meaning," *Synthese*, 17, 304–23; repr. in Davidson (1984), 17–36

Davidson, D. (1969), "True to the Facts," *Journal of Philosophy*, 66, 748–64; repr. in Davidson (1984), 37–54

Davidson, D. (1984), *Inquiries into Truth and Interpretation*, Oxford: Clarendon Press

Davidson, D. (1990), "The Structure and Content of Truth," *Journal of Philosophy*, 87, 279–328

Davidson, D. and G. Harman (1975), *The Logic of Grammar*, Encino, Calif.: Dickenson

Descartes, R. (1642), *Meditations upon First Philosophy*, see Haldane and Ross (1911–12)

Drucker, T. (ed.) (1991), *Perspectives on the History of Mathematical Logic*, Boston: Birkhäuser

Dummett, M. (1977), *Elements of Intuitionism*, Oxford: Clarendon Press

Dummett, M. (1978), *Truth and Other Enigmas*, Cambridge, Mass.: Harvard University Press

Dummett, M. (1981), *Frege, Philosophy of Language*, 2nd ed. London: Duckworth

Edwards, P. (ed.) (1967), *The Encyclopedia of Philosophy*, 8 vols. New York: Macmillan

Ellis, B. (1978), "A Unified Theory of Conditionals," *Journal of Philosophical Logic*, 7, 107–24

Ellis, B. (1984), "Two Theories of Indicative Conditionals," *Australasian Journal of Philosophy*, 62, 50–66

Feigl, H. and W. Sellars (eds.) (1949), *Readings in Philosophical Analysis*, New York: Appleton-Century-Crofts

Fenstad, J. E. (ed.) (1971), *Proceedings of the Second Scandinavian Logic Symposium*, Amsterdam: North Holland

Findlay, J. N. (1976), "*Mind* under the Editorship of David Hamlyn," *Mind*, 85, 57–68

Fitch, F. B. (1952), *Symbolic Logic, an Introduction*, New York: Ronald Press

Forder, H. G. (1958), *Foundations of Euclidean Geometry*, New York: Dover

Frege, G. (1894), review of E. G. Husserl, *Philosophie der Arithmetik*,
v. 1, in *Zeitschrift für Philosophie und philosophische Kritik*, 103,
313–32; selections, tr. P. T. Geach, in Frege (1952), 79–85

Frege, G. (1952, 1960), *Translations from the Philosophical Writings of
Gottlob Frege*, tr. and ed. P. Geach and M. Black, Oxford: Blackwell,
1st ed. 1952, rev. ed. 1960

Frege, G. (1956), "The Thought: a Logical Inquiry," tr. A. M. and
M. Quinton, *Mind*, 65, 289–311, repr. in Strawson (1967), 17–38
(orig. pub. as "Der Gedanke, eine logische Untersuchung," *Beiträge
zur Philosophie der deutschen Idealismus*, 1 (1918), 58-77)

Frege, G. (1960a), *The Foundations of Arithmetic*, tr. J. L. Austin, New
York: Harper (orig. pub. as *Die Grundlagen der Arithmetik*, Breslau,
1884)

Frege, G. (1964), *The Basic Laws of Arithmetic*, tr. M. Furth, Berkeley: University of California Press (orig. pub. as *Grundgesetze der
Arithmetik, begriffsschriftlich abgeleitet*, Jena, v. 1, 1893, v. 2, 1903)

Frege, G. (1969, 1976), *Nachgelassene Schriften*, 2 vols., ed. H. Hermes,
F. Kambartel, and F. Kaulbach, Hamburg: Felix Meiner

Frege, G. (1972), *Conceptual Notation*, tr. T. W. Bynum, Oxford: Clarendon Press (orig. pub. as *Begriffschrift*, Halle, 1879; also tr.
S. Bauer-Mengelberg, in van Heijenoort, 1967, 5–82)

Frege, G. (1976), *Wissenschaftlicher Briefwechsel*, Hamburg: Felix
Meiner

Frege, G. (1977), *Logical Investigations*, ed. P. T. Geach, tr. P. T.
Geach and R. H. Stoothoff, New Haven: Yale University Press

Frege, G. (1979), *Posthumous Writings*, tr. P. Long and R. White,
Chicago, Chicago University Press (tr. from Frege, 1969)

Frege, G. (1980), *Philosophical and Mathematical Correspondence*, tr.
H. Kaal, Chicago: Chicago University Press (sel. and tr. from
Frege, 1976)

Gabbay, D. and F. Guenther (eds.) (1983), *Handbook of Philosophical
Logic*, 4 vols., Dordrecht: Reidel

Gentzen, G. (1935), "Untersuchungen über das logische Schliessen,"
Mathematisches Zeitschrift, 39, 176–210, 405–31; tr. as "Investigations into Logical Deduction" in Gentzen (1969), ch. 3

Gentzen, G. (1969), *The Collected Papers of Gerhard Gentzen*, tr. M. E.
Szabo, Amsterdam: North Holland

Girard, J. Y. (1971), "Une extension du système de fonctionelles ré-
cursives de Gödel et son application aux fondements de l'analyse,"
in Fenstad (1971), 63–92

Gödel, K. (1930), "The Completeness of the Axioms of the Functional Calculus of Logic," with tr. by S. Bauer-Mengelberg, in
Gödel (1986), 102–23; see also van Heijenoort (1967), 582–91

Gödel, K. (1931), "On Formally Undecidable Propositions of *Principia Mathematica* and Related Systems," tr. by J. W. Dawson, Jr., in Gödel (1986), 144–95; see also van Heijenoort (1967), 596–616

Gödel, K. (1944), "Russell's Mathematical Logic," in Schilpp (1944), 123–53, repr. with an addition in Gödel (1990), 119–41

Gödel, K. (1986, 1990), *Collected Works*, 2 vols., ed. S. Feferman et al., New York: Oxford University Press

Goldfarb, W. (1989), "Russell's Reasons for Ramification," in Savage and Anderson (1989), 24–40

Grice, H. P. (1975), "Logic and Conversation," in Davidson and Harman (1975), 64–75, repr. in Jackson (1991), 155–75

Hacking, I. (1977), "Do-It-Yourself Semantics for Classical Sequent Calculi, Including Ramified Type Theory," in Butts and Hintikka (1977), 371–90

Hacking, I. (1978), "On the Reality of Existence and Identity," *Canadian Journal of Philosophy*, 8, 613–32

Haldane, E. S. and G.R.T. Ross (eds.) (1911–12), *Philosophical Works of Descartes*, 2 vols., Cambridge: Cambridge University Press

Harper, W. L., R. Stalnaker, and G. Pearce (eds.) (1981), *Ifs*, Dordrecht: Reidel

Harris, Z. (1968), *Mathematical Structures of Language*, New York: Interscience

Hempel, C. (1935), "On the Logical Positivists' Theory of Truth," *Analysis*, 2, 49–59

Henkin, L. (1949), "The Completeness of First Order Functional Logic," *Journal of Symbolic Logic*, 14, 159–66, repr. in Hintikka (1969), 51–63

Henkin, L. (1961), "Some Remarks on Infinitely Long Formulas," *Infinitistic Methods* (proceedings of a Warsaw symposium), New York: Pergamon, 167–83

Heyting, A. (1956), *Intuitionism: an Introduction*, Amsterdam: North-Holland.

Hilbert, D. (1899), *Die Grundlagen der Geometrie*, Leipzig (2nd ed. tr. L. Unger, La Salle: Open Court, 1971)

Hilbert, D. (1900), "Mathematische Probleme," *Nachrichten von der K. Gesellschaft der Wissenschaften zu Göttingen, Math.-Phys. Kl.*, 253–97

Hilbert, D. (1905), "Über die Grundlagen der Logik und der Arithmetik," in *Verhandlungen des dritten internationalen Mathematikerkongress* in Heidelberg 1904, Leipzig, 174–85 (tr. as "On the Foundations of Logic and Arithmetic" in van Heijenoort, 1967, 129–38)

Hilbert, D. (1926), "Über das Unendliche," *Mathematische Annalen*, 95, 161–90 (tr. as "On the Infinite" in van Heijenoort, 1967, 367–92)

Hilbert, D. and W. Ackermann (1950), *The Principles of Mathematical Logic*, 2nd ed., tr. L. Hammond et al., New York: Chelsea (1st ed. 1928)

Hintikka, J. (1959), "Existential Presuppositions and Existential Commitments," *Journal of Philosophy*, 56, 125–37

Hintikka, J. (ed.) (1969), *The Philosophy of Mathematics*, Oxford: Oxford University Press

Hintikka, J. (1973), *Logic, Language Games and Information*, Oxford: Clarendon Press

Hintikka, J. (1974), "Quantifiers vs. Quantification Theory," *Linguistic Inquiry*, 5, 153–72

Hodges, W. (1983), "Elementary Predicate Logic," in Gabbay and Guenther (1983), vol. 1, 1–131

Hofstadter, D. (1980), *Gödel, Escher, Bach: An Eternal Golden Braid*, New York: Vintage Books

Horwich, P. G. (1990), *Truth*, Oxford: Blackwell

Hunter, G. (1971), *Metalogic, An Introduction to the Metatheory of Standard First-Order Logic*, London: Macmillan

Hylton, P. (1990), *Russell, Idealism, and the Emergence of Analytic Philosophy*, Oxford: Oxford University Press

Jackson, F. (1979), "On Assertion and Indicative Conditionals," *Philosophical Review*, 88, 565–89, repr. in Jackson (1991), 111–35

Jackson, F. (1980–1), "Conditionals and Possibilia," *Proceedings of the Aristotelian Society*, 81, 125–37

Jackson, F. (ed.) (1991), *Conditionals*, Oxford: Oxford University Press

James, W. (1909), *The Meaning of Truth*, New York: Longmans Green

Jourdain, P.E.B. (1912), "The Development of the Theories of Mathematical Logic and the Principles of Mathematics," *Quarterly Journal of Pure and Applied Mathematics*, 43, 237–69

Kant, I. (1965), *Critique of Pure Reason*, tr. N. Kemp Smith, New York: St. Martin's Press (1st ed. (A), 1781, 2nd ed. (B), 1787)

Kant, I. (1974), *Logic*, tr. R. Hartman and W. Schwarz, Indianapolis: Bobbs Merrill

Kaplan, D. (1972), "What Is Russell's Theory of Descriptions?" in Pears (1972), 227–44, repr. in Davidson and Harman (1975), 210–17

Keenan, E. (1973), "Presupposition in Natural Logic," *The Monist*, 57, 344–70

Kleene, S. C. (1967), *Mathematical Logic*, New York: John Wiley

Kneale, W. C. (1936), "Is Existence a Predicate?" *Proceedings of the Aristotelian Society*, supp. vol. 15, 154–74, repr. in Feigl and Sellars (1949), 29–43

Kneale, W. C. (1956), "The Province of Logic," in Lewis (1956), 235–61

Kneale, W. C. and M. Kneale (1962), *The Development of Logic,* Oxford: Clarendon Press

Körner, S. (1960), *The Philosophy of Mathematics,* London: Hutchinson

Kreisel, G. (1962), "Foundations of Intuitionistic Logic," in Nagel et al. (1962), 192–210

Kripke, S. (1975), "Outline of a Theory of Truth," *Journal of Philosophy,* 72, 690–716

Lakatos, I. (ed.) (1968), *The Problem of Inductive Logic,* Amsterdam: North-Holland

Leblanc, H. (1983), "Alternatives to Standard First-Order Semantics," in Gabbay and Guenther (1983), v. 1, 189–274

Leibniz, G. W. (1989), *Philosophical Essays,* tr. and ed. R. Ariew and D. Garber, Indianapolis: Hackett

Lejewski, C. (1976), "Popper's Theory of Formal Inference," in Schilpp (1976), 632–70

Lemmon, E. J. (1966), "Sentences, Statements and Propositions," in Williams and Montefiore (1966), 87–107

Leonard, H. S. (1964), "Essences, Attributes, and Predicates," *Proceedings and Addresses of the American Philosophical Association,* 37, 25–51

Leśniewski, S. (1929), "Grundzüge eines neues Systems der Grundlagen der Mathematik," *Fundamenta Mathematicae,* 14, 1–81

Lewis, C. I. and C. H. Langford (1959), *Symbolic Logic,* 2nd ed., New York: Dover

Lewis, D. (1976), "Probabilities of Conditionals and Conditional Probabilities," *Philosophical Review,* 85, 297–315, repr. in Harper et al. (1981), 129–47

Lewis, H. D. (ed.) (1956), *Contemporary British Philosophy,* Third Series, London: Allen and Unwin

Lindström, P. (1969), "On Extensions of Elementary Logic," *Theoria,* 35, 1–11

Locke, J. (1975), *An Essay Concerning Human Understanding,* ed. P. H. Nidditch, Oxford: Clarendon Press (based on 4th ed., 1700)

McCall, S. (ed.) (1967), *Polish Logic 1920–1939,* Oxford: Clarendon Press

Mackie, J. L. (1973), *Truth, Probability and Paradox,* Oxford: Clarendon Press

Mac Lane, S. (1986), *Mathematics: Form and Function,* New York: Springer Verlag

Mac Lane, S., see Birkhoff and Mac Lane (1953).

298   *Bibliography*

Malcolm, N. (1960), "Anselm's Ontological Arguments," *Philosophical Review*, 69, 41–62

Marcus, R. B. (1961), "Modalities and Intensional Languages," *Synthese*, 13, 303–22

Martin, R. M. (1943), "A Homogeneous System of Formal Logic," *Journal of Symbolic Logic*, 8, 1–23

Martin-Löf, P. (1973), "An Intuitionistic Theory of Types," mimeographed, University of Stockholm

Mates, B. (1965), *Elementary Logic*, New York: Oxford University Press

Mendelson, E. (1964), *Introduction to Mathematical Logic*, Princeton: Van Nostrand

Mill, J. S. (1843), *System of Logic*, 2 vols., London: Parker

Monk, J. D. (1969), *Introduction to Set Theory*, New York: McGraw Hill

Montague, R. (1965), "Set Theory and Higher-Order Logic," in P. Crossley and M. Dummett (eds.), *Formal Systems and Recursive Functions*, Amsterdam: North Holland, 131–48

Montague, R. (1974), *Formal Philosophy: Selected Papers of Richard Montague*, ed. R. Thomason, New Haven: Yale University Press

Moore, G. E. (1899), "The Nature of Judgment," *Mind*, 8, 176–93

Moore, G. E. (1903), *Principia Ethica*, Cambridge: Cambridge University Press

Moore, G. E. (1953), "Propositions," in *Some Main Problems in Philosophy*, London: Allen and Unwin, 52–71

Moore, G. E. (1959), *Philosophical Papers*, London: Allen and Unwin

Mostowski, A. (1967), "Tarski," in Edwards (1967), v. 8, pp. 77–81

Nagel, E., P. Suppes, and A. Tarski (eds.) (1962), *Logic, Methodology, and Philosophy of Science*, Stanford: Stanford University Press

Nolan, R. (1969), "Truth and Sentences," *Mind*, 77, 501–11

Papineau, D. (1987), *Reality and Representation*, Oxford: Blackwell

Peacocke, C. (1976), "What Is a Logical Constant?" *Journal of Philosophy*, 73, 221–40

Peacocke, C. (1978), "A Reply to Bjürlof's Objection," *Analysis*, 38, 122–24

Pears, D. (ed.) (1972), *Bertrand Russell, A Collection of Critical Essays*, New York: Anchor Books

Peirce, C. S. (1932), *Collected Papers*, vols. 2–4, ed. C. Hartshorne, P. Weiss, and A. W. Burks, Cambridge, Mass.: Harvard University Press

Popper, K. (1947), "New Foundations for Logic," *Mind*, 56, 193–235

Popper, K. (1959), *The Logic of Scientific Discovery*, 2nd ed., London: Hutchinson

Post, E. (1921), "Introduction to a General Theory of Elementary Propositions," *American Journal of Mathematics*, 43, 163–85, repr. in van Heijenoort (1967), 265–83

Prawitz, D. (1965), *Natural Deduction: A Proof-Theoretical Study*, Stockholm: Almqvist and Wiksell

Prawitz, D. (1971), "Ideas and Results in Proof Theory," in Fenstad (1971), 235–307

Prawitz, D. (1973), "Towards the Foundations of a General Proof Theory," in Suppes et al. (1973), 225–50

Prior, A. N. (1960), "The Runabout Inference Ticket," *Analysis*, 21, 38–39, repr. in Strawson (1967), 129-31

Prior, A. N. (1964), "Conjunction and Contonktion Revisited," *Analysis*, 24, 191–95

Putnam, H. (1978), *Meaning and the Moral Sciences*, London: Routledge and Kegan Paul

Putnam, H. (1981), *Reason, Truth, and History*, Cambridge: Cambridge University Press

Quine, W. V. (1936), "Truth by Convention," in Quine (1966), 77–106, also in Feigl and Sellars (1949), 250–73

Quine, W. V. (1950), *Methods of Logic*, New York: Holt (rev. ed., 1959)

Quine, W. V. (1951), *Mathematical Logic*, 2nd ed., New York: Harper and Row

Quine, W. V. (1959): see Quine (1950)

Quine, W. V. (1960), *Word and Object*, Cambridge, Mass.: M.I.T. Press

Quine, W. V. (1966), *The Ways of Paradox*, New York: Random House

Quine, W. V. (1966a), *Selected Logic Papers*, New York: Random House

Quine, W. V. (1966b), "Russell's Ontological Development," *Journal of Philosophy*, 63, 657–67, repr. in Pears (1972), 304–14

Quine, W. V. (1970), *Philosophy of Logic*, Englewood Cliffs: Prentice Hall

Quine, W. V. (1990), *Pursuit of Truth*, Cambridge, Mass.: Harvard University Press

Ramsey, F. R. (1927), "Facts and Propositions," *Proceedings of the Aristotelian Society*, supp. vol. 7, 153–70

Resnik, M. (1970), "The Frege-Hilbert Controversy," abstracted in *Journal of Symbolic Logic*, 35, 182

Ruitenberg, W. (1991), "The Unintended Interpretations of Intuitionistic Logic," in Drucker (1991), 134–60

Russell, B. (1903): see Russell (1937)

Russell, B. (1905), "On Denoting," *Mind*, 14, 479–93, repr. in Feigl and Sellars (1949), 103–15, Russell (1956), 41–56, and Russell (1973), 103–19

Russell, B. (1912), *The Problems of Philosophy*, Oxford: Oxford University Press

Russell, B. (1919), *Introduction to Mathematical Philosophy*, London: Allen and Unwin

Russell, B. (1924), "The Philosophy of Logical Atomism," in Russell (1956), 175–282

Russell, B. (1926), *Our Knowledge of the External World*, 2nd ed., London: Allen and Unwin (1st ed., 1914)

Russell, B. (1937), *The Principles of Mathematics*, 2nd ed., London: Allen and Unwin (1st ed., 1903)

Russell, B. (1956), *Logic and Knowledge: Essays 1901–1950*, ed. R. C. Marsh, London: Allen and Unwin

Russell, B. (1959), *My Philosophical Development*, London: Allen and Unwin

Russell, B. (1963), *Mysticism and Logic*, London: Allen and Unwin

Russell, B. (1973), *Essays in Analysis*, ed. D. Lackey, New York: Braziller

Russell, B. and A. N. Whitehead (1910–13 and 1962): see Whitehead and Russell (1910–13) and Whitehead and Russell (1962).

Saarinen, E. et al. (eds.) (1979), *Essays in Honour of Jaakko Hintikka*, Boston: Reidel

Sainsbury, R. M. (1979), *Russell*, London: Routledge and Kegan Paul

Salmon, W. (1966), *The Foundations of Scientific Inference*, Pittsburgh: University of Pittsburgh Press

Savage, C. W. and C. A. Anderson (1989), *Rereading Russell*, Minnesota Studies in Philosophy of Science, v. 12, Minneapolis: University of Minnesota Press

Schilpp, P. (ed.) (1944), *The Philosophy of Bertrand Russell*, La Salle, Ill.: Open Court

Schilpp, P. (ed.) (1976), *The Philosophy of Karl Popper*, La Salle, Ill.: Open Court

Shaffer, J. (1962), "Existence, Predication, and the Ontological Argument," *Mind*, 71, 307–25

Shoesmith, D. J. and T. J. Smiley (1978), *Multiple-Conclusion Logic*, New York: Cambridge University Press

Stalnaker, R. (1968), "A Theory of Conditionals," *Studies in Logical Theory, American Philosophical Quarterly*, Monograph 2, 98–112, repr. in Harper et al. (1981), 41–55 and Jackson (1991), 28–45

Stalnaker, R. (1970), "Probability and Conditionals," *Philosophy of Science*, 37, 64–85, repr. in Harper et al. (1981), 107–28

Stalnaker, R. (1975), "Indicative Conditionals," *Philosophia*, 5, 269–86, repr. in Jackson (1991), 136–54

Stegmüller, W. (1964), "Remarks on the Completeness of Logical Systems Relative to the Validity Concepts of P. Lorenzen and K. Lorenz," *Notre Dame Journal of Formal Logic*, 5, 81–112

Stevenson, J. T. (1961), "Roundabout the Runabout Inference Ticket," *Analysis*, 21, 124–28

Strawson, P. (1950), "Truth," *Proceedings of the Aristotelian Society*, supp. vol. 24, 129–56

Strawson, P. F. (1952), *Introduction to Logical Theory*, London: Methuen

Strawson, P. F. (1957), "Properties, Concepts and Logical Truth," in Strawson (1974), 116–29

Strawson, P. F. (ed.) (1967), *Philosophical Logic*, Oxford: Oxford University Press

Strawson, P. F. (1974), *Logico-Linguistic Papers*, London: Methuen

Suppes, P., L. Henkin, A. Joja, and Gr. C. Moisil (1973), *Logic, Methodology, and Philosophy of Science IV*, Amsterdam: North Holland

Swing, T. K. (1969), *Kant's Transcendental Logic*, New Haven: Yale University Press

Tarski, A. (1933), "The Concept of Truth in Formalized Languages," ch. 8 in Tarski (1956/83)

Tarski, A. (1936a), "The Establishment of Scientific Semantics," ch. 15 in Tarski (1956/83)

Tarski, A. (1936b), "On the Concept of Logical Consequence," ch. 16 in Tarski (1956/83)

Tarski, A. (1944), "The Semantic Conception of Truth and the Foundations of Semantics," *Philosophy and Phenomenological Research*, 4, 341–75, repr. in Feigl and Sellars (1949), 52–84

Tarski, A. (1956, 1983), *Logic, Semantics, Metamathematics*, tr. J. H. Woodger, 1st ed. ed. J. H. Woodger, Oxford: Clarendon Press, 2nd ed. rev. and ed. J. Corcoran, Indianapolis: Hackett

Tennant, N. (1978), *Natural Logic*, Edinburgh: Edinburgh University Press

Tennant, N. (1987), *Anti-Realism and Logic*, Oxford: Oxford University Press

Thomason, R. H. (1965), *Studies in the Formal Logic of Quantification*, doctoral dissertation, Yale University

Thomason, R. H. (1970), *Symbolic Logic,* New York: Macmillan
Thomson, J. F. (1963), "What Achilles Should Have Said to the Tortoise," *Ratio,* 3, 95–105
van Benthem, J. and K. Doets (1983), "Higher Order Logic," in Gabbay and Guenther (1983), v. 1., 275–329
van Fraassen, B. C. (1975), *Formal Semantics and Logic,* New York: Macmillan
van Heijenoort, J. (1967), *From Frege to Gödel, A Source Book in Mathematical Logic,* Cambridge, Mass.: Harvard University Press
von Neumann, J. (1927), "Zur Hilbertschen Beweistheorie," *Mathematische Zeitschrift,* 26, 1–46
Wang, H. (1974), *From Mathematics to Philosophy,* New York: Humanities Press
Wessels, L. (1977), "Cut-Elimination in a Gentzen-Style Calculus without Identity," *Zeitschrift für mathematische Logik und Grundlagen der Mathematik,* 23, 527–38
Weyl, H. (1949), *Philosophy of Mathematics and Natural Science,* rev. ed., tr. O. Helmer, Princeton: Princeton University Press (orig. pub. as "Philosophie der Mathematik und Naturwissenschaft" in *Handbuch der Philosophie* in 1927)
Whitehead, A. N. and B. Russell (1910, 1912, 1913), *Principia Mathematica,* 3 vols., Cambridge: Cambridge University Press
Whitehead, A. N. and B. Russell (1962), *Principia Mathematica to *56,* Cambridge: Cambridge University Press
Williams, B. and A. Montefiore (eds.) (1966), *British Analytical Philosophy,* New York: Humanities Press
Wittgenstein, L. (1961), *Tractatus Logico-Philosophicus,* tr. D. F. Pears and B. F. McGuiness, London: Routledge and Kegan Paul
Wolf, A. (1938), *Textbook of Logic,* 2nd ed., New York: Collier
Zucker, J. (1978), "The Adequacy Problem for Classical Logic," *Journal of Philosophical Logic,* 7, 517–35

Index

Numerals in bold type refer to essays in this volume; where they appear, page references in that essay are, in general, not supplied for the entry in question. No references to the bibliography are given.